THE LONDON YANKEES

Other books by Stanley Weintraub

FOUR ROSSETTIS:
A VICTORIAN BIOGRAPHY

WHISTLER: A BIOGRAPHY

JOURNEY TO HEARTBREAK:
THE CRUCIBLE YEARS OF BERNARD SHAW

THE LAST GREAT CAUSE:
THE INTELLECTUALS AND
THE SPANISH CIVIL WAR

AUBREY BEARDSLEY:
IMP OF THE PERVERSE

PRIVATE SHAW AND PUBLIC SHAW

STANLEY WEINTRAUB

THE LONDON YANKEES

Portraits of American Writers

and Artists in England

1894–1914

HBJ

HARCOURT BRACE JOVANOVICH

NEW YORK AND LONDON

For Serrell Hillman

Requests for permission to make copies
of any part of the work should be mailed to:
Permissions, Harcourt Brace Jovanovich, Inc.
757 Third Avenue, New York, N.Y. 10017

Printed in the United States of America

Library of Congress Cataloging in Publication Data

Weintraub, Stanley, 1929–
The London Yankees.

Bibliography: p.
Includes index.
1. Authors, American—Homes and haunts—England—London.
2. Authors, American—England—London—Biography.
3. London—Intellectual life.
4. Americans in London.
5. Artists—United States—Biography.
6. Artists—England—London—Biography.
I. Title.
PS144.L6W4   810′.9′94212   78–22276
ISBN 0–15–152978–7

First edition
B C D E

CONTENTS

CONTENTS

ILLUSTRATIONS

Between pages 248 and 249

Mark Twain, portrait photograph by Alvin Langdon Coburn. From George Eastman House, Rochester, New York.

"To a Master of His Art," Mr Punch toasting Mark Twain, by Bernard Partridge, in *Punch,* June 26, 1907, p. 453.

Portland Place, London, England, photographed by Alvin Langdon Coburn for the *New York Edition* of Henry James's works. From George Eastman House, Rochester, New York.

Bret Harte in the nineties, a portrait photograph. From the Humanities Research Center, University of Texas at Austin.

Pearl Craigie. Portrait photograph reproduced in *Literature* (London), August 20, 1898.

The last photograph of Stephen Crane (with his dog, Spongie), taken at Brede in 1900. From the Barrett Collection, University of Virginia.

Henry Harland, Esq. (1896), by Max Beerbohm, from *Twenty-Five Gentlemen* (1896).

The trial of "Kate Frederic," courtroom sketch artist's depiction in *The Daily Graphic,* London, October 27, 1898.

Harold Frederic in his last year. From *Literature,* October 29, 1898.

Edwin Abbey at fifty-seven, painted by Sir W. Q. Orchardson, R.A., in 1909; reproduced in E. V. Lucas's *Edwin Abbey,* as frontispiece to Vol. II.

Romaine Brooks, *Self-Portrait,* oil on canvas, 46 ½ x 26 ⅞ inches. From the National Collection of Fine Arts, Smithsonian Institution, Washington, D.C.

Brown and Gold: Self Portrait, by James McNeill Whistler, c. 1900. From the National Gallery of Art, Washington, D.C. Gift of Edith Stuyvesant Gerry.

"Mr Joseph Pennell thinking of the old 'un," by Max Beerbohm, 1913, from *Fifty Caricatures* (1913). The pose is that of Whistler's *Carlyle,* with Whistler himself in the picture on the wall.

"The Queue outside Mr Sargent's" (1908), by Max Beerbohm, from Evan Charteris's *John Sargent,* 1927. The setting is 31 Tite Street. The fashionable ladies are waiting their turns for portrait sittings, while the four messenger boys are presumably bringing others' urgent requests for sittings.

Jennifer Churchill, portrait photograph by Herbert Barraud, c. 1895. From the National Portrait Gallery, Smithsonian Institution, Washington, D.C.

Jacob Epstein's *Rock Drill* (1913). Originally the plaster work was mounted upon the tripod of a mechanical drill. From the Tate Gallery, London, England.

Henry James at seventy, by John Singer Sargent. From the National Portrait Gallery, London, England.

Ezra Pound in 1913, photographed by Alvin Langdon Coburn. From George Eastman House, Rochester, New York.

Tomb of Oscar Wilde, by Jacob Epstein. Photographed by Samuel C. Sabean in 1969. From the Sabean Collection.

T. S. Eliot by Wyndham Lewis, pen-and-ink, undated, from Lewis's *Blasting and Bombardiering.*

Robert Frost in 1913. A portrait photograph taken in England, probably as publicity for his publisher. From the Jones Library, Amherst, Massachusetts.

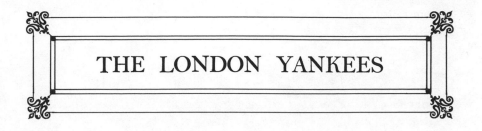

THE LONDON YANKEES

I bring you the spoils, my nation,
I, who went out in exile,
    Am returned to thee with gifts.

—Ezra Pound in 1912

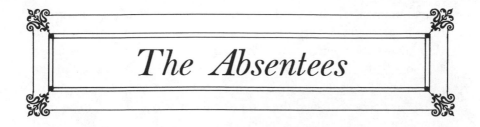

The Absentees

Anything is better than the vagabond artistic American of the nineteenth century, hanging round the picture galleries and talking Henry James or Frank Harris, according to taste.

—Bernard Shaw

THE FIRST TIME she met Henry James, Elizabeth (Mrs T. P.) O'Connor, the American-born wife of the London editor, remembered, he asked her how she liked the city that was her new home. She hadn't made up her mind, she said. London, James declared, permitted one "every independence of opinion and action, only you must contribute socially—beauty [*and he bowed very courteously to me, and I bowed very prettily to him*], or wit, or agreeableness, and then London accepted you."

"In Texas, where I was born," she told him, "they say a man is not asked his nationality, his religion, or his politics, but only if he is a good fellow."

"Ah," answered James. "Then London is the Texas of Europe."

Before there was even an American nation—or a Texas—there were London Yankees. From the earliest days of the infant republic, some Americans saw their horizons as too confined and their impact muted unless they circulated near the heart of English-speaking culture. In prerevolutionary America, many educated Virginians, South Carolinians, Bostonians, and Philadelphians felt more at home in London than in the most sophisticated cities of the colonies. For the purveyors of culture, from Boston to San Francisco, London, even as late as 1900, remained the center of the world that really counted, the place to become someone known and talked about in the shared language, someone whose knocks on American doors might be answered because London had already responded. As California novelist Gertrude Atherton felt in the 1890s, the refusals of New York publishers "convinced me that there was no hope for me in my own country, and I determined to go to England to live. If I made a reputation in the literary headquarters of the world, America would be forced to acknowledge me." Years before, Herman Melville's brother had taken the manuscript of *Typee* to London to look for a publisher so that the book might have a chance for success at home. Little had changed.

For the American aspiring to a creative life, London had a sentimental allure, a psychic value, a professional practicality. It meant the presence of the past as a working influence in one's daily life; and although there was a palpable past in a Rome or Florence or Paris, it was not accessible in one's own language, and the intellectual ambience was somehow askew. One could, conceivably, succeed where a foreign tongue was written and spoken; yet even the most gifted artist often encountered a formidable social barrier and an intellectual elitism into which it was difficult to gain admission, where, furthermore, the local tongue, as he employed it, exposed him as an intruder. As George Santayana, despite his Spanish birth one of the most cultivated of Americans, wrote William James from Paris in 1904, "The French people, if I may trust my impression and experience so far, are perfectly willing to let one alone. . . . [Only one of the] Frenchmen I have met has even called on me, or suggested that I should call on him."

In England, of course, Americans had advantages in being both within and without the society. "If you cannot be a duke with a large rent-roll in England," Price Collier wrote in 1909, "by all means be an agreeable American, for to one and the other all doors are open.

. . . No one is jealous of you, no one envious; no one suspects you of pride or vainglory, because being a sovereign yourself, you are equally at home with sovereigns or with the people. . . ." It was easy, then, to shed one's sense of difference. As Ezra Pound put it,

I did not begin with you,
I do not end with you, America.

Viewing the shared culture in terms of his artistic goals, Henry James explained to his brother, "I aspire to write in such a way that it would be impossible for an outsider to say whether I am at a given moment an American writing about England or an Englishman writing about America . . . and so far from being ashamed of such an ambiguity I should be exceedingly proud of it, for it would be highly civilized."

The Russian-born American writer John Cournos, who was in Ezra Pound's English circle and like Pound came from Philadelphia, found his first experience of London in 1912 unlike anything he had known earlier in Naples, Rome, Florence, Venice, or Paris: "The mood defies definition. It was as though I had been in London before, as though there were something in the notion of a previous existence. No sooner had I put my foot here than I felt strangely at ease and familiar with my surroundings, and had the oddly unaccustomed feeling of coming home. More singular still, . . . I quite definitely was aware that I should never leave London for a prolonged absence without experiencing the most excruciating pangs of distress. . . . It is irrational, I admit, and like irrational things, it had surely its roots somewhere deep in the soul."

Writing of himself in the third person, Conrad Aiken, of the same expatriate generation, saw England as "a window, the window which it had been his imperative need to find and to open: the window which looked into his own racial and cultural past, and thus bestowed upon him the sense of belonging, of being part of a moving continuum, the evolving series of civilized consciousness."

Richard Aldington, who was involved with a number of American expatriate writers and married one of them, would sarcastically describe (in *Stepping Heavenward,* 1931) his T. S. Eliot figure as arriving in London during "the calm effortless superiority of the Victorian sunset" and realizing "that he had found his spiritual home. Here, in the ancient matrix of his race, he felt that the genius within him would be recognized, would be effective in a way impossible in a cruder and more turbulent land. . . ." That this was not mere caricature is clear from what England was to Eliot's friend Aiken, who first encountered, in the Edwardian twilight, "the island which contained . . . all of the books which evoked the magic and the dark wonderful mystery of unknown London, the city of cities." To Eliot himself, London at its most attractive was the city of Sidney Paget's late-nineteenth-century illustrations of Sherlock Holmes. "I cannot even remember the name of the artist," he wrote, "but I remember the hansom cabs, the queer bowlers, Holmes's fore-and-aft cap, Holmes in a frock coat after breakfast. . . . But in the Sherlock Holmes stories the late nineteenth century is always romantic, always nostalgic, and never merely silly."

England, George Santayana wrote to his sister in 1901, was "not, as you naughtily say, the best possible world but it is the best actual country, and a great rest after [the turbulence of] America." In his memoirs he defined why he thought so as a young man, recalling a public school celebration of the Jubilee. "Externally," he wrote, "the flint walls and low buildings prepared me for mediaeval austerity; but at the Commemoration service in the chapel it was the soul of modern England that stirred under those Gothic arches and windows, and knelt or sang in those monastic stalls. Deeply moving was the singing by the whole School in unison of *God Save the Queen,* all the verses, under the spell of restrained emotion: fifty years of safety and glory behind, and before, for those young spirits, the promise and the uncertainties of a broad future. This was more than ten years before the Boer War, before the first hint of difficulty and limitation in British dominion. Nothing as yet impaired the sense of a glorious heritage committed to the care of the rising generation, to be maintained and enriched indefinitely. The pride of earth merged delusively and overpoweringly with the will of heaven."

A much different kind of London intoxicated Frank Harris, who had arrived there via Lawrence, Kansas. Even his penchant for overstatement does not diminish his recollection of how it *was,* for what was important was how it *seemed.*

. . . London when you are twenty-eight and have already won a place in its life; London when your mantelpiece has ten times as many invitations as you can accept, and there are two or three pretty girls that attract you; London when everyone you meet is courteous-kind and people of importance are beginning to speak about you; London with a foretaste of success in your mouth while your eyes are open wide at its myriad novelties and wonders; London with its round of receptions and Court life, its theatres and shows, its amusements for the body, mind and soul: enchanting hours at a burlesque prolonged by a boxing-match at the Sporting Club; or an evening in Parliament where world-famous men discuss important policies; or a quiet morning spent with a poet who will live in English literature with Keats or Shakespeare or an afternoon with pictures of a master already consecrated by fame; London, who could give even an idea of its varied delights?

On leaving London, Julian Hawthorne mourned that "it seems a cold and shivering thing to go anywhere else," and concluded that it had been both pleasant and fortunate for him that he spent the better part of his third and fourth decades in England. "For not often in English history have more men and women worth knowing gathered in London than during the last quarter of the nineteenth century." Despite the number of native English writers and artists who may have struggled in attics and garrets, there were always Americans, like the nearly forgotten Hawthorne, son of a famous father, who thought it more romantic and perhaps even more advantageous to risk professional frustration in London than to be sure of it at home in America. "It is the heart of the world," Henry James insisted, "and I prefer to be the least whit in its whirl, than to live and own a territory in any other place."

"I did not know, when I went to London," Van Wyck Brooks wrote, "how many aspiring writers had much the same idea at about the same moment. . . . Numbers of these . . . were to publish their first books in England, as I published mine. . . ." Yet he felt, at that time, that "the American writer could neither successfully stay nor go,—he had only two alternatives, the frying-pan and the fire; and the question was therefore how to change the whole texture of life at home so that writers and artists might develop there." But to change it, one had to become a known quantity at home. When one realizes that, in the twenty years before the First World War limited such options, the career of Robert Frost or T. S. Eliot or Ezra Pound needed London for its springboard, or that Mark Twain left America for London hopelessly in debt, his career in ruins, one has a better idea of the assumed powers of English fumes and fogs to nurture or to restore American genius.

Whether American artistic and literary careers were enhanced by London, or just viewed in a different light, can only be conjectured. Would Stephen Crane have survived to rise again to the level of *The Red Badge of Courage* had he not tried to become an English country squire? Would Harold Frederic have been a novelist at all if London had not provided him distance from the upstate New York he analyzed ruthlessly in *The Damnation of Theron Ware?* Would Bret Harte have written any differently in the bosom of his little-loved family in Plainfield, New Jersey, than in the Lancaster Gate sanctum from which, as an English gentleman, he turned out stories of a vanished West? Would the notorious *Yellow Book* have brought a sense of the avant-garde to English arts and letters, and become the quintessence of what we now view as the English 1890s —or existed at all—if a young and obscure American novelist, Henry Harland, had not left New York for the larger professional vistas of London? What would English painting have been like without Whistler's anglicizing of Impressionism and Sargent's overwhelming impact on portraiture?

The London Yankees is only a record of what was. Still, questions are answered, if only implicitly, in these pages. Did such Americans, from artist Benjamin West in the early days of the republic to poet Robert Lowell in the latter half of the twentieth century, feel exiled from their country? How did their experience affect England, and how did it reverberate in America? To what extent were Americans already established in London willing and able to help advance the careers of their compatriots? For better or worse, how important a factor in the life and work of the expatriate was the experience of London? And what was it like to be an American writer or artist there?

In some cases London would make the man and artist; in other cases the environment swallowed up the man. Transplants can be rejected by the body, or take hold so completely and imperceptibly that one assumes the transplant to be native tissue. With human transplants another possibility exists—the translation to another environment without any perceptible change in either person or environment. Expatriates often brought with them disagreeable mannerisms which stuck, or acquired others which they thought were suitable to the locale. As Bernard Shaw complained, "Anything is better than the vagabond artistic American of the nineteenth century, hanging round the picture galleries and talking Henry James or Frank Harris, according to taste." Yet as Ford Madox Ford had observed, those Americans in his orbit "had all become Londoners because London was unrivalled in its powers of assimilation—the great, easy-going, tolerant, loveable old dressing-gown of a place that it was then." And, he added sadly, after 1914 "it was never more to be so."

Still, the ultimate accolade was not the recognition of successful assimilation as an Englishman, but the recognition that one had accommodated one's Americanism to the appropriate traditions. As Ezra Pound declared, "If a man's work require him to live in exile, let him suffer, or enjoy, his exile gladly. But it would be about as easy for an American to become a Chinaman or a Hindoo as for him to acquire an Englishness . . . that is more than half a skin deep." And John Alford in 1913 would praise Pound—these were the days before his crankiness overshadowed other aspects of his personality— as "a unique phenomenon for he has succeeded in being an American, a man of culture, and a poet, all at the same time."

To Ralph Waldo Emerson a generation earlier, a person in Pound's situation would not have been classified as an American. Contemptuously—or defensively—he had declared in 1878, "They who find America insipid—they for whom London or Paris has spoiled their own homes—can be spared to return to those cities. . . . They complain of the flatness of American life; America has no illusions, no romance. They have no perception of its destiny. They are not Americans." In 1899, in a column entitled "American Literature in Exile," William Dean Howells, at the time the most respected name in American letters, published in a London paper his contention that the absence abroad of such creative talents as Whistler, Sargent, and James made them not exiles but the vanguard of a culture that was becoming more international. Besides, he rationalized, "qualitatively," in the cases of the people he named, "and in Mr. Bret Harte, Mr. Stephen Crane, Mr. Harry Harland, and the late Mr. Harold Frederic, as well as in Mark Twain, now temporarily resident abroad, the defection is very great; but quantitatively it is not such as to leave us without a fair measure of home-keeping authorship." He professed another cause for unconcern. "If any good American," he cautioned, "were distressed by the absenteeism of our authors I should first advise him that American literature was not derived from the folk-lore of the Red Indians, but was . . . a condition of English literature, and was independent even of our independence."

There were enough creative American expatriates who were then in London to give pause to observers, and it is the artistic and literary impact of the experience of London and environs on some of these American artists and writers, on literature and art back home, and on the host culture in the twenty years before the First World War which is the subject of this exploration. Some "London Yankees" turn up only as supporting players; others do not emerge from the shadows at all. No claim is made for representative experience, because each confronted a different situation molded by personality and circumstance. Yet the geography of exile reshaped the American experience and markedly altered our cultural legacy.

"Save for the voice and certain small differences of manner which gave them a flavour of their own," Virginia Woolf wrote complacently in the London *Times Literary Supplement* in 1908, "Americans sink into us, over here, like raindrops into the sea." Except in the town houses of Lancaster Gate, where "John Oliver Hobbes" had covered the ornate dining room table with pages of her mannered fiction, indistinguishable from the native product, and Bret Harte, down the street, had evoked a romantic frontier California from his small upstairs room, she appears to have been mistaken as prophet. It was not that easy to absorb a London Yankee.

CHAPTER I

Tedworth Square

I suppose that London has always existed. One cannot easily imagine an England that had no London.

—Mark Twain in 1897

EARLY IN 1897 an American newspaper ran a five-column headline, "Close of a Great Career." Beneath it was the story that Mark Twain, abandoned by his wife and daughters, at sixty-one was living in London in wretched poverty. Disgusted by the baseless libel yet truly down on his luck, Sam Clemens raged that only a man was capable of such lying and vileness, not a dog or a cow. But he made out a list of things which had gone wrong. The cook's sweetheart was dying, one of the maids was losing her sight, the porter had pleurisy, a friend's baby had died, another friend had fractured his skull. Besides, returning from a visit to the friend in the hospital, Clemens's cab had nearly run over a little boy. "Since bad luck struck us," he concluded, "it is risky to have anything to do with us."

The list omitted the worst disasters. Bad investments had left him with a six-figure debt, and to extricate himself from his creditors while earning money to pay his bills (dollar for dollar, as his wife,

Livy, insisted), he had gone on a round-the-world tour the year before, arranged by the indefatigable Major J. B. Pond, the Barnum of
lecture agents. Bankruptcy had affected Clemens's pride more than
his life-style, and the tour westward from Vancouver (where Pond
bade him good-bye) to New Zealand, Australia, India, South Africa,
and other places where English was spoken and read, had resembled
a royal progress. He and Livy had examined their accounts and their
needs very carefully, he had allegedly told Robert Barr, whose *Idler*
magazine had serialized *The American Claimant* a few years earlier,
and they found that "the only things on which they could economize
were *Harper's Magazine* and a cheaper closet paper."

At every port there were newspapermen, and Clemens, knowing
that controversy sold tickets and filled seats, provided quotable lines.
While Logan Pearsall Smith, who had already settled in as an expatriate, was telling another London Yankee, Joseph Pennell, that
the English concept of an American was "an ideal built up from Bret
Harte and Mark Twain," Clemens was busy on the other side of the
globe explaining that Harte was "sham and shoddy." Australian
papers were quick to respond. According to the *Argus* it was amazing that the author of *A Tramp Abroad* and the "Jumping Frog"
should consider the author of "Truthful James" and "The Luck of
Roaring Camp" a writer of "shoddy," and the *Sydney Morning
Herald* took Clemens's attack on his "brother writer" as additional
evidence that "authors are perhaps the very worst judges of authors." The great surprise to Australian reporters, however, was
Clemens's bald assertion that although he didn't like the man, he did
expect to meet Harte in London. He didn't, although Harte was
there.

Nothing in London went as anticipated. On the last day of July
1896, Clemens's steamer, the *Norman,* arrived in Southampton,
where his publisher, Andrew Chatto, had forwarded letters from
America, six copies of the Chatto edition of *Joan of Arc,* a royalty
check for £446 7s. 9d., and a letter expressing pleasure "that you and
Mrs Clemens are once more back in the old country." They had been
traveling more than a year.

It had been arranged that Katy Leary, who had long been in the
family service, would accompany the younger daughters, Jean and
Susy, to England, and in preparation Clemens and Livy proceeded to

London and located a furnished house in Guildford, in the Surrey suburbs to the southwest. A week later came a letter from Katy. Susy, at twenty-four the apple of her father's eye, a bright and beautiful young woman who had gone to college at Bryn Mawr, was "slightly ill—nothing of consequence." Unconcerned at first, Clemens wrote Chatto on August 12 to accept his "kind invitation to a chop or a steak, when I might take your instructions regarding 'Tom Sawyer, Detective' & make a suggestion for a new issue of your other [Mark Twain] books. . . ." But two days later, now troubled by no word from Connecticut about his daughter, he telegraphed Chatto that he might return to America the next day. Still, he did not, never imagining that the "slight illness" would become meningitis, leaving Susy blind and raving in her last days in the Clemens home in Hartford.

With no response to a cable for further news, Livy and their daughter Clara left Clemens to his business and began packing to return to the *Norman,* "in case the news should be bad." The ship was to leave Southampton for New York the next day at noon.

Finally came a cablegram saying, "Wait for cablegram in the morning." This was not satisfactory—not reassuring. I cabled again, asking that the answer be sent to Southampton, for the day was now closing. I waited in the post office that night till the doors were closed, toward midnight, in the hopes that good news might still come, but there was no message. We sat silent at home till one in the morning, waiting—waiting for we knew not what. Then we took the earliest morning train and when we reached Southampton the message was there. It said the recovery would be long but certain. This was a great relief to me but not to my wife. She was frightened. She and Clara went aboard the steamer at once and sailed for America to nurse Susy. I remained behind to search for another and larger house in Guildford.

That was the 15th of August, 1896. Three days later, when my wife and Clara were about halfway across the ocean, I was standing in our dining-room, thinking of nothing in particular, when a cablegram was put into my hand. It said, "Susy was peacefully released to-day."

It is one of the mysteries of our nature that a man, all unprepared, can receive a thunder-stroke like that and live. . . .

There was no longer any need for a larger house at Guildford. Still, Clemens remained there, completely stunned, until his grieving family returned from America, when they moved temporarily to

Ford's Hotel in Manchester Street on September 11. The Chatto firm house-hunted for them while they attempted to come to terms with their bereavement. At least once, Clemens emerged to visit the new Chatto quarters near St Martin's Church and the National Gallery, recording in his notebook how the chiming of the St Martin's clock reminded him of the tune he had "heard . . . to weariness from every church clock in Australia, & now and then in India & Africa." But obviously there had been other explorations, for notebook jottings suggest that the Mark Twain sense of humor and interest in life were slowly returning. "England is the land of neat and pretty and shapely and polite housemaids," he observed on September 22. ". . . All the dogs here wear muzzles. Of course, they prefer it."

On October 3 the family moved to 23 Tedworth Square in Chelsea, a quiet backwater above Queen's Road* but only a short stroll from the fashionable artists' and writers' residences on Tite Street, Cheyne Walk, and the Embankment. The red brick corner house, four narrow floors with a servants' level below stairs, was occupied without fanfare. Chatto's partner, Percy Spalding, had arranged for the lease. It was to run until the following July, at five and a half guineas a week, half a guinea more than Clemens claimed he could afford, but in his bereavement he was not prepared to quibble. He wanted to hide away until he was ready to see people again. (Frank Bliss, his American publisher, would not be given his London address until the following May.) In his notebook he observed, "In London it takes five weeks to find a house (furnished) that will suit both your convenience and your means. Five more to find a cook." He was appalled that a good cook required thirty-five pounds a year including beer money, yet even then the family would change cooks three times in as many months, perhaps because the household atmosphere was so lugubrious. "We already had maids," Clemens noted, "or maybe it would have taken eleven weeks to get them. Got a good man the first day to do odd jobs—carry up coal, black boots, scour knives, etc. He is the authorized messenger of the block and has to show a good character before the police will appoint him."

From the second-floor bay windows Clemens could watch "young

* Now Royal Hospital Road.

men and maids" hugging and kissing in the park, and was relieved not to be the target of curious attention when he went for his walk up to the busy King's Road at Markham Square, where there happened to be a pub on the corner. Huddled into his sorrow, he was a thin and shrunken vestige of the famous Mark Twain. As, in a better mood, he told the Savage Club a few years later, when he had first come to London he was six feet four: "Now I am 5 feet 8½ and daily diminishing in altitude. . . ."

London, he told his notebook, "is a collection of villages. When you live in one of them with its quiet back streets and its one street of stores and shops, little bits of stores and shops like those of any other village, it is not possible for you to realize that you are in the heart of the greatest city in the world." As a result, it took three weeks before the first reporter found him. Clemens was sure that the Chelsea librarian must have provided the tip. There was no interview. Then a Water Company representative arrived to deliver notice that if the owner of the house did not pay his overdue bill the water would be cut off. "They know that you will pay . . . ," he noted, "and take it out of next [month's] rent rather than have your water cut off." There were problems to city dwelling, but the seclusion largely was successful, and Clemens late in October was able to exorcise some of his ghosts by beginning a new travel book, to become *Following the Equator* in America and *More Tramps Abroad* in England.

He still liked to think of himself as poor, and wrote E. C. Stedman in New York that he had sent his resignation from the Authors Club "solely because I am in debt and must economise even in trifles when I am spending other people's money." But he retained his Players Club membership, he explained, because it was his home whenever he was in New York and therefore an "economy" for his creditors. To his friend and financial adviser, Standard Oil financier H. H. Rogers, he noted on November 6 the election of "Brer McKinley" as President. "I supposed he would [win]. Now, then, let us have a quiet spell for a while, if we can." But to Mrs Rogers he wrote to urge on her husband the creation of a college fund for a young girl just turned sixteen. "For and in behalf of Helen Keller, stone blind and deaf, and formerly dumb," he prefaced it. "It won't do for America to allow this marvelous child to retire from her studies because of poverty." Clemens had met her when she was fourteen. She was now ready for Radcliffe and had scored astonishingly high on the entrance examinations. Perhaps Clemens was especially moved by the memory of Susy, blind and isolated from the world in her last days, as he asked that Rogers and his wealthy associates "put their hands down through their hearts into their pockets" to assure Helen Keller's education. Rogers took care of it. His friend in London was grateful.

They did not celebrate Thanksgiving Day at 23 Tedworth Square. Clemens's notebook recorded instead recollections of Susy, yet he kept his gloom out of *Following the Equator.* Christmas came and went in similar fashion, although the commercial neighborhoods of London were bright with holiday cheer. "The square and adjacent streets," he wrote on Christmas morning, "are not merely quiet, they are *dead.* There is not a sound. At intervals a Sunday-looking person passes along. . . . The family have been to breakfast. We three sat and talked as usual, but the name of the day was not mentioned."

In 1896–97 Mark Twain lived in a world that was only incidentally the London he loved. Sorrow pervaded Tedworth Square, and the literary and artistic activity which enlivened Chelsea had no place in his life. (Katy Leary's judgment about their former Tite Street neighbor, Oscar Wilde, who had gone to jail the year before, was that "he was a very bad man . . . , so bad you couldn't talk about what he had done.") "I don't mean that I am miserable," he wrote William Dean Howells; "no—worse than that—indifferent. Indifferent to nearly everything but work. I like that; I enjoy, & stick to it. I do it without purpose & without ambition; merely for the love of it." He wrote because he needed to earn dollars, but otherwise his self-assessment was accurate; and much of what he wrote, except for *Following the Equator,* was unpublishable. Often he would rise at four or five in the morning, and would write compulsively for hours in hopes of shutting out the brooding demons who forced him to think about his dead daughter, but his notebooks are evidence that every device failed. They include numerous self-pitying references to Susy, including one in which he felt denied by fate of the oppor-

tunity of seeing Susy in her coffin. He began to live in a world of
dreams and daydreams which substituted for a world gone sour, and
the dreams found their way into his notebooks and fragments of fiction, some of them clearly a reaction to the loss of Susy, others the
release of a self he suppressed when awake. "Everyone is a moon,
and has a dark side which he never shows to anybody," he confided
to his notebook in Tedworth Square. In one of his dreams, he noted,
a young "negro wench . . . made a disgusting proposition to me."
He accepted the existence of a "dream self" which could do things
and think thoughts which the unliberated waking self would never
dare. "I go to unnameable places," he wrote; "I do unprincipled
things; and every vision is vivid, every sensation—physical as well
as moral—is *real.*" The dream self appeared at social gatherings in
a nightshirt, forgot his lines on the lecture platform, lost his way in
"the corridors of monstrous hotels." He seemed to seek out a condition on the edge of madness where he could, pen in hand, conjure
up memories of Susy, or force his imagination to devise writing ideas
at a time when his conscious creative energies were numbed. One recommendation to himself from the London notebooks, obviously inspired by his longing for Susy, suggests the painfully surreal *Dream
Play* which Strindberg would write in 1901:

Write a novel in which part of the action takes place in heaven and
hell, the next upon the earth. Let a woman in heaven watch the sweep of
the ocean of fire at close quarters—a person passes by at very long intervals only; the ocean is so large. It is a solitude—so is heaven. She has
sought for her daughter for a long time—she is watching hell, now, but
not expecting her daughter to be there. Musing, she hears a shriek, and
her daughter sweeps by. There is an instant of recognition by both—the
mother springs in, perceiving there is no happiness in heaven for her
any longer.

His daughter Clara recalled his outbursts to her mother at Tedworth Square about the price one paid to be a temporary inhabitant
of the earth.

"Do you remember, Livy, the hellish struggle it was to settle on making that lecture trip around the world? How we fought the idea, the horrible idea, the heart-torturing idea. I, almost an old man, with ill health,

carbuncles, bronchitis and rheumatism. I, with patience worn to rags, I was to pack my bag and be jolted around the devil's universe for what? To pay debts that were not even of my making. And as a reward for our self-castigation and faithfulness to ideals of nobility we were robbed of our greatest treasure, our lovely Susy in the midst of her blooming talents and personal graces. You want me to believe it is a judicious, a charitable God that runs this world. Why, I could run it better myself."

On Sundays, Clara remembered, "Father would take Jean and me for a walk by the side of the river or into Regent's Park. But everywhere we met an atmosphere of world-loneliness. Poor women seated aimlessly and alone on benches, even when the air was cold and damp. A stray cat, a stray leaf, a stray—— Oh, everything looked adrift and unattended. It was on such days that Father created the habit of vituperating the human race." Clemens's misanthropy had hardly begun there, but everything Clemens saw now reinforced his cynicism, and it did not improve matters for him that Jean, the younger of his two surviving daughters, might suddenly, while walking along the Chelsea Embankment with him, be struck by an epileptic attack. The world was a hateful place—even his beloved London. Yet the world was not entirely bleak, although Clara's selective remembrances suggest little else. Clemens, through Chatto's son Andrew, arranged that the girls could indulge in the new passion for cycling, purchasing, for twenty pounds (despite his straitened circumstances), two "Swift" bicycles with which Clara and Jean were "charmed." And Clara had a hired piano upon which she practiced more and more as the need for solemnity receded, a *Times* reporter living nearby even complaining, by May, of the noise—as he worked a night shift and slept by day. Clemens consulted Spalding, who advised ignoring the complaint, and Tedworth Square continued to resound with Clara's keyboard virtuosity.

On rare occasions Clemens invited a close friend, J. Y. M. Mac-Alister, a former physician who had founded the *Library* and wrote on health matters, to visit and "smoke some manilas," but the offer was a private one which did not include seeing the mourning family—"still hermits," he apologized. But he promised a fire in his study, and conversation. Occasionally he went out to dinner with literary friends. Bram Stoker, of *Dracula* fame, Anthony Hope Hawkins,

author of *The Prisoner of Zenda,* and American liberal preacher
Moncure Conway were three whose company at the table he enjoyed;
and he sometimes dined with Andrew Chatto and with Sir Henry
Morton Stanley, the American correspondent who found Livingstone
and after a career of adventure in Africa had acquired a seat in
Parliament.

He visited Henry James in Kensington, who explained that he
was teaching himself to dictate directly to a typewriter—the term
then in use not only for the machine but for the person who punched
the machine's keys—because he had heard that Clemens had taken
to dictating. The author of *Tom Sawyer* and *Huckleberry Finn* had
even purchased a Remington as early as the late 1870s, soon after the
new American invention had been placed on the market, and had
been the first author to submit a typewritten manuscript to a publisher. His typescript, however, had been made from the handwritten
text, and he still kept his distance from the device. James "makes it
go," Clemens wrote to Howells, "but if there could be anything
worse for me than a typewriter, it would be a human typewriter."

Few saw Clemens at home and fewer knew where it was, permit-
ting him still to take his daily stroll unnoticed among the colorful
denizens of Chelsea he liked to refer to as "Shakespeare people." His
notebook entry for February 18, 1897, showed him in a typical
mood. "Brilliant morning (very rare). Some of the people looked
glad to be alive. But not many. Walked an hour in the King's Road,
as usual, between Markham Square and the Chelsea Polytechnic—
back and forth. Shakespeare people all on hand as usual."

A few days earlier Clemens's old friend Poultney Bigelow, who
had once lived at Cheyne Walk, persuaded him to take tea with
Bigelow's former neighbors, Lord Monkswell and his wife, Mary.
Cautioned that she should invite no curious guests, because Clemens
was in "deep mourning for a daughter, & lived 'perdu,'" Lady Mary
nevertheless let her brother Henry make his weekly call as long as he
pretended he lived there. The strategy worked, and Clemens, arriving alone, "very thin & small, & with a profusion of fair hair nearly
turned white," talked to the small admiring circle, Lady Mary "sitting quite in his pocket." She had "carefully thrown his books, two
fat red vols., in a careless manner, on the table close to his tea cup,"

19

and was certain that they did not escape his "eagle eye." Whatever the reasons, Clemens warmed to his company, talking about "the attractiveness of old legends, ghosts & apparitions; his eyes blazed and he shook his long white hair."

On April 13 he recorded in his notebook, "I finished my book to-day," and two days later sent some leaves of unused manuscript to his friend MacAlister; but *Following the Equator* appeared unsatisfactory when he and Livy (his severest critic) reread it, and he holed up again at Tedworth Square. "Finished the book again—" he noted on May 18, "addition of 30,000 words." Still, a lot of material intended for the book remained in the discard heap, Clemens explaining to Rogers, "A successful book is made not of what is in it, but what is left out of it." More, in fact, was left out of the American version than the English text. Andrew Chatto toned down none of Clemens's philosophical asides or aspersions upon British imperialism, although what Clemens called "a whole raft of reprint matter" was expunged, including a number of printed pages torn from an Australian book, his substitution for flagging inspiration. Wary of careful English readers, Chatto also insisted upon correcting the date of Fiji's cession to England and upon consulting *Whittaker's Almanac* for the English professional record throw of a cricket ball.

Since it was unlikely that *Following the Equator* would itself extricate Clemens from debt, he began flirting with the idea of returning to New York briefly to deliver a benefit lecture at the Waldorf for which choice seats were to be auctioned off "at Jenny Lind prices." But the gaudy scheme was contrary to the code imposed by Rogers and upheld by Livy, which required the author to earn dollar for dollar. He would have to lecture, Livy insisted, "in the old way and at the ordinary prices." A hard winter of traveling would undermine Livy's health, and he had no stomach for it either. A month later he turned down an alternative proposal from Major Pond of fifty thousand dollars and all expenses for 125 nights in America.

Still another tactic was tried. James Gordon Bennett's *New York Herald,* getting wind of Clemens's troubles, organized a Mark Twain subscription fund, a debt of gratitude, it editorialized, "for the sunshine spread among the American people by the writings of the author." The *Herald* began the campaign with a thousand dollars matched by another thousand from Andrew Carnegie. No wonder rumors circulated that Mark Twain was either living in poverty in London or had already died there.

On June 2, a reporter named White, representing the *New York Journal,* arrived at 23 Tedworth Square with two cablegrams from his paper, which he showed Clemens:

IF MARK TWAIN DYING IN POVERTY, IN LONDON, SEND 500 WORDS.
IF MARK TWAIN HAS DIED IN POVERTY SEND 1000 WORDS.

Clemens suggested, in substance, a shorter response:

James Ross Clemens, a cousin, was seriously ill here two or three weeks ago, but is well now. The report of my illness grew out of his illness; the report of my death was an exaggeration. I have not been ill. Mark Twain.

An interview with him appeared in New York a few days later, making light of the rumors:

"Of course I am dying," Mark Twain smiled grimly. "But I do not know that I am doing it any faster than anybody else. As for dying in poverty, I had just as soon die in poverty here in London as anywhere. But it would be a little more difficult, because I have got quite a number of friends, any one of whom would be good for a month's provisions, and that would drag out the agony a fairly long time.

"No, I assure you I am as well as ever I was. You see you must not attach too much importance to my wife's remark that I was not in a condition to receive visitors. That simply means that I was in bed. Now most women think that if a man does not get up before twelve o'clock there must be something wrong with him, and as I never get up before then, my wife thinks that I am not in good health. As a matter of fact when you were announced I told her to have you shown up to my room, but you can never persuade a tidy woman to show a stranger into an untidy bedroom, and so that did not work.

"I said to her, 'Show him up, send some cigars up. I am comfortable enough!'

" 'Yes,' she said, 'but what about him?'

" 'Oh,' I said, 'if you want him to be as comfortable as I am make him up a bed in the other corner of the room.' That did not work, either, so I thought the best thing to do was to get up and come to see you.

"Poverty is relative. I have been in poverty so often that it does not worry me much. A more serious matter is the money owing to other people, not by any fault of mine, and yet owing to them by me. . . . But I do not trouble about the rumors that go about in regard to me. . . . I keep on ploughing away and working and working and hoping and hoping, but the idea of being in poverty does not either trouble me or frighten me."

(What are you working about, just now?)

"Oh, my journey about the world. Everybody has done his little circumnavigation act, and I thought it about time I did mine, so I have been getting it ready for the press since I have been here, and therefore, for the matter of that, the book is just my impressions of the world at large. I go into no details. I never do for that matter. Details are not my strong point, unless I choose for my own pleasure to go into them seriously. Besides, I am under no contract to supply details to the reader. All that I undertake to do is to interest him. . . ."

On July 24 the *Herald* announced that its subscription fund had grown (only) to $2,601.65. That day a reader sent a dollar and proposed that everyone who had read *Huckleberry Finn* do likewise. By then Rogers, who had observed the sluggish returns, cabled Clemens, "All friends think *Herald* movement mistake. Withdraw graciously." From London the object of the increasingly embarrassing campaign, who had kept what he assumed was an acquiescent although detached silence, had written Bennett, who was in Paris, "I have grown so tired of being in debt that I often think I would part with my skin and teeth to get out." But he was parting with something which Livy Clemens felt was even more valuable—his pride. Clemens may have been the most popular writer in America, but that fame would not translate itself into a popular subscription to extricate him from the $190,000 disaster of the Paige typesetting machine or from the failure of the publishing company he let his nephew mismanage. He wrote to the *Herald* to put an end to the fund raising. "My wife," he then wrote Carnegie, "won't allow me to accept any money as long as I am not disabled."

As the *Herald* campaign was being wound down, Clemens, apparently in good humor, earned some American dollars by reporting the Jubilee festivities. His lengthy dispatch was an extended love letter to London, with its central feature an imaginative reconstruction of an earlier but apparently equally colossal and colorful procession, the parade in 1415 celebrating Henry V's victory over the French at Agincourt. Finally, he concluded, "That was as much of it as the spirit correspondent could let me have; he was obliged to stop there because he had an engagement to sing in the choir, and was already late." Then he grew serious, pointing out, as other writers also would, that "in a good many ways the world has moved further ahead since the Queen was born than it moved in all the rest of the two thousand [years of British history] put together." Two weeks later the Clemens family vacated Tedworth Square and moved to the Continent, spending the remainder of the summer in Switzerland before settling in Vienna, where Clara hoped to study piano under Theodor Leschitzky. Besides, living in style in Austria with American dollars was cheap, he wrote Howells. They could live in the finest hotel in Vienna, with four bedrooms, a dining room, a drawing room, three bathrooms, and three "Vorzimmers" (including all food expenses) for $600 a month, less than half of comparable New York costs. And through the later nineties the Clemens fortunes were improving, his copyrights in England and America alone bringing in $200,000 a year by the end of 1898. On December 30 he told Howells, "I have been out & bought a box of 6-cent cigars; I was smoking 4½ before."

Eager to pay off all his debts, Clemens bubbled over with ideas for quick profits, from inventions which were impractical to book schemes which convinced no one. To Chatto he suggested that he preface a collection of translations of French journalistic pieces on the Dreyfus case, at a 25 percent royalty to himself, not only because he was eager to capitalize on the interest in the trial, but because he saw Captain Dreyfus as another martyr to injustice on the order of Joan of Arc. Deflating the idea, the overcautious Chatto thought "the feelings of the British public are not sufficiently stirred by the Dreyfus affair. . . ." With no interest likely in America, Clemens could only mourn to Chatto that it would have been "a most killingly readable book." Casting about for subjects which might benefit from a Mark Twain by-line, Chatto recommended instead "a killingly readable book of your own writing," which was more than Clemens could provide, as each idea for a major work aborted into useless fragments, unfinished manuscripts, or articles he could later collect into a substitute for the large-scale work for which he no longer had the inner resources.

Despite the advantages of Vienna, living in a country where English was not the prevailing language was exile. In May 1899 they would return once more to London, where they would remain (but for a summer in Sweden) until October 1900. It was a happier period. They settled first at 30 Wellington Court, Albert Gate, near Regent's Park. Since their apartment was too small for a writing room, Chatto & Windus supplied space in its own offices at 110 St Martin's Lane, to which Clemens repaired happily on the open top level of a horse-drawn omnibus. There he produced no extended writing—he was past that—but only magazine articles and speeches for rounds of dinners and entertainments at such clubs as the Whitefriars, the New Vagabonds, the Beefsteak, and the Authors; such events as the annual Fourth of July Dinner of the American Society, a benefit banquet for the Royal Literary Fund, and a welcome-home dinner for actor Sir Henry Irving. No longer living *perdu* as in Tedworth Square, and no longer in financial embarrassment, he had returned to London as the representative hero of the American experience.

Also, Twain was vastly quotable, and even his seemingly absurd commentaries on the world betrayed uncommon sense. *Punch* headed a column soon after he arrived "The Twenty-First Century Publishing Company, Limited," and went on, "This company has been formed to carry on the ordinary business of a publisher on the system devised by the eminent American humorist, Mark Twain, in a moment of seriousness. Instead of issuing books within a few months of their completion, the Company will not publish any work until a century after the death of the author. All unpleasantness, opposition, and fear of litigation on the part of the author's contemporaries will thus be avoided, In the case of an author who may wish to receive remuneration for his work, the necessary deeds will be drawn up by the Company's solicitors to secure for his heirs, or their assigns, a share of the profits or a royalty on each copy sold." The mock announcement followed Twain a step further: "The Company cannot treat with any impecunious writer whatever who might be misguided enough to desire some profit for himself during his lifetime."

Everyone in London who counted wanted Mark Twain to dinner, or to speak after dinner, or to accept an honorary membership or office. The Savage Club made him its fourth honorary member, its previous three having been the Prince of Wales, Arctic hero Fridtjof Nansen, and Henry M. Stanley. At its dinner for him on June 9, Clemens responded to the toastmaster by observing, "I was sorry to hear my name mentioned as one of the great authors, because they have a sad habit of dying off. Chaucer is dead, Spenser is dead, so is Milton, so is Shakespeare, and I am not feeling very well myself." Three evenings later he was accepting membership in the Authors Club, where he confided that his American originality as a writer was only his English literary heritage. "They must not claim credit in America for what was really written in another form so long ago. They must only claim that I trimmed this, that, and the other, and so changed their appearance as to make them seem to be original. You now see what modesty I have in stock. But it has taken long practice to get there."

At the Whitefriars Club dinner for him in the huge banquet room of the Hotel Cecil on June 16, among the two hundred guests were the American ambassador, Joseph H. Choate, and the senator-elect from New York, Chauncey Depew; but the gathering was largely one of London journalists and editors, one of whom, Louis Frederick Austin of the *Illustrated London News,* in introducing Clemens, cited the parallel between Mark Twain and Sir Walter Scott, both of whom had honorably paid debts incurred by business failures through the earnings of their pens. "I do not know anything so sad," Clemens responded, "as a dinner where you are going to get up and say something by and by, and you do not know what it is." But he recalled a Whitefriars dinner twenty-five years before, when editor George Augustus Sala had arrived late and was almost instantaneously called upon to give a speech, which he did, impromptu. "He went into the whole history of the United States, and made it entirely new to me. He filled it with episodes and incidents that Washington never heard of, and he did it so convincingly that although I knew none of it happened, from that day to this I do not know any [American] history but Sala's." Eventually he rambled on to Senator Depew and the ambassador, and although Choate, like Sala a quarter-century before, had not yet arrived, Clemens had an observation prepared which he determined upon despite the tardiness of his compatriot. "And here we three meet again," he declared, "as exiles on one pretext or another, and you will notice that while we are absent there is a pleasing tranquility in America—a building up of public confidence. We are doing the best we can for our country, and we never serve it to greater advantage than when we get out of it."

The round of welcoming dinners included one on June 29 for both Mark Twain and Olivia, tendered by the New Vagabonds Club, largely peopled by actors, writers, and artists. Music hall comedian George Grossmith did the introduction, after which Clemens, first paying a tribute to Livy's role in his writing ("My wife puts the facts in, and they make it respectable"), noted with mock ominousness, "A sermon comes from my lips always when I listen to a humorous speech." Threatening his audience of one-time bohemians with a moral lecture, he announced, "I will [now] read you a written statement upon the subject that I wrote three years ago to read to the Sabbath schools." Then, with the timing of a London music hall comic, he emptied each of his pockets inside out, searching for the alleged speech. "No!" he apologized with mock chagrin. "I have left it at home."

On July 3 he lost something else—not a speech but a hat—and milked the episode for years afterward in his writings, speeches, and small talk. He had been at a luncheon at which another guest was the eloquent champion of temperance Basil Wilberforce, Canon of Westminster Abbey and Chaplain of the House of Commons. There were few issues on which the two men might have agreed, but they did have one thing in common, as Clemens wrote Howells:

This afternoon he left a luncheon-party half an hour ahead of the rest, & carried off my hat (which has *Mark Twain* in a big hand written in it). When the rest of us came out there was but one hat that would go on my head—it fitted exactly, too. So I wore it away. It had no name in it, but the Canon was the only man who was absent. I wrote him a note at 8 p.m., saying that for four hours I had not been able to take anything that did not belong to me, nor stretch a fact beyond the frontiers of truth, & my family were getting alarmed. Could he explain my trouble? And now at 8:30 p.m. comes a note from him to say that all the afternoon he has been exhibiting a wonder-compelling mental vivacity & grace of expression, etc., etc., & have I missed a hat?

The next day Clemens suggested to an audience, alluding to Wilberforce and the incident of the hat, "So I judge I was born to rise to high dignity in the Church somehow or other, but I do not know what he was born for." The hat affair began a friendship with the future Archdeacon Wilberforce which their very different attitudes toward whiskey did not sever.

For the annual Fourth of July dinner of the American Society (again at the Cecil), Ambassador Choate arrived on time, and announced patriotically in his address to the assembled expatriates and guests, "You may be Americans or Englishmen, but you cannot be both at the same time." The audience applauded dutifully, but many there knew it was not so. Some had lived in England for decades; some had taken English citizenship, and even titles; some dressed, in Bret Harte fashion, like English clubmen or country squires. Still, they saw no conflict in their dual loyalties except on such rare, worrisome occasions as the Venezuela boundary affair, and then threat of war made them more Yankee than ever. Clemens passed quickly over what he called the "sentimental, patriotic, poetic side" of the national holiday. "It has a commercial, a business side that needs reforming." He had not been "home" for years to see the day of Independence celebrated, nor had many of his hearers; yet he inveighed against his country in language which suggested that time and distance had not made him wax sentimental about what he thought to be a blot on the American example of behavior. "See what it costs us every year with loss of life, the crippling of thousands with its fireworks, and the burning down of property. It is not only sacred to patriotism and universal freedom, but to the surgeon, the undertaker, the insurance offices. . . ."

Only once was he at a loss for words. At a London party given by Sir Gilbert Parker he was introduced to a twenty-five-year-old writer, half American in ancestry, who had already earned a reputation as a soldier-correspondent, having published journalism on the insurrection in Cuba and books about his service with the Malakand Field Force in India in 1897 and with Kitchener's Nile expedition in 1898. As young Winston Churchill strolled off with Clemens into another room for a few moments of private talk, each with his inevitable cigar, other guests wondered which one would do the talking. Each was known to prefer a monologue to a conversation, but experienced listeners predicted that the old veteran would prevail. The pair returned, and Churchill, asked if he had enjoyed himself, answered with an eager "Yes!" Clemens, taken aside privately, answered the same question with "I have had a smoke." Yet when Churchill came to New York in December 1900 on a lecture tour, Clemens agreed to deliver the introductory speech. Perhaps it was his way of getting his own words in first.

Because Clemens hoped that his daughter Jean's ailments might respond to the manipulation of osteopath Henrick Kellgren, the family left the Knightsbridge flat for the remainder of the summer to be near Kellgren's clinic at Sanna in Sweden. The "Swedish movements" became a panacea Clemens recommended for all ills (he submitted to it himself), and he was awed by the beauty of the northern sunsets, which he said often brought tears to his eyes. But by October they were back in London, where Jean Clemens vainly continued her treatments, and her father returned to his articles and stories for American newspapers and magazines, and notes for after-dinner speeches. Promoting the osteopath to Henry James at one dinner, Twain completely baffled the Master. As James put it in a letter to his sister-in-law Alice, Mark Twain had given him "muddled and confused glimpses of Lord Kelvin, Albumen, Sweden and half a dozen other things on which I was prevented from afterwards bringing him to book."

When he had been hidden away at Tedworth Square, he had written his friend the Reverend Joseph Twichell in Hartford, "I have many unwritten books to fly to for my preservation." And he had compulsively begun story after story in Tedworth Square, adding to the pile of unfinished manuscript while on the Continent—dream fragments, autobiographical epitomes, sequels to his adventures of Tom Sawyer and Huck Finn—writing as if the very act would stave off not only his self-accusations about Susy but the conclusion he had already come to in his subconscious that the vein of American experience he had been mining for forty years had given out. In London in the autumn of 1899 he worked further on yet another version of "The Mysterious Stranger" and completed a long piece on Joan of Arc he had begun while in Sweden. It had been written on invitation from T. Douglas Murray, a wealthy barrister and amateur historian who had commissioned a woman to translate the official record of the trials and rehabilitation of the Maid, which years before had been published in a French text by Jules Quicherat. The Mark Twain introduction (because Clemens had published a popular book on Joan in 1896) was intended to guarantee the book's commercial success; however, Murray would spend nearly a year anglicizing (in red ink) the Twain prose and punctuation, and making the diction more elegant, changing *fight* to *struggle, brief* to *short,* and *go back* to *return.* Clemens called him a "literary kangaroo" and wrote Murray a long, vituperative letter accusing him of "reducing simple & dignified speech to clumsy & vapid commonplace." Eventually he withdrew his piece. Murray published the translation under his own name in 1902 and Clemens's essay appeared belatedly in *Harper's* in December 1904 as "Saint Joan of Arc."

Canon Wilberforce, also interested in Mark Twain on Joan, tried to lure him into his drawing room to talk on the subject "to the Dukes & Earls & M.P.'s." Clemens put him off, although the canon assured him that he would not steal his hat this time, and Clemens apologized in a note: "You mustn't think it is because I am afraid to trust my hat in your reach again, for I assure you upon [my] honor it isn't. I should bring my other one."

October had brought Clemens back not only to England, but to an England, like his own United States, at war. "Privately speaking," he wrote Howells early in the new year about the struggle with the Boers in South Africa, "this is a sordid & criminal war, & in every way shameful & excuseless. Every day I write (in my head) bitter magazine articles about it, but I have to stop with that. For England must not fall: it would mean an inundation of Russian & German political degradations which would envelop the globe & steep it in a sort of Middle-Age night & slavery. . . ." But he was also for the man defending his home, and confessed, "My head is with the Briton, but my heart & such rags of morals as I have are with the Boer." He saw the American war with Spain which had begun in

1898 as equally imperial and expansionist, writing to Twichell in January 1900, "Apparently we are not proposing to set the Filipinos free & give their islands to them; & apparently we are not proposing to hang the priests & confiscate their property. If these things are so the war out there has no interest for me."

Much of positive and personal importance to Clemens was nevertheless going on in America in his absence. A uniform edition of Mark Twain was being published in New York, with Columbia pro- ︎ fessor Brander Matthews providing a biographical and critical introduction which constituted a literary establishment seal upon his achievement. There was also an "Author's Preface," for which Clemens wrote that anything he said could be construed as immodesty, except that "by law of custom" such a preface was in order. "I find no reason [for the collection] that I can offer without immodesty except the rather poor one that I should like to see a 'Uniform Edition' myself. It is nothing; a cat could say it about her kittens." What had attracted more attention was his article "Christian Science and the Book of Mrs. Eddy," which had appeared in the October (1899) *Cosmopolitan*. For months, letters from laymen and ministers would cross the Atlantic heaping praise or blame. He was either un-American or a champion of formal religion—neither posture a very familiar one to him. *Cosmopolitan* editor John Brisben Walker, delighted with the furor, sent him an additional two hundred dollars above the price agreed to for the piece, crowing, "It seems to me that you have knocked Christian Science in this country flat." To Twichell the author of the essay wrote, paradoxically, "I cannot help feeling rather inordinately proud of America for the gay and hearty way in which she takes hold of any new thing that comes along and gives it a first-rate trial. Many an ass in America is getting . . . benefit out of X-Science's new exploitation of an age-old healing principle— faith, combined with the patient's imagination—let it boom along! I have no objection. Let them call it by whatever name they choose, so long as it does helpful work among the class which is numerically vastly the largest bulk of the human race, i.e., the fools, the idiots, the pudd'nheads." (Henry James would be more caustic about the American importation, telling E. M. Forster when they first met in 1908 that Mary Baker Eddy "succeeded by saying to herself,

'Hitherto things have been done gratis, for the poor; I will provide for the rich and charge accordingly.' ")

Although Clemens had settled in as a Londoner, even to the point of agreeing to be a witness at the House of Lords committee hearing on copyright in April 1900, there were insistent teasing reminders of the usefulness of an American base of operations. From New York S. S. McClure had made a tempting offer of one-tenth interest in a new periodical he wanted to establish, the *Universal,* if Mark Twain would become editor; further, Clemens would receive an added one-twentieth interest for each of the two succeeding years if he remained as editor. Negotiations dragged on through the first half of 1900, with the token time Clemens was to devote to the work enlarging itself in subsequent McClure letters. It would have been an excuse to return, and Clemens confided to Rogers, who was an intermediary in the scheme, "I am tired to death of this everlasting exile."

Being a Londoner while the Boers were winning, and the newspaper casualty lists were both embarrassing and alarming, was less pleasant for Americans in the spring of 1900 than it had been a year earlier. "For three months," Clemens wrote Twichell, "the private dinner parties (we go to no public ones) have been Lodges of Sorrow. . . ." But at one private dinner his host was one of his favorite historians, W. E. H. Lecky, and at another it was Irish theater patroness Lady Gregory. It was happier, he thought, to be among the Irish then, for their "ease and sociability and animation and sparkle and absence of shyness and self-consciousness" he found to be "American." It was obvious that he was becoming restless for home.

Reports that Mark Twain was leaving London were pervasive, and Clemens at the annual banquet of the Royal Literary Fund at the Cecil on May 2 gave some credence to the rumors. "I am now on my way to run for the presidency because there are not yet enough candidates in the field, and those who have entered are too much hampered by their own principles, which are prejudices. I propose to go there to purify the political atmosphere. . . ." He would also speak at a gala dinner welcoming Sir Henry Irving on his return from an American tour, a rare recorded episode in which Mark Twain and Bret Harte (then frail and seriously ailing) were in the same room in London at the same time. But the old collaborators and antagonists apparently did not meet across the many tables decorated with floral representations of the Union Jack and the Stars and Stripes.

By then Clemens had learned that the McClure proposition had fallen through, and Livy, who had written her sister that she dreaded reopening the Hartford house, with all its disheartening memories, was glad to postpone departure. Besides, Jean was still under the Kellgren treatment. They began looking for more spacious quarters in which to spend a London summer.

Early in July the family vacated the Knightsbridge flat for Dollis Hill House, in what was at the time considered Kilburn, a then-rural setting in the northwest suburbs across the Finchley and Edgware Roads west of Hampstead Heath. For Clemens, the days at Dollis Hill, with its great old oaks under which sheep grazed in the patches of shade, were among the supreme moments of his life. A few years later he could write to Howells, who was planning an overseas journey, "The summer in England! You can't ask better luck than that." To Twichell he boasted, "From the house you can see little but spacious stretches of hay-fields and green turf. . . . Yet the massed, brick blocks of London are reachable in three minutes on a horse. By rail we can be in the heart of London, in Baker Street, in seventeen minutes—by a smart train in five." Yet not everything was perfect. To the editor of *The Times* he complained that although the newspaper was printed at four o'clock in the morning his copy did not reach him until five in the afternoon.

America teased further. Columbia professors Willard Fiske and Brander Matthews visited for tea, and, Clemens wrote Twichell in August, "it was a breath of American air to see them. We furnished them with a bright day and comfortable weather—and they used it all up, in their extravagant, American way. Since then we have sat by coal fires, evenings." Dollis Hill was, he thought, as the summer waned, "nearer to being a paradise than any other home I ever occupied." He had never been part of a Yankee colony in London and took transplantation well; but the family stuck to their plans to sail for New York.

Clemens abhorred the packing and removal, which he described to W. H. Helm, a London newspaperman who had often shared a bench in the shade with him, as "not so much choice between a re-moval & a funeral; in fact a removal is a funeral. . . ." He offered only perfunctory assistance, but Dollis Hill House was closed at the end of September, and the family put up at what Clemens described to J. Y. M. MacAlister as a "Family Hotel."*

They are a London specialty, God has not permitted them to exist elsewhere; they are ramshackle clubs which were dwellings at the time of the Heptarchy. Dover and Albemarle Streets are filled with them. The once spacious rooms are split up into coops which afford as much dis-comfort as can be had anywhere out of jail for any money. All the mod-ern inconveniences are furnished, and some that have been obsolete for a century. The prices are astonishingly high for what you get. The bed-rooms are hospitals for incurable furniture. I find it so in this one. They exist upon a tradition; they represent the vanishing home-like inn of fifty years ago, and are mistaken by foreigners for it. Some quite respec-table Englishmen still frequent them through inherited habit and ar-rested development; many Americans also, through ignorance and super-stition. The rooms are as interesting as the Tower of London, but older I think. Older and dearer. The lift was a gift of William the Conqueror, some of the beds are prehistoric. They represent geological periods. Mine is the oldest. It is formed in strata of Old Red Sandstone, volcanic tufa, ignis fatuus, and bicarbonate of hornblende, superimposed upon argil-laceous shale, and contains the prints of prehistoric man. . . .

The steamer *Minnehaha*—an appropriately American name—sailed on October 6 and arrived in New York on October 15. Clem-ens had been abroad more than nine years. "If I ever get ashore," he told one of the reporters who sailed out to meet the ship as it entered the harbor, "I am going to break both of my legs so that I can't get away again."

In 1904, when Howells had been congratulated by Clemens on being able to spend a summer in London, the reason for the journey had been to receive an honorary degree from Oxford. For Clemens it was "a secret old sore of mine" that he had not been equally honored, but he kept his feelings to himself. In April 1907, however, came Mark Twain's turn, an honor he attributed to private lobbying

* It was actually Brown's Hotel, in Dover Street.

by his friend Moberly Bell of *The Times,* but he was enthusiastic about accepting the degree whatever its origin. It was, he said before leaving for England early in June, "a loftier distinction than is conferrable by any other university." Three Americans had been tapped by the university's new chancellor, Lord Curzon, for honorary doctorates: Ambassador Whitelaw Reid, Clemens, and Thomas Edison. Edison declined, saying that he was too busy in his laboratory at Menlo Park, New Jersey, to spare time for the trip. When the cablegram had arrived confirming the invitation, Clemens told a young journalist who was assisting him, Albert Bigelow Paine, "I never expected to cross the water again, but I would be willing to journey to Mars for that Oxford degree."

Olivia Clemens had died, after a long illness, three years before. With her no longer at his side, and cables bearing invitations pouring into 21 Fifth Avenue from London, Clemens engaged a secretary, Ralph W. Ashcroft, a young Englishman, to accompany him. It had become obvious to him that this would not be a vacation trip but more in the order of a triumphal return home. On June 8, forty years to the day since his first voyage across the Atlantic, on the *Quaker City,* he embarked upon his last, assuring reporters climbing aboard the *Minneapolis* for a final interview, "I may never go to London again until I come back to this sphere after I am dead, and then I would like to live in London. I spent seven years there, and I am going back to see the boys."

At the Tilbury docks he was hailed by longshoremen as he disembarked. It was necessary to go from there to central London by rail, and his friend MacAlister was at St Pancras Station to meet him. Also there was Bernard Shaw, who had come to meet Archibald Henderson of the University of North Carolina, a mathematics professor who, despite the irrelevance of that field to literature or theater, was writing Shaw's biography under the playwright's direction, and who had also sailed from New York on the *Minneapolis.* Clemens and Shaw were introduced, and since each admired the other's work, they agreed to lunch together. A curious throng gathered to witness the encounter between the only two living satirists whose names were household words, but MacAlister pushed his friend through the crowd and into a cab, which deposited them at Brown's, the very "Family Hotel" in which the Clemens ménage spent its last days in London in 1900. In 1900 Brown's famous guest was a subdued Sam Clemens quietly slipping out of London. Now mail and visitors made a chaos of the hotel lobby, and the public Mark Twain, wearing a derby and—as a concession to his seventy-two years—spectacles, and carrying a cotton umbrella ("the only kind the English won't steal"), held court for reporters and informed them that he had arrived to show Oxford "what a real American college boy looks like."

An assistant secretary had to be engaged immediately, and the burgeoning pile of invitations answered. Henry M. Stanley's widow, predicting the results, urged, "You know I want to see you and join right hand to right hand. I must see your dear face again. . . . You will have no peace, rest, or leisure during your stay in London, and you will end by hating human beings. Let me come before you feel that way." Archdeacon Wilberforce wrote, "I am only a humble item among the very many who offer you a cordial welcome in England, but we long to see you again, and I should like to change hats with you again. Do you remember?" Mrs Edith Draper of Ormskirk, Lancashire, wrote to ask for a photograph for her husband, a railway clerk, to whom she gave a Mark Twain book every Christmas and birthday. "He is never tired of reading them and they keep him at home many a time when he would be out at night." Clubs he had belonged to, and others longing to host him for the first time—the Atheneum, the Garrick, the Savage, and others—had left invitations or cards of membership at Brown's, and the leading photographers put in claims for sittings. Clemens agreed to pose for perhaps the best of them, the London Yankee Alfred Langdon Coburn, who produced a white-suited Mark Twain against a background of sunlit windows which made him appear to be inhabiting a world less real than London.

Breakfasts, luncheons, teas, and dinners were crowded with old friends—Lady Stanley, J. Henniker Heaton, Marjorie Bowen, Anthony Hope, Conan Doyle, Edwin Abbey, Edmund Gosse, Henry Lucy, Bram Stoker, Norman Lockyer. Even the theft of the Ascot racing cup did not diminish Mark Twain's newspaper coverage, although some placards advertised both stories as if they were related, with "MARK TWAIN ARRIVES" and "ASCOT CUP STOLEN" providing Clemens with material for opening several after-dinner talks. Nothing he did was too minor for newspaper attention, and when he emerged from an elevator in a brown bathrobe and crossed Dover Street to the Bath Club, the news quickly reached New York and resulted in a cable from Clara: "MUCH WORRIED. REMEMBER PRO-PRIETIES." Undisturbed, he answered, "THEY ALL PATTERN AFTER ME."

On his fourth day in London, June 22, he traveled to the King's garden party at Windsor Castle, only one of hundreds of celebrities so invited. Emerging from the train at Windsor Station with Henniker Heaton, Sir Henry Campbell-Bannerman (the Prime Minister), Sir Mortimer Durand, Fridtjof Nansen, and Ellen Terry, he drove through streets lined with cheering crowds; and although they may have been cheering the Prime Minister, Clemens bowed repeatedly right and left as if he were a visiting head of state. Later, a newspaper reported that he had impertinently clapped Edward VII on the back, and kept his hat on while talking with the Queen, as if these were American irreverences, and Clemens defended himself:

One newspaper said I patted his Majesty on the shoulder—an impertinence of which I was not guilty; I was reared in the most exclusive circles of Missouri and I know how to behave. The King rested his hand upon my arm a moment or two while we were chatting but he did it of his own accord. The newspaper which said I talked with her Majesty with my hat on spoke the truth, but my reasons for doing it were good and sufficient—in fact unassailable. Rain was threatening, the temperature had cooled, and the Queen said, "Please put your hat on, Mr. Clemens." I begged her pardon and excused myself from doing it. After a moment or two she said, "Mr. Clemens, put your hat on"—with a slight emphasis on the word "on"—"I can't allow you to catch cold here." When a beautiful queen commands it is a pleasure to obey, and this time I obeyed—but I had already disobeyed once, which is more than a subject would have felt justified in doing; and so it is true, as charged. . . .

The next day, at Wilberforce's, he was quietly invited into the library, where there waited an unprepossessing man Clemens had never seen before. "Mr Pole," said the archdeacon, "show to Mr Clemens what you have brought here." Pole unrolled the length of white linen and revealed a saucer-shaped silver vessel which appeared to be overlaid with green glass. It was, said the archdeacon, the Holy Grail, and he explained that Pole, who claimed clairvoyant powers, had dreamed with great vividness the location of the Grail, and with another Englishman of peculiar powers, a Dr Goodchild of Bath, had located the relic. It was as if Mark Twain had been transmigrated back in time, as had been his Connecticut Yankee, into the days of Arthur. He thought about the difference between the vessel before him and its traditional shape, and took for granted that the contrast precluded any fraudulent intent. He handled it reverently, and later recalled:

I am glad I have lived to see that half-hour—that astonishing half-hour. In its way it stands alone in my life's experience. In the belief of two persons present this was the very vessel which was brought by night and secretly delivered to Nicodemus, nearly nineteen centuries ago, after the Creator of the universe had delivered up His life on the cross for the redemption of the human race; the very cup which the stainless Sir Galahad had sought with knightly devotion in far fields of peril and adventure in Arthur's time, fourteen hundred years ago; the same cup which princely knights of other bygone ages had laid down their lives in long and patient efforts to find, and had passed from life disappointed—and here it was at last, dug up by a grain-broker at no cost of blood or travel, and apparently no purity required of him above the average purity of the twentieth-century dealer in cereal futures; not even a stately name required—no Sir Galahad, no Sir Bors de Ganis, no Sir Lancelot of the Lake—nothing but a mere Mr. Pole.

Later a committee of eminent laymen and ecclesiastics examined the relic with more skepticism, and Mr Pole disappeared into deserved obscurity; but for a moment the desire to believe had moved Clemens to a rare moment of reverence.

On June 25 the Society of the Pilgrims gave a luncheon for Clemens, at which he recalled being told by Charles Eliot Norton of Harvard about a visit to Charles Darwin, during which Norton had been permitted in Darwin's bedroom, crowded with books and rare plants. "The chambermaid," said Darwin, "is permitted to do what she pleases in this room, but she must never touch those plants and never touch those books on the table by that candle. With those books I read myself to sleep every night." The books were by Mark Twain. "There is no question in my mind," Clemens recalled answering Norton, "as to whether I should regard that as a compliment or not. I do regard it as a very great compliment, and a very high honor, that that great mind, laboring for the whole human race, should rest itself on my books."

He also recalled the incident of Archdeacon Wilberforce's hat, and what had happened since:

And there is in that very connection an incident which . . . is rather melancholy to me, because it shows how a person can deteriorate in a mere seven years. It is seven years ago. I have not that hat now. I was going down to Pall Mall, or some other of your big streets, and I recognized that that hat needed ironing. I went into a big shop and passed in my hat, and asked that it might be ironed. They were courteous, very courteous, even courtly. They brought that hat back to me presently very sleek and nice, and I asked how much there was to pay. They replied that they did not charge the clergy anything. I have cherished the delight of that moment from that day to this. It was the first thing I did the other day to go and hunt up that shop and hand in my hat to have it ironed. I said when it came back, "How much to pay?" They said "Ninepence." In seven years I have acquired all that worldliness, and I am sorry to be back where I was seven years ago.

Immediately after the Pilgrim luncheon Clemens left for Oxford, where, in the Sheldonian Theatre the next day, Curzon read out the citation, *"Vir jucundissime, lepidissime, facetissime* . . . Most amiable, charming and playful sir, you shake the sides of the whole world with your merriment." Wearing his Oxonian scarlet robe, Mark Twain marched afterward in the morning sunlight with Rodin, Saint-Saëns, and Kipling, with Prince Arthur (the brother of the King), with the Prime Minister, and with the stern General William Booth of the Salvation Army, to lunch with Lord Curzon at All Souls' College. "Mark Twain's Pageant," one of the papers called it, after the new doctor of letters the crowd had singled out as its hero. But although so proud of his scarlet vestments that he often flaunted them back in America, he mistakenly wore black evening dress that night for dinner in one of the colleges. He was the only ungowned guest. "When I arrived," he said, "the place was just a conflagration

—a kind of human prairie-fire. I looked as out of place as a Presbyterian in hell."

There was hardly an afternoon or evening without a banquet and an expected speech by Mark Twain, and in the jumble of days and meals he felt that he had made a botch of some of them, in particular after the Lord Mayor's dinner at the Savage Club, at which he began by claiming that his entire visit had become one of having to rehabilitate his character after the burglary of the Ascot cup. But he concluded on the most poignant note of the visit—his recognition that at seventy-two it was almost certainly his last. "And now I am going home again across the sea," he said. "I am in spirit young but in the flesh old, so that it is unlikely that when I go away I shall ever see England again.* But I shall ever retain the recollection of what I have experienced here in the way of generous, most kindly welcomes. I took in the welcome you gave me when I entered the room, and I am duly grateful for it. I suppose I must say good-by, and in saying good-by, I do so not with my lips but with my whole heart."

He still had a week to go, but postponed sailing a further week. On the Fourth of July he was again at the American Society's dinner, at the Cecil, where again he inveighed against the violent profanation of the holiday by fireworks and firewater in the forty-six states. There was, he observed, a daylight Fourth and an after-dark Fourth. "We honor the day all through the daylight hours, and when the night comes we dishonor it." And then he suggested a further link between the nations he loved in the holiday in which Americans took so much pride—that it was actually "an English institution . . . born at Runnymede in the next to the last year of King John," to celebrate the liberties gained in the Magna Charta. At the Savage Club two evenings later, after Scott Stokes had observed that while his friend Harold Frederic—a late member—lay dying, Stokes had read to him from the books of Mark Twain, Clemens returned to the allusion. "I did not know Harold Frederic personally," he confessed, "but I have heard a great deal about him, and nothing that was not pleasant, and nothing except such things as lead a man to honor

* It was a realistic prediction. He died three years later.

another man and to love him. I consider it a misfortune of mine that
I have never had the luck to meet him, and if any book of mine read
to him in his last hours made those hours easier for him and more
comfortable, I am very glad and proud of that." The American
novelist and correspondent had died in 1898 just as Clemens and his
daughter had returned to London from their Swedish cure. The
scandal surrounding his death had rocked literary circles, but for
the occasion polite reticence was in order, even about that American
importation, Christian Science.

One day there was lunch at Adelphi Terrace with Bernard Shaw,
who had invited his biographer Henderson (who would also write
a book on Mark Twain) and Max Beerbohm, and the conversation
largely consisted of exchanges of compliments and anecdotes. No
mention was made of Shaw's as yet unpublished, and perhaps still
unwritten, short story, "Aerial Football, the New Game," about a
bishop who has difficulties in entering Heaven, or of a nearly forgotten and unpublished story by Clemens, "The Late Rev. Sam Jones's
Reception in Heaven." His "Captain Stormfield's Visit to Heaven"
would appear in *Harper's* in December, and as he checked his proofs
he was startled by the parallels in Shaw's tale, which had been published in *Collier's Weekly* that November. "Mental Telegraphy?"
Clemens wondered, and began a piece on the subject. Not only did
their styles intersect, but several details strikingly suggested mental
transference, in which Clemens was a profound believer. "So, I said,
'Mr. Shaw must have gotten those incidents out of my head when I
was in England last summer, by thought-transference. . . .'" He
rambled along on the subject for several hundred words more, then
thought better of publication. But he did not throw the scrap away.

The last major event for Mark Twain, but for a banquet at the
Liverpool Town Hall, to which he was escorted by editor "Tay Pay"
O'Connor, was a dinner given to him by the staff of *Punch,* which
had already saluted him with a full-page cartoon by Bernard Partridge, in which Mr Punch ladles out a drink from a huge punch
bowl set before Clemens and drinks to his health. Phil Agnew, *Punch*
editor, welcomed him at 10 Bouverie Street in Whitefriars, and sitting down with them in the historic office dining room where Thack-
eray and his successors had supped were Owen Seaman, Linley Sam-

bourne, Francis Burnand, Henry Lucy, and other writers and artists on the staff. Once dinner was served, Agnew's eight-year-old daughter, Joy, emerged from the cupboard in which she had been hidden to recite a welcoming speech and present Clemens with the original of the cartoon. He was charmed, and the men insisted that Joy, despite the hour, and *Punch* rules about females in the house, remain for the first two courses.

On July 13, 1907, Clemens embarked for New York on the *Minnetonka*. The crowd at the pier hoped for yet another speech, but he was exhausted, and only wrote out a brief farewell message for the reporters. The London *Tribune* editorialized that the ship which bore him away "had difficulty in getting clear, so thickly was the water strewn with the bay-leaves of his triumph." And indeed there was some difficulty, but with an obstacle less resilient than a bay leaf. Two days out the *Minnetonka* collided with the bark *Sterling,* but neither was seriously damaged. Publishing the news on July 23, the *New York Times* reported that Dr Clemens, aroused by the impact, had "grabbed his bath-robe, and rushed to the deck to see what the trouble was. Some of the passengers say that he thought he had grabbed his bathrobe, but that in reality he had put on his Oxford gown in the darkness."

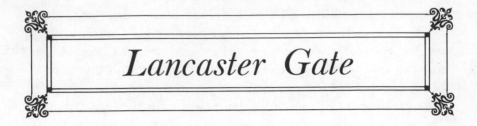

CHAPTER II

Lancaster Gate

The tall rich heavy house at Lancaster Gate, on the other side of the Park and the long South Kensington stretches, had figured to her, through childhood, through girlhood, as the remotest limit of her vague young world.

—Henry James, *The Wings of the Dove* (1902)

EXTERNALLY, Lancaster Gate had an ambience of comfortable gentility rather than showy fashion. At number 69, for example, lived retired Indian civil administrator Sir Richard Strachey, whose gaunt, precocious son Giles Lytton was often home from public school on sick leave. Every week the van from the circulating library would deliver half a dozen novels to Sir Richard's door, perhaps even the latest title by Bret Harte, or by Pearl Craigie under her well-known pseudonym, "John Oliver Hobbes." Deaf and doddering, Strachey very likely had no idea that Lancaster Gate was being overrun by authors or tainted by scandal by such Americans.

Up and down Lancaster Gate in July 1895, the gossip below stairs had probably shifted from the elderly American gentleman-writer who lived at number 109 with a lady not his wife to the young American lady-writer who lived at number 56 without her husband. The lady novelist was then in the process of divorcing her husband in a case which *The Times* described as "an exceedingly filthy one, . . . most of its details . . . utterly unfit for publication in a newspaper." Stylishly coiffed and attired, with a drawing-room wit almost without peer among her sex, she was one of the adornments of the tall and spacious row of town houses just above Kensington Palace Gardens, since fallen upon evil days and converted into genteel hotels and inexpensive rooming houses. But however elegant, Mrs Craigie had written for the notorious *Yellow Book,* then so much in the news because of the disgrace of Oscar Wilde, and was the daughter of the American entrepreneur who had made Carter's Little Liver Pills a household word in England.

The white-maned, distinguishedly mustached and boutonniered Francis Bret Harte, who appeared unlikely to do anything unfit for publication in a London newspaper, seemed older than his fifty-nine years and gave the impression of having spent most of them in gentlemen's clubs in Pall Mall. In truth, he belonged only to several which he could not afford, and had spent his best-remembered years in raw, rough northern California as editor of a frontier journal, the *Overland Monthly.* Only because the house belonged to Madame Marguerite Van de Velde, the well-to-do widow of a Belgian diplomat, could Bret Harte afford a fashionable Lancaster Gate address; he had the run of it, although ostensibly he had only a room, as permanent guest. Harte had been American consul in Glasgow, until President Grover Cleveland discovered it by happening upon one of Harte's frontier tales. He didn't like the story, and Harte was fired; but the ex-consul did not take the next boat back to America. Leaving Scotland was no problem: he had spent most of his time in London anyway, despite repeated State Department warnings. "I cannot help feeling," he once wrote from Glasgow, "that I am living by gaslight in a damp cellar with an occasional whiff from a drain, from a coal heap, from a moldy potato bin, and from dirty washtubs." His Scottish stories, in which Glasgow reappeared as St Kentigern, had good words only for the local woolens and whiskey, both of which were essential to his survival there. In London, he wrote his wife, Anna, he was someone, while in America he was "completely 'played out' " and would not be able to make a living. In due course, he assured her, "We could . . . consider the question of *our all living here.*" He did not mention Marguerite Van de Velde.

As long as Monsieur Van de Velde, chancellor of the Belgian

legation in London, was alive, the threesome evoked speculation and gossip, although nothing to affect Madame's reputation. After all, she had nine children, evidences of a wifely fidelity beyond reproach; but even London gossips could not have imagined that most of the entries in Bret Harte's own private diary, morocco-bound with clasp and lock, were in Marguerite's handwriting. Whatever their contents, it suggested a level of intimacy beyond anything Arthur Van de Velde may have had in mind. "You ask me how I live," Harte had once written his family in New Jersey. ". . . The nearest approach I have to a home is, naturally, not where it ought to be—at Glasgow. I suppose I am most at ease with my friends the Van de Veldes in London. A friendship of four years has resulted in my making their comfortable London home my home when I am in London; their country home at Bournemouth my home whenever I can get a leave of absence for a few weeks in summer. I have a room there always known as mine, and always containing something of mine, summer or winter. I have surely told you about this family in previous letters. There are nine children in all and nearly as many servants. It is the most refined, courteous, simple, elegant, and unaffected household that can be imagined. The father and mother are each foreigners of rank and title; Madame is the daughter of Count de Launay, the Italian Ambassador at Berlin. Arthur Van de Velde is the Chancellor of the Belgian Legation. They have adopted me into their family— Heaven knows how or why—as simply as if I had known them for years. Perhaps there is a kind of sympathy in the fact that they are intensely *un-English,* and Madame as a girl thirty years ago visited America with her father and loved it."

Early in the nineties, with her sons grown and out of the house (one of them, Frank, in England), Anna pressed to come to London with their two daughters, but Harte warned her off, always with expressions of an affection he had not felt for decades.

To come here to London to a hotel, or even to lodgings—living as you ought to live as my wife—even in the plainest way, would cost more than my income would permit, and much more than for me to come to New York—or rather to New Jersey or the country for an equal length of time. I have been able to live in London solely because I lived with

the Van de Veldes, half as guest, under circumstances that enabled me to
send you three thousand dollars a year. That three thousand dollars
would not give you the same *comfort* here as in America. But it *may be
possible* to find something out of London, or in the vicinity where we
could make at least a *temporary* home; for I should never consent to have
my daughters educated or even reside permanently in England.

The *ménage à trois* had occupied 15 Upper Hamilton Terrace
until Arthur Van de Velde died, when the surviving family moved to
Lancaster Gate. So did Harte. He may have suggested that London
was a dreadful place for his daughters, but one can read that only as
self-protection, keeping "Dear Nan" away. His genius, which had
been dormant after his move east from California, had been revived,
he felt, by Marguerite's confidence in him, and whatever else went
on upstairs in Lancaster Gate which was not confided to his diary,
Madame Van de Velde was his typist, his critic, his audience. She
could not keep him from wasting his time on the illusory rewards of
turning his stories into unproduced plays (she herself had collaborated with someone else on a vehicle for Sarah Bernhardt). Yet he
was also regularly turning out stories set in Sierras he created anew
from memory and managing to get agent A. P. Watt to place them
in the *Strand,* the *Idler,* the *Graphic,* or other papers which took his
nostalgic pictures of frontier life for the real and current thing. And
he needed to earn little more than he obligated himself to send
home, since he was a guest in the bosom of the Van de Velde family,
if not in the bosom of Madame herself.

In his correspondence one of the most private of men, Harte seldom exposed his feelings about anything beyond literary business,
trivial family chitchat (in lieu of more serious family affairs), social
engagements, and the weather. But Marguerite Van de Velde permitted one revealing letter to be published, a note he sent her—his
"Prime Minister"—to accompany a gift:

My Dear Friend,—When I beg you to accept the enclosed portfolio
I do not for a moment ever expect it to supplant the memory of the old
one which is endeared to me by the recollection of the hours you have
spent over it in deciphering my exasperating manuscripts and making
them intelligible to the printer, or in giving them another chance for
immortality by clothing them in the language of your own native land.

I am only trying to symbolize in this little gift something of my gratitude to you as amanuensis, translator, critic, and above all—friend.

I am not King of France or I should quote to *my* Prime Minister the words of Louis to Richelieu: "Lord Cardinal, you must take up again the *portfolio* you have laid down. In all my empire there is none worthy to follow you." Always, dear friend, yours most gratefully,

Bret Harte

The most profound feelings of which he was capable had clearly been reserved for her, and his devotion was reciprocated.

Few writers in London had Harte's advantages of a smoothly managed town house in winter and country retreat in summer, with no financial strings attached. He could devote all his time to writing, without the need to grub at hack work. He could take, and often did, a full month to pen, in his minute hand on four-by-eight-inch note-paper, a short story, Marguerite then carefully pasting each pair of sheets together to make a larger page from which to type. For the most part his fiction was still set in the gold-rush country in northern California, although at the same time as he was writing "Mr. Jack Hamlin's Meditation" or "A Night on the Divide" he was also turning out "The Ghost at Stukely Castle" and "Baxter on the Free Kirk Council." That the former were of higher quality than the latter suggests that time and distance had only mellowed rather than faded his memories of the West. He was writing even more dryly and ironically than before, eschewing much of his earlier sentimentality. And, with the exception of his chronic urge to write for the theater, he remained stubbornly attached to the short story form, unwilling to chance work of longer range or experimental form. He had a ready audience for his familiar formulas and for it perfected his limited canvas, content to demonstrate his mastery of small effects, his ear for nuances of speech, his eye for characteristic mannerisms. The belief that he did no work of artistic merit after he left California was inaccurate. From London he mined with verve the shallow thematic vein with which he had earned only indifferent success in his last years in America. And he regularly earned praise for his artistry, as when Andrew Lang, editor of the prestigious *Longman's,* declared that some of the writing in Rudyard Kipling's first book, *Departmental Ditties,* was worthy of Bret Harte (whom Kipling had actually read in public school).

The phenomenon puzzled Henry James as late as 1898, when *Tales of Trail and Town* was published. Writing his "American Letter" in the *Literature* supplement of *The Times,* he thought he detected a "school of Bret Harte" in younger American writers, but wondered more "what he has learned from himself" than what others had learned from him. Harte had been, he marveled, "his own school and his own pupil. . . . Removed, early in his career, from all sound, all refreshing and fertilizing plash of the original fount of inspiration, he has, nevertheless, continued to draw water there and to fill his pitcher to the brim. He has stretched a long arm across seas and continents. . . ." How had Harte "kept in touch"? James could only raise the question. "Is Mr. Bret Harte's supply of the demand—in an alien air, I mean, and across the still wider gulf of time—an extraordinary case of intellectual sympathy, sympathy keeping alive in spite of deterrent things? Has he continued to distil and dilute the Wild West because the public would only take him as wild and Western, or has he achieved the feat, at whatever cost, out of the necessity of his conscience? But I go too far: the problem would have been a subject for Browning, who would, I imagine, have found in it a 'psychological' monologue and all sorts of interesting things."

One of Harte's stories written in England, "An Apostle of the Tules," led John Hay, who had been both his admirer and protector in the State Department, to write him that he was just arriving at the peak of his creative powers. But, sheltered as well as encouraged by Marguerite Van de Velde, he remained insulated from meaningful new experience. Although he poked fun at English reverence for old buildings and even ruins, and for coats of arms and family crests, he happily soaked up information about historic places, and enjoyed long weekends in the country houses of the titled, where he willingly spun yarns to whoever would listen. And he would create conversation about himself, for when he was away from Lancaster Gate, he would receive a little box every morning containing a carnation, a rosebud, or a bunch of violets for his buttonhole. Madame knew his tastes and knew how to make her presence palpable.

Harte was a brilliant talker, and would work out ideas for stories while he entertained. One night in a wild part of the West, he would reminisce, he took a room overnight in a new hotel—such as hotels were in those parts. After he had settled comfortably in his bed he was aroused by sounds of scuffling punctuated from below by occasional pistol shots. But he refused to stir from his room. In the morning he made his way downstairs and found the proprietor behind the bar with a pleasant smile on whatever portions of his face were visible beneath a black eye and a cheek-to-forehead bandage.

"Well, landlord, you had rather a lively time here last night," Harte opened.

"Yes," said the proprietor pleasantly, "it *was* rather a lively time."

"Do you often have such lively times about here?"

"No," he said, reflecting on the query. "The fact is we've only just opened, and last night was about the first time that the boys seemed to be gittin' *really acquainted.*"

Late in 1895, as ill health began to slow him down and make him less talkative, he spent more time in the London equivalent of his beloved stately homes, the Royal Thames Yacht Club, just off Piccadilly, where the only water nearby was the pond in Green Park. He had no interest in clubs or yachting, he confessed, but he was left alone. "If I go to a literary club," he explained, "I am asked all sorts of questions as to what I am doing, and my views on somebody's last book, and to these I am expected to reply at length. Now my good friends in Albemarle Street talk of their yachts, don't want my advice about them, are good enough to let me listen, and I come away refreshed by their conversation." It was how he wanted it. He refused to mine such opportunities for writing as he had in Glasgow years before, preferring in London the narrow, comfortable grooves of the receding frontier.

Illness also caused him to withdraw more from old friends and former haunts. He was suffering from facial neuralgia and a chronic sore throat, the beginnings of his fatal illness. But in the security of Lancaster Gate he was always ready to churn out another story, and in the nineties collected them in books at the rate of nearly one a year, *In a Hollow of the Hills* in 1895 and *Barker's Luck* in 1896.

When Harte had moved in with the widowed Marguerite, no amount of evasion or rationalization could explain the domestic situation satisfactorily to Anna. The letters ceased on both sides, although he seems to have continued sending her money. Whether because of the rift at home or gossip in London, toward the end of 1895 he moved, at least technically, to a bachelor room at 74 Lancaster Gate, down the street. The letters resumed.

Perhaps to confront the innuendo head-on, Madame Van de Velde—an author herself—contributed an appraisal of her charge to the *New York Sun,* ostensibly refuting hints in the States that Harte had sold out to English respectability, but implying as well that other innuendos were equally invalid. He was uncompromisingly American, and patriotic to the core, she insisted, and he was, besides, a dedicated writer who daily practiced his art. What followed seemed closer to home:

When this mass of silly gossip is sifted the bare and simple truth remains that Bret Harte leads a quiet, simple, dignified, and useful existence; that he goes into society less than any other conspicuous American living in London; that he never threw over the humblest of acquaintances for the highest or richest; that he is ever ready to oblige or assist a compatriot; that he faithfully and perseveringly devotes a portion of each day to his profession; and that he often has not known how his health and strength would enable him to meet the many engagements thrust upon him by publishers and editors.

At 109 nothing had really changed, and the old relationship, whatever its nature, continued. Harte still had his bedroom and its adjacent library, and—as long as he could ring changes upon the old plots—a place to publish whatever he wrote. As an author he was one of the most fortunate of men. Editors requested a story and suggested a theme or setting, and he would tailor something to taste. Mark Twain had found temporary new sources of inspiration in other locales—England in *A Connecticut Yankee at King Arthur's Court* and Austria in *The Mysterious Stranger*—and had drawn on his travels when America failed him. Bret Harte saw himself as a different kind of professional. He could mine his experiences in Scotland or in Germany, but if publishers wanted something Californian he could write "Californian Christian stories, Californian juveniles, Californian sentiment, humor, adventure, mystery." And he could take professional pride in the finished product. Avant-garde new journals like the *Yellow Book* were not for him, nor he for them.

He knew none of the mostly young Americans who wrote for them, not even his elegant neighbor at number 56. The appeals for advances, the futile rounds of a much-traveled manuscript from publisher to publisher, were not part of Harte's life, well ordered as it was by Marguerite Van de Velde and A. P. Watt. Heath Joyce, editor of the *Graphic,* would ask for a story. He didn't care what sort of story it was, he explained, as long as there was a real live bear in it. As long as the bear was there, Harte could do as he pleased. The result was "Miggles," which slightly disappointed Joyce:

During the meal we heard a noise like the rubbing of a heavy body against the outer door of the house. This was shortly followed by a scratching and a sniffing at the door. "That's Joaquin," said Miggles, in reply to our questioning glances, "would you like to see him?" Before we could answer she had opened the door, and disclosed a *half-grown* grizzly, who instantly raised himself on his haunches, with his forepaws hanging down in the popular attitude of mendicancy, and looked admiringly at Miggles, with a very singular resemblance in his manner of Yuba Bill. "That's my watch-dog," said Miggles, in explanation. ". . . Lord love you! he trots round with me nights, like as if he was a man."

"It was only a half-grown one," explained the editor. "Still, better than no bear at all." Soon he asked for a sequel, as a letter from Harte to Watt makes clear:

October 8, 1895

Dear Mr. Watt,

I enclose herewith the story for the "Graphic" entitled "A Night on the Divide." It runs a little over six thousand words. I have taken "a bear incident" (although I have treated it *half humorously*), as the editor suggested. But it is the same grizzly bear that "Miggles" made a pet of—and as such ought to find favour with the general reader. Kindly advise me of its receipt. . . .

The next year he was complaining, as usual, to Anna about how bad conditions in London were, yet how much more difficult life would be in America. After a rare trip to the Continent he wrote her, "I am afraid I cannot stand the whole winter here; year after year it seems the more terrible, and the days of semi-darkness harder to bear. Yet everything I get, in the way of criticism, advice, or com-

ment, from America, tells me how utterly *alien* I and my writings
have become in my own country—and how I must depend upon ap-
preciations and standing here. When Max Nordau, the celebrated
German philosopher and novelist, lately wrote that I was the 'Columbus of American fiction' (whatever that means!), and that my countrymen did not appreciate me sufficiently, I thought it might strike
some echo in America—but, alas! I have not seen even an allusion
to it in my American publishers' *advertisements!*—while here it was
copied largely and discussed." And he enclosed, as usual, his monthly
check.

When he had lost his consulate and made no effort to return, he
had promised Anna that he would provide her in America with the
equivalent of his $3,000 annual salary. He knew he would have to
earn it by his writing before he could retain anything for his own
upkeep. Through the years, until his last illness, the check or cable
for $250 arrived each month, and often there was an extra $50 in
November or December for Christmas gifts. It was never easy despite
his guest status at 109 Lancaster Gate, for he wrote slowly and
meticulously—more slowly than ever as his energy flagged and he
was racked by neuralgia, sciatica, rheumatism, toothache, gout, lum-
bago, dyspepsia, an ulcerated throat, and tonsillitis. Some of the
ailments might have gone away had he abandoned the fog and chill
of London, but all that gave his life purpose was there.

When Hamlin Garland, a young writer from what was left of
the frontier, and a self-styled Naturalist, came to London in 1899,
he carried two letters of introduction from the respected William
Dean Howells, to Bret Harte and to Mark Twain. Harte, Garland
was told on arrival, was unlikely to be found in the society of other
Americans, and indeed the young writer first saw him across the
room at a tea, where Yankees hardly ever gathered. He wore a cut-
away, striped trousers, a fancy vest, with watch chain, lavender spats,
and a monocle screwed into his right eye. His appearance was "almost precisely that of the typical English clubman of the American
stage," and Garland hesitated about making an approach. But he introduced himself, and was invited to 74 Lancaster Gate. Harte was
careful about appearances.

Garland arrived prepared to dislike Harte, and was not disappointed. He offered his introduction to be read, and was invited to sit down while Harte inserted his eyeglass and read Howells's letter. "His whole appearance," Garland decided, "was that of an elderly fop whose life had been one of self-indulgent ease. His eyes were clouded with yellow, and beneath them his skin was puffed and wrinkled. Although affable and polite he looked and spoke like a burned-out London sport." Putting the two pages of Howells's letter down, Harte asked for news of "the boys"—his writer-contemporaries left behind in the States. When the talk shifted to California, Harte acknowledged that the place he remembered no longer existed. "Sometimes," he confessed, "I wish I had never come away." As Garland left, Harte followed him down the steps to the sidewalk, still asking about American friends—Thomas Bailey Aldrich, E. C. Stedman, Charles Dudley Warner. At the corner Garland turned for a last look at the house he had left and saw the old man, white head bent, still standing silently by his own doorway, his hand on the railing.

Although Garland was moved by the sadness in the voice of the old man, Harte, who received a bad press in the States, earned nothing better from his American visitor. "In his mind, as in mine, he was an exile, an expatriate, old and feeble and about to die, estranged from his family and from all his American friends. He was poor and the subject of gossip. His books were no longer in demand. He had lived here too long, . . . and it was reported that he was living on the bounty of a patron."

Soon afterward Garland found Mark Twain at his "small but exclusive hotel," and presented his more prized introduction. In reputation Twain had become "the largest and most significant figure in American literature." Still, he did not appear the "rugged force" Garland had expected. "I was shocked," he remembered, "by the changes which had come to him. His shaggy hair was white and a stoop had come into his shoulders. . . . As he talked to me he appeared to forget me. He looked over my head at some far-off landscape." And his conversation filled with invective as he checked off the iniquities of his former friends in America, finally confiding coldly to Garland, "For many years I have been writing a kind of diary in which I have set down from time to time exactly what I think of the men and women I have met. It can't be published while *I* am alive. It can't be published while Mrs Clemens is alive. It can't be published while *any of the people mentioned* are alive; but when it *is* published that blankety blank blank will turn in his grave!"

Fortunately Garland did not mention his other letter of introduction, or his interview with Harte, for Harte was almost the only bitter enemy Twain had failed to excoriate. In 1876, in America, they had collaborated on a play, and had fallen out, with Mark Twain unhappy about his partner's dilatory working habits, heavy drinking, and sneering—so Twain claimed—at his life-style and his wife. Harte was, Twain accused, "a born bummer and a tramp . . . a loafer and an idler." Later he added that Harte "hadn't any more passion for his country than an oyster has for its bed; in fact not so much and I apologize to the oyster. The higher passions were left out of Harte; what he knew about them he got from books." Even without the usual attacks on Harte, however, Garland was awed by the virtuoso performance and in his notebook that night summed up Mark Twain as "a really great soul."

In the last year of the old century, word filtered through literary circles that a biography of Harte, unauthorized by him, was in progress. Edgar Pemberton offered to rush out an authorized one as antidote, in case it were needed, and Harte agreed to the idea. If the concern proved anything, it was that despite Garland's view, he was not forgotten, although his old *Overland Monthly,* still going strong in 1898, had published a parody, "Plain Language to Bret Harte," which satirized his faulty recollection of physical detail as the Sierra foothills and shantytowns receded into mythic haze. What outraged the writer most of all was not that Harte was unaware of how California had changed,* but that he had forgotten even the color of the poppies on the hillsides overlooking San Francisco:

* One of the changes unknown to Harte was evidenced by the appearance in London the next year of a product of the San Francisco artistic community, Isadora Duncan. She had grown up in the circle of poet Ina Coolbrith, once a friend of both Mark Twain and Bret Harte. Miss Duncan had moved east to open a dancing school in New York, but after it was leveled by fire she sailed, with her brother Raymond and their mother, to London. Some difficult months followed, including days during which they lived on penny buns from the refreshment room at the British Museum, where Isadora was studying Greek

. . . But what kills me plumb dead
Is to see where he's writ

That our poppies is red—
Which they ain't red a bit,
But the flamingest orange and yellow—
Oh, Bret, how could you forgit!

Whatever Harte's inaccuracies, his vision of the American West had mapped it for countless English readers. One of them, according to Gertrude Atherton, was a duke who visited the wealthy Californian Milton Latham at his country estate near San Francisco. The guests had already gathered in the drawing room in their dinner jackets and Paris gowns when the English butler announced, "His Grace, the Duke of Manchester." None had ever seen a duke before, and were baffled when he strode in wearing thigh-high boots over his trousers, and a red flannel shirt. And he was very likely less than amused to see the company attired in lavish London dignity, but he explained that all he knew of California had been gleaned from the stories of Bret Harte, and that he had furnished himself with what he believed to be the appropriate Western costume, so that his hosts would feel at ease. The apology was taken as a huge joke, and everyone recovered quickly from the embarrassment, Mrs Atherton—who claimed to have been among the guests—remembered. Yet whether or not her tale was apocryphal, it suggests the measure of influence Harte's fiction possessed in places where he was regarded as the recorder, not the romanticist, of the Far West.

In London, if not in New York, he was regarded as fit subject for biography; and since he was grateful for the benign approach to

---

dancing as it appeared in pottery and sculpture. Then "an extremely beautiful woman in a large black hat" discovered Isadora and Raymond, barefoot and in skimpy Greek tunics, dancing at midnight in Kensington Square, near the house in which they were living. "Where did you come from?" asked the lady. "Not from earth at all," said Isadora, "but from the moon." "Well," said the lady, "whether from the earth or the moon, you are very sweet; won't you come and see me?" She was the actress Mrs Patrick Campbell. Through "Mrs Pat," Isadora, only twenty-one in October 1899, found patrons and audiences—and the beginnings of the fame which would establish her as a cult figure in Paris a year later.

his work that was ensured by having Pemberton as his Boswell, he wrote an appreciative letter intended to give the book his imprimatur, thanking Pemberton for sparing him "the alternative of taking my own life in an autobiography." It was dated August 31, 1900, a time in Harte's life when it was beyond his powers to undertake such extended writing. His chronic neuralgia and "ulcerated" sore throat had become so severe that he forwent the cigars he usually smoked as he wrote in favor of "*very* mild" ones. Still, almost every year another collection of his short fiction emerged, with *Under the Redwoods* the volume for 1901. But he was clearly failing. The sore throat was cancer, which he could not admit to himself, but he warned Anna in May 1901 that she had to expect his income to be "more and more uncertain." "I could not get a substitute to write for me. With the ailments I have, I am writing much more slowly each year—and I have *no income* but from my pen. You must forgive my repeating this, but I do not think either you or Ethel or Frank realize in your plans, or consider how precarious is the living I am making."

Anna had become much more of a burden when late in 1898, after thirty years of separation, she had left Plainfield, New Jersey, and recalled Bret to his duties as a husband. Their son Frank was now married and living in Caversham in Berkshire, west of London. The best Bret could do was keep her away from Lancaster Gate. He made no effort to leave his bachelor domicile or his more spacious quarters down the street at number 109, and Anna avoided her rival. Harte visited his wife uneasily and with studied infrequency in Berkshire. In their middle sixties, they were strangers. He still closed his letters with the perfunctory "Affectionately," but the feeling behind the word had evaporated years before. Even the monthly remittance, as he had warned, had now dwindled. Henceforth it would be thirty pounds.

Constant pain made writing an agony, yet he had to produce for his market, and composed parodies which suggested no signs of flagging zest. His "Rupert the Resembler" even showed that he was keeping up with things, as Anthony Hope's best-selling *Prisoner of Zenda* had become a stage success beyond London and into the provinces. Stoically, he wrote two brilliant "Starbottle" tales (the humorous "Colonel Starbottle for the Plaintiff" and the dramatic "A Ward of Colonel Starbottle's"), and experimented again with operetta, doing the lyrics for musical adaptations of his "At the Mission of San Carmel" and "The Strange Experience of Alkali Dick." Almost daily he worked with Hungarian composer Emanuel Moór, as they metamorphosed "Alkali Dick" into *The Lord of Fontenelle,* reading aloud what he had written or revised, and listening to his collaborator's new music. Still mesmerized by the theater, he was convinced that he could turn California into gold at the box office although he had little to show from thirty years of trying except the enmity of Sam Clemens.

In 1901 Harte was spending as much time with doctors and dentists as with his work, and his physicians, knowing that cigars were his last solace, forbore removing them. He was in constant pain and subsisted on soups and "slops," finally submitting to surgery in March 1902 which confirmed the inoperable cancer. No one told him of a luncheon given by William Dean Howells a few weeks earlier for another expatriate writer, novelist and *Yellow Book* editor Henry Harland, who had made a rare return visit to New York. Mark Twain had dominated the conversation, which he directed for no apparent reason onto Bret Harte, whom he excoriated as a "whelp" and a "blackguard." "Do you know what that blankety-blank two-faced hound did?" he asked. "He came to Elmira to get my endorsement of him as consul to Glasgow, and told me with glee that he had secured the support of both [political] parties!" No such visit had ever occurred, but Twain's enmity was sufficiently implacable that he very likely had come to believe his own story.

To recuperate, Harte returned to Lancaster Gate, with Marguerite Van de Velde to care for him. Anna was not invited to visit, nor did she, and he declined, with his usual kindly evasion, her offer to have him come to Caversham. On April 17 he seemed to rally. Dragging himself to his desk, he croaked to Marguerite, "I'm about to write the best story I've ever written!" At the top of the sheet he posed a tentative title: "A Friend of Colonel Starbottle." Starbottle, pompous, jaunty, and verbose, was Harte's symbol of the anachronistic chivalry of the Old South, and a major figure in twenty earlier stories, but he could think of nothing further to say. Finally, writing despite the pain which clutched at his throat, he managed to complete two brief, barely legible paragraphs before sinking back into his bed.

On May 5 he tried again, but before any words could come, his throat welled with blood. That afternoon, with Madame Van de Velde at his side, he died.

In Frimley Churchyard in Surrey, in the shadow of the square-topped steeple, Anna Griswold Harte and Marguerite Van de Velde, as mourners, confronted each other for the first and last time. There was no question as to who was in charge of the obsequies. It was Marguerite's country church, and her claim was recorded later on the red granite tombstone under Bret Harte's name and vital statistics:

IN FAITHFUL REMEMBRANCE
M. S. VAN DE VELDE

To Anna, Harte left all his assets—his copyrights and £360 6s. 9d.

Elsewhere on the crescent that is Lancaster Gate, at number 56, lived another American writer, one who was not able to escape from an unsatisfactory marriage by putting an ocean behind her. For Pearl Richards Craigie, who had come to England from Massachusetts as a child, London was home. There was no alternative domicile in America, although she had visited there often with her father, a patent medicine entrepreneur who had brought Yankee elixirs and pills to England and become president of the American Society in London. In July 1895 the Craigie scandal had crowded Bret Harte's decorous arrangement with Marguerite Van de Velde out of local gossip, for the young Mrs Craigie—she was nineteen when she married in 1887—charged adultery and cruelty, and the sordid details, too "filthy" for publication, were nevertheless aired in the courtroom.

Standards of filth were somewhat different in the last decade of the nineteenth century, and what had outraged *The Times*'s court reporter can no longer be ascertained; however, it may have been because Reginald Walpole Craigie, in contesting the charges, pleaded "condonation of his adultery and cruelty, if any; connivance of his adultery, if any; conduct on the part of the petitioner conducing to his adultery, if any." To deny her estranged husband's assertions, Pearl Craigie employed four attorneys, including two Q.C.'s, twice the legal talent mobilized by Reginald Craigie, and as part of the

ordeal she spent nearly five hours under cross-examination, collaps-
ing once.

Sensitive and delicate in the best Victorian tradition, she had not
been an easy wife for Craigie to manage. The match seemed right out
of a Henry James novel. She had been an American heiress not quite
out of her teens whose father, John Morgan Richards, maintained a
town house in London and a country estate on the Isle of Wight, and
had bought the proprietorship of the prestigious weekly the *Academy*. Craigie, twenty-nine, although only a clerk in the Bank of England, managed to be a dashing man-about-town. Vows were exchanged in the venerable church which still bisects Lancaster Gate
and looks out over the Park. A wedding trip to Cannes followed, but
it was abbreviated when the bride became seriously ill with a knee
inflammation which forced her return, on a litter, to England. The
Jamesian idyll, if it ever began, was already over.

For six months they lived with Mrs Craigie's doting father and
peculiar mother, whose religious fantasies would have landed a
poorer woman in an institution. When Pearl was sufficiently recovered to be able to take care of herself, the couple moved with relief
to their own flat in Oxford Street and began sampling the fashionable London society in which Craigie thrived. For a while Pearl also
enjoyed being a part of it, and wrote sketches, "The Note-Book of a
Diner-Out," under the pseudonym "Diogenes Pessimus" for a
weekly, *Life*. The fact that she wrote, and the choice of pen name,
revealed more about her than the frivolous doings she chronicled.
She was restless as a mere society wife, and had deep philosophical
yearnings she could not, at twenty, understand. Nor could Reginald
Craigie, who liked wine and women, and was so enamored of his
splendid physique that to her horror he would parade nude before
his bedroom mirror. He apparently paraded in similar undress elsewhere as well, for Pearl showed less interest in his body than in
studying Greek and medieval literature and philosophy. After her
son John was born in August 1890, she divided her time between
motherhood and literature, taking a home at High Barnet, then
just outside London. Reginald Craigie preferred high society and the
pleasures of the bottle and the flesh. When he failed to turn up for
long periods, Pearl would take her child and his nurse to Lancaster
Gate. By May 1891 the separation was complete.

"Ideals, my dear Golightly, are the root of every evil," says a character in Mrs Craigie's first book. "When a man forgets his ideals he may hope for happiness, but not till then." It was advice she took herself. Her Ideal Husband had evaporated before Wilde wrote his play of that title, and Pearl Craigie put her world-weary cynicism, at twenty-four, into her fiction and into her faith. After publishing her witty, brittle *Some Emotions and a Moral* (1891) in Fisher Unwin's new "Pseudonym Library"—where the oblong yellow volume was a striking success—the author added a second set of new names by becoming a Roman Catholic. The "Pseudonym Library" required a pen name, and although Pearl Craigie never attempted to conceal her gender, she chose "John Oliver Hobbes." As she explained, "I chose the name of John because it is my father's and my son's; Oliver because of the warring Cromwell; and Hobbes because it is homely." Also, she noted that she was an admirer of the philosopher Hobbes, for his rationalism saved her from "maudlin sentiment," and that Oliver was a name which "filled the mouth." And she told an American reporter that "Hobbes was the ugliest name I could think of." But that was after the name had become essential to her work. "My jealousy of that creature is not to be expressed," she told an audience at a New York club. "However much I enjoy this party I know perfectly well it is not for me but for Hobbes. But for him I should never have been here. I will not say I dislike Hobbes—but even a woman is human."

That her first explanations of Hobbes were peculiar was proved by her conversion in 1892, for rationalism and Romanism had little in common, and for the newly rechristened Pearl Mary-Teresa Craigie, conversion seemingly committed her to her estranged husband. Morally and spiritually, divorce became unthinkable and remarriage impossible. Yet she "read herself into the Church," Father Gavin, S.J., one of her clerical friends, insisted. "Her conversion . . . could not be ascribed to sermons, still less to the attraction and beauty of the Church's liturgy and public services. She became a Catholic by study and conviction and in obedience to her conscience."

"If the gods have no sense of humour," John Oliver Hobbes concluded in her second novel, *A Sinner's Comedy,* "they must weep a great deal." Privately she must have wept a great deal herself. On the surface her flippant, artificial, almost inhuman novels breathed

fashionable *fin de siècle* aestheticism. But as Vineta Colby, her best
modern critic, has described it, "Love and life are treated with a
chilly detachment that serves to emphasize both their comic and
their tragic irony. The selfish and shallow characters survive and
prosper and are comically absurd. The sensitive and sincere characters are destroyed." Her next novel, *A Bundle of Life* (1893), dedicated to Walter Spindler, an artist and Isle of Wight neighbor who
was hopelessly in love with her, included a self-portrait as Lady
Mallinger, a charming young widow who married unhappily at
eighteen but was rescued by her husband's death—perhaps a bit of
wishful thinking on the part of the author. "The world liked my
husband," says Lady Mallinger; "he ate too much, drank too much,
and made too merry with other people's lives. No one knows what
I have suffered." Pearl Craigie kept her suffering less to herself.
Physically frail since her illness at nineteen, she hid the fact under
smart, feathered hats and Watteau gowns, but complained of pal-
pitations and shortness of breath which sometimes resulted in a
fashionable, Victorian, ladylike faint. "A great part of the book,"
she confided to readers of the preface to the second edition of *A
Study in Temptations* (1893), "was composed under the strain of
bad health, and all of it in circumstances of peculiar anxiety. If the
author had written as he felt or thought, the result would have been
far from amusing."

Mrs Craigie's home life in Lancaster Gate was far from amusing,
although she had a surfeit of friends of both sexes, publishers eager
to receive her writings, and the funds to fulfill her every material
desire, whether for hats or holidays. Even her reviews generally
pleased her, within the limits of the literary pose she had chosen, and
by 1894 she was the subject of a playful rhyme which circulated
about London:

> John Oliver Hobbes, with your spasms and throbs,
> How does your novel grow?
> With cynical sneers at young Love and his tears,
> And epigrams all in a row.

Life with the eccentric Mrs Richards was difficult, but writing
elsewhere proved impossible. Traveling in Italy or France meant the
logistics of governess and child and assorted baggage; the family

home at Ventnor on the Isle of Wight, Old Park, was good for letter writing, but the sun shone too often for even "a stroke of work" to be accomplished. Both at Old Park and Lancaster Gate, John Richards entertained lavishly—it was good for business. Because he was interested in the fortunes of his *Academy* as well as Bromo Seltzer, Mrs Allen's Hair Restorer, Carter's Little Liver Pills, and his line of Colgate products, he also invited literary people, Henry James once greeting him in the drawing room, obsessed by one Richards product, with "How are you, Mr Carter?" The fashionably cluttered salon, with its Morrisian flowered wallpaper, also included framed religious mottos, a statue of St Joan, and a placard inquiring "What Would Jesus Say?" When Mrs Craigie encountered guests staring at it, she would shrug and say, "Oh, that's mother's." A few years later, when war between America and Spain loomed, religion and patriotism warred within Mrs Richards, who considered herself at times a direct emissary of God, and who spoke often, amid the puzzlement of visitors, to her unseen friends among the prophets of the Bible. To His Eminence at the Throne of St Peter she dispatched a peremptory telegram: "POPE, VATICAN, ROME. STOP WAR. RICHARDS." There was no response, but the United States handily defeated the enemy.*

Despite her mother's peculiarities, Pearl often preferred to write not in her bedroom-study on the third floor, where she often worked through the morning in bed, dictating letters to her secretary Zoe Procter, but at the huge dining-room table at Lancaster Gate, where she could spread out her papers, particularly the playscripts which had become her new interest. Playwriting was also her link to a romantic interest, novelist George Moore. There were always men in Pearl Craigie's life, although her husband had quickly lost *his* enthusiasm. Not classically pretty, but with large liquid eyes, slender figure, and elegant clothes, and a conversational charm and wit that made her competed for at dinner parties, she attracted writers and artists and politicians, and could be seen on the arm of Arthur Balfour or George Curzon, whose back brace produced a haughtiness of carriage even beyond his intentions. She was "safe" as a female com-

---

* The King of Spain also received a "STOP WAR" message. Laura Richards would often add such personal homilies to her telegrams as "HAVE FAITH IN ONIONS," which tested the stoicism of the girl at the "cage" in the local post office.

panion because she was unlikely to put any marital pressure upon a gentleman; however, her parents kept urging her to a divorce, particularly to legalize her custody of her son. But she was also safe in a way that men may have been less eager to discover. Whatever charm she directed at a male companion, to his disappointment it was unlikely to lead to the bedroom. Whether Reginald, or religion, or merely a low sexual temperature was responsible, she suggested possibilities which proved not to be there.

For Moore, whose tales about his amorous exploits were sometimes true but more often not, the Craigie affair was a drama with many acts, each ending in an anticlimax. Not the most attractive of men—at forty-one his flaxen hair and pale face resembled straw on an egg—he nevertheless had no difficulty finding interested women, and sought out Mrs Craigie when Arthur Symons told him (it was 1893) that the author of *Some Emotions and a Moral* was actually an attractive young woman. "That—that was a different matter!" he told Barrett Clark in 1922. "I saw her some days afterward at the theatre and thought she was amazingly beautiful. Well, one thing led to another, and I fell in love with her." The courtship was carried on via literary collaboration, Moore working with her at Lancaster Gate on a one-act adaptation from the French, *Journeys End in Lovers Meeting,* which became a curtain raiser in two London productions, and the Wildean *The Fool's Hour,* an act of which went into the first *Yellow Book.* But the play remained as incomplete as their relationship.

Moore told the story fictionally as "Lui et Elles" in 1921, describing the lady as a writer who signed her name mannishly as "Mark Anglewood," and with whom he worked in the sitting room of the tastelessly furnished mansion of her wealthy but "commonplace" parents, "filled with engravings of Doré pictures and marble statues." Pearl—"Agate" in Moore's tale—encourages his attentions but after stimulating his hopes, rejects him as a lover:

By some word or letter, sometimes even by acts she would dissipate suspicions, I might also say the belief, that my courtship would bring me to her bed. To be quite truthful, she hinted in the beginning that sex relations did not appeal to her, but such hints are so common among women that one attaches no real significance to the confession, or interprets it in the opposite sense, that sex relations are the one thing of interest to them. No one's talk turned oftener on the subject of sex than Agate; she admitted sex to be her subject; her brain was certainly possessed of it, and though sometimes it seemed about to descend from her brain when we returned from the theatre in the family brougham, I was not sure that our relations would become less and less restrained.

Undiscouraged, because "Agate" appears to tease him and lead him on, Moore submits to her urging (as he had to Pearl's) to go to concerts and to study the piano. Yet finally he is told, while strolling with her in Green Park, that she does not wish to see him again. It was, according to Zoe Procter, "a curious sentimental interlude. Having once seen him in the drawing room at Lancaster Gate looking, as I told her, like a fat white worm, I could not believe that they had taken country walks together and eaten the green leaves of young hawthorn, in what she called 'a sort of sacrament.' "

"She was horrible," he told Clark. "We saw each other every day for six months. . . . We were very intimate but she would never allow me actually to become her lover. I was frantic." The result, as told in "Lui et Elles," is almost certainly fact rather than fiction:

At last my stunned brain awoke, and I saw she was enjoying my grief as she might a little comedy of her own invention, conscious of her prettiness in black crepe de chine, with a hat to match. We were walking towards Kensington. I on her right side next the railings, and the ill-repressed smile that I caught sight of under her hat cast me out of myself; a great selfquake it was, and my left foot, flinging itself forward, hit her nearly in the center of her backside, a little to the right. She uttered a cry, and I met her look, which curiously enough was not a detestation, for lack of perception was not Agate's failing; and I think she took pride in the fact (I know she did later) that her power over me should have caused me to put off all conventions. . . .

Later, Moore confided that Pearl Craigie had intended to snare Lord Curzon, with whom she was indeed friendly, but that Curzon had spurned her for another American heiress in London, Mary Leiter of Chicago. The rationalization was very likely wrong, for Mary Leiter, like Curzon, was her lifelong friend, but Pearl Craigie, despite her Catholicism, began to think about a divorce.

Whatever the reasons for her legalizing her break with Reginald Craigie, despite his warnings that he would fight in court and expose her to embarrassment, Pearl did not seem to have remarriage among them. The opportunities were there. "I can't live without men's society," Moore quotes her as saying. "If I am deprived of it for about a week I begin to wilt." Later—for Moore was eventually drawn back to Pearl, and she toyed with him further before they quarreled again—she wrote to a friend that some male (probably Moore, but unidentified) had observed to her, "I never feel any anxiety about *your* relations with your men friends, because I am sure that you are *constitutionally* incapable of an indiscretion!" When she read the comment to friends, they questioned whether she had been insulted or whether it was the funniest thing they had ever heard, one man observing that she had recently been the subject of discussion at his club, where, Pearl reported, "They said my 'charm' was that of an enchanting boy . . . (I make no *demands,* in fact!)—so different from that of most women. . . . They all agree that I am a little paragon!!" The picture which remains is that of a woman who wanted sexual excitement without any of its consequences, as Moore drew her in 1895 in "Mildred Lawson," one of his stories in *Celibates,* where the heroine "dangles" her admirers: "She didn't want to marry but she would like to have all the nicest men in love with her."

Like Pearl Craigie, too, Moore's Mildred Lawson dresses "as if she were going to a garden party," wears "large hats profusely trimmed with ostrich feathers which suited her so well," and is worn down by emotional strain which never appears upon her public face. "Give me a passion for God or man, but give me a passion," she cries out, tossing on her bed. "I cannot live without one." Life is a burden she regularly considers putting down. "I often think I shall commit suicide. Or I might go into a convent."

As Pearl prepared for the divorce hearing she was indeed despondent, dreading the scandal and notoriety that might undo her socially and professionally. She gave in more and more to the depression which accompanied her fatigue. "I am tired out," she wrote to Moore just before their break. "I seem the feeblest creature in the world: twenty-six years of life have left me with nothing but a desire for rest and a long sleep. Today I paid three long calls and have had

to talk to ten people on sixty subjects. People teach me nothing. . . .
Tired, tired, tired, TIRED!!"

Craigie v. *Craigie* opened on July 3, 1895. Mr Murphy, Q.C.,
aware that he not only had to prove a husband's misconduct but dis-
prove the countercharges of condonation, connivance, and unreasonable delay in petitioning for dissolution of the marriage, opened by
stating that he had to present a very painful case. It had not come
to trial earlier because the petitioner had quailed at public airing of
the sordid details, which she was certain would have desolated her
parents. In their first year of marriage, while the young bride was in-
valided and on crutches, her husband had "abused and treated her
badly. He had also threatened her with a pistol. . . . In 1890 the
respondent struck the petitioner, and in March, 1891, he told his wife
that he had become acquainted with another woman." She did not
immediately inform her parents, Murphy noted, only doing so when,
that May, she left her husband's home to live permanently apart
from him. It was then that he addressed to her father what *The
Times*'s reporter called "a very unctuous and piously worded docu-
ment, in which he admitted his shortcomings as to temper, and spoke
of the respondent in terms of exalted praise." He also addressed
similar documents to his wife, entered into evidence in court, in one
of which he alleged that she had given him permission to commit
adultery if he wished to. In the witness box a shaken Pearl Craigie
denied the assertion, and added that she was constantly terrified by
her husband's violent conduct. He had threatened to shoot her; he
had locked her in a bedroom; he had thrown her books in the fire;
he had tried to strangle her. What was obvious but unspoken, however, was that Reginald Walpole Craigie had often pressed vainly
for his due as a husband and had reacted violently to his frustration. All that was elicited was the petitioner's contention that she
had never "set him at defiance."

To Florence Henniker, a minor writer and sister of Lord Crewe
(reputedly another suitor), Pearl wrote candidly of her ordeal as
witness:

I must thank you for your words of sympathy. The ordeal on Wednes-
day was a severe one, but I have been shewn so much kindness & given

so much encouragement that half its bitterness is already past. The thought of my child sustained me during the trial—the horror of which the Times only hinted at. I have seen other reports which were—from the circumstances of the case—garbled & inaccurate. For four hours & a half I was under cross-examination: I fainted once & yesterday after the verdict was given I was carried out of the court-room half insensible. I can only realize the result of the case today—& now in a vague sense only. I cannot help thinking that when a woman is in the position of plaintiff she should be spared such suffering. I felt so grieved for my parents who were present & could only think that if I had a son or a daughter so tortured under my eyes—I should die of sorrow. It nearly killed my father when I became insensible. He & my mother are simple people of the old school—homely, devoted to each other, living only for their family & kind deeds. It was death to me to see them in that courtroom listening to such desolating & revolting facts of life as I had to tell. It was to spare them that I bore so much for four years in absolute silence. And yet it all had to be told! This is the irony of so-called self-sacrifice. It is too often made in vain—I am leaving town & hope soon to feel stronger.

After Pearl's appearance, and collapse, the trial was adjourned until the next day, when as the court began its sitting, Mr Edward Carson, Q.C., asked to speak for the respondent. Carson, a shrewd attorney who only two months earlier had successfully defended the Marquess of Queensberry against Oscar Wilde's libel suit, precipitating Wilde's fall and imprisonment, knew he had no case. Bearing in mind some observations made by his lordship on the subject of corroboration, he told the court, he had had a conversation with his client on that point. There was no way, he had told Craigie, that the charge of condonation could be corroborated, and had advised him accordingly. His client would no longer defend the action.

The court commended Carson for the course he had adopted, and the jury promptly found the respondent guilty of adultery and cruelty. A divorce *nisi* was granted, with costs. Pearl Craigie had been vindicated as well as set free, but to Ellen Terry she wrote: "The strain has been very great. I can hardly realise the verdict at present. I feel that the trial is still going on—that it is going on for ever and ever! The sensation is hideous. But I have got my child." Still, when she entered him at Eton in 1899, she was forced to write to his housemaster, Arthur Benson, "With regard to the boy's religious instruction: he may not be brought up as a Roman Catholic. I have the sole guardianship and custody of the child, but the English law is very decisive on *that* point." She had not won everything.

Whatever others assumed would happen, she put any thought of remarriage aside. In her novel *The School for Saints* (1897) her heroine, Brigit, insists, when her father tells her that a divorce can be arranged and another husband found for her, "As I have no rights [as a woman] I may remain true to my marriage vows. The word divorce has no meaning for me. I am a Catholic. I implore you to let me go."

Pearl Craigie exorcised the demons by writing and traveling. She determined to write a play, and to visit America. It was important to get as far away from London as was practical; and a reason presented itself when her earlier plays were to be performed in Philadelphia, Washington, Boston, and New York. She was a celebrity, and savored the acclaim although the productions fell short of expectations. She was also a connoisseur of hotels, and in December 1895 discovered New York's Waldorf, which she felt, in a surge of native pride, spoiled her forever by comparison to European establishments. But the play conceived as a comedy for Henry Irving about a middle-aged married couple, the male lead to be a "Disraeli type," underwent a sea change although Irving had encouraged the work. In London in 1896 she duly drafted a play but then kept only the characters and one of the projected scenes, while turning the scenario into an ambitious novel.

The School for Saints was planned to be her masterpiece. She cut down on her dinner parties and country house weekends to work at it, while her parents objected that she was perversely losing her opportunity to remarry. She did not take Mrs Richards ("our curse") seriously, but her impatient father followed his lectures by cutting off her allowance. The "indirect reproof," as she called it, only resulted in her taking, temporarily, rooms in a Kensington convent, a flat at the fashionable Albany, and a separate house on the Isle of Wight. Her writing had earned enough to make her independent, and almost everything she wrote included some declaration of disillusion with marriage and abhorrence of divorce. Besides, she was

now more ill than before, and to her way of thinking, doubly unmar-
riageable. "Art must indeed be a disease," she once wrote to Father
William Brown, one of her confidants. "My own sufferings baffle
description." In the later nineties she spent days in bed with exhaustion, often after a collapse. She was taking heart stimulants by day,
and Trional and Veronal to enable her to sleep at night. Richards
relented.

Although she was often able to write only two hours a day, and
that in bed, she read deeply in religion and history for her novel, and
traveled to Tours, Paris, and Brittany to examine possible settings.
She was not merely going to draw a Disraeli-like hero, but do so in a
Disraelian novel including, among other real-life personages, Disraeli himself. The result would be not a single politico-religious
novel, on the order of her idol's *Lothair* or *Tancred,* but two, *The
School for Saints* (1897) and *Robert Orange* (1900). The eight hundred pages of political intrigue and period romance strayed from
Disraeli to Ouida, all of it padded by unbelievably long letters and
unreal entries in journals. She had tried to create a hero who strode
through the secular and spiritual terrain of the mid-nineteenth century. Orange's destiny, his vocation, is the church but not until he has
first been exposed to such wordly temptations as sex, power, and
reputation—Mrs Craigie's school for saints. Her goal, writes Vineta
Colby, "was to write Newman's *Apologia* with the spirit of Disraeli's
Lothair, in the modern, updated style of Oscar Wilde's drawing
room comedies. Her failure was inevitable."

Punch satirist Owen Seaman, who later produced an affectionate
parody of *Robert Orange,** wrote to her in August 1900 that he had
just been reading the novel, and "I think if I did not know you I

---

* "Robert Porridge," in *Borrowed Plumes* (London, 1916):
Robert was passing through that crisis which is inevitable with those in whom the
ideals of childhood survive an ordered scheme of ambition. His head was his Party's;
but his heart was in the "Kingdom under the sea," Lyonesse or another, not in the maps.
He spent long hours of vigil over Jules Verne's *Twenty Thousand Leagues,* in the original. . . . Dépaysé by arbitrary choice, his adopted name of Porridge stood merely for
the cooked article, the raw material being represented by his family name of Hautemille,
a stock unrivalled in antiquity save by the Confucii and the Tubal Cains; and to the
last even in the intervals of the most exalted abstraction, he was prey to poignant irri-
tation when the comic journals (ever ready to play upon proper names) anglicized it
phonetically as Hoatmeal. He repeated the *Chanson de Roland* verbatim every night in
bed.

should be a little afraid of meeting you. There is only George Meredith besides you, that could have written it." Another London critic, the American Vincent O'Sullivan, called Orange "that cold, dull phantasm, a penny-in-the-slot machine for aphorisms," yet both novels were commercial successes in a pre-electronic age when readers were less impatient. The reception of the cliff-hanging *School for Saints* encouraged her to write the second half of the story. But between the appearances of the novels, "John Oliver Hobbes" returned to the theater. Henry Irving still wanted his play, and for him she wrote her Wildean *The Ambassador,* produced at the St James's in the summer of 1898, with George Alexander, Fred Terry, and Violet Vanbrugh also in the stellar cast. As the applause at the opening was punctuated with shouts of "Author! Author!" Pearl Craigie, resplendent in white satin, stepped forward. "Where's John?" someone called; when the audience began to understand, the shouts changed to "Pretty John!" It was her first success at sole authorship of a play, and it tempted her into other, more ambitious attempts, against which critic Max Beerbohm, who had succeeded Bernard Shaw at the *Saturday Review* drama desk, warned her. That she saw life, Max thought, "only through a haze of pretty sentimentalism and prettier cynicism" was just the right "equipment . . . for the writing of comedies. . . . I hope she will not be induced to despise her true gift. . . . I have noted with concern that in her recent books she has shown a certain restiveness, a certain contempt for her own métier."

The next plays were more ambitious and less successful. Of *The Wisdom of the Wise,* produced in November 1900, Beerbohm wrote in disappointment, "Why, then, is her comedy so dull? The dialogue is as delightful as ever, showering off its innumerable little bright sparks of wittiness and prettiness. But the characters who speak it! They do not exist. They are the vaguest puppets, there to work out the basic idea, percisely through jigging of their joints; they are not human characters to illustrate the idea in a human manner. Their antics are tolerable, and seem even like human movements, so long as the idea is in process of expression. But this period is very brief." The audience at the first night had booed, yet the author had bravely come forward anyway to take her call. Later she explained in the *Pall Mall Gazette* why she had courted execration. "As I had given the public my very best—the result of two years of care, thought and observation—I felt I had no reason to slink away like a thief in the night." Afterward her stage triumphs became successively more modest, and Beerbohm theorized that "all that is good" in her writing was done by Mrs Craigie. "All that does not seem to 'come off' was done with the striving toward virility—done by John Oliver Hobbes."

Perhaps because she did sometimes realize that she was misusing a small but genuine talent, she tried less to be an Oscar Wilde or a George Meredith, but the need to be somehow connected to the theater drove her again into working with her old nemesis George Moore, who visited her at her father's newest Isle of Wight residence, Steephill, in 1904. Her role was less collaborator than editor and refurbisher, but although it was agreed at the time that both would sign it, there was another falling out, and Moore had the play set in type under his name alone as *Elizabeth Cooper*. (Earlier working titles had been *The Three Lovers* and *The Peacock's Feathers*.) While the reconciliation lasted, Moore wrote Edward Dujardin from Steephill that "in the morning she walks on the terrace and in the garden in the most delicious costumes *à la* Watteau, rose-colored silks and flower-decked hats." But soon she was writing her publisher, Fisher Unwin, about Moore: "He is not a gentleman and he is mad. . . . Seriously, I believe his brain is touched. His conversation with men and women guests at Ventnor was found highly offensive. . . . I had to soothe some enraged husbands. . . ."

Moore's side of the story, confided to Barrett Clark in 1922, was that Mrs Craigie told him at Ventnor that she was still waiting vainly for Lord Curzon. "It seems that the Lord's wife was an invalid and P—— wanted the lady to die, so that he might marry *her*, but she refused to die. That was why P—— came back to me."

Mrs Craigie's letters suggest that Curzon had been interested at one time, but married one American heiress when the other was unavailable. Pearl's separation without divorce, and then her conversion to a faith which did not recognize divorce, effectively cut her off from hopes of Curzon, for whom her Roman Catholicism might have been more of a bar to his ambitions than Mary Leiter's Mennonite ancestry. Yet Pearl seemed to harbor the feeling that if she could not have him, no one else might have him either. She nursed continuing hopes about him, and jealousy of Mary, which she had the poor judgment to confide to Moore, whose autobiographical inventions often appear to have at least a basis in fact.

A curious clue is that when, in 1902, she was about to go to India as guest of Lord and Lady Curzon, she was actually considering breaking her vow not to marry again because Walter Spindler—with whom long intervals of silence had followed their frequent quarrels —"will not stand more temporizing." Inevitably she blamed her re- newed refusal on her religious scruples, although it may have had more to do with her desire to see what the state of the Curzon mar- riage—and Mary's health—was; and she sailed with Owen Seaman (an admirer who did not include marriage in his plans) to the Delhi Durbar, at which Curzon, as Viceroy of India, was to formally an- nounce the accession of Edward VII. In articles commissioned by the *Graphic* in London and *Collier's* in New York, most of the material destined for reuse in her book *Imperial India,* she described the color- ful parades, banquets, and investitures which dramatized British over- lordship of the subcontinent. But opportunities in India to renew the old intimacies with George and Mary Curzon were almost non- existent, and when back in England she reacted by rashly renewing her old intimacies with Moore, he had his opportunity for revenge. Moore had the unscrupulousness of the artist who would use or abuse anyone if he could refashion the material in a way he consid- ered art. When he was not abusing Mrs Craigie privately for intimat- ing false expectations, he would use her as material for his fiction, describing in *Evelyn Innes* and its sequel, *Sister Teresa* (1898 and 1901), a woman modeled sufficiently on his old friend to cause her to write to Fisher Unwin, "I have not had the courage to mark the objectionable passages. The whole tone is false and an abomination. . . . The heroine isn't convincing—there never was such a girl. . . ." Yet there must have been to cause her to react with such outrage.

She was even more unhappy over Henry James's *The Wings of the Dove* (1902), in which the heroine, Milly Theale, a rich and beautiful but apparently consumptive young American girl in London, has been accepted as James's nostalgic elegy for a dead cousin. Pearl saw herself; and in the scheming lover Merton Densher she identified Owen Seaman. Reacting indignantly, she wrote Treasury official T. R. Higgs that it was "appalling to find a man of James's intellect filling nearly six hundred pages (of fine type) with squalor crowned by an obscenity which is dense only by reason of its clumsiness. . . ." To Father Brown she wrote that she had confronted James himself with her suspicions:

Henry James has sent me *The Wings of the Dove*. Clearly, the man is meant to be Seaman. It is hard upon him. With James I took the bull by the horns. I said, in acknowledging the book, "I know Densher. But he is far more child-like than you have made him." He [James] may take it that I mean "Densher" is an eternal type of the weak smug Englishman. All the same, the book was a bit too close to facts. We are given Venice: * hints are given of my style of dressing: he makes me out to be suffering from a mysterious incurable malady (a popular delusion) and makes much of the fact that I *look* well: I have no air of the invalid.

No one else seems to have recognized Mrs Craigie in Milly Theale, or *Punch* journalist Owen Seaman in newspaperman Merton Densher (who was almost certainly based on Morton Fullerton), but Pearl was sensitive to talk about her distinctive clothes and her mysterious collapses. What she left unsaid was a more obvious relationship to *The Wings of the Dove*. "The tall rich heavy house at Lancaster Gate, on the other side of the Park and the long South Kensington stretches" (presided over by Kate Croy's redoubtable aunt, the suggestively named Maud Lowder) in which much of the action of the novel takes place, was very likely her own, and Mrs Lowder's "looming" presence seems a respectable version of the showy and eccentric Mrs Richards. "It was an oddity of Mrs. Lowder's that her face in speech was like a lighted window at night, but that silence immediately drew the curtain," James wrote, and it was "by her personality that Aunt Maud was prodigious, and the great mass of it loomed because, in the thick, the foglike air of her arranged existence, there were parts doubtless magnified and parts certainly vague." She has "a strong will and a high hand," and—a hint at the mercantile

---

* Like James, both Owen Seaman and Pearl Craigie enjoyed Venice, and were often there together.

source of the family wealth—her "own room, her office, her count-ing-house, her battlefield, her especial scene, in fine, of action, [is] situated on the ground-floor, opening from the main hall. . . ." She would have been

an extraordinary figure in a cage or anywhere; majestic, magnificent, high-coloured, all brilliant gloss, perpetual satin, twinkling bugles and flashing gems, with a lustre of agate eyes, a sheen of raven hair, a polish of complexion that was like that of well-kept china and that—as if the skin were too tight—told especially at curves and corners. Her niece had a quiet name for her—she kept it quiet: thinking of her, with a free fancy, as somehow typically insular, she talked to herself of Britannia of the Market Place. . . . There was a whole side . . . the side of her florid philistinism, her plumes and her train, her fantastic furniture and heaving bosom, the false gods of her taste and false notes of her talk, the sole contemplation of which would be dangerously misleading. She was a complex and subtle Britannia. . . .

Mrs Lowder's "vast drawing-room" and the "prodigious extent" of the Lancaster Gate mansion, with its "massive florid furniture, the immense expression of her signs and symbols," awe the impecunious Merton Densher, although he rationalizes that his hostess is "colos-sally vulgar." He "had never dreamed of anything so fringed and scalloped, so buttoned and corded, drawn everywhere so tight and curled everywhere so thick. He had never dreamed of so much gilt and glass, so much satin and plush, so much rosewood and marble and malachite. But above all it was the solid forms, the wasted finish, the misguided cost, the general attestation of morality and money, a good conscience and a big balance." Mrs Lowder "*was* London, *was* life," but she appears to be also Mrs John Richards of 56 Lancaster Gate—Pearl Craigie's mother—at whose lavish table Henry James had dined and at whose receptions he had studied the fauna of late Victorian society and filed his observations for later use. He had not only given the game away by making her a "colossally vulgar" Lon-don Yankee, but many of her guests are Americans, one of them young Milly Theale, for whom the "great historic house" had "be-yond terrace and garden, as the centre of an almost extravagantly grand Watteau-composition, a tone as of old gold. . . ." Milly is impressed by the introductions to charming people, by "walks through halls of armour," by pictures, tapestries, and the "assault of reminders that this largeness of style was the sign of *appointed felicity."*

Certain words in *The Wings of the Dove* echo later through George Moore's fictionalizations of Pearl Craigie and her background —*agate, Watteau* . . . Had he sensed James's code? Although the Lancaster Gate mansions have declined into a faded respectability of flats and inelegant hotels, the vulgar brilliance of the setting in which "John Oliver Hobbes" felt caged will survive as long as there are readers for James's novel.

Lesser fictional variations on Pearl Craigie's life appeared posthumously. The English-born American writer Henry Logan Stuart drew in *Fenella* (1911) the daughter of a rich American resident in London who purchases a literary journal, the *Parthenon,* to promote her literary ambitions. (C. Lewis Hind, editor of the *Academy* when John Morgan Richards was proprietor, declared that the magazine never puffed her novels.) Further, Althea Rees is a Catholic convert who has gone through a notorious divorce trial:

Even after her conversion she liked to play at heresy—to be the *enfant terrible*—to have grave monsignori wag their fingers half reprovingly at her. Her religion remained intensely personal, and she was never impressed, as some worthy converts have been, by the spectacle of the Church as a "great, going concern." Its dogma oppressed her; she was not strong enough, physically or nervously, to endure its elaborate ritual, and would often leave her seat in church, suffocating, in the very middle of high mass. What she liked best was to creep away at high dusk, when the world is busied with shopping and tea, and before some dimly-lit altar in Farm Street or Brompton, to set herself adrift upon an ocean of sentiment that, with a little more conviction and a little less self-consciousness might almost have become ecstasy.

More biting was Gertrude Atherton's *Ancestors* (1907). Mrs Atherton, who spent many years in London, did not carry her grudges lightly. At a garden party in the nineties, Mrs Craigie had "turned her back on me pointedly one night when she was receiving with the hostess at a literary party." Until then she might have been only "a short dark woman who would have been plain but for a pair of remarkably fine eyes," but Mrs Atherton was suddenly certain that it was no coincidence that the paper owned by Mrs Craigie's father regularly "slammed" her novels. "Until I appeared," Gertrude Atherton wrote later, "[she] had been the only American literary pebble on the [London] literary beach." Pearl Craigie never knew she had been in a rivalry for preeminence among American literary ladies in London, for *Ancestors* appeared after her death, portraying an "astonishingly clever" American woman, Julia Kaye, daughter of vulgar, social-climbing parents, who is known for her epigrammatic writing and for snubbing her American sisters who come to England to poach upon her literary territory.

It was true that few of Pearl Craigie's friends were from the American colony; however, her closest woman friend was the best-known American woman in London, Lady Randolph Churchill, who in New York had been Jennie Jerome. Although they had known each other before 1895,* Lord Randolph's drawn-out and agonizing death that January (what was alleged to be syphilis had destroyed his nervous system, leaving him stumbling and insane) made the intimacy of the two women more possible, for after the July divorce hearing Mrs Craigie, too, had a life to put back together.

Twenty-seven in 1895, she was thirteen years younger than Jennie, who despite her troubles looked as young and beautiful as ever. It was a friendship of unequals, despite the shared confidences and close associations which followed, Pearl writing Jennie such notes as "Are you quite sure that there will be room for me this evening? . . . I should go in any case, solely for the pleasure of seeing you. . . ." Each needed the other, and Jennie Churchill, attempting to create a professional life for herself after years of scandals and disasters, had found a person who would stake her to the life-style and status she wanted to maintain in John Lane. In 1898 he was eager to found a new magazine to replace the floundering *Yellow Book*. It would be the new flagship of his firm, and with Lady Randolph Churchill as editor he would have instant prestige and established connections. She pressed for the concept of an international literary magazine; Lane was willing to experiment if she would guarantee as her total liability any losses on the first four numbers.

Young Winston shared his mother's enthusiasm about the venture:

* Pearl's son, born in 1890, was even named John Churchill Craigie.

. . . you will have an occupation and an interest in life which will make up for all the silly social amusements you will cease to shine in as time goes on and which will give you in the latter part of your life as fine a position in the world of taste & thought as formerly & now in that of elegance & beauty. It is wide & philosophic. It may also be profitable. If you could make £1,000 a year out of it, I think that would be a little lift in the dark clouds.

But Winston also warned her that "a bad name will damn any magazine," and recommended a search for a title with class about it. One of her former lovers suggested *Anglo-Saxon,* which enchanted her, but Pearl Craigie, already working closely on the projected magazine, warned her that someone else had registered such a title, and that the owner "will wait, probably, until your circulars, advertisements [are out] . . . & then apply for an injunction, claiming damages and compensation. . . ." Jennie's solution was to add *Review* to the title, and to begin planning the first number. The *Anglo-Saxon Review* would be a glorified *Yellow Book,* expensively bound and priced, but at a guinea (then about five dollars) a copy, could she, with no experience in such matters, make it go? Pearl reassured her:

Dearest Jennie, What do you mean by calling yourself uncultured, un-literary & old? You must be "going crazy"—to use our country's cheerful idiom. You are perfectly charming & your judgment in artistic matters is distinguished. These things you know in your heart, already, so I cannot be accused of flattering you. . . .

At Lancaster Gate, at a dinner party, she found what she needed, an editor—Sidney Low, then the literary editor of the *Morning Standard.* But Jennie, with Pearl Craigie, made most of the editorial decisions, putting a John Oliver Hobbes play (*Osbern and Ursyne*) into the inaugural issue, as well as a story by Henry James, a poem by Swinburne, an article by the Prime Minister, Lord Rosebery, another (on wireless telegraphy) by Oliver Lodge, and a long article called "A Modern Woman." Through the hectic months of planning the two women were drawn even closer together, even beginning a series of charity concerts in which they played together with Mademoiselle Maria Janotha, once court pianist to the German emperor and a favorite of Queen Victoria. Both American women had studied music as girls in Paris, and although they were not of Janotha caliber, they held their own in Bach's Concerto in D Minor for Three Pianos with the orchestra of the Royal College of Music. Several years later they were still performing together, playing a Beethoven trio at a reception for the new Queen Alexandra. Pearl had first hesitated about performing, claiming she was out of practice, but then took lessons from a well-known piano teacher, a Signor Bisacchia, who observed that Mrs Craigie "plays with her brain."

In the midst of the *Robert Orange* novel which she hoped would assure her reputation, with other playwriting ventures and with a heady social life that kept her a figure of lively gossip, Pearl Craigie made herself the informal coordinate publisher of the *Anglo-Saxon Review,* suggesting stories and contributors, finding Jennie an efficient secretary, remaining intimate on a social and personal level despite their disparity in outlook on almost everything, one being ascetic in matters of sex and religion and the other a sensual being to whom a passionate male was as necessary as breathing and to whom the spiritual life meant nothing. But the glossy and expensive *Review* they worked so hard to establish needed commercial success more than social acclaim, and one critic called it *"The Yellow Book in court dress and bedroom slippers,"* and the *New York World* warned, "You pay five dollars for this magazine. It may be good, but you can buy the *World* for a cent." Pearl sounded a note of confidence:

As for criticism, if one gives work to the general public, one has to accept the fate of an Aunt Sally, so far as the journalists are in question. They detest every educated influence. . . . They fear the brightening of the average intelligence—for in the imbecility of the mob (well-dressed and otherwise) is the hack journalist's strength. But the times are changing rapidly. The mob—as a mob—is becoming well-read, even philosophical, the Press in England has less power, and the country more power every day.

After the first four quarterly numbers, Lane was glad to have Jennie offer to withdraw the magazine, which he had felt might succeed "on a different line" as a quarterly for two shillings sixpence—an eighth of the price. Further, he suggested shrewdly, most subscribers could not be expected to remain beyond a second year. It would be best to wind up the publication with the eighth number. With Lane gone, Jennie listed Mrs George Cornwallis West as a publisher. It was her new name. At forty-five she had married a young officer only two weeks older than her son Winston. It did not help the fortunes of the *Review*. The eighth issue was a Coronation number, with a frontispiece portrait of Edward VII and a piece on the monarchy by Frederick Greenwood and articles by Bernard Shaw, Jennie's brother-in-law Moreton Frewen (on conservation of fish), her son Winston (on the cavalry), and her friend John Oliver Hobbes, and one of her own on "Decorative Domestic Art." Obviously the *Review*'s purse had become more limited, for there was little other reason to make most of the contents a family affair, and Jennie and Pearl discussed such alternatives as a monthly or even a weekly, or buying a going journal and jettisoning the *Review*. With only John Morgan Richards, of all the wealthy possible investors approached, willing to risk his money, it was allowed to die after the tenth issue. Lane had been right. Jennie turned to promoting the careers of her husband and her son. Pearl put renewed energy into her fiction and into planning a series of public lectures which would take her to America.

Busy with books and plays and articles early in 1902, she even had a telephone installed at Lancaster Gate in the interests of efficiency. She enjoyed working hard, she wrote her son John at Eton, and was only cross when she was too ill to do it. And she was often ill. When her father opened the American Exhibition at the Crystal Palace on the last day of May 1902, she was there, but when he went to the American Society's annual July 4 banquet she pleaded "the crowd and the stuffiness." Yet she forced herself to confront crowds, lecturing to two thousand people in Edinburgh in November 1902. In 1903 she carried her philosophy to Glasgow and Birmingham, the *Morning Post* reporting the Birmingham lecture. Being away from London often had become necessary because her mother was now so difficult to live with. As she explained to friends, despite her affection for "the poor dear Gov'nor," she could no longer *work* at home or endure the strain of Mrs Richards's behavior. To T. R.

Higgs she confided that there was never any organic malfunction found by her doctors, "but my pulse goes wrong." And when it did she would collapse.

Still she went to the Durbar in India, produced a novel a year, traveled about England and Scotland lecturing (and published volumes of her lectures). She had become, in more ways than one, a stylish stage presence; she could make a great deal from lecturing, and, she told her friend "Tip," she was considering doing more of it since Unwin was not promoting her novels as effectively as she wanted. She had run up considerable debts in maintaining her doctors and her life-style. "I fancy Papa thinks a great deal goes to R.C. charities," she confided, letting Richards continue to assume as much while her lecture engagements provided necessary cash. Yet they worked her to exhaustion. "I don't believe I shall live much longer," she wrote a friend in February 1905, noting again her concern about her pulse. ". . . For many years I have been trying to cheat exhaustion; my mind is as active as ever but I can't struggle against this fatigue. My life has been sad and eventful. I have lived two lives in one: I take everything to heart and I have thought far too much. . . . My knowledge of the world has not embittered me, but it has *tired* me."

Despite the dire foreshadowings, she left for the United States early in November 1905 for a long lecture tour, and before sailing added £5,000 to her insurance policy, bringing the total payable to her son to £18,000. To "Tip" she claimed that her ailment was (to use modern terms) a tubercular pericarditis which flared up as a result of nervous exhaustion. It affected her pulse and felt like a dull, painful swelling in her chest. Only "powerful drugs" alleviated the symptoms, and until they did she was "fit for nothing." Given such concerns, her decision to attempt a lengthy lecture tour through a quarter of the United States in midwinter appears almost suicidal. And she might very well have been attracted by the prospect of dying in the land of her birth.

Henry James's advice to Jennie Churchill when she had contemplated a lecture tour in America was "It doesn't matter what you say—they only want to *look* at you!" If Jennie had transmitted the Master's prophecy it would again have been accurate. At each city

and town the arrival of John Oliver Hobbes, in ermine and silk, became an occasion. She had never thought or acted, as far as she knew,
as an American, except for residual instinctive loyalties; but she had
retained her American citizenship. Now she took it as her mission to
mitigate prejudices about speakers from "the other side" who had
shocking manners and bad voices; however, Max Beerbohm in paro-
dying her platform style suggested that she was in demand for her
elegant ex cathedra performance more than for her content, which
escaped most listeners. "Balzac, Turner and Brahms," "Dante and
Goya," or "Dante and Botticelli" juxtaposed names and ideas which
seemed paradoxical or even irrelevant to Max, who imagined her delivering a talk on "Isaiah, Watteau and Strauss":

Perhaps in this distinguished audience there will be some who will
wonder why I have grouped these three great men together. My . . .
private motive (between you and me and Papa's Little Liver Pills) is
that I have nothing whatever to say that has not already been said about
Isaiah or Watteau or Strauss—nothing, that is, to say above the level
of any high-school girl who has dipped into a popular encyclopedia—
whereas by making a trio of them I can seem to be doing something very
thoughtful and profound—or rather I can seem throughout my lecture as
if I were *going* to be very illuminating about the differences between
these three great men, and about their points of resemblance; and when at
length I suddenly resume my seat, I shall smile round on you so sweetly,
with such modest brilliance, that you really won't be able to realise that
I have merely succeeded in making fools of you, and a fool of myself.
My hat, at which so many of you are looking, cost 17 guineas. And now
to the subject of my lecture.

Isaiah was a Prophet, Watteau was a Painter, Strauss is a Musical
Composer. . . . There have been very few feminine Prophets. In the
nature of women there seems to be (I say it with a giggle) something
that prevents them from prophesying. But Isaiah was not a woman.
Isaiah was a man. . . . It is likely enough that, in his boyhood, people
did not foresee his future eminence. There were people who did not
foresee mine. And yet here I am. Watteau, when he grew up, was essentially a *Court* Painter. He delighted in all that is graceful and gay and
distinguished in the outer aspects of life. In this he was very different
from Rembrandt, who probed deep into character. That is what *I* do, but
then I don't only do that, you bet your bottom dollar: I've got culture,

but I'm a right smart Amurrican gurl, and don't you make no darned error about it. . . .

In New York she lectured at Barnard College (where she was introduced by former American ambassador to England Joseph Choate), met John Drew and Ethel Barrymore, and went to the opera with the Vanderbilts. In Washington she was the guest of Mary Curzon's parents in their mansion on Dupont Circle (telling the Leiters untruthfully that their daughter was "looking splendidly"—she would die in London that July at thirty-six); and she would be invited to the White House by Theodore Roosevelt. There were crowds at every stop, as people were eager to see whether she was as elegant in person and as clever in talk as the characters about whom she wrote. Appearances arranged by her lecture agent took her to Bryn Mawr College and Philadelphia, Chicago and Indianapolis, Boston and Providence. At each stop, often after long nights on a train, there were interviews, receptions, and meetings, as well as articles to write and file to newspapers in New York for which she had rashly agreed to report on her journeys across America. And there were deadlines to meet for the serial installments of her novel *The Dream and the Business,* which was already appearing in England. By the end of January 1905 she was too exhausted to continue. "I could not live in this country," she wrote Father Brown. "It is marvellous, stimulating, all kinds of things, but it is very crude." Breaking her contract (she was to lecture through March), she sailed back to England, completing her novel from her bed, despite what she called a heart attack. "I thought I was dying last Saturday and I am sorry I did not," she wrote a friend in March. "Please don't think I want a long illness and horrors. I want to die in harness and at work. . . ."

She was now failing rapidly, but no one seemed to notice any change because for years her life had been one of frenetic activity followed by exhaustion and collapse. Still, she wrote a friend, "[Doctors] told me some years ago that I should go out like a candle: my heart was broken by grief long ago, and although it is sound physically, and I *ought* to live by all the rules of the physical game,—the laws of the spiritual game are more determined—if more elusive."

Her routine of dinner parties, travel abroad or to the Isle of Wight, country house weekends at such manors as Lady Warwick's in Sussex, and theater-going in the West End required more and more days in bed to recuperate. When, at Lancaster Gate, she would encounter her ex-husband on the street or in the post office—he had remarried and lived nearby—the day would be darkened. George Moore was still spreading rumors about her, and even the devoted Father Brown at Vauxhall broke with her briefly when he felt that his intimacy with her might be construed as imprudent. "Ill-natured people," he explained lamely (by letter), "would make capital out of my being often seen alone with a lady." She slashed a wrist, which was hardly in keeping with Roman Catholic principles about self-destruction. Like most such attempts the result was a messy failure. She explained unconvincingly to Mélanie, her maid, that she had stopped a nosebleed. When she next appeared in public, on June 17, 1906, as guest speaker at a dinner in honor of Ellen Terry, ever elegant, she wore a lace sling.

Her life was going to pieces, but stubbornly she began a new novel. To her publisher she observed, preparing him for it, "I can't attempt to cope with the 'Jungle' public. Sensationalism is not my line. I am an artist." It might have been dialogue from one of her novels or plays. "Jungle" was a reference to the shocking novelistic exposé of the Chicago stockyards by a fellow American, Upton Sinclair, just published. Her fictional world was as remote from midwestern abattoirs as the artificiality of her writing style was from Sinclair's Yankee journalese. The world was changing rapidly and she realized that there was no retreat into the past. When Father Brown made amends she wrote him that "nothing [was] so pitiful as a maimed . . . friendship—patched up." Then Mary Curzon died in July. Papa and well-meaning friends reminded her that Curzon was again available. She was thirty-eight. Even if she were to be widowed, and thus free in the eyes of the church to marry, she told Brown, "there is nothing *now* in marriage which calls me. If I had an illusion or so, it might be different."

On August 2 she inquired about her son's listless work at Eton, and his master at Godolphin House reported that it was difficult for John to "act self-reliant." He was without apparent needs or wants, except for golf, and when at Easter she had seen little of John she hinted to him that she might write an essay someday "on the Solitude of Devoted Mothers." Whether he liked it or not, she was planning a motoring holiday in Scotland with him to begin on August 15, and returned from Steephill on August 12, after the usual family acrimony, to prepare. The next morning a maid at Lancaster Gate found her dead in her bed, a rosary in her hand.

Despite the opposition of her father, an inquest was held that ascribed the death to cardiac failure.* To make matters worse, Richards insisted to reporters that his daughter never took drugs of any kind, and denied all knowledge of her heart condition. Both statements were true as far as they went since she had once written "Tip" that she had never explained anything about her ailments to him, and that of course Mama was "hopeless on such subjects." George Moore suggested privately that she had taken a drug overdose in a suicide attempt, and a curious request in her will specified cremation; but since she had also requested "the rites of the Roman Catholic Church," she was interred in St Mary's Cemetery, Kensal Green, following a requiem mass at the Jesuit church at Farm Street. Mama did not attend. The estate was probated at £24,502.

On May 22, 1907, the Strachey House at 69 Lancaster Gate was put up for auction although Lytton wanted the family to let it furnished to some wealthy American "and live on the proceeds for the next ten years." Since there were no bids at the floor price upon which Lady Strachey insisted, it was sold privately that September. The American literary presence at Lancaster Gate was gone.

* Very likely (in modern terms) an interatrial septal defect which would permit her to reach adulthood, although with recurrent problems of exhaustion, and which would eventually cause right-sided heart failure and death (according to the textbooks) "in the fourth or fifth decade."

CHAPTER III

Cromwell Road

To have a quality of his own, a writer must needs draw his sap from the soil of his origin.

—Henry James on Henry Harland (1898)

IF THERE WAS an elder statesman among literary Americans residing in London, it was neither Mark Twain, whose years in the city were numerous but nonconsecutive, nor Bret Harte, who was a pariah among Yankees. Henry James, who had lived in London even longer than Harte, was different. Recognizing the Master's status, a Kensington neighbor and disciple had come to call on a Sunday afternoon early in 1894, accompanied by an even younger friend. Their mission was to enlist James's interest, as he recorded in his notebook, "in a periodical about to take birth . . . on the most original lines and with the happiest omens, . . . to sound the note of bright defiance." Although bright young defiance had never been James's métier, his wounded spirit was ready to respond to flattery. A two-year venture into playwriting had just resulted in the rueful confession of defeat which he was then preparing for a volume of unproduced plays. For a piece of fiction as long as James cared to make it, Henry Harland offered him the lead place in the inaugural issue.

"The project, modestly and a little vaguely . . . set forth," confessed James, "amused me, charmed me, on the spot." But "the bravest of the portents that Sunday afternoon" worried him: Harland's young companion, the thin, hatchet-faced Aubrey Beardsley, was to be "in charge of the 'art department.'" James remembered meeting him once before, and had encountered "an example of his so curious and so disconcerting talent," for which the Master's appreciation had "stopped quite short." He agreed to furnish something, while hinting strongly that he would be relieved if Beardsley did not feel it necessary to accompany his "comparatively so incurious text" with a perverse illustration.

The presence of Harland as editor reassured James that the magazine would maintain a tone of prudence and decorum. Besides, the pair assured him, Oscar Wilde would be excluded as a potential contributor; and John Lane, its publisher, James knew, tempered the firm's enterprise on behalf of new and startling talent with sound business instincts. As E. F. Benson later put it, Lane "had no objection . . . to thin ice, provided he felt reasonably sure that it would not let him through."

The key to acquiring Henry James had been his need for a literary success. He had informed Harland that his price was ten pounds per thousand words, although for a very long story he would settle for less. (He had just completed one and anticipated problems with its publication.) James's income from America and his writing earnings barely maintained his modestly expansive life-style. His young American protégé had come at the right time.

A prospectus promised that the *Yellow Book* would "seek always to preserve a delicate, decorous and reticent mien and conduct," while having "the courage of its modernness" in not trembling "at the frown of Mrs Grundy." In March the announcement appeared, appropriately on bright yellow paper, and decorated with an elegantly elongated Beardsley female. A list of Harland's expected contributors followed, including Henry James and "John Oliver Hobbes," but also promising a dozen who never did appear, ranging from the ever-unreliable Frank Harris to the future "hermit of Peking," Edmund Backhouse, then an Oxford student.

Cultivating his potential contributors as well as likely critics, Harland held Saturday evening at-homes, often very curious affairs, at 144 Cromwell Road. In the gray winter months of 1894, evenings at the Harland flat, lit by lamps and candles although electricity had already come to more fashionable addresses, consisted of animated conversation about art and music and writing and sex, punctuated only rarely by food or drink. Henry James's own well-appointed fourth-floor rooms at De Vere Gardens were not electrified until 1895, and one tale which went the rounds about the Master's magnetism with the ladies (who saw him as exuding a vitality that was unthreatening) was that at an evening party at Grosvenor House, the first of the great London establishments to install the new luxury, the lights suddenly went out. Just as suddenly they came on again, "to discover—so the story went—thirteen ladies clinging to Mr. James."

Of the candle-lit evenings at less fashionable Cromwell Road, Evelyn Sharp, then young, wide-eyed, and intense, remembered, "We did not care much what conventional society thought of us, so long as we could succeed in pleasing our editor's fastidious taste in letters and avoid the two cardinal sins of banality and insincerity. I suppose we were as much interested in sex as young people are in all periods. . . . The personal and often unconventional relationships of acquaintances were discussed sometimes with a frankness that at first embarrassed a country-bred person like myself, but [a generation later] would not embarrass a schoolgirl. . . ."

In the nineties, "indifferent amateur music" was giving way as indoor entertainment to the self-amusement of talk; but Aline Harland had a piano and a pleasing soprano, and sang French songs, and Leonard Sickert sang German and Italian songs, which guests at Cromwell Road accepted as a temporary interruption to the more pleasing music of conversation. Cleaving the chatter as well as the song was not easy, but Miss Sharp remembered the occasion when Henry James came to tea and "we sat in dumb humility" while Harland's *maître* "walked up and down the room seeking the word he wanted for the completion of his sentence. I am sure we all knew the word, but the sacrilege which would be implied in our intrusion upon his mental travail by mentioning it was undreamed of. It was, of course, an immense honour to have been invited to worship at the shrine; but the atmosphere cleared pleasantly when he left and our editor became himself again."

Borrowing what he could of his mentor's ceremonial magic, Harland had become London host to whatever visiting American writers passed through, partly to retain literary connections with publishers and critics in Boston and New York, and partly to enlist new talent. Hamlin Garland recalled an evening when Harland was "strenuously entertaining," punctuating his "shocking reactionary sentiments" on American democracy and English society with stories about how he outwitted sheriffs who came to collect overdue bills or repossess merchandise. He was always "just a jump ahead of the wolf," he boasted, and while Aline frowned, Henry explained how he had engaged a constable in political talk "whilst the piano was being salvaged down the back stairs." Garland could not take his host's professions of conservatism seriously, "for all the women of his party drank and smoked, which was new and very 'radical' to me." Another Cromwell Road visitor was "an American female called Agnes Repplier," who "asked to be introduced, I fancy, for the purpose of making herself disagreeable," Mary Chavelita Dunne ("George Egerton"), author of *Keynotes,* wrote haughtily to John Lane. "I have an idea she was the girl you sat next to at H. Harland's dinner." The date was July 8, 1894, at the height of *Yellow Book* prestige. Miss Repplier, from Philadelphia, was never published in the *Yellow Book.*

The most unpleasant, although not entirely untrue, account of the Harlands at Cromwell Road came from a small, bespectacled former seminarian, Frederick Rolfe, who had been expelled from his studies for the priesthood for offenses ranging from larceny to buggery and had tried writing as one escape from poverty. Although the professional frustrations he blamed upon Lane and Harland were not all the product of paranoia (another Rolfe disability), his masochistic tendencies led him to undermine most of his opportunities. He wrote formidably to editors as "Baron Corvo," although his actual address was usually seat B4 in the British Museum Reading Room during the day (where he was working on *Stories Toto Told Me,* his thinly disguised tales of homosexual adventures with Italian village boys), and flophouses or a bench on the Embankment at night. The charm of the stories appealed to Lane and Harland, who invited Rolfe to visit, and he arrived bearing his worldly goods tied up in a colored handkerchief and his writings in a shabby portfolio.

Harland apparently offered him five pounds for a pair of stories, eventually raising the amount to seven pounds. Rolfe assumed he was to get ten pounds for the pair—five for each. After waiting months for his check, and receiving only seven pounds, he not only needed the full ten pounds but wanted payment in guineas. The extra shilling in each pound meant much to a writer who lived on the edge of starvation. Although Lane was an imaginative, innovative publisher, more courageous than most in London, and his editor, Harland, was a sensitive literary man, when it came to money both were cautious and tight-fisted.

Even before Rolfe had met Harland, he had regarded him with anti-Semitic contempt, assuming on the basis of the early New York novels published as "Sidney Luska" that Harland was a covert Jew; and his bitterness was intensified by the contrast between the editor's fashionable clothes and the Baron's frayed and filthy ones. Still, Rolfe accepted a lunch of eggs and bacon at Cromwell Road, and even took a sovereign as an advance against a Toto story, while Harland prophesied that a book of such Toto tales would bring Rolfe, who had just been in the Holywell workhouse for lack of funds, seven hundred pounds in six months. In the meantime Rolfe was invited to parties at Cromwell Road, although pert, topknotted Ella d'Arcy, who acted as appointments secretary as well as subeditor, relegated him to the afternoon soirées, which were, she said, to the evenings "what the Luxembourg is to the Louvre," and she recalled him as a "disquieting creature" who left "singularly lively traces of his presence in Harland's armchairs."

"Never were there such evenings," Miss d'Arcy rhapsodized, "as those long ago evenings in Cromwell Road! I see [Harland] standing on the hearth-rug, or sitting on the floor, waving his eye-glasses on the end of their cord, or refixing them in his short-sighted eyes, while assuring some 'dear beautiful lady!' or other how much he admired her writing, or her painting, her frock, or the colour of her hair. He would re-christen a golden red-headed woman 'Helen of Troy'; he would tell another that her eyes reminded him of 'the moon rising over the jungle,' and thus put each on delightfully cordial terms with herself . . . and with him." But Rolfe only recorded being silent and watchful as he drank his afternoon tea and ate his farthing bun while Harland "skipped and hovered and sat on his hind leg everywhere, like a cricket, a bluebottle, a toad clickety-clacking, buzzing and rarely dumb."

Nursing his revenge for the empty promises and the poor takings from the Toto stories which Harland and Lane did publish, Rolfe put both men into his autobiographical novel *Nicholas Crabbe,* in which Harland became "Sidney Thorah" and Lane "Slim Schelm." Despite its sour temper and its inaccuracies, no better picture of literary life at 144 Cromwell Road exists.

Crabbe waited a couple of minutes in a large and very dainty drawing-room. There were a couch and a piano and lots of weird and comfy chairs, and a feminine atmosphere. Sidney Thorah suddenly fell in, with a clatter and a rush; and began to talk-on-a-trot. He was a lank round-shouldered bony unhealthy personage, much given to crossing his legs when seated and to twisting nervously in his chair. He had insincere eyes, and long arms which dangled while he was silent and jerked and waved when he spoke. He spoke a great deal, in eager tones inlaid with a composite jargon which was basically Judisch but varied with the gibberish of newly-arrived American students of the Latin Quarter. He wore a fawn-coloured dressing-suit and a silk handkerchief; and Crabbe, noting the big jacinth on the little finger and the wide upturned nose, suspected an apostate Jew.

Thorah . . . never looked his guest in the face; but made play with his eye-glasses, fiddled with his slippers and the fringes on carpets and chairs, provided cigarettes, and finally settled down with one leg tucked under him and the other dangling in a manner which indicated mitral regurgitation. He evidently was a hard man on trousers. All the time, he was darting side glances; and his shrill clamour lashed Crabbe like sleet. He talked of books and people. His conversation was amazingly witty, pleasant, ephemeral, and insincere. . . .

Presently, Thorah wished to make his visitor known to the sub-editor of the *Blue Volume.* She was an intellectual mouse-mannered piece of sex, inhabiting a neighbouring flat; and a verbal message brought her. The men carried on the conversation while she played the chorus. Thorah at last introduced the question of ways and means. Crabbe described his interview with Schelm. . . .

The sub-editor nodded silent sympathy; and would have squeaked a tale upon request. Thorah said that there was lots of work going begging: the thing was to get to know the proper people. He offered to arrange a hundred introductions; and, when Crabbe rose to go, asked him to accept a sovereign. . . .

Thorah clamorously asseverated that Crabbe ought to (and must) have a patron, a new Maecenas to give him an easy mind and a fair field for the cultivation of his genius. Crabbe found the notion not unpleasant, provided that it was understood that a *quid pro quo* would be given when success was reached. Thorah was in love with his idea; and would try to give it form. The husband of the tall fair handsome friend whom Crabbe had met, for example, and he was a financier in the city and a patron of Whistler and Otomaro. Why should he not be a patron of Crabbe?

Dinners ensued; and an all-one-summer-night party in a garden in Kensington, when the flower-beds were outlined with fairy-lamps and everything was lovely and amusing. . . .

Harland could be quite as impossible in real life when he was playing impresario. He and Aline ("Eileen" in Rolfe's novel) were lavish with suggestions and invitations, but the suggestions were often vague and the invitations, unless Miss d'Arcy kept account of them, equally airy. They were known to have invited friends to dinner and then—unless it were a Saturday—forget all about it, so that guests turned up at Cromwell Road in evening dress at eight o'clock to find the pair sitting down at the kitchen table over two chops. Blandly, Harland would wave his hand and confess, "You know, Aline, I never remember a word of anything that happens when I am drunk." Another time, three guests arrived to be taken to dinner, only to find the Harlands quarreling about where to go. Finally Henry turned on Aline and sulked, "All right, we won't go anywhere at all!" And their guests missed out on their dinner.

One dinner Harland and his co-editor did provide was a banquet for the contributors to the *Yellow Book,* on publication day, Monday evening the fifteenth of April 1894, in an upper room of the Hotel d'Italie, at 52 Compton Street in Soho. At each place was a *Yellow Book.* Its notoriety had preceded it, for five shillings—a book price —itself would have called attention to the magazine, and the editors had also provided joint, widely read interviews. Besides, their publisher's censorship of Beardsley's allegedly scandalous drawings was a rumor which quickly spread and, unlike most rumors, was accurate. John Lane had learned from Beardsley's striking illustrations to Wilde's *Salome* that every sketch had to be scrutinized carefully. The diligence had forestalled trouble, for a disarmingly captioned drawing of a fat woman proved on further examination to resemble—unfavorably—the pretty but plump "Trixie" Whistler.

On the morning of the fifteenth Frederick Chapman and his stock boy Lewis May had filled the little bow window at 6B Vigo Street, under the sign of Sir Thomas Bodley's head, with copies of the new quarterly. Publishing and bookselling partners Elkin Mathews and John Lane possessed an ultrarespectable location. Only a few footsteps from Regent Street and the Royal Geographic Society, they were also close to the seat of the English art establishment in Piccadilly, Burlington House, making the unkind remark, precipitated by the first *Yellow Book,* "uncleanliness is next to Bodliness," all the more ironic. The shop was, May remembered, "a little box of a place" with books shelved "from floor to ceiling. At the far end was a sort of screen, behind which, above a trap-door leading to a cellar, sat the cashier." At the window itself, he thought that morning, they had created "such a mighty glow of yellow at the far end of Vigo Street that one might have been forgiven for imagining for a moment that some awful portent had happened, and that the sun had risen in the West."

The shop's crowded bow window still survives, in a fanciful portrayal by Aubrey Beardsley, with Elkin Mathews as a nearsighted Pierrot, peering lovingly at his wares. Although the gaunt, dandified Beardsley, who worked in a compulsive fever of inspiration, would die of tuberculosis in less than four years, he would outlive the *Yellow Book.* His publishing partner, whose consumption was less rampant, would survive slightly longer. At thirty-three, Henry Harland was nearly a dozen years older, and at least that many times as sophisticated in the ways of the London cultural world. Born in Brighton in 1872, Beardsley still bore the naïveté of the young genius come to London from the town. Harland carried himself as the cosmopolitan whose natural habitat was Regent Street and Piccadilly.

He was born, he claimed, in St Petersburg, Russia, and "passed most of his childhood in Rome, old Papal Rome," although "most of his youth" was spent in France, and "two or three years of his early manhood [were spent] in America. . . ." He also suggested at times that he was an illegitimate son of Emperor Franz Joseph of Austria, "and that if he had stuck to the Irish College in Rome he would have been given a cardinal's hat before he was 25." Further, he laid circuitous claim to an English baronetcy, although he modestly never used the title.

Harland's actual background was much less exotic. He was born in 1861, probably in Brooklyn, and grew up in New York and nearby Connecticut, son of a lawyer and a painter. His godfather was editor and critic Edmund Clarence Stedman, who would furnish useful introductions as Harland was finding his way into the writing profession. With a family of comfortable means, and with literary connections including not only Stedman but William Dean Howells and publisher S. S. McClure as well, Harland soon considered City College of New York too modest an institution to contain him. After trying free-lance writing unsuccessfully, he spent a year at divinity school at Harvard before dropping out to be a private tutor. Since he wanted to write, Stedman urged Europe upon him as a means of broadening his experience, and early in 1883 he went to Rome. Italy ended his interest in becoming a Unitarian minister, and he began to drift toward Catholicism, but when he returned to New York and to dull work as a law clerk, he wrote a novel which suggested that he was a Jew. *As It Was Written,* about a young Jewish musician's life, was offered to a publisher through Stedman, and was accepted. For added authenticity Harland had used the pen name "Sidney Luska." "Every young Jew I had ever heard of was named Sidney," he said, "and Luska I thought a good name because it didn't mean anything." Other novels with Jewish themes followed, but also *An Account of the Fortune of Mr. and Mrs. Thomas Gardner,* a thinly disguised account of his marriage written under his own name.

Aline Merriam, whom he had married in 1884, was an authentic cosmopolitan. Charming, talented, and ambitious, and a year older than her husband, she was the daughter of Americans who had chosen to live in Paris, and on a visit to them after her marriage, her parents introduced the couple to French literary life. It was a timely connection, for Harland's career needed new direction. Once *The Yoke of the Thorah,* advocating intermarriage and assimilation, was serialized in *McClure's,* outraging Jewish sensibilities, his cover as "Sidney Luska" was blown. New York became unattractive as a place in which to improve his literary fortunes.

Paris proved equally inhospitable. A writer writing in English needed appropriate literary sponsors. The Harlands moved to London in 1889, Aline complaining to Stedman of "the darkness of this sunless and misty city," but through the loyal Stedman, Harland met the dean of London Yankees, Henry James. "Sidney Luska" could now be left for dead. In London he could write English as a "living language," for there, he later claimed, one "hears the language which he writes, spoken by living people all about him. . . . Only an English dialect is spoken in America." However beneficial the setting, London proved wrong for his lungs. A doctor, on examining Harland's chest, warned him erroneously that he had only two years to live, and needed a milder climate. Stubbornly, he remained, but the likelihood of Harland's literary fame seemed, to Henry James, remote. Harland, he confided to Edmund Gosse, had "literary longings unaccompanied by the *faculty.*"

Four years in London had changed all that. He was making connections, he wrote Stedman. "Whistler is the best friend we have made here: a most eccentric, kind-hearted, brilliant, delightful creature." And he added other names, some mere one-time acquaintances whose alleged friendship Harland added to the myth of himself he was already manufacturing. His lungs, despite the concern of his physicians, were no worse, and his writings, if not up to James's standards,* was getting into print. He had written a three-volume novel in the English fashion and a book of short fiction inspired by French masters. One of his stories in the Maupassant manner was being written on commission for *Black and White,* a new magazine which used both new art and new writing, and in France he had seen the *Revue Blanche.* On New Year's Day, 1894, with a soupy yellow fog keeping them indoors, Beardsley and Harland had sat before a glowing coal fire at Harland's flat, and imagined a maga-

---

* Vincent O'Sullivan called Harland a "lemonade Henry James."

zine of their own, one which would be hospitable to the "new movement" and as elegant as a book. The next day they had an appointment in Vigo Street with John Lane, who had begun as silent partner to Elkin Mathews and was now becoming the dominant proprietor. Beardsley proposed the *Yellow Book* as a working title, and the suggestion stuck; one morning a few days later Lane discussed format with Harland and Beardsley, displaying specimens of type, paper, and cloth in the leisurely setting of the Hogarth Club in Bond Street.

Arthur Waugh, then a young subeditor at the *New Review,* remembered the *Yellow Book* as the most poorly kept secret in London, as he listened in at a meeting at his own club, the National Liberal, where Harland and Lane had come to inform Edmund Gosse—a senior member of the critical establishment—of their intentions. The Bodley Head, already reputed to be the sign under which decadence bloomed, needed an organ of respectability. Beardsley had fixed upon the daring color of yellow—associated with allegedly wicked French novels—but Harland, as a follower of Henry James, was a guarantee to Lane of a safer sort. That afternoon Harland and Lane, "so far as Lane could get a word in edgeways," Waugh wrote, prophesied that the venture would represent the best that was being done in England in "prose and poetry, criticism, fiction and art, the oldest school and the newest side by side, with no hall-mark except that of excellence and no prejudice against anything but dullness and incapacity. . . ."

Word of the new magazine had spread as the editors solicited material and prepared a prospectus. One group of potential contributors met with the editors and publisher at the Hogarth early in February, where Frank Harris—an Irish-American—and George Moore—an Irishman—insisted that literary criticism worth the name did not exist in England. Lane disagreed, and named names. At any rate, Beardsley observed, there were no art critics in England except Joseph Pennell, and he was an American. The message was clear: it would take more than native English talent to make the *Yellow Book* the highbrow commercial success its creators had in mind. Also, the cachet of a Henry James had to be balanced by cautious suggestiveness elsewhere among the contents; yet the thin ice which was Beardsley's contribution may have been one reason why some of the

Establishment figures represented in the first *Yellow Book* were not present at the Hotel d'Italie to toast its instant success.* Whatever James's timidity, he loved a grand social occasion and was away unavoidably in Venice. Very likely he would have been the lion of the evening, which made it all the more ironic that the leading place in the opening number had gone to his long tale, "The Death of the Lion." It reflected a typically Jamesian perspective upon literary life. Nothing succeeds for writers, James well knew, like success, and nothing shattered the personal privacy in which the writer wrote more effectively than that very success. James's hero is lionized to death.

The Master contributed to several later numbers as well, while confessing uneasiness about some of his bedfellows in "the small square lemon-coloured quarterly," and gratitude to Harland for allowing him so much space. He felt that such freedom for the writer was "the millennium" for the short story and indicated, on the part of the editor, "the finest artistic intelligence." Still, he wrote to his brother William from Italy in May that he hadn't sent a copy, "although my little tale which ushers it in appears to have had, for a thing of mine, an unusual success. I hate too much the horrid aspect and company of the whole publication. And yet I am to be intimately, conspicuously associated with the 2nd number. It is for gold and to oblige the worshipful Harland."

He and Harland shared, James later explained, the French ideal of "the beautiful and blest nouvelle," and his three long stories for the *Yellow Book,* ranging from fourteen to twenty thousand words, were among his finest in that genre. All had in common, he observed, their concern with the literary life, "gathering their motive, in each case, from some noted adventure, some felt embarrassment, some extreme predicament, of the artist enamoured of perfection, ridden by his idea or paying for his sincerity." Ironically, the *Yellow Book* was James's own "felt embarrassment," arising from the predicament of his financial concerns—reduced advances on his novels and the failures of his plays—and the playing to his pride of Harland's "worship."

Although the Jamesian presence was Harland's respectability in-

* Within a month it was in a fourth printing.

surance, the editors had shrewdly added his compatriot John Singer Sargent. Once his pictures had raised eyebrows in Bond Street, yet Sargent, whose most pressing problem was whom he would find time to paint, now represented cautious distinction. "Harland tells me," Beardsley had written James, "that you very kindly promised to lend your portrait by Sargent to the *Yellow Book.* Will you give me authority to go to your rooms and take it away as I am now making up No. 2. Of course I will have it carefully returned as soon as the block is made." Unaware in his innocence of the Master's uneasiness, Beardsley then crowed, "Have you heard of the storm that raged over No. 1? Most of the thunderbolts fell on my head. However I enjoyed the excitement immensely." The connection of the painter and writer was more appropriate than either Harland or Beardsley knew, for James had confided to his notebook (April 25, 1894) that he had committed himself to another long story for the *Yellow Book,* and had fixed, "on 2nd thought," upon "the idea of *The Coxon Fund*—asking myself if I can't treat it in a way to make it go into that limited space. I want to do something very good for the Y.B., and this subject strikes me as superior. The formula for the presentation of it in 20,000 words is to make it an *Impression*—as one of Sargent's pictures is an impression. That is, I must do it from my own point of view—that of an imagined observer, participator, chronicler. I must picture it, summarize it, impressionize it, in a word —compress and confine it by making it the picture of what I see."

Unlike James, Sargent would elect not to reappear in the *Yellow Book,* which was too flashy and vulgar for his taste. "From an aesthetic point of view," he wrote to Gosse in April 1894, "I dislike that book too much to be willing to seem a habitual contributor."

"The writer who brought me in touch with Harland and the *Yellow Book,*" Douglas Ainslie recalled, "was Henry James." They would meet at the Athenaeum Club and talk "about literature and life." James had no compunction about sending new writing talent to his disciple, now in a position to pay struggling writers for their wares. Harland never let on how difficult it was to extract pence, let alone pounds, from Lane to pay contributors, but he struggled to maintain editorial independence while writing letter after letter to Lane to beg funds to pay his *Yellow Book* authors, even resorting to listing, among contributors and their expected remuneration from Lane, "Henry Harland. He gives his story for the love of the *Y.B.,* though the *Idler* gives him £3:3:0 a thousand words and the *New Review* pays him £2:2:0." Lane had insisted that two hundred pounds was all he would pay for writers' fees in any issue, and Harland was forced to juggle "cheaper poems," and to exhort Lane, "If you ask any editor in England what he thinks would be a fair average price per page for literary matter of the standard published in the *Yellow Book,* he will tell you at the lowest 15 shillings. Yet I am getting you 300 pages, all of the stuff good, much of it coming from men of high rank, at the rate of 13/4 a page. . . ." By "high rank" Harland meant such proper English critics as Edmund Gosse, Dr Richard Garnett of the British Museum, and Professor George Saintsbury. Only Garnett turned up, quietly, at the *Yellow Book* dinner.

As art editor, Beardsley, too, courted respectability, printing two studies by Sir Frederick Leighton, president of the Royal Academy. The gesture failed to appease the staid *Times,* which thundered that the artistic note of the first number appeared to be "a combination of English rowdyism with French lubricity." Quickly the unhappy Sir Frederick visited the Bodley Head (soon to be referred to in *Punch* as the Sodley Bed) to tell Lane that he had been accused by his friends of embarrassing serious art, and that he had promised "never to appear in such company again." Such qualms never disturbed another artist often called upon by the *Yellow Book,* Joseph Pennell, a Philadelphia Quaker who lived with his writer wife, Elizabeth (another Philadelphian), just below the Strand at Charing Cross in a tiny house in Buckingham Street. As a writer about the arts and as a line draftsman, Pennell found himself enough in demand to ignore criticism. But he, too, had been away on an assignment at the time of the inaugural dinner. Elizabeth appeared at the head table in his place.

Irascible and feisty, Joseph Pennell had rankled over not being invited to be the *Yellow Book*'s art editor. Where were Harland's Yankee—or artistic—loyalties? Born in 1857, Pennell, whose ancestors came to Pennsylvania in 1684, had lived in England since the middle eighties. One of Harland's oldest American friends in London, Pennell knew all the artists in England worth mentioning, and was an illustrator of great elegance, although as a critic he often used a more blunt instrument, despite traditional Quaker eschewing of violence. It was Pennell who, after Aline Harland had introduced him to the frail and marvelous boy, a clerk in an insurance company office, had written him up in the first issue of the *Studio,* a piece which, embellished by the boy's drawings, had made Beardsley famous at twenty-one. While Pennell persevered in his loyalties to his protégé, Beardsley had made it easy. He confided his inexperience, consulted with Pennell about contributors, and reproduced a Pennell etching in the first number. And when Pennell had to choose between Beardsley and Harland—the latter a fellow American—he remained loyal to Beardsley. When Harland had to carry on the *Yellow Book* alone, and the dying boy took on the art editorship of the rival *Savoy,* Pennell offered it his etching of the grand, sweeping curve of Regent Street, done in his finest architectural manner.

Harland made a continuing effort to secure Americans for his list. He had not forgotten his background, however he disguised it, but he had few connections among Americans resident in London except through Henry James, who seemed to know everyone. One compatriot who appeared in the inaugural issue and at the dinner in Soho he might not even have identified as a Richards of Massachusetts, the elegant Mrs Pearl Craigie. Since she was "John Oliver Hobbes," her appearance lent some irony to the fact that the lead story in the *Yellow Book,* by her friend Henry James, satirized the transvestite world of contemporary writers. In "The Death of the Lion" the well-known romantic novelist Dora Forbes is really a bald, bushy-mustached man, who "only assumes a feminine personality because the ladies are such popular favourites." Meanwhile, the formidable novelist Guy Walsingham turns out to be "a pretty little girl who wore her hair in what used to be called a crop."

The "Hobbes" contribution to the issue was an act of a play on which she had been working with George Moore. Like Sargent, she quickly turned uncooperative, writing Moore that Harland wanted her "to write a poem, story, an article, anything, for the next number," but that she had "never seen such a vulgar production." Other

Americans would appear later in Harland's pages—at least one in most issues—but few of them appeared to have achieved anything more remarkable than to have been born on Harland's side of the ocean.

Perhaps the most accomplished American was novelist and *New York Times* London correspondent Harold Frederic, who had a melodramatic story in the seventh number. A less-known newspaper-man, whose reverent sonnet on Meredith would appear in the third issue, was William Morton Fullerton. Twenty-nine when the first *Yellow Book* appeared, he had come to London from Harland's hometown, Norwich, Connecticut, but had grown up in Waltham, Massachusetts, where his father was a Congregational minister. In 1886 he had graduated from Harvard, where, with George Santayana and Bernhard (as he was then) Berenson, two other students destined to become expatriates, he helped found the *Harvard Monthly.* After two years as literary editor of the *Boston Advertiser,* he had gone to England with his classmate Richard King Longfellow, a nephew of the poet, and after a few months of free-lancing had made several important conquests. He had found a job on the staff of *The Times,* a friend and sponsor in Henry James, and an aristocratic mistress in Margaret Brooke, the Ranee of Sarawak. She had a house in London, far from her "white raja" husband, and was fifteen years older than Fullerton. Henry James had introduced them, with no anticipation of the consequences. (He had also introduced Fullerton to Harland.)

The sonnet was among the least interesting of Fullerton's writings. His diary was full of sensual dream visions of statuesque, full-bosomed females (he was slight and five feet six), described in orgasmic detail, and his letters to the Ranee were full of impassioned descriptions of souls and lips mingling. After several passionate years, Margaret Brooke realized that it was no longer possible to conceal her gray hairs, and so did Fullerton. He located a plush *Times* assignment at the Paris office, where he continued his research on the female figure, covered the Dreyfus case, and wound down his liaison with the redoubtable Ranee. Edith Wharton, another of Fullerton's older women, would come along in 1907.

Young Norman Hapgood, out of Harvard in 1893, was also devoted to James. Harland duly accepted Hapgood's essay on Stendhal for the fourth number. The *Sketch* called it "the best thing" in the issue, and *Bookman* in New York praised it. Later Hapgood sold a piece on Choderlos de Laclos and his *Liaisons Dangereuses* to Harland, but it was never printed, for by then disaster had overtaken the *Yellow Book.* Yet both were part of what Hapgood called "the literary debauch I was taking, . . . [which] had something that helped to round out the world-outlook of a young American from the middle-west." When he returned to America he went on to the *Chap-Book,* which modeled itself on the *Yellow Book,* and in 1900, still only in his thirties, he became editor of *Collier's* in New York. The *Yellow Book* had been a good springboard.

The *Yellow Book*'s fortunes, and Harland's reputation, continued to rise during the year as the three additional volumes which had followed the inaugural issue had respectable press runs and grudgingly respectful notices. The *Speaker* had been deliberately offensive, imagining the publishers to have urged their writers, "Be mystic, be weird, be precious, be advanced, be without value," and it was that review in particular which had frightened Mrs Craigie away from further relations with the *Yellow Book.* Yet the notoriety had only stimulated sales. If any signs of smugness appeared on the faces of "Harry" and Aline as they conducted writers and artists and critics through the throng of guests in the Cromwell Road flat on a Saturday evening, it had to be understood in context. As Aline wrote E. C. Stedman in New York, the *Yellow Book* had been "mercilessly abused by the critics who had been incensed by our presumption in trying to do a new, original, better thing than had yet been done . . . , and by our impertinence in proclaiming that we intend to do so. As we have succeeded in spite of their unfriendliness we bear them only the slight grudge and small amount of contempt one cannot help feeling for meanness unspeakable. . . . It is impossible to tell you the bitterness, hatred and malice rife in the London art world—how each big fish lives by devouring the little fishes as fast as they become half big enough to hold their own. It is all so heartsickening that we are glad to get away from London and out of it for a fortnight, when we shall be obliged to go back again & face the world and the devil. . . ."

They returned not only to continue Harland's editorial activity but because London was the place where success in literature was possible, despite the parable of the fishes. The problem was that critics appear to lie in wait for a catastrophe upon which to capitalize, and for Harland, and even more for Beardsley, an unanticipated storm descended just as the fifth volume was about to be released in April 1895.

Deliberately snubbed by Harland and Beardsley, and never asked to contribute to the *Yellow Book,* Oscar Wilde had called it, in revenge, "horrid," "loathsome," "dull," and—worst of all—"not yellow at all." But that month Wilde was arrested and taken to Bow Street police station. The angry crowd which gathered outside noticed that he was carrying a large book bound in yellow. Although it was a French novel—Wilde would not have wanted deliberately to give the magazine the approbation of being seen in public with him—the misunderstanding "killed *The Yellow Book,*" John Lane later mourned, "and it nearly killed me." Crowds gathered under the sign of the Bodley Head and hurled stones through the window. Lane was in America on business, and Harland was in France on a holiday, having put the issue to bed and left the follow-up work to Frederick Chapman. With a delegation of Lane's most respectable authors clamoring to have Wilde's books withdrawn from the Bodley Head list, and Beardsley sacked for good measure—because he had illustrated Wilde's *Salome* and was connected in the public mind with the incarcerated Oscar,* the man in London he most disliked—Chapman cabled Lane, not Harland, for advice. Beardsley was fired, and

---

* Once Wilde went to Pentonville Prison, a letter dated September 11, 1895, addressed to J. B. Manning, the prison's governor, and signed "The Few American Friends," was received. The anonymous friends expressed concern over the impact of prison life upon Wilde's genius and offered Manning a bribe of £100,000 to connive at Wilde's escape, £50,000 more for the release of Alfred Taylor, a Wilde accomplice in finding willing boys, and an additional £50,000 "to pay some people in the prison to look the other way." If Manning were to go along with the bribe he was to place an advertisement in the personal column of the *New York World,* and then retain the notepaper on which the penciled message was written for a response to the American group, as it had a code word in red ink on the back. Further, he was warned that for his own safety "the matter is private and must be so for ever," and that if he did not agree to the proposal, he was to "forget that you have received this." He apparently kept his word to forget. The manuscript did not surface until 1962. What Americans were involved —if the letter were not a hoax—remains unknown.

the most obvious traces of his hand were removed from the issue. Two weeks late, with the help of Miss d'Arcy, and Harland's suggestions from Paris by mail, the purged *Yellow Book* reappeared. It would never be the same.

Fudging, dishonorably, the reasons for the departure of his art editor, Harland wrote of Beardsley to Edmund Gosse, "Yes, his absence from the YB is deplorable; but what is one to do with a capricious boy whose ruling passion is a desire to astonish the public with the unexpected? He'll be in the July number, I hope, larger than ever." Harland knew otherwise, but labored mightily to retain a sense of daring within the new, circumspect limits. He published the work of such promising young authors as H. G. Wells and Arnold Bennett, and another long story by Henry James, "The Next Time," in which the hero—a projection of the author?—was an ironic failure because in his attempt to produce best-selling fiction he could only succeed in creating uncommercial artistic successes.

Plagued by the bad publicity which followed Beardsley's expulsion and Wilde's imprisonment, the *Yellow Book* continued to lose contributors and readers, as well as its reputation for expressing freshness in contemporary art and writing. Even new American contributors were few. In the sixth number there was only Charles Miner Thompson, who wrote boys' stories for the *Youth's Companion,* and produced for Harland "In an American Newspaper Office." It proved even to Thompson that his forte was boys' stories. Harold Frederic helped save the seventh number, but after that the decline was rapid. There remained only the mysterious, foreign-sounding Renée de Coutans, who signed her name to short stories in the tenth and twelfth numbers, "A Lady Loved a Rose" and "Natalie." She was Aline Harland. Her husband was having difficulty filling the increasingly bland issues, and appeared himself under the pseudonym of "Robert Shews" in the eleventh, with a forgettable story titled "The Elsingfords."

Harland's acknowledged fiction was better—adroitly constructed and artificial in sentiment, with a charm that did not survive its period. But it was, according to James, the "Europe of the American mind." In an essay on his pupil in the *Fortnightly* early in 1898, James emphasized Harland's sense of "dispatriation." As he explained it, using the opportunity of a review of Harland's collected short fiction, *Comedies and Errors,* "To speak of a writer as detached, one must at least know what he is detached from, and in this collection of curiously ingenious prose pieces there is not a single clear sound of the fundamental, the native note. . . . There is not a single direct glance at American life in these pages, and only two or three implied. . . . I have found half the interest of *Comedies and Errors* to be the peculiar intensity of that mark of the imagination that may best be described as the acute sense of . . . 'Europe.' . . ." What James saw as Harland's strongest quality was his perception of "the feelings of things," a "disencumbered, sensitive surface." Harland, thought the more Europeanized James, was "lost in the vision, all whimsical and picturesque, of palace secrets, rulers and pretenders and ministers of bewilderingly light comedy, in undiscoverable Balkan States, Bohemias of the seaboard, where the queens have platonic friendships with professional English, though not American, humourists; in the heavy, many-voiced air of the old Roman streets and of the high Roman saloons where cardinals are part of the furniture; in the hum of prodigious Paris, heard in the corners of old cafés; in the sense of the deep English background as much as any of these; in a general facility of reference, in short, to the composite spectacle and the polyglot doom."

Must a writer, James had wondered at the start, "draw his sap from the soil of his origin"? Harland, despite his purchases of James's work and his willingness to publish James's young disciples, would find James's criticism of him valuable exposure but no puffery. Harland, judged James, was "a little too much everywhere" to have drawn successfully from his own roots. As an artist one had to be a citizen of somewhere before one could be a "citizen of the world."

James became acquainted with another stateless American writer when his *Yellow Book* stories "The Death of the Lion" and "The Coxon Fund" appeared in his collection he titled *Terminations.* A young Oxonian of Philadelphia Quaker background, Logan Pearsall Smith, was so impressed that he impulsively offered James his own frail book. It was, James recalled, a "labored, imitative, rather lifeless" work which he promptly mislaid in the Underground, probably by leaving it on his seat, but he guiltily bought a replacement and asked the young American over to De Vere Gardens. His praise was tepid but kind; he guessed correctly that Pearsall Smith would never become an artist in fiction. When the young author confessed that his ambition was "to do the best one could with one's pen," the elder writer offered him a lesson which seemed to come out of Jamesian fiction. "My young friend," he said, "and I call you young—you are disgustingly and if I may be allowed to say, nauseatingly young—there is one thing that, if you really intend to follow the course you indicate, I cannot too emphatically insist on. There is one word—let me impress upon you—which you must inscribe upon your banner, and that"—he stopped for an impressive pause—"that word is *Loneliness.*"

Pearsall Smith was not yet ready for an introduction to Harland. He never appeared in the *Yellow Book.* But he appears in spirit beneath the heavy overcoat in which Whistler painted the Count de Montesquiou—a substitute during many of the tedious sittings—and he remains a memorable stylist in prose for the volumes he titled *Trivia* (1902, 1921). James would see much more of him.

The Master had reappeared in the twelfth *Yellow Book* in January 1897. After promising *What Maisie Knew* to Harland, he had settled for something he could finish more quickly, "She and He," an essay-review based upon the Alfred de Musset–George Sand correspondence. Two months after it appeared Harland was still begging Lane to send James his fifteen guineas and his editor his editorial fee. Still later Harland was again requesting his fee. "Do please send me a cheque will you?" he urged Lane. "I'm stony-broke! And why don't you ever come to 144 Cr. Rd.?" Both Lane and his editor knew the answers. The *Yellow Book* was losing money as each issue succeeded the last in predictable fashion, despite the new names. The lack of any striking new talent dramatized how much there was wrong under the sign of the Bodley Head. One of the *Yellow Book*'s weaknesses had become its employment as shop window for writers appearing under Lane's imprint. It had become obvious to a critic for *The Times,* who observed acidly that "The principle upon which *The Yellow Book* is edited would seem to be that at intervals of every three months a section of the reading public is seized with a craving for fresh work by Mr Henry Harland, Miss Ella d'Arcy, and others of the little school of writers whom the Bodley Head has brought into notice. The contributions, therefore, tend to run largely in the same groove." That had not been the original goal of Harland and Beardsley, and was not entirely accurate; but it was the fate of the quarterly not only to be a brief display case for the talents of the best writers of the nineties, but also, in a way they had not intended —and contrary to what Harland and Beardsley had happily predicted that New Year's Day in 1894—for "any and all of ourselves that nobody else could be hired to print."

The thirteenth number, dated April 1897, was not only late in going on sale; it was the last. No valediction from the editor announced the end—only the failure of the next issue to appear in July. In the April number, however, the end was sufficiently clear. There were no pieces from such regulars as James, or from such occasional contributors as Buchan, Bennett, Frederic, Wells, Gissing, or even from the eccentric "Baron Corvo." The major new name was that of a young Irish poet who had written for the *Savoy* until it folded, W. B. Yeats. Joseph Conrad, another writer on his way up, not realizing it was too late, mulled over sending a long story he had just completed, "The Return," since the *Savoy,* which had taken his "The Idiots," had failed after a year. No one had announced the demise of the *Yellow Book,* and when it ceased to stir controversy, contributors, and purchasers, it was succeeded by other, less pretentious publications. In the reorientation of literature which followed the Wilde scandal, this was perhaps inevitable.

The *Yellow Book* was not meant to be faddish, or to foster any clearly defined "movement," but neither was it intended to be "respectable" in the Victorian sense of the word. For thirteen quarterly appearances, it responsibly served the transition from Swinburne-Wilde decadence and Victorian reticence to the artistic use of realism. It epitomized the literature of the nineties as no other publication did. As Harland later summed up its achievement, "During this time we made most of the London critics gasp a bit and we forced the recognition of any number of principles and ideas for which we had been striving. It let down the bars of prejudice and tradition in the London publishing offices and so it served its turn."

Although Aline Harland had broken into print via the *Yellow Book,* the pseudonymity of the stories left her with no reputation but that of staunchly supportive wife. Her letters reinforce the picture of a clever, strong-willed woman, willing to press her husband's cause in any way possible. Although his tuberculosis seemed at least temporarily arrested, she had no idea how long she could keep him from the grave, and the tension which that realization created may have helped, on her part, to reinforce their marriage. With Harland, the period of relative good health, and the beginnings of success for his ambitions, may have produced the opposite effect. The evidence exists that the editor of the *Yellow Book* was willing to use his literary position to try out his sex appeal on other women. Rolfe had suspected a dalliance with Harland's loyal subeditor, Miss d'Arcy, who lived conveniently nearby, but at least once, Aline was away long enough, perhaps in France, for Harland to use Cromwell Road safely as his return address for a flirtation. Olive Custance was twenty-two (in 1896), dark-haired, and pretty, and had sent the *Yellow Book* some poetry from her home in Norfolk. Harland fell in love with her photograph at the Bodley Head office. Her writing was "exquisite," he told her, and before long he scheduled her verse for volume seven and Lane was planning to publish a slim volume, *Opals.*

When Harland tried to arrange a meeting in Cambridge, not far from her home, Miss Custance wanted to know what he looked like. He had no photograph, he explained, but described himself as a "middle-aged man" of thirty-four, and produced a familiar fiction of exotic birth and upbringing. Otherwise he was reasonably accurate, picturing himself as "rather tall (five feet eleven), very thin, with a dark skin, dark hair rapidly turning grey (almost white on top), and grey eyes with an unmistakable snub-nose between them. For the rest, a short, pointed beard, rather prominent cheek-bones, and a pince-nez. . . . Not at all an English face,—a Slav type of face. . . ."

They met, and Harland's surviving letters thank heaven that he had lived to meet that "splendid thing, a strong, passionate, authentic woman . . ." whose poetry was "the singing of a soul." Then the strong, passionate Aline returned to Cromwell Road. Olive Custance, who had fallen in love with the handsome young John Gray (Wilde's "Dorian") when she met him at sixteen, and written him passionate poems, unaware that his sexual interests lay in another direction, remained unattached. In 1902 she eloped with still-handsome Lord Alfred ("Bosie") Douglas, who had decided, after his embarrassments with Oscar, to try the other sex. The marriage was not a success. But she may have had her romance with Harland. In any case, she preserved the evidence all of her life.

Harland was less taken with California novelist Gertrude Atherton, who was attractive, formidable, four years his elder, and widowed. George Atherton, dapper and useless, had drained the family finances and gone off on a schooner to Tahiti, where he died and was embalmed in a barrel of rum for the return voyage. After she arranged for the transfer of her husband from cask to casket, Mrs Atherton had left San Francisco for New York with her manuscripts, having begun writing fiction as an escape from boredom as well as a way out of debt. When the publishing world there seemed much too closed a society to crack, she went on to Paris and then to London, where Harland refused for the *Yellow Book* a story, "The Striding Place," which she claimed to have written before getting out of bed one morning. It was, he insisted, "far too gruesome." Mrs Atherton insisted to the end of her days that it was the best short story she ever wrote, and had no trouble selling it to the *Speaker*. Still she went to John Lane with her novel *Patience Sparhawk,* where, without Harland to urge on publication, the book was delayed for two years. When it made Lane money, he was delighted to take on her *American Wives and English Husbands,* which established her as yet another writer who could cope successfully with what James called "the international theme."

With the *Yellow Book* venture over, Harland could afford contacts which would have been out of the question a few months earlier—in particular, Oscar Wilde. Having served his full sentence, Wilde was in self-exile in France, living off the charity of friends and followers, and an allowance from his wife's family. When the *Yellow Book* had begun, with Wilde excluded, his closest crony, Robert Ross, would earn guffaws from Oscar for his imitation of Harland's nervous mannerisms, high voice, and constant need for wifely support.* "Harland is here," Wilde wrote to Ross from Paris in April 1898. "I dined with him and his wife at Pousset's last night. Remembering your delightful imitations I could not help shouting with laughter from time to time. 'Isn't he *wonderful*, Aline?' reappeared every five minutes, but they were both very nice. I dine with him again on Saturday."

Harland's holidays in France became longer as London needed him less and his weak lungs suffered further from the fogs and fumes of the city. As early as the first summer of the *Yellow Book*, Dieppe, just across the Channel, with its old castle and new casino, Norman marketplace, and new bathing quay, had become a favorite, and inexpensive, watering hole for English writers and artists in aesthetic circles, and in 1898 and 1899 Harland continued to holiday at a modest *pension* behind a signboard that announced, surprisingly (given his fluency in French), "English Spoken." But he was still dependent upon John Lane's undependable remittances, and the boardinghouse was cheap.

On holiday or in England Harland seemed convinced that he was a typical cultivated Englishman, yet when he would claim Rome, Paris, or St Petersburg as his birthplace, rather than London, he would explain his residence there with the theory that a man should never live in the land of his birth. Still, he was hurt when, on the Continent, where he wanted to appear most British, he was identified as an American—except by Americans. The English clientele of his *pension* found his enthusiasms un-English and puzzling. He would greet a visitor, Evelyn Sharp, with "Darling of my heart! Child of my editing!" And he would wander about distractedly looking for his wife, shouting, "Where's Aline! Has anybody seen Aline?" As Miss Sharp put it, "Even if they could have confessed to the impropriety of knowing the first name of a comparative stranger's wedded wife, they had not seen Aline."

Harland's un-English emotionalism was at its peak in the summer

* Ross, who was reputed to have initiated Wilde into homosexuality in the mid-1880s, may have found the apparent closeness of the Harland marriage offensive, something suggested by a Max Beerbohm letter to him labeling as Ross's "delusion" the idea "that everybody abuses the poor Harlands. Surely they are a fairly popular couple—as couples go" (August 1896).

of 1899, when he was again in Dieppe and the second trial of Captain Dreyfus was in progress. The boardinghouse rocked with his outbursts at the continuing miscarriage of justice, and although he had, in conversation there, once moved his birthplace to Paris, "for the moment he was not being born in Paris," and Miss Sharp remembered hearing him threaten to take his next holiday in Germany "or somewhere Teutonic where these outrages could not happen." But the weeks in France had become necessary antidotes to the months in the flat in Cromwell Road where the words came more easily, even when the locales about which he wrote were vaguely Continental.

At about the time of Aubrey Beardsley's death, at twenty-five, early in 1898, Harland's concern with his own health had flared anew. He and Joseph Pennell became co-chairmen of a private solicitation of funds for Aubrey's mother, and he was quoted as saying that his own lungs felt as if they were full of holes punched in them by the ferrule of someone's umbrella. It was even rumored that Harland had bought an oak coffin and kept it in his bedroom as a reminder of the little time left to him to complete his great works. Shedding his mustache and goatee (which had become white), and switching from pince-nez to ordinary spectacles, Harland looked increasingly frail. He and Aline even became Roman Catholics, more out of aesthetic than spiritual impulses, one might surmise; yet he became increasingly devout, and began to people his fictions with warm-hearted priests and saintly bishops while turning full circle into a cranky and gratuitous anti-Semite. He had "become all but a Jew himself," he had written to Stedman in 1885, in the days of "Sidney Luska," but now considered himself, he confessed to an interviewer, "a bigoted Papist."

No great works materialized from the conversion, but in 1899 he did complete a romantic novel set in Italy, written, he told Lane, "in my most engaging and distinguished manner." Eventually titled *The Cardinal's Snuff-Box,* it became one of the best-selling books of 1900. Harland knew it was good. It ended happily, he assured Lane; it was "full of colour, sparkle, atmosphere"; it was "RIPPING."

After many delays, the failure of Lane to make good on advances, and Harland's bedridden condition at Cromwell Road at the time the final proofs needed correction, *The Cardinal's Snuff-Box* appeared in May 1900. Harland was disgusted with the result. Lane had cut every corner to keep expenses down in the production of what Harland considered his masterpiece. The "cheap and nasty" binding made it look like a book by Jerome K. Jerome, he complained bitterly from his bed. *His* readership, he insisted, was "the cultivated, the bookish public"—which required an uncut, better-bound product. Otherwise, "the failure of the book is assured beforehand."

If the binding was shoddy, the text inside was no better, a coyly told tale about an expatriate English novelist in an idyllic, pastoral Italy who falls in love with the beautiful, widowed Duchessa Beatrice (herself an Englishwoman), who thereupon wins Peter Marchdale to the true faith with the aid of her benevolent uncle, Cardinal Udeschini. The book was a prodigious success. By September *The Cardinal's Snuff-Box* had sold over fifteen thousand copies in England, and more in America; but Lane was dragging his feet over providing Harland with a check for £100 in advance of the first royalty statement. The next year the Harlands were finally comfortable. Earnings for the novel during its first year of publication were £1,320 10s. According to the usually reliable *Bookman,* the author would earn £14,000 (then seventy thousand uninflated and little-taxed dollars) from the novel; and soon the Harlands would move from Cromwell Road to the more fashionable Kensington Place Mansions, in De Vere Gardens, which had the cachet of being the one-time address of Harland's aging *cher maître,* Henry James.

In the year of Harland's triumph, Lane was to publish Frederick Rolfe's second book of Toto stories, *In His Own Image.* When Harland saw it before publication, it bore a dedication to him and to Aline. According to Rolfe, Harland insisted that if the book were to be dedicated to him, a certain "flavour" would have to be removed. With a show of innocence Rolfe inquired what it was. "Pederasty," said Harland, bluntly. Rolfe became red in the face and blustered, "That's quite gratuitous. What a frightfully degenerate imagination you must have. Now mark me: I won't make or permit to be made, a single alteration." He was a fool, Harland told Rolfe. Publication of the book as it was would mean that he would no longer be welcome at Cromwell Road or at the homes of Harland's friends. In effect it meant literary isolation. Harland meant to keep him in the "mire of poverty," Rolfe insisted. He vowed to alter the dedication rather than the book, and they parted in mutual indignation.

In the wake of repeated printings of *The Cardinal's Snuff-Box* Harland quickly forgot the ubiquitous Rolfe. In two years he turned out two additional novels, *Mademoiselle Miss* and *The Lady Paramount,* each filled with similar forgettable ingredients, and selling copies on the strength of the earlier success; and toward the close of 1902 he paid his first visit in many years to the place in which his literary career had begun, New York. It was, he wrote Lane, a "noisy, confused, but most hospitable town," certainly a more friendly place to the returned Henry Harland than it had been to the departing Sidney Luska in 1889. But the American language, he complained, was a "foreign importation," unsuitable for writers. "I fancy," he told an interviewer, "a year on end in New York might remove one's ability to write English at all."

It would be his last contact with that American soil which Henry James had observed was missing from his art. (It would still be missing in 1904 when he published his last book, *My Friend Prospero.* "Have you read the Harland book yet?" Reggie Turner would write to Max Beerbohm. "Even the reviewers seem to recognise the story. He will have to invent another plot.") Leaving America for London in February 1903, Aline wrote to the Stedmans from their ship, the *Ivernia,* that she was "very low in my mind at parting," but that Harry "finds he works best in his own habitat in London."

Illness ended their dreams of building a country place and of entertaining again, as in the old days at Cromwell Road. Even the reappearance of some less splendid ghosts from the grand days of the *Yellow Book* had not tarnished the memory—but for one, the ubiquitous "Corvo." The brazen Rolfe had sent his manuscript of *Nicholas Crabbe* to Lane—the "Slim Schelm" of the book. Lane forwarded it to Harland, for whom Aline wrote on July 5, 1905, that it was his opinion that the novel was criminally libelous, and that sending it to Lane—a publisher—constituted legal publication. Lane, Harland urged, must keep the typescript until he had his solicitor pressure the author into declaring in writing the falsity of the venomous statements and into promising to destroy all copies of the book. Lane wrote accordingly, and Rolfe answered sweetly that *Nicholas Crabbe* was a romance and nothing more.

By then the "Sidney Thorah" of Rolfe's book was past caring, although he was putting what was left of his energies into yet another Italianate, "lemonade Henry James" novel, *The Royal End,* which would have as heroine an expatriate American woman who confronts her sense of displacement abroad and who almost certainly emanates from Harland's revisit to the New England of his youth. Slipping rapidly, Harland went from a Bath chair at the seaside to an invalid's room at the Villa Solaro in San Remo, the resort on the Italian Riviera that was the last resort of so many English consumptives. There on a December morning in 1905, Henry Harland died at forty-four.

Before sailing for America with Henry's mother, who still lived at Sentry Hill—the "Barracks Hill" of the unfinished novel—in Norwich, Connecticut, Aline wrote pitiful letters to friends about her husband's "terrible year" of agony. Then she returned to London, where for three decades more she signed her letters, including many to the Bodley Head, requesting payment of long arrears in royalties, as "Aline, Lady Harland." Posthumously, the first and only editor of the *Yellow Book,* who had begun writing as a pseudonymous East Side New York Jew, had metamorphosed in Aline's fantasies into "Henry Anthony, Fifth Baron Harland." It was an appropriate subject for a Henry Harland novel.

CHAPTER IV

Croydon Police Court

It is difficult to realise that in the enlightened days of the nineteenth century, sensible and intelligent people should bind themselves to such an absurd course of [medical] procedure. The fact remains that a valuable and intellectual life has been thrown away. . . .

—W. P. MORRISON, coroner for the Croydon district of Surrey,
November 8, 1898

WHILE the *Yellow Book* suffered from allegations of scandal in its contents, real scandal surfaced in the lives of many of its contributors, from Pearl Craigie to Harold Frederic. More English readers discovered Frederic in the newspaper transcripts from Croydon Police Court in 1898 than had learned of him from his fourteen years of writing in London. "Homefield," his rustic home near Kenley, just south of Croydon on the Brighton line, was fourteen miles from Charing Cross Station. Off a crooked lane only five hundred yards from the main highway, once a Roman road, it was a square, two-storied structure surrounded by gardens and green lawn, in which an American rocking chair and English wicker table sat, in fair weather, for Frederic's fiction-writing sessions. The squire of Homefield, befitting someone of his status, had a solid, spacious residence in the city as well as one in the country—"Old House," on Dunsany Road in Brook Green, Hammersmith. One fact about Frederic's domestic arrangements, however, was somewhat out of the ordinary: at Old House resided Mrs Frederic and her children, and at Home-field one found another "Mrs Frederic" and *her* children.

Novelist as well as London correspondent for the *New York Times,* Frederic knew everyone of mark, and his burly figure was seen wherever anything of interest was going on. But Saturday after-noons were reserved for the National Liberal Club, in Whitehall Place, where he wrote his long weekly cable interpreting the news for the Sunday editions in New York. It cut into his weekends, reserved for his legal family in Hammersmith (weekdays found him commut-ing to Homefield), but relations with Grace Frederic had been strained for years. Her husband had even sounded out American lawyers about a divorce on grounds of "incompatibility of temper," although long into the nineties the outward evidences of felicity at Old House appeared whenever friends did. In Hammersmith, Fred-eric's study, with its twelve-foot-high bookshelves, its reserves of tobacco (Arcadia mixture) and Appollinaris water, and its first-edition set of Dr Johnson's dictionary, suggested the writer at work, yet most of his writing was done weekdays in the shadow of Kate Lyon, the other "Mrs Frederic." Thus it was inevitable that Frederic should growl through his heavy mustache at journalist G. B. Burgin, who had come at the suggestion of the *Detroit Free Press*'s cor-respondent, the Canadian-born Robert Barr, who wrote as "Luke Sharp." "Barr knows very well that, for family reasons, I can't be interviewed for your 'Lions in their Dens' series. The reasons don't matter, but if you want this interview, I'll see one of you at the National Liberal."

Grace, sweet and gentle, passively tolerated what she could not alter, and spent her time with their four children. Ruth, their daugh-ter, was her father's favorite, at twenty not only a beautiful young woman but sophisticated enough to meet him at the National Liberal for dinner or even to visit at Homefield, from which she returned with checks signed "Kate Frederic" for support of the London house-hold; and when Frederic was unable to go to a premiere on which he was to report for the *Times,* Ruth would wear her hair up, put on evening clothes, and proxy for her father, who would compile a dispatch from her notes. Somehow she got on with Kate Lyon, whom her father had probably met in 1890 in the easy camaraderie of writers and scholars in the British Museum, when he was thirty-four and she was thirty-seven (but passing for thirty-four). Like Grace, she was from a small town in upstate New York. Kate had gone to a teacher training school in Chicago and was better educated; yet she had given up teaching to follow a married sister to England and help care for her four children. By 1891 she was living with Frederic, and the next year Helen, the first of their three children, was born. Heloise would follow in 1893 and Barry in 1894.

Supporting two families was not easy. Frederic liked to live comfortably and to entertain without stint, as an English gentleman should. His *New York Times* salary was unchanged over the years, but he had managed to use it prudently by turning many of his European journalistic assignments into books—on pogroms in Russia in 1892, on the Kaiser in 1891. And he churned out fiction, one novel, *The Return of the O'Mahony* (1892), with an Irish heroine modeled after Kate, whose mother was an O'Mahony. Kate and the suburban household flourished; Grace and the London household withered, although Frederic did his duty for the first several years of the relationship by spending the requisite number of days and hours there. The legitimate family was provided for at six hundred pounds a year; Frederic's earnings averaged about three thousand pounds annually, and he spent all of it. At Hammersmith the atmosphere was tense but correct when the children were present; when he was there Frederic was restless, eager to leave for work in the City or at his club, and work was all that kept the leases on two homes paid and the account in the Lincoln Bank in New York solvent. Discreet loans and advances from agents and publishers were often necessary; sometimes desperate letters replaced discretion. Even his best novel did no better than his potboilers, for *The Damnation of Theron Ware* (1896; *Illumination* was its English title) was published by Stone and Kimball in Chicago, which then proceeded to go bankrupt. Yet when Stone reorganized his company, Frederic loyally offered him another novel, *Gloria Mundi,* after it was serialized in *Cosmopolitan* and had generated some guaranteed income.

It was important for Frederic to be published in America, not only for the income produced, but because he continued to consider himself an American and had a lively loyalty to the States. In London he was a pillar of the American Society, founded early in

115

1895, and delivered one of the toasts ("The Society") that year at its first Thanksgiving Day dinner. There the postprandial toast of "The Queen" was followed by that of "The President of the United States" and the singing of "The Star-Spangled Banner," and visiting American editor R. Watson Gilder (of the *Century*) gave the major address, which was immediately forgotten when Robert Barr toasted "Thanksgiving Day" in a humorous speech in which he alleged that his research had uncovered the fact that every country had some sort of Thanksgiving Day except Scotland, for a Scot had nothing to be thankful for until he got out of the country, after which he would join in the local thanksgiving.

Being an American in London seldom meant concealing or rejecting one's land of origin. When, for example, George W. Smalley retired in 1895 as *New York Tribune* correspondent in London, it was Frederic who presided at the testimonial dinner at the Holborn Restaurant, and the guests included not only Ambassador Bayard but Henry James and Bret Harte. The American Society was paralleled by a Society of American Women, to which Americans from Mrs Craigie to Lady Randolph Churchill belonged, and Jennie Churchill in a burst of patriotism would later, when the Boer War began, charter a hospital ship to take to South Africa which she would christen the *Maine,* after the American battleship whose sinking precipitated the Spanish-American War. But late in 1895 the dual loyalties were suffering their greatest strains in decades, over the boundary dispute between Venezuela and British Guiana. When Britain threatened to enforce its claims, President Grover Cleveland insisted that the Monroe Doctrine applied, and both big powers made ugly noises about war through the winter of 1896. Patriotism among London Yankees reached such a pitch that Bret Harte "earnestly avowed his intentions of instantly returning to his own country, should hostilities break out," although he had carefully kept the Atlantic between himself and his wife for twenty years. But there were also divided loyalties. "The American outbreak has darkened all my sky," Henry James wrote English critic W. E. Norris. "One must hope that sanity and civilization, in both countries, will prevail," he wrote his brother in great anxiety. "But the lurid light the American newspapers seem to project on the quantity of resident Anglophobia in the U.S.—the absolute war-hunger as against this country

—is a thing to darken one's meditations. Whence, why does it, today, explode in such immense volume . . . and whither does it tend? It stupefies me—seems to me horribly inferior and vulgar— and I shall never go with it. . . . I had rather my bones were ground into British powder!" His sense of separation from his own country —he had been away for twelve years—made the news from America seem, he confessed to William Dean Howells, "as if it came from China or another planet."

The *New York Journal* wondered whether the "American wives" who had married influentially in England might put some pressure on the government, as they also included, in addition to Lady Randolph Churchill, Mrs Joseph Chamberlain, the Duchess of Marl-borough, and the future Lady Curzon, whose husband was then undersecretary of state for foreign affairs. "I am wondering what I should do," Mary Curzon wrote her mother, "if England and America followed Cabot Lodge's advice, and went to war about Venezuela. I should wear the American flag under my jacket if I could not wear it on the outside as the wife of an English official. One's country is always one's country. Laws may change one's nation-ality, but they cannot change the heart, and mine is *and ever will be* American."

Frank Harris, then editor of the *Saturday Review,* called on Frederic to discuss how Americans in London might intervene, the outcome being an editorial declaring "that in case of war England would cease to exist as a power among the nations, and to run such a risk for a paltry stupidity in Venezuela was so absurd as to be criminal stupidity." Lord Salisbury, the prime minister, sent for him, Harris claimed in his memoirs, which usually inflated his political impact as well as his sexual prowess. "The Americans," he remem-bered warning the Prime Minister, "are crazy with the sense of the greatness of their country and the rapidity of its growth. In my opinion they would beat the world in arms today. They are the best organizers of labor in the world, and that is equivalent to being able to produce the best armies and navies."

In any event, Britain retreated into arbitration, and some of the credit may go to Americans who were not eager to see the conditions of their existence in London undergo any drastic upheaval.

Harris and Frederic were friends because they were useful to

each other. It was difficult to take charge of any company or conversation if the formidable Frederic were present, while the booming-
voiced, bushy-mustached Harris had ego requirements and buc-
caneering instincts which made it difficult to trust him or even
tolerate him. According to publisher Grant Richards, then beginning
his career in London, there were "plenty of people who, in their dislike of Frank Harris, his manners and methods, . . . maintained
that he never wrote his stories. The favourite attribution was to
Harold Frederic. . . . But those who knew Harris best in those
early days when he descended on London and edited in succession
the *Evening News* and the *Fortnightly Review,* and especially those
who, like my uncle, heard him tell the stories before he actually
told them in print, would have none of it. It is true that midway
in his career as a writer of fiction he began to go off—Frederic had
died by that time—but this fact proves nothing."

Frederic would write occasionally for Harris's *Saturday Review,*
but would publish wherever he could. He welcomed visiting American editors for the contacts they provided, and produced enough copy
to give a number of English and American publishers the opportunity
of listing him. He scattered his material with one thought paramount:
the more publishers he had, the more advances on future earnings
he could secure. His books were reviewed widely and well on both
sides of the Atlantic, but their sales were disappointing. In quest of
a big financial success he began a dramatization of *Theron Ware*
with Brandon Thomas, his close friend and author of the wildly
successful farce *Charley's Aunt,* but it was quickly shelved, and on
his own Frederic completed a psychological drama, *Destiny,* but
could not get it produced. In London William Heinemann wrote him
one May, "Your request for £30 puts me into a fix. My partner
[Sidney Pawling] finds that you have had nearly £50 more than your
books have earned in loans and unfortunately the books are bringing in very little." Like most authors Frederic blamed inadequate
promotion, writing Scribners in New York in 1894 for an advance
on a new book and to complain that "men who do work much inferior to mine get advantages in advertising and in cognate things
which my books, poor devils, may not hope for."

As an expatriate writer he could only complain from afar, and could not walk in and pound his large fists on a desk. But when a Scribner came to London, Frederic suggested a weekend at Home-field—not the "proper" Hammersmith home—to enjoy the "rustic scenery" and his lilacs, this after a previous half-year's royalty statement which enclosed only $30.42 representing the earnings for five books. He had outgrown his anger, he confided, but the pain would not go away, and he puzzled over what he could only see as systematic neglect. Uneasy about the irregularity of the Kenley household, the publisher declined. It did not change Frederic's opinion of his own writing. When G. B. Burgin, aware of Frederic's double life, remarked to him that a man should be judged not by his life but by his work, Frederic snapped, "Enough of that. Whatever my life has been, my pen has always been on the side of the angels."

Readers of *Theron Ware* were not sure of that, especially if they were of the sort who believed in angels—or devils. What Frederic had done was to react sourly to the small-town Methodist ambience of upstate New York. The town of Octavius is a smaller Utica. Its religious divisions stem from the divisions between immigrant Irish Catholic and "native American" Methodist. As a trustee of Theron Ware's church informs his callow young minister,

"We are a plain sort o' folks up in these parts. . . . We ain't gone traipsin' after strange gods like some people that call themselves Methodists in other places. . . . We don't want no book-learnin' or dictionary words in our pulpit. . . . What we want here, sir, is straight-out, flat-footed hell—and the burnin' lake o' fire an' brimstone. Pour it into 'em, hot an' strong. . . . And then, too, our folks don't take no stock in all that pack o' nonsense about science, such as telling the age of the earth by crackin' up stones. I've been in the quarry all my life, an' *I* know it's all humbug."

Frederic, who loved Ireland and its people* and often vacationed there, had still other reasons for making his liberal congregation a Catholic one. He wanted to put Kate into it as heroine, and she became Celia Madden, of Irish origins. A church organist, Celia was

---

* His *Yellow Book* story "The Truce of the Bishop" (vol. 7, October 1895) was set during the British burning and plundering in the west of Ireland in the days of Queen Anne, and left no doubt about where his sympathies lay. It was also a graphic, eloquent piece of fiction.

to speak for the late Victorian gospel of beauty espoused by the aesthetic writers and artists of the nineties, many of whom Frederic saw converting to Catholicism far less for its theology than for the attractiveness of its ritual. As she admits, frankly,

"But I'm not religious at all, you know. . . . I'm as Pagan as—anything! Of course there are forms to be observed, and so on; I rather like them than otherwise. I can make them serve very well for my own system; for I am myself, you know, an out and out Greek . . . much more in sympathy with the Greek thought, the Greek theology of the beautiful and the strong, the Greek philosophy of life, and all that, than what is taught nowadays. . . .

"I am a Catholic. . . . But I should explain that I am a Catholic only in the sense that its symbolism is pleasant to me. You remember what Schopenhauer said—you cannot have the water by itself: you may also have the jug that it is in. Very well; the Catholic religion is my jug. I put into it the things I like. . . ."

The irony was that Kate had brought with her from America the new, and native American, gospel of Christian Science. It would complicate Frederic's life far more than would his two families. Mary Baker Eddy's Boston-based church was still largely unknown in London. Bret Harte's niece and her friend, visiting from America, gave him his first inkling of it. "They are both enthusiasts of a new kind of religious 'fad' which they tell me," he wrote the wife of his illustrator, A. S. Boyd, "is sweeping America, called 'Christian Science.' They wonder I have never heard of it . . . They have books upon it, they expound it to *me*. Our conversation is not flippant nor wildly entertaining."

In the spring of 1896 *Theron Ware* was a sensation in both England and America. By September Israel Zangwill was writing in the *Critic* that Frederic had "set the Thames on fire with his *Illumination.*" Soon young Arnold Bennett, full of optimism after his own appearance in the *Yellow Book* (in the issue *before* Frederic's contribution), would be writing to his friend George Sturt that he was working on a first novel in which "my great revival scene in the Wesleyan Methodist chapel . . . is to beat Harold Frederic in his own chosen field." Frederic's novel was on best-seller lists on both sides of the Atlantic, and although he reached the height of his

London fame with it and even earned badly needed pounds which sustained his life-style some months longer, fame did not alter it. But even in leaner times, the tensions did not show. Critic C. Lewis Hind recalled seeing Frederic in the years before *Illumination,* at a party in the Chelsea studio of American-born portrait painter J. J. Shannon (later Sir James Shannon, R.A.). It was Show Sunday, when pictures destined for Royal Academy exhibition were placed on easels for friends to admire and art critics to get a preliminary view. After the crowd thinned, Hind remained for supper, and asked who was the big man who seemed to know everyone and had a generous supply of gossip and stories. It was Harold Frederic, Hind was told, the *New York Times's* man, "but his real game is novel writing. You should read his *Seth's Brother's Wife* and *In the Valley."* Later in the evening there were shouts for a song by Frederic, who obligingly moved to the piano, his table napkin still dangling from his waist ("he was rather an untidy man"), and "sang a series of American college songs roisterously, boisterously, yet, when the occasion demanded it, with feeling and emotion. The Americans present joined in the chorus, and the English folk emitted harmonious sounds."

"What college was he?" Hind asked. "None." And his neighbor at the table explained that Frederic went from grade school to a reporter's job, becoming editor of the *Utica Observer* when he was twenty-four. "It's like Harold Frederic to know the college songs. He's an adept at universal information. Why, he knows these songs better than most college boys."

The next week there was an article by Frederic in W. E. Henley's *National Observer,* giving a humorous account of the evening, but identifying none of the participants. He had turned the occasion, as was his custom—and need—into coin. He had to, and with his authoritative voice and commanding presence he could sell almost anything to a London editor if he did it in person. The system was simplicity itself, he explained to a friend at his club who had been unable to market anything to Clement Shorter, then editor of the *Sketch.* "My dear man," said Frederic seriously, "Shorter is one of the best editors in the world, and one of the best fellows. All you are saying simply shows that you don't know how to deal with him.

When I have a story that I want to sell to Shorter, I wear that big, yellow, shaggy ulster which comes down to my heels. I turn the collar up over my ears. I put on that disreputable hoodlum cap I got in America twenty years ago, and draw it down over my eyes. I take a blackthorn stick given to me in Ireland, as thick as your thigh. I don't announce myself, but walk into his room, close the door, and set my back against it for a moment, until Shorter has had time to focus his glasses on what is before him; then I take three strides to his table, and rapping gently on it with my blackthorn, thunder out in a deep, harsh voice: 'Shorter, I have a story to sell you!' He buys it right away."

With *Theron Ware* Frederic had written himself out of American subjects and would turn to English ones, less effectively. But home had not receded from his consciousness altogether, for Hind also recalled another dinner, at the home of a charming woman who wrote forgettable poetry under the name of "Graham R. Thomson," where he walked in and discovered Frederic "seated at the piano singing folk songs and Negro spirituals. He was having refreshments at the same time: the cup was on the candle stand, and a piece of bread-and-butter and a piece of cake were on his knee. The crumbs of each decorated his waistcoat. . . . He sang the Negro spirituals with true darky feeling, and I remember that a song about Clementine was encored three times."

As always in the mid-nineties, Frederic had come alone. It was not unusual for artists and writers to leave their marriages—not merely their wives—at home, and Frederic in any case would not take Grace and could not take Kate. But he again put Kate in his next novel, his first one with an English setting, so English that he had his hero, not yet completely sober after a night of revelry, meet his new love on Westminster Bridge at eight o'clock in the morning. *March Hares* was a short book: Ruth Frederic, visiting Homefield for the weekend in November 1895, dutifully counted the words (47,568) before her father sent the manuscript to his publisher under a pseudonym—"George Forth"—explaining that he didn't want the whimsical fiction competing with *Illumination*. It was an open secret that it was Frederic's work, but Henry Harland, writing his usual critical column (as the "Yellow Dwarf") for the *Yellow*

Book in July 1896, declared, tongue in cheek, that it was too well written to have been done by an American. Frederic had "proved," he wrote, "that he can . . . write able, unreadable *Illuminations* in classic Americanese. But he could no more flitter and flutter and coruscate . . . in the . . . fashion of George Forth, than he could dance a hornpipe on the point of a needle."

Except where artistically necessary, Frederic was unevasively and loyally *American,* once declaring, in a letter to the editor of the *Daily Chronicle,* about its condescending reviews of American books, "Our literary standard is in no respect lower than yours, it is different, that's all." Pointing out some of the differences between English and American usage, he concluded that variations were "the modern outgrowths of a separate national, or rather continental, existence," and that it was an English reviewer's right to sniff at such Americanisms only when he encountered them in a purportedly "English" book. But it was "quite another matter when he picks out at haphazard any example of unintelligible or slip-shod composition in an eminently British book, and says it may be 'tolerable American.' That I take to be sheer impertinence."

A year after his "George Forth" masquerade Frederic was working on a Jamesian novel to be called *Gloria Mundi;* and then he had his favorite heroine, Celia Madden, reappear—in a London setting —in a novel he first sold to the *Saturday Evening Post* as a serial, *The Market Place.* There Celia, playing opposite a rising business executive, Joel Thorpe, has matured beyond the capricious sensuality which had inflamed Theron Ware. Of course it was Kate again. But the novels were more than vehicles for his fantasies about Kate. They were crowded with issues which also permeated the early plays of Bernard Shaw—socialism, commercial immorality, the hypocrisies of the social system, the "new woman." Frederic's notes for *Gloria Mundi* show the range of the problems he planned to confront in his new fiction: "Big Estates, Business, Man at 40, Religion and Education, Art, The Sex Passion, Woman, England, The Army Set, and Children."

Perhaps because of his instincts for organization, which made possible the balancing act he performed, Frederic's two homes and two families and two occupations—journalistic and literary—were

not nearly enough for him. He had become London sponsor for a
young American writer who had moved to England with an older
woman to whom he was not married but whom everyone called
Mrs Crane; and the couples quickly became close companions.
Stephen Crane, on the strength of his prospects after *The Red
Badge of Courage,* rented a large Surrey home at Ravensbrook,
within easy riding distance of Homefield, and the two families went
on a holiday together in the autumn of 1897 in Ireland. Stephen
soon was ill, but the holiday seemed unspoiled, and the men began
planning a joint household in Ireland, Frederic arranging to lease
a house the following spring overlooking Dunmanus Bay. Writing
to his younger friend as "My Dear Boy," he described the house as
having two sailboats at its dock, seven bedrooms, and a bath with
hot and cold water. He thought of the property "solely with reference to your sharing it with us," and indeed upkeep in the west
of Ireland would have been light compared with the London suburbs.

As the friendship with Crane deepened, Frederic began to realize
that the communal life would be impossible. "Patience is my long
suit," he once confided, but Cora was an energetic terror, inviting
anyone she thought useful to Stephen's writing career, although
they had little or no money even to purchase adequate food for
themselves, let alone all the guests; and Stephen's weak lungs were
worsening, making him a special problem, although when he was
out of bed he threw himself into Cora's plans with equivalent frenzy.
Frederic needed order. He had somehow contained his existence
although by every physical law it should have exploded apart. Diplomatically, he wrote to Cora to explain that it was his "stupidity"
that led to the suggestion, which he now perceived as a blunder.
The two households, he explained, had each defined for itself "a
system and a routine" which, if they were put under one roof, would
bring them to grief. He worried "that the bond would be injured
much more easily than the habits would be harmonized." The friendship survived intact.

At Homefield one day Robert Barr asked to see the typescript of
Frederic's newest novel, but as he sat down in the back garden, near
the greenhouse, to read it, Frederic said, "Just a minute until I get
you fully equipped, and then you can go ahead." He ran into the

house and emerged a few moments later with a poster-sized chart. "There," he said, tossing it onto a table beside Barr, "this will help you understand the story as you go along." It was a complicated chart "with long horizontal lines, having shorter perpendicular pen strokes descending from them, and names hung onto the ends of these, like clothes on a hook," resembling, Barr thought, the tables in history books explaining the descent of the royal house. "That's the genealogical tree," Frederic explained, "of all the characters in *The Market Place.*"

Barr objected. "How can people who don't exist have genealogical trees, or ancestors, or anything of that sort?"

"They don't exist! Who don't exist? Thunder! They exist quite as much as my grocer does, and you would think he existed if you had to pay his bills. You see, in that novel I have taken characters from *Theron Ware,* and characters from *Gloria Mundi.* I've got to keep track of these people, and not get them mixed up. I must know their relationships, and perhaps trace them back to some ancestor whose idiosyncrasies are going to crop up in different form here and there as the story progresses."

When Frederic projected his next book, after *The Market Place,* Barr also recorded that conversation, again leaving out only the expletives which garnished every Frederic dialogue where women were not present.

"I've got a corking ideal for a novel," he cried, bringing down his fist on the table with a vehemence that made the room tremble. "You see, my roots go back into Germany; the name 'Frederic' shows that. My ancestor came over to America during the Revolutionary War, a Hessian in the employ of Great Britain,—a hired man, as it were, of war. He shot for pay, and not for patriotism.

"I can imagine him a big, swaggering bully, who didn't give a hang for either side as long as he got his money and enough to eat and drink. Then look at his position; it's unique in history. Here are the Americans fighting for liberty, with all the stubborn courage and carelessness of privation which that belief calls forth; here are the British, equally honest and determined in the faith that they are putting down disloyalty, a rebellion against King and country; then here is our hired man, who despises both sides, who would as soon shoot an Englishman as an American, taking equal pleasure from either act; who looks upon both as the same brand of fool; who doesn't know, and doesn't want to know, what they are fighting about.

"All the books that have hitherto been written on that struggle are partisan, either British or American, and, so far as they are partisan, are valueless. I propose to write a book from the point of view of that hired man. I shall clear my mind of all sympathy with America, and all prejudice against Great Britain; I shall turn back the clock a century, and be that hired man while I write. I shall give an impartial account of the incidents I take part in, but have no particular interest in, not caring a Continental which licks [which], and give my views to these two sets of idiots, speaking the same language and industriously cutting each other's throats, both alike foreigners to me.

"But if the American question is indifferent to me, the American girl isn't, and so I shall become acquainted with one during the campaign, marry her, and settle down in America as my ancestor did. How does that strike you as the outline of a story?"

Barr agreed that there were great possibilities in the plot, but Frederic went off instead to Ireland to fish, and on his return late in 1898 complained of feeling ill. Still, he went on much as usual, signing a contract for an unwritten new novel, rushing off to the club to write his *Times* dispatches, and sniffing about London for news. (But by then he had ceased his once-regular visits to Hammersmith.) The new novel, to be called *Kenley,* would precede the one he had ambitiously outlined to Barr, and would be, he wrote publisher Frederic Stokes in America, about two young Americans from Boston who go to England, "where the boy rises to be one of the great painters of his time, and the girl comes, loaded with the praises of Milan, Paris, St. Petersburg, &c., to take London by storm as a prima donna. . . . It will be a book of character studies of painters, opera singers, actors, and the like, in the London of our day. It seems to me it ought to be not only my best book but the one most likely to achieve big popular success.

Jimmy Whistler, Frederic knew, had gone from Massachusetts boyhood to European success as a painter, and it may have been the germ of his plot, but first there was his newspaper and magazine copy to produce, and the early proofs of *Gloria Mundi* to read. In his favorite knickerbockers he would putter around the greenhouse and garden at Homefield, then recline in his favorite chair, cover himself with a wolfskin rug to shut out the damp, put a glass of whiskey on the table, and light up a pipe or cigar, while Kate or Ruth or his literary assistant Scott Stokes would read back to him his latest piece returned from the typist, and he would stop them occasionally to substitute a word or phrase. But he could no longer push himself, having returned from Ireland feeling tired, rather than exhilarated, after the holiday. At Dunmanus Bay he had apparently suffered a minor stroke, but had returned without realizing why he felt the way he did. Having a guest overnight at Homefield, he thought, might drag him out of his unaccustomed lethargy. It was also his way of paying social debts or cementing professional friendships, and he was not done with them, especially when the colleague professed no social queasiness about visiting the home of the "other" Mrs Frederic. Thus he invited yet another American in London, Gelett Burgess (of "Purple Cow" fame), to Homefield, via the Club, where Burgess was to meet him "at five or six next Saturday" with "the least little hand bag." They would go together to Surrey. "The more comfortably you dress," Frederic added, 'the happier we shall be, and the worse your clothes are the less they will put me to shame." The date of the letter was June 16, 1898. Burgess may have been the last guest Frederic was to bring to Homefield. After that the invitations would be made by Kate.

Through the early summer of 1898 Frederic was ill at Homefield but did nothing about it. He had to keep earning. He had once thought of a way out of writing potboilers and journalism, the way of Hawthorne in Liverpool and Harte in Glasgow. One could concentrate on serious fiction by finding an American consulate as sinecure. He knew the American minister in London (and earlier ones), and had worked for the election of President Cleveland with businessman Oscar Straus, who had afterward been rewarded with a diplomatic post in Constantinople. To Straus, in 1892, then minister to Turkey, Frederic had appealed for strings to be pulled to acquire the consulate in Liverpool ("I would make a good consul . . ."). It had never come, perhaps because the potential for scandal of his private life even then was an open secret.

Always eager to see how American writers were succeeding in London, he had more opportunity, in his exhausted state, to read, and encountered a Gertrude Atherton novel. His hesitation, he explained in a warm letter on July 10, was that his experiences with the publisher of the *Yellow Book* had not encouraged him to pick up other products of the firm:

It is only the other day that "Patience Sparhawk" came into my hands (I fear my long delay in getting it was due mostly to my deep disinclination to put an added penny into John Lane's unclean pockets), and since then I have read "American Wives and English Husbands." Since I have never before written spontaneously to an author I didn't know about his work, I fancy that the latter book must really have impressed me more than I am able to explain to myself—much less to you. It has a kind of vitality of its own which forces recognition even if it eludes analysis. When I had finished it I said, "There is this at least about it: she has a clearer vocation to write novels than any woman I know of;" and I trust you will pardon me for repeating it as the thing which best describes what is in my mind.

Another thing that is definite in my mind is that you are going to do much greater things. The gap between "Patience" and "American Wives" is truly Californian in its dimensions. And on this head, if I knew you, I should harangue you about the peril, not perhaps of writing too much, but of writing too easily. You have in an extreme degree the talent of lucidity—but melody is an acquired gift with all but the laurel-wreathed few. Do take the pace a little more slowly, and listen with a more solicitous reflective ear—and get the trick of drawing *sound* out of the ink bottle. I adjure you thus cheekily, because I want you to beat all the other women out of their boots. In essentials you do it now, but if you write "United Statesian" and things like that, the critics will never find themselves realizing this truth. . . .

The weekly columns continued to be cabled to the *New York Times,* with John Scott Stokes acting as his legs in gathering information. As usual they were published with a "Comment of London" or "Gossip of London" or "What London Hears" title followed by a more descriptive subtitle: "Keen Interest Felt in London over the Victory at Santiago," or "The Death of Mr. Gladstone Shakes the Hearts of All Men."

On August 12, he had a severe stroke, with partial paralysis on his right side, twisting his face and stilling his writing hand. There were also obvious cardiac complications. But he was only forty-two, and vigorous men of that age did not have strokes, he may have thought. Stubbornly, he refused to see a doctor until the next day, when Dr Nathan Boyd of Kenley was called in. Boyd was a neighbor with a medical degree who had not practiced in a decade, and whose wife, with Boyd's consent, had been attended twice by a Christian Scientist—perhaps the reason Kate had turned to him. But Boyd realized that Frederic was beyond spiritual skills, and he had quickly consulted Dr Robert Brown. Kate had other ideas. She employed an illiterate Greek who worked for the Cranes, Adoni Ptolemy, to dress and undress Frederic, to help him in and out of bed, to take him for walks and short drives in the countryside. Ptolemy also fetched cigars and champagne, although the idea horrified the doctors. But to Kate the doctors were unnecessary. There were Christian Science practitioners in London.

Frederic himself indicated that he was of two minds about doctors, especially when they recommended he give up drinking and smoking, for Christian Science permitted eating and drinking whatever one liked; and the doctors, sensing a practitioner of Mrs Eddy's doctrine in the wings, modified their rules to permit a glass of whiskey and water and a daily bottle of German beer. But it was too late. On August 16 Kate had sent an exultant telegram to Mrs Athalie Mills in London: "Victory! Send someone to stay immediately. Must be strong and wise. Not Mrs Boyd's healer. Send at once. Terribly urgent. [Kate] Frederic." After a second telegram late that afternoon a healer arrived—Mrs Mills herself. Visiting the bedside, she informed Frederic that the precondition of her treatment was the dismissal of his doctors. Only after that could she put into practice the teachings of *Science and Health* (available from Boston at seventeen shillings sixpence), which declared that "Science is the wisdom of the Eternal Mind as revealed through Jesus Christ who taught the power of Mind to overcome the illusions of sin, sickness and death." Feeble but alert, Frederic at first wanted to have it both ways, and Mrs Mills apparently decided to tolerate the physicians, for he paid little more attention to her than he did to Dr Boyd, Dr Brown, and Dr Montagu Murray of London, who was called in by the others and who encountered Mrs Mills on the platform at Kenley Station, and urged her not to interfere. Physicians continued to visit occasionally, and Mrs Mills remained out of sight, but advice about diet and medicines was ignored. Kate would bring Frederic his meals, and on good days Ptolemy would assist him into the garden, where he smoked and drank his whiskey and water until the sun went down. Cora Crane came to take the three children to Ravensbrook, and relieve Kate of their care, and Ruth was summoned from Hammersmith to help. Friends also came down from London, but seldom could they see him without Kate being present, although Frank Harris suggested quietly that he would send for a Dr Willoughby. Harris did, and Frederic explained to the doctors what pressure he was under to refuse medical advice: "I could not do anything else, could I? They pressed me so." Yet he once told Murray, "Doctor, I have an intellectual contempt for milk." And when one of the doctors advised a male nurse attending Frederic to let the patient struggle out of bed if he insisted, in order to prove that he was really helpless—"Let him get out, and let him fall— then perhaps he will let you nurse him"—Frederic duly crawled out of bed, leaned against a wall, and fell down. "Now, Mr Frederic," said the nurse, "come back to bed." "No," said Frederic, "I am going down stairs [even] if I have to slide down."

Stubbornly, Frederic was continuing his cabled columns to New York, although little else. Scott Stokes would come down from London with material, and go over an appropriate subject—peace prospects in the Far East, the Dreyfus case, English and French military activity along the Nile. How much of the final cable was actually dictated to Stokes, and how much was written by him under Frederic's name, is unknown. But they continued, weekly, as if nothing had changed, until October 16, Stokes alternating his reading from cables with passages from Mark Twain.

There were scenes with Kate whenever doctors visited. Each time the doctors retreated, and Frederic was consoled by whiskey and cigars, and the fact that visits from Mrs Mills to read (silently) from Mary Baker Eddy were slackening off, although when she did return it was also to pocket a healer's fee of a guinea a week from

Kate. "Absent treatment"* was considered just as efficacious as if Mrs Mills were projecting her will on the scene. Then on September 21 Mrs Mills returned to stay. Frederic grew progressively weaker. Brandon Thomas came and found him with a whiskey in his good hand, and Barr and other friends arrived, generally finding Frederic in the garden, where he looked less like a patient. But he was failing from progressive heart disease, and William Heinemann, alerted to Frederic's condition, rushed to Homefield with the cover of *Gloria Mundi,* which his author had helped design. It was all of the finished book which Frederic would see. A month after Kate had first called for a practitioner, Dr Boyd at Barr's urging wrote a letter to Kate and also telegraphed his concern to Frank Harris and Cora Crane. He was fully satisfied, he said, that she was acting from the highest motives, but her efforts to cure Frederic through Christian Science could only lead to harm. If medical treatment were withheld and Frederic died, he warned, the result would be public scandal, an inquest, and criminal proceedings. Stubbornly, Kate replied, "I am going to do it absolutely."

On October 17, although a London specialist, Dr Ludwig Freyberger,† was summoned by telegram, when he arrived Kate had changed her mind and blocked his path. Freyberger shrewdly informed Kate that he would not leave unless she would sign a statement absolving him from any blame. She gave way, and Frederic, seeing a physician, was evidently glad. "Kate," he said weakly, "I have never told you that I believed that damned Christian Science does me any good. That damned Mrs Mills bores the head off my shoulders, and I will now have medical treatment." It was obvious to Freyberger that the patient was dying, and he insisted that Kate

---

* Mark Twain would write, between 1903 and 1906, articles for *Cosmopolitan* and other journals which, when he was in England in 1907, he would publish as a book, *Christian Science.* The diatribe opened with his blackly humorous description of having received both the "near" and the "absent" treatment from a visiting lady practitioner from Boston for broken bones received in Austria in a fall.

† The Viennese-trained Freyberger (1865–1934), who as a Socialist saw social causes as responsible for many illnesses, was best known as physician to Karl Marx's collaborator Frederic Engels and second husband to his protégée, Louise Kautsky.

sign a pledge not to interfere with medical treatment. It took her
a day to agree, reluctantly. Elated, Ruth Frederic sent a telegram to
a friend, meant indirectly for her mother in Hammersmith, "Victory! Doctors in. Please tell at old house." Mrs Mills stamped out
when the doctors came in with two nurses from Guy's Hospital.
But it was far too late. A half-hour after midnight the following
day, October 19, Frederic died.

For Robert Barr the sun in the sky had been extinguished.
Frederic was not only his closest friend; his wife Mabel was Kate's
sister. "Those who know the desperate pain of seeing the dead face
of a great leader and friend," Barr wrote with anguish, "will forgive
these lame words in which I tell of this cruel thing. I loved him
with his large, tender heart and rough big voice, his great brain,
his vast plans for his own dear country and the Ireland of his
dreams."

Two days later an inquest was held in Kenley. Ruth Frederic
identified the body, and Kate Lyon—no Frederic to the law—was
called to the stand as were the three doctors who had been help-
lessly involved in the case. Kate admitted not only to calling in
Mrs Mills for Frederic, but for herself: "I wished to be made strong,
to bear up."

"You spoke to Mr Frederic about Christian Science?"

"Yes, and I told him that material remedies were antagonistic
to it."

In the witness box Dr Freyberger agreed that material remedies
had been ignored, and attested that when he was first called in by
Dr Brown the patient could have been "in a fair way to recovery"
if his "unreasonable way of living" had not been permitted, and
medical care accepted.

There were two additional days of testimony, including that of
Mrs Mills, who according to the inquest record "thought that the
deceased had a belief that he was seriously ill; but she never gave
the matter any consideration, knowing that all was well with God."
Under cross-examination she admitted that she had never made a
physical examination of the patient, and denied that she had received
more than fourteen pounds in fees.

"Was that paid in a cheque?"

"No."

"Is a cheque contrary to the principles of Christian Science?"

"No."

"Do you have any banking account?"

"No. Sufficient unto the day is the evil thereof."

The questioning led to Christian Science principles, the barrister representing the Frederic estate (in effect, Grace Frederic) finally asking, "Then according to your system the cure is not affected by death?"

"No," said Mrs Mills, "death is a mere belief. Jesus Christ said that if we believe in His teaching we shall not see death."

"Whether a patient lives or dies your cure is equally effective? The patient, in fact, is not affected by the unfortunate fact that he dies?" Mrs Mills agreed. A patient's illness, she countered, was only as real as he made it.

There was a fourth day of hearings, at which Adoni Ptolemy appeared, and at which novelist Richard Whiteing declared that Frederic had spoken to him about Christian Science, saying something about his having heard that wonderful things were being done by believers; and Oswald Baron attested that the previous year, when his friend Frederic had suffered a slight illness, "he told witness he was going home to be treated by faith, and that he would not have a doctor." Frank Harris asked if he could give evidence, and told the jury that the year before, Frederic and his family had visited him at his home in the country, where the question of Christian Science came up. "I laughed at him and said that I utterly disbelieved in it." Later, however, Harris remembered, Frederic's little daughter was "stung over the eye by a bee. I said that I would immediately send for a 'blue' bag, as it would relieve the pain. Harold said, 'No, old boy, I don't think so. The pain will do the child very little harm, and she will be the better for it.' I said, 'Better be hung. The poor child is crying: it's disgraceful of you not to help her.' Harold replied, 'It's part of the discipline of life, Frank. A little pain isn't bad for a young child.' I thought it was rather a curious bit of philosophy."

Harris's intentions were obvious. If anything wrong had happened to Frederic, it was his own doing, and was consistent with his outlook. "Was his mind clear?" Harris was asked. Yes, he said, although Frederic's "way of speaking" was rather unusual. But Ruth Frederic, recalled to the witness box, remembered that on the occasion of her little brother's illness "her father himself called in Dr Miller to him, and paid the bill."

In summing up, the coroner observed that although it was up to the jury to decide upon the existence of criminal responsibility, "no words of mine could in any adequate measure convey to Mrs Mills my utter abhorrence of the so-called treatment, and it is difficult to realise that in the enlightened days of the nineteenth century sensible and intelligent people should bind themselves to such an absurd course of procedure. . . . The fact remains that a valuable and intellectual life has been thrown away merely for the want of proper medical care." He then asked whether there were any questions from the jury, and a juror unhappy with Mrs Mill's testimony declared, "It's no good asking; you don't get any answer."

The jury retired at five-thirty, taking with them the long letter written by Dr Boyd to Kate Lyon and the telegrams sent by her to Mrs Mills. In less than an hour they returned with a verdict of manslaughter against Miss Lyon and Mrs Mills. The coroner, W. P. Morrison, issued a warrant, and as the ladies left the hearing they were arrested by the police observer at the proceedings, Inspector Cameron. Brandon Thomas offered to furnish Kate's bail pending a trial, but she and Mrs Mills were held over at Kenley Police Station for action the next day. The pace of justice was swift in 1898.

In his *Saturday Review,* Frank Harris editorialized loyally on the "contemptible verdict," declaring that Frederic was a "wilful man of genius . . . always impatient of guidance or control" and that Miss Lyon had devoted herself to Frederic "as if he had been her God," and should have "at least the poor satisfaction of knowing that her wonderful devotion and loyalty to the man we all loved has not been everywhere misunderstood and derided."

On November 9 the trial began in Croydon Police Court. There were reporters from more than a dozen newspapers—*The Times, Daily Telegraph, Daily News, Daily Mail, Morning Post, Daily Chronicle, Daily Graphic, News of the World, Evening Standard,* and various weeklies and local papers. Miss Kate Lyon gave her age as forty-two, identified herself as "of no occupation," and declared her address to be Ravensbrook, Oxted—the Cranes' home, as she had already been evicted from Homefield as having no legal right of residence there. Mrs Athalie Mills gave her age as forty-five and her occupation as Christian Scientist. They were charged jointly with "feloniously killing and slaying Mr Harold Frederic by neglecting to provide him with proper medical treatment whilst in their charge. . . ." Kate had been accompanied to the dock by Cora Crane, Frank Harris, and Scott Stokes, who took seats in the courtroom. Mrs Mills was alone. When the charge was read by Alderman R. V. Barrow, the defendants made no reply. Since no police objection was offered to bail, Harris and Stokes agreed to furnish it for Miss Lyon, and Leonard Cunliffe and Major Rowley for Mrs Mills. The case was then adjourned for a week.

Meanwhile further details of Frederic's private life were becoming public as rival appeals for funds were addressed to the public, one for Grace Frederic's children, the other for Kate's, and a two-fold ethical debate arose in England as an outgrowth of the Frederic affair. The first was the right of Christian Science as a professed religion to withhold medical care as a tenet of faith. "Christian Manslaughter" was the heading of one editorial. In the other case, clergymen, educators, journalists, artists, members of Parliament, and writers of letters to the editor had begun questioning whether Frederic's illegitimate offspring had any right to charity. "Wake up and be ashamed of yourself, you unfeeling sinful girl," Bernard Shaw's mean-spirited Puritan Mrs Dudgeon had chastised her illegitimate niece Essie in *The Devil's Disciple* the year before, ". . . your father hardly cold in his grave. . . . Your history isn't fit for your own ears to hear." In 1898 that spirit was still alive offstage in London.

Kate was not only under indictment: she and the children were penniless. Frederic's will had neatly divided his estate by leaving his American copyrights and royalties to Kate and his English copyrights and royalties to Grace, but neither were worth much and Frederic had often borrowed, besides, against future income. To cap it all, with Stephen away to cover the war in Cuba, and little writing income reaching England, Cora Crane, with Frederic's second family as an added burden, was served at Ravensbrook with court summonses for unpaid bills by her grocer and butcher. Still she pressed an appeal for funds to counter a public plea from the lawful Mrs Frederic, in whose name a printed circular was distributed by a committee headed by *Daily Chronicle* editor W. J. Fisher ("Honorary Secretary and Treasurer") with Heinemann's partner Sidney S. Pawling as co-trustee. Frederic, it noted, had "left his widow and four children entirely without resources," and with his English copyrights and revenues "so heavily mortgaged . . . it must be some considerable time before any income, however small, can be looked for from this direction." There was no mention of the "other" family, prompting Cora to plead with Fisher to permit some of the funds to be used for Kate's children. "We, the executive," Fisher responded, "dare not divert any portion of it without the sanction of the Committee and the subscribers."

Undeterred, Cora then wrote to each of the signers of the appeal to ask for separate donations, pointing out that Kate's children were also Frederic's. In some cases money arrived by return mail. Playwright A. W. Pinero observed ironically that it was a pity that the first subscription had not made explicit "the whole sum of the human legacy bequeathed by Mr Frederic to the world." Novelist Julia Frankau ("Frank Danby") added to her contribution a note that she was "personally acquainted" with Mrs Mills, "who I *know* to be a thief and a liar and whom I believe to be also a constructive murderer. . . ." George Gissing (living then with a common-law wife) subscribed, with a note of admiration for Kate as Frederic's "true companion, his real wife," who "enabled him to do admirable things." Joseph Conrad, a close friend of both Crane's and Frederic's, wrote Cora that she was "the only Christian in sight in this whole affair," but "the exact truth is I've only £8 in the bank and am in debt to publishers so heavily that I can't go to them for more. Or else I would do it, believe me." Bernard Shaw contributed five pounds but added his feeling that in theory "all extra orphans" should be repudiated. The feeling was generally shared, but without following Shaw's example of a check to repudiate the theory in practice, for many reacted skeptically to the rival appeal. Novelist Hall Caine (author of *The Christian*) wrote Cora that he wished to postpone any contribution until he looked into the other fund. He understood the justice of her plea and would not make a moral issue of the children. "What I had to say on Frederic's walk in life, I said to the man himself while he was alive. It would seem to me that the time is gone by for further discussion of that subject. A man's children are his children, and that is all that remains to be said on the subject." Henry James, who had signed Fisher's appeal for Grace's children, contributed five pounds for Kate's, and then months later, when Stephen Crane had returned, added fifty more. "Deeper than I can say," he wrote Cora, "is my commiseration for those beautiful little children." (He never knew that Frederic had once called him "an effeminate old donkey . . . who insists on being treated as if he were the Pope. . . .") Years before, Crane had written a poem that included the line "Charity, thou art a lie." Had he been back in London then he would have found his sentiments reinforced by Cora. Many of those appealed to offered nothing but their moral outrage, and it was in that atmosphere that Kate's trial continued.

At Croydon County Police Court on November 21, 1898, Mr Horace Avory made an opening statement for the Crown. Introducing the case, he went through the litany of physicians' visits and rebuffs. Dr Boyd, he noted, "at that time formed the opinion that the deceased's mind was affected by his illness, and that he was hardly responsible for what he was saying."

A month later there was no improvement, Avory pointed out, but the doctors' instructions were still not being followed; rather, the period was being used by Miss Lyon and Mrs Mills to persuade the deceased to adopt Christian Science healing. "On September 21 Mrs Mills was installed in the house, and commenced what was called her 'treatment.' . . . From that day Mrs Mills came to the house frequently—three or four times a week—sometimes staying all night. Her 'treatment' . . . appeared to have consisted of allowing and encouraging the deceased to eat and drink as much as and whatever he liked, to smoke as much as he liked, and [to] act, in fact, in all respects as if there were nothing the matter with him. He was undoubtedly allowed champagne, to take long drives, . . . and to stay up late at night—in fact, to do just what he ought not have done in the circumstances of his illness, for at this time, while this so-called 'treatment' was going on, he was suffering from a stroke of paralysis, rheumatic fever, and embolism of the brain."

This continued, Avory concluded, until—four weeks later—a

friend who visited was shocked by Frederic's deterioration and prevailed upon Miss Lyon to again permit the doctors to attend him.
"Drs. Brown and Freyberger were accordingly recalled, and found
[the] deceased in a dying condition. . . . It was only after great
persuasion that Miss Lyon [had] allowed the doctors to come. She
wished to [further] postpone their visits, stating that it was very
awkward their coming in that day, because the deceased was in a
state of 'chemicalization.' " What that meant, Avory could not imagine, but he called the term "rubbish." About thirty hours later, he
reminded the court, Frederic died, and the autopsy confirmed that
death was "undoubtedly accelerated by the so-called 'treatment,' and
also that in all human probability Mr Frederic would have been
cured, or, at all events, that his life would have been prolonged for
many years, had the medical treatment not been interfered with." He
was unwilling to discuss any religious aspect of Christian Science,
"for the simple reason that no religious belief was any answer to a
breach of the law. . . . The fundamental principle of this so-called
creed might properly be called a 'crank.' " And Avory, in order for
the court to "appreciate" what Christian Science meant, called attention to one passage in *Science and Health* "containing their doctrine
and creed": "There is no pain in truth, and no truth in pain; no matter in mind, and no mind in matter. . . ." It was, said Avory, "a
jargon of unmeaning phrases, and it was melancholy to think that a
person in a serious illness should be taken in hand and, as Mr Frederic himself said, have his head bored off his shoulders by such rubbish as this." He proceeded to read extracts from Mrs Mills's testimony at the inquest, where Mrs Mills declared that since death had
occurred while the doctors were at the house, and she had been driven
from it, she had no responsibility in the matter. That she was not "in
attendance," as she put it, was "a paltry quibble" to Avory. "If that
was a specimen of Mrs Mills's sincerity she must be condemned as a
humbug, because Mr Frederic was then dying under her." As this was
an unusual and, so far as he knew, unprecedented case, he ventured
to remind the court of the principle of law involved—that if a person
held herself as capable of treating sickness or disease, she was bound
to bring to the discharge of that duty a competent degree of skill;
and that if such person undertook the charge of a sick person, and in

the opinion of the jury was guilty of gross neglect through ignorance or inattention, that person was guilty of manslaughter. And he sought a conviction in the first degree for Mrs Mills and in the second degree for Miss Lyon.

The first witness called by Avory was Ruth Frederic. In the early part of August when she saw her father at the National Liberal Club, he appeared to her very ill. At Homefield she saw Mrs Mills read from her Christian Science book only to herself. Miss Lyon did permit her father all the food he wanted but would not allow him to have all he wanted to drink. He went for long drives, at least once with Mrs Mills. Yes, Mrs Mills left the house on October 17 when she heard that two doctors were coming. Yes, Kate Lyon only admitted the doctors after great pressure. Mr Lawless, counsel for Mrs Mills, asked whether during his illness her father had appeared intelligent—and sane. Yes, up to the hour of his death. Did she witness any "present treatment"? No, she never saw Mrs Mills do anything which appeared to be treatment, but she once heard the lady expound her views to Mr Frederic. No, she never saw Mrs Mills give her father whiskey, but he insisted on having cigars and did indeed receive them.

Dr Boyd was called, and testified that Frederic at first offered no objection but two days later "roundly abused" him, saying that Boyd was killing him, and that Christian Scientists would cure him in two days. Under cross-examination by Lawless, Boyd admitted to not having practiced in ten or eleven years.

Avory then summoned Dr Freyberger, who confirmed that the deceased had suffered from recrudescent inflammation of the valves of the heart and embolism of the brain, and that he had given explicit instructions on diet to Miss Lyon. When he saw the deceased a week later, Frederic appeared improved, but still later the doctor found him in the garden in a state of fever and with the disease palpably worse. On the next visit, on September 20, he found Frederic's condition grave, and Frederic confided when Miss Lyon was out of hearing that medical advice had not been taken because "the Christian Science people" said they could cure him, but not while he had doctors. As a consequence Freyberger's visits ceased. When he next saw Frederic four weeks later the patient was dying. Yes, it was he who was told by the deceased then that Mrs Mills bored his head off. Was his death accelerated by neglect and the refusal to permit medical treatment? Yes, his life "in all human probability . . . would have been prolonged."

When the trial continued on November 29, Dr Robert Brown of Kenley confirmed that so far as he could judge from his visits, no medical directives had been carried out, and most were severely flouted. Frederic, for example, was permitted to go on a drive to Redhill, which kept him out more than four hours. He had heard, Brown said, of a Christian Scientist being called in, and knew that treatment recommended by physicians was not being followed, yet he found that Frederic was making an "extremely satisfactory" improvement in the first weeks after his stroke.

"What happened on September 16?"

"I found him on the lawn, and found him hot and feverish. . . . He denied that his temperature was really higher, but that it was due to warmer underclothing." Brown then recalled telling Kate Lyon in Frederic's presence three days later that he was aware of her refusal to permit proper treatment, and that Frederic ought to be in bed and Dr Freyberger sent for again.

"Was death due, in fact, to neglect of these precautions?"

"Yes."

Mr Lawless, representing Mrs Mills, cross-examined Brown and elicited from him the confession that the patient had been indeed a difficult person to control, and "was not amenable to medical directions." He forbade the patient to smoke, but found him smoking each time he saw Frederic. From the sixteenth to the twentieth, Brown admitted, he and Freyberger were permitted access to the patient, yet Frederic was getting worse, and when he returned on the twenty-first, "I should not have been surprised if he had died as we were talking."

"Is that true?"

"Yes, he was downstairs when he should have been in bed, and he had a relapse of rheumatic fever, which would, presumably, affect the valves of the heart." He forbade the patient to go out for a drive, Brown added, but Frederic went anyway.

Thomas Mathew, cross-examining for Miss Lyon, drew a response that as far as Brown could see, Miss Lyon was "an affectionate, kindly woman, trying to do all she could for Mr Frederic." But Brown also recalled the conditions of neglect he saw, although he professed to be unaware whether Kate was "talking Christian Science" to Frederic all the time.

Next on the stand was Miss Lottie Sayer, who identified herself as "lady help" to Miss Lyon. She had seen signs of ill health in Frederic as early as the previous March, when he complained of the lingering effects of what he called fish poisoning. She recalled the summoning of Dr Boyd as having been suggested by Frederic himself, and also that Mrs Mills had come to the house only four or five times before September 23, but she understood from Miss Lyon that Mrs Mills was giving "absent treatment" at other times. "She came three or four times a week, and once or twice a week stayed the night. . . . On October 11 he went for a drive with Miss Lyon and Mrs Mills for about five hours. This was only eight days before he died." Frederic was permitted to smoke cigars and drink Munich beer with his meals, and have whiskey and water, "sometimes two or three times in the afternoon." He went out regularly for carriage rides, Miss Sayer went on, sometimes being away for hours. "Once Mr Frederic drove to Redhill and had tea at the Railway Hotel. He had cold meat and ale."

"Rather a high tea, wasn't it?" said Mr Avory. Amid the laughter, order had to be called for in the courtroom. "Perhaps," said Miss Sayer, assuming an answer was required. But the answers came reluctantly, and the witness was reminded by Mr Avory that she was "doing no one any good by this attitude: the truth was bound to come out." Yet she could add little more except to verify what others had said. She could not describe Mrs Mills's treatment nor did she know how it applied, but gathered that it was "purely mental." But she, too, reiterated that Frederic was a "self-willed man" who would insist on having what he wanted. She had heard him speak of Christian Science for about two years. He had also spoken of doctors, and was not very complimentary.

"Come, did he abuse them?"

"No more than anyone else."

Again there was laughter in the courtroom, after which Miss Sayer was asked if she could recall anything which Mrs Mills had said about medicine. She remembered that Mrs Mills had said that being examined by doctors was all rubbish. She had also heard the remark about Mr Frederic's being in a state of "chemicalization."

Next to appear was Mrs Cora Crane, who could not recall meeting Mrs Mills until October 11, a week before Frederic died, when he arrived in a carriage at her home in the company of Mrs Mills. Frederic had appeared weaker each time she saw him in the last month of his life, and on the Monday before his death he had appeared so ill when she visited Homefield that on her own responsibility she had telegraphed to Dr Freyberger. Kate Lyon had told her that although she had every faith herself in Christian Science she would consent to having a doctor if her friends thought it necessary. Cora had also heard the term *chemicalization* used to refer to Frederic's condition at the time.

"Did you understand that the term was synonymous with dying?"

"Oh, no."

Avory had discovered that Kate had treated Stephen Crane, after a carriage accident, for a broken nose, and asked Cora about it.

"What did she do?"

"She thought." (*laughter*)

"Did your husband's nose get better under the process?"

"I don't know. It's well now." (*laughter*)

The court was adjourned for another week. When it sat again, Avory suggested to the bench that the charges against Miss Lyon be dropped but that they be continued against Mrs Mills. Miss Lyon, said Avory, "May have been, and probably was actuated more by misguided affection for the deceased than by Christian Science." Lawless then addressed the bench on behalf of Mrs Mills, who he said had done her duty as her religion spelled that duty out, and added that failures in the application of Christian Science were attributed by Christian Science healers to their own human shortcomings rather than to any fallibility in the teachings they practiced. People were not perfect; only Jesus was. Further, Lawless recalled to the bench that the testimony of every witness, including the physicians, was that Frederic remained an intelligent, forthright, commanding presence until the day of his death, making his own decisions. No one spoke for him any more than anyone wrote his books for him. All that can be said against Mrs Mills was that she did not force open Mr Frederic's mouth and compel him to take medicine and drugs against his will.

Avory replied for the Crown, but his enthusiasm for the case had faded. He asked for a private consultation with the magistrates, who then declared that in the opinion of the bench the manslaughter charge was not strong enough to continue it against Mrs Mills alone. Both defendants were ordered discharged. Frederic was dead, but freedom of conscience—at a price—had prevailed in England. Frank Harris, who had pompously offered to pay half of Kate's legal expenses, had absented himself from Croydon Police Court as the trial wound down, and—predictably—defaulted on his promises, leaving Cora, who was nearly destitute herself, with Kate, her children, and her debts.

Grace Frederic would survive her husband by only a few months, dying of cancer on March 17, 1899. She had become so reclusive that few had known she was even ill. Kate Lyon, after living precariously in London with her children, moved to Chicago in 1904 where she lived under the name of Mrs Forman. Through Frederic's American copyrights and her own writing she eked out an existence into her late seventies, after which the trail disappears.

In leaving America, Harold Frederic had escaped the puritanical rigidities of the hell-fire religion he had examined in *The Damnation of Theron Ware;* yet what hastened his end had been a new religion, itself fresh from America. He had not even escaped the flames. His body was cremated.

CHAPTER V

Brede Place

*Stephen said that a solemn feeling of work came to him there;
so I am delighted.*

—Cora Crane to Edward Garnett from Brede Place, 1899

WHILE CORA, Stephen Crane's "wife," was standing by Kate "Frederic" almost alone, Crane shuttled between New York and Cuba, taking in the war with Spain and puzzling over his ambivalence about returning to London. Facing, with the Marines, disorganization and death at Siboney or Guantánamo, Crane was a hero cited by the Corps for bravery. Facing the prospect of the possessive and loyal Cora in England, and the loss of his regained independence, he was more timid. "How do you persuade anybody to do anything by cables and letters?" he wrote to a friend on November 28, 1898, from New York. "I am very anxious to have Mrs Crane come to this country. Mrs Crane is very anxious to have me come back to England. We are carrying on a duel, at long range, with ink." But Cora knew what he refused to confront: he could not introduce her to his staid family in New Jersey as Mrs Crane, even if she were legally entitled to his name.

Sophisticated but flashy, and a half-dozen years his elder, Cora

144

gave every evidence to perceptive Americans of what she had been
—the honey-haired proprietress of the Hotel de Dream, a Jacksonville nightclub and house of joy, whom Stephen—twenty-six in 1898
—had met on his first trip to Florida and Cuban waters. She had
cared for him after the disaster at sea he afterward turned into fiction in "The Open Boat," and he responded by offering to rescue her
from the life he assumed she led only with reluctance. A sentimen-
talist about women, Crane could stand on the sidewalk all night
pathetically gazing at his true love's window and he could declare
to yet another true love, "It is better to have known you and suffered, than not to have known you." He was drawn to older women,
often married ones, and was chivalrous to ladies of the streets,
whether or not he bedded down with them. And Cora Howorth
Stewart was no Shavian Mrs Warren, vulgar and happily crass. Despite her Boston origins and Florida profession, she considered herself an English lady upon hard times, separated from an aristocratic
army captain who refused to divorce her. Crane would protect her
with his name; abroad, he assumed, no one would be the wiser.

Although he yearned at the time for a filibustering expedition to
Cuba where he could engage in a private military action, he knew he
had to wait for the then inevitable war with Spain over the island.
Meanwhile, Greeks and Turks were fighting each other, and Hearst's
New York Journal offered the author of *The Red Badge of Courage*
a contract to cover the war. It was better than no war at all. Crane
took Hearst's dollars, and Cora, to England en route to Greece.

Crane had quickly gravitated into the orbit of resident American
writers in London, and Harold Frederic had fixed on Stephen as
more than a newspaperman. *The Red Badge* was as respected in
England as in America. Crane, he thought, was the best hope of the
American novel. Frederic recalled first hearing about *The Red
Badge* from Henry James, whom he disliked, and whose recommen-
dation "deterred [me] from reading it for some days. . . . With his
usual lack of sense or generosity he described the book as an imita-
tion of Zola's *The Downfall* which it resembles as much as I do Miss
Ellen Terry." Frederic's dispatch to New York about the success of
The Red Badge in England would establish Crane's reputation in
America in ways local fame could not effect.

Crane was enchanted with London, and Frederic saw to it that he met publishers and writers who could persuade him that an author meant something more there than in the narrow and uncouth canyons of New York. There was nothing insincere about Frederic's admiration although in his characteristic bluff manner he led his new friend into the Savage Club late in March 1897 (according to Thomas Beer) "as if he invented the boy." On the last day of March they were together at a luncheon at the Savoy given for Crane by American correspondent Richard Harding Davis, and there Crane met James Barrie, Anthony Hope, and Justin McCarthy. He was "very modest, sturdy and shy," Davis wrote his mother. "Quiet, unlike [what] I had imagined," but with a "bi-roxide blonde who seemed to be attending to his luggage."

"Mr Stephen Crane," observed editor Arthur Waugh in his "London Letter" of April 2 in the *Critic,* "has flitted through London this week on his way to the insurrection in Crete, but his visit was of the briefest. Indeed, it was characterized by extreme and refreshing modesty, being conspicuously free of the tendency to self-advertisement which is so often characteristic of the Novelist's progress. . . . He seemed much pleased with the reception of his work in England and jokingly remarked that he was off to Crete because, having written so much about war, he thought it high time he should see a little fighting. Which proves him a man of humor—an excellent thing in letters."

The four brief days in London were crowded. Finding Crane attractive, his publisher, William Heinemann, visualized a series of future masterworks, and Heinemann's partner Sidney Pawling quickly arranged for Crane also to represent the *Westminster Gazette,* which meant more income from war reporting and (from the Heinemann standpoint) more visibility in England. Harold Frederic —himself a Heinemann author—traveled to Dover to see Crane and Davis off, while Cora and her companion from Jacksonville days, Mrs Charlotte Ruedy, discreetly shared a separate compartment on the boat train until Davis parted from them in Paris, intending to go to Greece by a different route.

By April 8 Crane, having sailed from Marseilles, was off Crete in the Bay of Suda; Cora was still on the longer sea route to Athens via Constantinople. By the time Crane himself reached mainland

Greece, the war was almost over, with the demoralized Greeks victims of the mismanagement and incompetence of Crown Prince Constantine's officers. All of Crane's early dispatches were full of stirring optimism, but there was an armistice in mid-May and Crane returned by sea to Marseilles with the young Ptolemy brothers, whom he had picked up as refugees. In early June, with his enlarged retinue, Crane was back in England, and Arthur Waugh reported in his column in the *Critic* that the novelist "was seen on the Strand yesterday afternoon," and that Crane's new book, *The Third Violet,* was being treated kindly by London critics. A thin work about an artist's frustrated love, *The Third Violet* sold modestly on the strength of the author's reputation. Still, one less respectful London reviewer hoped "that instead of violets Mr Crane will give us war— war—war." Frederic was ready with the same opinion: Crane had to turn his Greek experience into a novel.

On Frederic's urging, Crane decided to settle in the London area, and while his new friends (one of them editor Edward Garnett) helped search the Surrey suburbs for something suitable—which meant within easy access of their own residences—the Cranes, with Mrs Ruedy, settled into furnished rooms in Limpsfield. Before the end of June they had found "Ravensbrook Villa," a pretentiously named brick corner house, with a brook that was more of a culvert, in the adjacent village of Oxted, in a low, damp area below a chalk cliff. Few locations could have been worse for Stephen's chronically weak lungs, but all around him were literary acquaintances, American and English, and London in the summer of the Diamond Jubilee was brilliant and inviting.

He had determined to bluff out the deception of a marriage, and kept his secret from all but a few intimate friends; yet Crane told some he had been married in Athens, others he had been married in America, and still others that he had married in London with H. G. Wells as one of his witnesses. It made little difference. For Frank Harris's *Saturday Review* he wrote several "London Impressions" that July and August, contrasting the raucous noise of New York with the decorous drone of London, and symbolizing the traditionally slower pace of English life in the ascent and descent of a London lift with the dignity of a coffin being lowered into the grave, its "elevator boy" an elderly gentleman with a great white beard: "I saw that the lift had been longer on its voyage than I had expected."

In England Crane was a celebrity, even among other celebrated Americans. His new friend Harold Frederic had seen to that as far back as January 1896, in a dispatch headlined in New York "Stephen Crane's Triumph. London Curious about the Identity of America's New Writer." *The Red Badge of Courage* would become, Frederic wrote, "one of those deathless books which must be read by everybody who desires to be, or to seem, a connoisseur of modern fiction. If there were in existence any books of a similar character, one could start confidently by saying that it was the best of its kind. But it has no fellows. It is a book outside of all qualifications." Now Frederic worried that "the boy" was too frail in health—he reminded many of Stevenson—to repeat the effort unless he quickly buckled down to new work. Yet Frederic had been right at the start. *The Red Badge* was unique and there was no way for its author to go in that direction. In any case "Stevie" was urged to write a novel based on his Greek experience, and in November 1897 he began what would eventually become, although it languished on his desk more than it was picked up, *Active Service,* a novel about a lovesick journalist who risks his life covering the war against the Turks.

Even at the beginning, the novel failed to sustain Crane's own interest, and he returned to a long short story, "The Monster." With the expanse of the Atlantic providing the distance he needed for objectivity, his mythical American town of Whilomville, about which he had written earlier tales, seemed more grotesquely real. "The Monster" became a tale of a Negro hostler who in rescuing his son from a fire is horribly burned but saved by the local physician only to change in public image from hero to faceless horror ostracized by the community. The story was finished, after some false starts, in a week of interrupted evenings in Ireland with Frederic.

Crane had attempted an ambitious tale about the quality of pity, but his American agent, Paul Reynolds, found it quickly rejected. As an editor at the *Century* explained, "We couldn't publish that thing with half the expectant mothers in America on our subscription list!" Even to Frederic the story was a mistake, and he advised Crane to throw it away. (Yet Crane, for all his reputed fidelity to detail, had only written of the Negro, "He had no face.") According to Sanford Bennett, a minor French-Canadian writer who became a friend to both Crane and Frederic, Crane defended his story passionately, banging the butt of a long Mexican revolver on the furniture for emphasis. Why should people be frightened by a story "with some sense in it"? He was concerned, as he would always be in his most thoughtful fiction, with the problem of moral choice in a world of disintegrating traditional values, while Frederic, who had a practical knowledge of the market in London and New York, did not believe in art if it would not sell.

It was a highly productive period for Crane, the second half of 1897 including such other stories as "The Bride Comes to Yellow Sky" and "The Blue Hotel." Despite the incursions of friends, acquaintances, and those who wanted to bask in his fame or eat and drink at his expense, he was managing to get writing accomplished, but he had coined a name for the invaders, many of them Americans. They would usually be called, as long as Crane remained in England, "Indians," although sometimes the parasites—the lowest form of hangers-on—were "lice."

During the productive summer of 1897, Crane earned nearly two thousand dollars, but complained to his agents and publishers that he had seen little of it; and he actually had to go to J. B. Pinker, his London agent, to borrow against his earnings. By December, Crane's helpless good nature and Cora's desire to win friends for him and his work had bogged him down in entertaining at heavy cost to his literary output and his bank account. At tea in John Hay's house in London, he told the American ambassador on being congratulated on his success, "I wish success paid me a salary, sir."

As Ford Madox Hueffer (afterward Ford) put it, noting the hugely inflated rumors of Crane's writing income floating about at the time, literary London "was filled to about capacity by the most discreditable bums that any city can ever have seen. They pullulated mostly about the purlieus of the Savage Club, but you would find them in Bedford Park and you would find them in Limehouse. And no sooner did the word go round that there was in Oxted . . . a shining young American of genius, earning twenty pounds for every thousand words that he wrote, and ready to sit up all night dispensing endless hampers of caviar, *foie gras,* champagne, and oysters in season. . . . The reverberations were terrific. London was at that time full of American reporters. It was the fat time for war correspondents, and they all went through the Savage Club—to the Balkans, to Athens, to Vladivostok by the Trans-Siberian; and innumerable lame ducks, bad hats, *tristes sires,* and human detritus from New York to Tin Can, Nevada, were left by the tide between Fleet Street and Adelphi Terrace, which was the Mecca of the Bohemian out-at-elbows. And, merely to be reputed to have known that Fortunate Youth was to have parcels of that flotsam drift into one's doorstep."

Crane's real problem was that the heady literary atmosphere of London and environs tempted him (and Cora) into living at a pitch which required paying for it out of advances for works still unpublished and sometimes even unwritten. One project which might have made money but which failed to survive his move across the Atlantic was a promised collaboration with Clyde Fitch, then the most successful American playwright. Fitch made a number of long visits to London, but no play with Crane resulted. To his agent Paul Reynolds in New York, Crane wrote for help in securing an advance from S. S. McClure for *Active Service* and to apologize for a hack story based on a Greek incident, "Death and the Child." "I would not have done it if I was not broke. For heaven's sake raise all the money you can and *cable* it, *cable* it sure between Xmas and New Year's. . . ." He and Cora also wrote Sunday newsletters from London under the name "Imogene Carter" which she had used in Greece. They were published around the country as well as in the *New York Press* in the autumn of 1897, the series—ten articles in ten papers —bringing in four hundred dollars at four dollars an article. "Rotten bad" was Stephen's description of the columns on fashion, sport, society, drinking habits, and gossip, but they needed the money. Ravensbrook was no showplace, Oxted no exotic setting, but the Cranes made do. As they wrote in one of the weekly newsletters, "Life in an English country house is perhaps the most delightful manner of living in the world, and society must be forgiven if it grows silly over it. . . ." The two American nonconformists had themselves succumbed.

By December, when Crane pleaded with Reynolds for advances,

he confided that his English expenses "have chased me to the wall."
At one point he had to flee to Brown's Hotel in Dover Street "to
finish some work," as he wrote a friend, adding, "Cora just now
wires me that she has got rid of some people who have been board-
ing with us for three days, so I can go home." He liked being a
guest himself, and was amused by English ignorance of America, a
condition he found difficult to rectify. "I told a seemingly sane man
at Mrs Garnett's," he wrote James Huneker in New York, "that I
got my artistic education on the Bowery and he said, 'Oh, really? So
they have a school of fine arts there?' " One of Crane's own visits to
Frederic at Homefield (in October 1897) proved longer than expected. Going in style to a birthday breakfast, he and Cora were
hurt when the hired carriage, improperly harnessed, overturned.
They remained a week while Stephen's broken nose mended without
the assistance of a doctor ("Kate will make you right," Frederic assured his friend), and then were carried off for three more weeks to
Frederic's favorite fishing village in Ireland, on Dunmanus Bay,
near Bantry. And Crane also visited back and forth with Joseph Conrad, talking and smoking half the night and sharing each other's
writings, with Conrad especially interested in impressing Crane with
Nigger of the Narcissus, which seems, consciously or not, to have
been influenced by *The Red Badge.* "If I've hit you with the death of
Jimmy," Conrad assured him, "I don't care if I don't hit another
man." Crane was duly impressed, arguing with Frederic over its
merits. "You and I and Kipling couldn't have written the *Nigger!"*
Crane insisted, emphasizing his point by crashing the butt of his revolver into a dessert plate.

Another regular visitor was Ford Madox Ford, a neighbor, who
once waited at Ravensbrook with Cora for Crane to return from a
visit to J. B. Pinker in Arundel Street. As Cora could tell from the
full hamper of foie gras, caviar, champagne, and claret Stephen had
hauled from London, the news was good, and he confided his coup to
her while leaning against a doorpost, his hat tilted across his eyes. He
had been cautious about coming into the room, worried that the
other figure there was the bailiff. Local tradesmen had not only cut
off his groceries but gone to the law, because the Cranes were purchasing everything on credit and had no ready cash.

As Ford, who seems not to be embroidering the facts in his usual manner, recalled, Crane wanted someone to share his future good fortune. "So, till breakfast next morning, he went on passionately telling me that he didn't give whatever it was the then fashionable slang not to give for corner lots and battle-fields; that I ruined, ruined, ruined my verse by going out of my way, in the pre-Raphael-ite manner, to drag in rhymes which made *longueurs* and diluted the sense. . . . And he produced from the hip pocket of the riding-breeches into which he had changed from his town clothes, a Colt revolver, with the foresight of which he proceeded to kill flies. . . . He had spilt a little champagne over a lump of sugar on the table and flies had come in companies. He really did succeed in killing one, flicking the gun backhanded with his remarkably strong wrists. Then he looked at me avengingly and said: 'That's what you want to do instead of interring yourself amongst purple pre-Raphaelite pleo-nasms. . . . That's what you learn out in the West. . . .' "

Since his readership considered him narrowly as a writer about war, Crane, putting idealism aside, decided that he might cure his chronic lack of money by concocting a potboiler, *Great Battles of the World*. Kate Frederic was enlisted to research material in the British Museum, a task familiar to her from years past, and produced data on the final battle of the War of 1812 at New Orleans. Harold Frederic also sent material, addressing it to Stephen as "My Dear Boy," in the same letter making his offer of a joint household in Ire-land he was afterward to withdraw with some embarrassment. Con-rad, too, would suggest a joint household—"say in Brittany for three months or so." But the Cranes could not have made such an arrange-ment work; impulsive and improvident, they would have quickly caused several warm literary friendships to explode in acrimony. (Once Crane walked out on Frederic after an argument, leaving *him* at Ravensbrook.)

But to one friend, bearded like Conrad and as complicated in his speech and small courtesies, Crane was unfailingly gentle: Henry James. Thomas Beer tells of an episode in February 1898 when Crane, Frederic, and James gathered in a London hotel as guests of an American visitor and suffered the impromptu entertainment of a tipsy lady who claimed to be imitating Yvette Guilbert. "Crane with-drew the elderly novelist to a corner and talked style until the fan-

tastic woman poured champagne into the top hat of Henry James.
. . . Frederic was amused. The wretched host . . . was too young
and too frightened to do anything preventive and Crane, coldly tact-
ful, got the handsome creature out of the hotel, then came back to aid
in the restoration of the abused hat." Others there thought that
James's tedious pomposities were amply repaid by the act, but Crane,
in a letter afterward, defended the Master. "I agree with you that Mr
James has ridiculous traits and lately I have seen him make a holy
show of himself in a situation that—on my honour—would have
been simple to an ordinary man. But it seems impossible to dislike
him. He is so kind to everybody. . . ." James responded accordingly.
Few London Yankees were more loyal to each other than the one-
time Bowery bum and the cultivated old bachelor from New York
and Boston.

In the spring of 1898 Crane was writing at both the top and the
bottom of his form. In February he had put his frontier story "The
Blue Hotel" on the steamship *Majestic* addressed to Paul Reynolds,
calling it "a daisy." It was, but the quality magazines, *Scribner's* and
Atlantic Monthly, rejected it, and it went instead to *Collier's Weekly*
where Crane was paid only three cents a word for a story of ten
thousand words, one of the best he had crafted and one of the finest
pieces of short fiction by an American. In April, Doubleday and Mc-
Clure would bring out his *The Open Boat and Other Stories of
Adventure,* and the next year "The Blue Hotel" would be put between covers in *The Monster and Other Stories,* but he poured out
his financial woes to Reynolds while praising him for handling his
American affairs effectively. "A ten pound note even fills me with
awe. You must understand as my confidential agent that my settle-
ment in England cost me in the neighborhood of $2000 worth of
debts. Your payments from the Harpers knocked a comfortable hole
in them but I must have about $1200 more."

A way to find the dollars he needed turned up while Crane was
rushing out more hack writing for English and American journals.
The mysterious explosion which sank the battleship *Maine* in Cuban
waters had led to war with Cuba, and a war meant war reporting. At
the height of the irresponsible American newspaper campaign for an
invasion of Cuba, Henry James had written his brother, sadly, "I

confess that the blaze about to come leaves me woefully cold, thrilling with no glorious thrill or holy blood-thirst whatever. I see nothing but the madness, the passion, the hideous clumsiness of rage, of mechanical reverberation; and I echo with all my heart your denouncement of the foul criminality of the screeching newspapers." His young friend Crane had no deep patriotic motives about what was clearly a sleazy conflict, but he could not afford to miss it. As Joseph Conrad remembered it, Crane had come to him one afternoon late in April to seek help in finding sixty pounds with which to get to Cuba "before the sun set, before dinner, before the 'six forty' train to Oxted, at once that instant—lest peace should be declared and the opportunity of seeing a war be missed. I had not sixty pounds to lend him. Sixty shillings was nearer my mark. . . . Crane's white-faced excitement frightened me. Finally it occurred to me to take him to Messrs Blackwood & Sons' London office. There he was received in a most friendly way. Presently I escorted him to Charing Cross, where he took the train for home with the assurance that he would have the means to start 'for the war' next day."

To wheedle the funds from Blackwoods it was necessary for Conrad to mortgage his own future literary earnings as security, while Sanford Bennett furnished an additional ten-pound note. Crane left an ominous message for Bennett: "Sorry not to have seen you. I have raised the wind and sail tomorrow. Nothing I can do for Harold. Barr will look after him. . . ." Harold Frederic, in Ireland, was already experiencing the first symptoms of the ailment which would fell him several months later, and Crane had recognized death in his face before anyone else had perceived it.

With Stephen suddenly gone, Cora joined the Frederics on Dunmanus Bay, bringing with her Mrs Ruedy, Adoni Ptolemy, and three dogs. In late summer there would be a new exchange, as the "Frederic" children went to Ravensbrook while Kate watched Harold die. Nearly nine months would pass before Stephen's return, but Cora was determined that he would come back to a more attractive setting than the damp brick pile at Ravensbrook. A suggestion came from Edward Garnett. Crane's fellow expatriate Lady Randolph Churchill had a brother-in-law, Moreton Frewen, who had knocked about America himself, and who owned the once-stately Brede Manor, near

Rye, which he might lend at nominal rental in return for upkeep to the buildings and grounds. Cora then met Jennie Churchill's sister Clara at the Society of American Women in London, where the former proprietress of the Hotel de Dream and the aristocratic Jerome sisters were social equals. Resident Americans with literary or artistic credentials in any case enjoyed many of the opportunities of England's stratified class structure without suffering most of its obvious disadvantages.

The vision of Stephen as squire of an authentic and venerable manor house tantalized Cora no less than that she would be its chatelaine. Yet how many of her letters he received about her dream of Brede is unclear. When he wrote at all, it was to say that he was not receiving her letters, and she was constantly writing or cabling someone in America to forward or reforward them. He apparently did not want to receive them, or own up to receiving them. Feigned ignorance gave him more freedom of action, as he moved between New York and the Caribbean, fought in the jungles and on the beaches with the Marines, or holed up in Havana writing about Cuba or the earlier war in Greece. Meanwhile Richard Harding Davis secured the newspaper scoops—all but one—and enhanced his reputation and his bank account. When the Americans invaded Puerto Rico, Harding Davis and Crane were with them. While Harding Davis slept—Crane was supposed to awaken him—Crane coolly crept forward of the advance posts into the town of Juana Díaz. As he ambled into the first street he came to, smoking a cigarette, his khaki suit, slouched hat, and leggings were all that were needed to drive the first man who saw him into retreating to arouse the garrison. Within ten minutes, Harding Davis later reported, the *alcalde* surrendered the town to its lone occupier. "Crane told me that no general in the moment of victory had ever acted in a more generous manner. He shot no one against a wall, looted no churches, levied no forced loans. Instead he lined up the male members of the community in the plaza, and organised a joint celebration of the conquerors and conquered . . . that overflowed from the Plaza into the by-streets and lashed itself into a frenzied carnival of rejoicing."

The next morning, eight hundred troops led by a colonel cautiously entered the town, intending to take it by surprise. With them was Harding Davis. "The colonel's astonishment at the sight of Crane was sincere. His pleasure was no less great. He knew that it did not fall to the lot of every colonel to have his victories immortalised by the genius who had written *The Red Badge of Courage.* 'I am glad to see you,' he cried eagerly. 'Have you been marching with my men?' Crane shook his head. 'I am sorry,' said the Colonel. 'I should like you to have seen us take this town.'

" 'This town?' said Crane in polite embarrassment. 'I'm really very sorry, Colonel, but I took this town myself before breakfast yesterday morning.' "

Crane was back in Cuba when the Protocol of Peace was announced on August 12, 1898. Having tired of the pitiful comedy that was the war, but not ready to return to London, he had quit early, almost certainly never collecting all of the three thousand dollars of the fee he had agreed upon to report the war for Joseph Pulitzer in the *New York World.* Enjoying Havana, Crane was spending some of the happiest months of his life in a boardinghouse, penciling sketches of Cuban life for the *New York Journal* and stories for Paul Reynolds, who had instructions not to reveal his whereabouts. Without mail or money from Stephen, Cora kept up as good a front as she could, given her financial catastrophes, the Frederic tragedy, and the stories from America beginning in September that Stephen had disappeared without trace from his quarters at the four-story Grand Hotel Pasaje, a building modern enough to boast electricity. On the twenty-fourth Cora appealed to Stephen's friend Ambassador Hay "to use your influence to find him. . . . I am almost distracted with grief and anxiety." But Hay was back in America on vacation, before assuming his new post as American secretary of state, and Cora heard nothing. She wrote also to the British consul in Havana, cabled Secretary of War Russell A. Alger, and implored Reynolds, "I am in *great* distress of mind as I can get no news through the *Journal* office here. Mr Crane's affairs here need his attention. I am in great need of money. And I fear we will lose our home here if I cannot get money to pay some pressing debts. The *Journal* is behaving very shabbily. . . ."

Crane had quietly moved to Mary Horan's lodging house, from which he neglected Cora both by accident and by design while he

enjoyed a total freedom made possible by isolation and remittances
from New York. But the cable to the secretary of war finally exposed him, after which he offered General J. F. Wade in Havana
regrets "at having caused so much trouble" and continued to ignore
appeals from England. The mystery distracted Conrad from his work
as he was financially involved, and for him Crane's defaulting would
be a disaster. Cora intimated to Jessie Conrad that she worried that
another woman might be involved, and was assured unconvincingly
of Stephen's fidelity. Finally Blackwood received a Cuban war tale,
"The Price of the Harness," via Reynolds, whom Crane told, "I
love this story." By then it was already November. Cora had still
heard nothing except for a laconic cable scratched out to satisfy
General Wade.

With Ravensbrook besieged by creditors, Cora was desperate. If
she were legally married, her husband would be responsible for the
debts piled up in England. If the truth should leak out, she herself
would be liable. She desperately needed to be accepted as "Mrs
Crane," and feared that Stephen's noncommittal cable meant he did
not plan to return. To protect herself as well as to save Stephen from
himself, she enlisted Robert Barr to help her raise funds to sail for
Havana and fetch Crane home. The effort came to nothing. No one
would risk the money as she could not legally promise Stephen's
future writings to anyone, if there were to be any writings beyond
what was already tied up by loans and advances, and she had no
property not about to be seized by the bailiffs. To add to her woes,
Harold Frederic was dying and Kate would soon be tried for manslaughter. At least there was one blessing: the "Indians" from London remained away as if the house were under quarantine.

As Cora suspected, there was another woman. In Washington
Stephen had met with an old flame, Lily Brandon Munroe, formerly
of Asbury Park, unhappily married and seeking a divorce. Away
from her in Cuba he penciled pages of sentimental love lyrics to his
"lost one," pondering whether she remembered a time when their
love "was to thee thy all." It seemed briefly like a romantically
quixotic gesture to abandon everything in order to huddle back into
his past. Meanwhile, London newspapers reported that Crane was
suffering from yellow fever in Havana (it was malaria), and Cora

bravely announced to anyone who would listen that her Stephen would be coming home soon to live at Brede Place.

Finally Crane quit Havana, which had been a convenient place to hide from both women. Underground and alone, he had shed the notoriety that had followed him to England, and had achieved, almost perversely, the tranquillity in which to write for which he had first fled America for England. But little writing of any value had come to him. He had exhausted as much of his fund of personal experience about Cuba as he cared to turn into dollars, and appeals were being transmitted to him from friends such as Conrad, who was ashamed of Stephen's abandonment of Cora, and Jack Stokes. It was Scott Stokes who provided the real push, cabling on November 14, "Money shortly through General Wade." He was sending fifty pounds from Heinemann through military channels to make sure Crane knew that they in London knew he had received it.

With nothing more to do in Cuba at any rate, he cabled in return that he was sailing for New York, which in London suggested the first leg of a return home. Yet in New York such friends as critic James Huneker and Richard Harding Davis found Crane weary and gray and unwilling to come to terms with his future. On November 23 he and Huneker were in Hoffman's Bar in Delmonico's Hotel, when Crane noticed some old journalistic enemies and decided to leave. One, Thomas McCumber, a photographer, gossiped loudly that Crane had tried to get himself killed in Cuba. Why? someone asked. Because, said McCumber, he was dying of syphilis.* Richard Harding Davis, off in a corner, listened. Crane, said another, was leaving America "for America's good; he is a drug addict." Davis towed the loudmouth out of the bar and took a swing at him outside. Crane had heard this before, having written Robert Barr from Key West, "Now I owe Harold [Frederic] an apology for laughing when he said they would tear me in pieces the minute my

---

* It may well be that Crane had decided that he was indeed dying of something, as he appears to have made a trip to Saranac Lake, New York, to Dr Trudeau's tuberculosis sanatorium, for a checkup in the summer of 1898. When Cora inquired about the report, Trudeau wrote her (September 16, 1898), "Your husband had a slight evidence of activity in the trouble in his lungs when he came back here this summer, but it was not serious and he has improved steadily, I understand. . . ."

back was turned. Hi, Harold! I apologize! Did you know me for a
morphine eater? A man who has known me ten years tells me that
all my books are written while I am drenched with morphine. The
joke is on me."

What quickly became clear to Crane was that the United States,
New York in particular, was unfriendly country. Even the police
were demonstratively hostile, remembering that Crane, the author of
Maggie, had once intervened on the side of streetwalkers who were
being shaken down by plainclothesmen for protection money. There
was even a suggestion from police authorities that he be booked
somehow on a trumped-up charge, and at least once when he was
with friends, police abused the party, threatening Crane with "Come
round to the station, you drunken bum!" But there was a priest in the
party, and at the sight of the collar a policeman mumbled something apologetic and disappeared.

Sometime in December he took the train to Washington, probably to see Lily. Whether it had been to say good-bye to Lily or to
recheck his chances, on December 20 he cabled Cora that he was returning. *Blackwood's Edinburgh Magazine* had just published "The
Price of the Harness." On Christmas Day she wrote Moreton
Frewen, "The horror of the last few months is almost at an
end. . . ." On the last day of the year, Crane's brother Edmund
accompanied him to the dock to catch the steamer *Manitou.*

The ship reached Gravesend on January 11. On the thirteenth,
from Ravensbrook, Crane sent Conrad a telegraph order for fifty
guineas, and soon after, Sanford Bennett received his ten pounds.
Yet Crane owed a year's rent on Ravensbrook, and encountered a
pile of duns from a Surrey solicitor representing the local butcher,
grocer, and other creditors, as well as Whitely's in London, to
whom he owed an unpaid balance of nearly a hundred pounds for a
piano. The steady Pinker was brought into the emergency as
guarantor that payments would be made, "time not specified." As
Crane put it to Pinker, he needed a buffer as "This will enable me
to move almost at once to Brede and get a fair chance at myself."

Once he had traveled down to Brede with Cora, Stephen regretted his months of indecision, for the baronial Brede Place, with
all its splendid inadequacies, seemed to fit him as if tailored for his

curious needs. The man who in New York felt an affinity with the street girls, in Washington labored under the illusion that old loves can be reawakened with untarnished ardor, and in Havana was captured by the otherworldliness of Mary Horan's decaying lodging house, was ripe for the romance of ancient Brede. Cora saw it as conferring social status, and Stephen—an aspiring squire himself—may have seen it as something more. In presenting a copy of *Maggie* to Hamlin Garland in 1893, Crane had noted that it "tries to show that environment is a tremendous thing in the world and frequently shapes lives regardless." He may have visualized in Brede a setting in which high literary art could gestate.

From the station at Hastings, the Cranes had driven to the manor house and wandered about until dusk, when they improvised from their hamper a supper of ham and eggs at the kitchen fireplace. "We are going to move Heaven and Earth to get there," Cora wrote Edward Garnett. "Stephen said that a solemn feeling of work came to him there; so I am delighted." It was, said Garnett, "the lure of romance that always thrilled Crane's blood, and Brede Place had had indeed, an unlucky, chequered history." The oldest wing of the manor, Stephen wrote Sanford Bennett, was begun in 1378. But the Oxenbridge family, associated with it for centuries, had sold it in 1619 after which it deteriorated, for Sir Edward Frewen, who bought it early in the eighteenth century, already had a country seat nearby at Northiam. Close to the Channel coast, the uninhabitable house became a smugglers' nest, and smugglers very likely encouraged the stories of its being haunted, to frighten away the curious. Yet the gaunt, empty house, its windows black and broken, its gardens and fields a tangle of weeds, excited the Cranes. The cavernous stone pile breathed history, although it was civilized neither by bathrooms nor running water nor electric lights, and there was no source of heat other than the huge fireplaces which greedily devoured logs carried in throughout the day—like the water—by servants. With no toilets, only bedside thunderjugs, visiting gentlemen would later relieve themselves in the shrubbery outside.

Somehow—it must have taken more than Pinker's efforts—the Cranes found the wherewithal to begin putting Brede into livable condition, moving by train and wagons on Sunday, February 12.

Stephen quickly furnished the most essential room—a study in the
cubicle over the porch—and began churning out copy for Cora to
type and transmit to Pinker. Eventually he would put the Brede
setting into "The Squire's Madness" and his novel *The O'Ruddy,*
where there are tales related of old Sir Goddard Oxenbridge tramping through the night "in two sections." Although Sir Goddard's
altar tomb is in the Brede church, more than a mile away in the
village, in *The O'Ruddy* Crane has a caretaker at the manor house
explain, "Bullets wouldn't harm him, nor steel cut him, so they
sawed him in two with a wooden saw down by the bridge in front.
He was a witch of the very worst kind, your honour. You hear him
groaning at the bridge every night, and sometimes he walks through
the house himself in two halves, and then everybody leaves the place.
And that is our most serious danger, your honour. When Sir Goddard takes to groaning through these rooms at night, you'll not get
a man to stay with you, sir; but as he comes up from the pit by the
will of the Devil we expect his Reverence to ward him off."

The O'Ruddy, the composition of which would be the agony of
Crane's Brede years, may have been suggested by Harold Frederic's
The O'Mahony, also set in the Ireland they had visited together. But
for months Crane had nothing to show of it but a thumbnail outline
of the first four chapters, which eventually he did not follow. Instead he worked on a dozen things simultaneously, including a
Spanish-American War play he never finished, set on an English-
owned estate in Cuba, a vague transplantation of Brede. A play
suggested large and quick profits, but he did not have the professional resources to bring it off, and he did not call in Clyde Fitch.
Instead, alternative pieces proliferated, keeping Cora busy.

How she found time to do Stephen's typing, on a wayward machine which had no right-hand margin release, and thus required
lines with missing final letters to be filled in by hand on ribbon and
carbon copies, is remarkable in itself. She explored the countryside
for cheap old furniture and bedding, refinished some of it herself,
cooked many of the meals, and entertained a burgeoning guest list,
while Stephen, often late at night when everyone else had gone to
bed and there was no one to share talk and a bottle, penned short
stories about "Whilomville," war sketches about Cuba, the remain-

ing half of *Active Service,* and whatever short pieces could be written quickly and sold as quickly. He was "writing against the clock," according to R. W. Stallman, his biographer, "without time to let themes ripen in his mind, and he could not afford to tear up a first draft or start on a better line. To obtain advances from Pinker he was writing things that came easily to him. . . ." Like Bret Harte, Crane was becoming, in Howells's phrase, "a trained bear of the magazines." Crane used the term twice himself.

During the first three weeks of February his advances from Pinker came to two hundred pounds, and although it was largely Pinker who staved off the bailiffs, Crane in the confusion and urgency of his need offered "The Blue Hotel" to yet another English agent, W. M. Colles, and duplicated some offers to Paul Reynolds in New York, so that Pinker finally had to write tactfully to Cora—usually Stephen's business manager—that "Editors are not pleased if I go and talk a great deal about a story and ask them to pay special attention to it, and then withdraw it."

Finally part of *Active Service* was typed—all that Crane had written in the long, confused weeks in Cuba. Forwarding twenty-two short chapters to Pinker on April 25, Cora hectored the harassed Pinker to make sure that he did not permit editors to keep Stephen's copy more than two weeks. Coming to a decision quickly meant cash, and while inwardly there was perpetual panic at Brede, outwardly Cora and Stephen radiated fiscal confidence. In a letter in which Stephen had attempted to borrow five hundred dollars from his brother William, he wrote, "We are living very quietly, devoting all our attention to my work. My wife is very helpful to me and feels the same interest in my stories that I feel myself. This makes it easier and if the month of March don't wipe me off the earth I hope by this time next year to be fairly rich so much confidence do I have in the different life I am now leading. . . ."

To Mrs Frewen, Stephen wrote that he and Cora "love Brede with a wildness which I think is a little pathetic," and, he added, every day, despite the spring rains, "it seems more beautiful to us." But with Stephen's recurrent malaria and tenuously arrested tuberculosis, the lowlands of East Sussex and Kent were as badly chosen for a residence as was possible. "I formed a very disagreeable impression of Brede," Ford Madox Ford recalled melodramatically. "It seemed to be full of evil influences, to be very damp, and to be hopelessly remote . . . , with its deep hollows, dank coppices, and precipitous hop-fields . . . full of hobgoblins and miasmas." But to Clara Frewen, Stephen found whatever happened at Brede "delightful": "During these late heavy storms the whole house sang like a harp and all the spooks have been wailing to us. It is rather valkyric. The servants are more impressed than we would like them to be and we have not yet found maids who will sleep in the house." To Moreton Frewen, inviting him in May to visit, he added, "If you can stay the night we will be very glad and can put you up comfortably. The ghost has been walking lately but we cannot catch him. Perhaps when the real Frewen sleeps under his roof he may condescend to display himself to all of us."

Residents took the Brede ghost seriously both before and after the Crane residency. A girl who lived there in the 1960s believed that she once saw the impression of someone moving restlessly about on a bed there, although there was no one in the bedroom. A woman who had lived nearby for decades felt in the 1970s that there was still something eerie about the place, although by then the weathered gray hulk had been sumptuously restored and, surrounded by a velvety lawn, looked more stately than it ever had appeared in its ancient prime. In 1898 the drafty shell, with many of its rooms un-furnished and unoccupied, and unlit even by flickering candles, lent itself to nervous fears. Novelist A. E. W. Mason recalled sleeping in a room at one end of which were double doors which he innocently opened after dark and "found that if I had taken one step forward I should have stepped down about thirty feet into the chapel, this [bedroom] being the private pew or box of the owners of the house." Rushes on the floors instead of carpets—this for economy rather than authenticity—added to the medieval atmosphere, and in Mason's room bats flew about until he snuffed his candle, whereupon they settled down to share the room with him. He slept badly.

Mark Barr, met by Stephen at the Rye railway station with a wagonette drawn by bay horses named Hengist and Horsa (because they were "true Kentishmen"), was told that the ghostly visitations were said to occur chiefly in a circular room in a tower at the far end of the house, where creaking footsteps were heard at night. Also, it was said, the door of the room would open mysteriously, the latch lifted by invisible means. Barr bedded down in the room, listened to the moaning of the wind, and heard the door he had latched swing open. He lit his candle and closed the door. Again it swung open. This time he checked the lock more carefully, and running his finger over the worn wooden hasp on the door realized that over the years the notch had been rubbed nearly smooth. The slightest draft would cause it to slide loose. He slept soundly; securing a file and deepening the notch the next day laid that particular ghost for good, but he kept silent about his prosaic encounter with the occult. So did nineteen-year-old Edith Ritchie, Stephen's niece, who came to live with them in June 1899 and enjoyed cultivating the illusion of a ghostly presence at Brede, but knew better. "Outside my windows," she wrote in a memoir fifty-five years later, "was thick ivy in which white owls roosted, and their hoo-hoo-hoos were eerie if you didn't know where they came from. The room had three doors, leading to other rooms or halls. When I went up to dress for dinner, I would carefully close each door. A moment later I would look fearsomely over my left shoulder. Door number one would be open. Then, over my right shoulder, door number two open and, a little further to the right, door number three. I always turned slowly and always had the same spooky feeling. But the doors, I knew, were not really bewitched. They all had old slippery wooden latches which had to be pegged to stay shut. When I was lying in bed at night, I seemed to hear babies crying, or a coach-and-four would come trundling from a distance, the horses' hoofbeats pounding louder and louder over my head. I loved it, because it was the wind making the rafters creak and groan."

With the nostalgia of time and distance, Edith Ritchie Jones blurred over the tensions at Brede, which in any case had been kept from her when possible. Brede was an idyll: "I never heard money mentioned when I was there. I never saw an uninvited guest." As the Cranes lived into their second year at Brede the influx of Indians actually did subside and the weekend surfeit of guests did appear to be there because Stephen and Cora wanted them, Stephen after all the fun and games paying for it by writing doggedly in his cluttered room over the porch. Edith never saw the letters to Pinker which accompanied the potboiling pieces, pleading for "sure and quick money." Rather, she saw an impulsive and warmhearted pair, deeply in love with each other, sensitive, protective, Stephen with "gray eyes and tawny hair and mustache, both rather shaggy," and Cora with hair "pure gold" and "skin exquisite," radiating "great dignity and quiet charm" despite her stocky figure and her curious garb. "I haven't any more clothes than a rabbit," she would say, and affected at Brede "a kind of tunic and skirt, which she made herself. Some were made of cotton, some of wool, some of silk or velvet. She always wore sandals. She had brought home the original pair from Greece and had them copied by the cobbler in the village. She had a suit and blouses and shoes which she wore when she went to town, and a lovely black evening gown. But she certainly never spent money on herself. Stephen usually wore knickers at home and he always forgot to put on his garters. Cora said his stockings were accordion-pleated."

Some of Crane's intimates called him "Baron Brede." Delighted with the hundred-acre park which enclosed Brede, he would saddle a horse and take a morning canter "within the fence" as if he were not an interloper living on local credit. Cora often referred to him teasingly as "the Duke," and indeed he would dress formally for dinner like an English gentleman who was lord of his manor. Yet, wrote Ford, "when the fit took him, he would assume the dress and speech of an American plainsman and pace the sunk lanes of his demesne, a picturesque figure with his shock of hair, piercing eyes and rather weak mouth, his rough attire of cowboy shirt and breeches, with revolver swinging at his hip." Often, Ford thought, Crane's imaginative life left him remote from Brede. "I don't mean to say that he was homesick for a bench in Union Square. He didn't have to be; he was always there, surveying the world from that hard seat. He picked his way between dogs snarling over their bones in the rushes of the medieval hall, but he was thinking how to render the crash of dray horses' hooves and the rattle of the iron-bound wheels on the surface of Broadway where it crosses Fourteenth Street. Or he was lost in the Bowery. Or Havana. Or the Oranges."

While Crane played at being a country squire, he complained that Mark Twain, in London, was acting like a society clown. Yet he saw Clemens only once while both were in England, when they met at the Savage Club on the evening of July 3, 1899. "The wild, free son of nature," Crane carped, was now a stuffed shirt in "collars and a coat." Both had "gone English" in their separate ways, and it was more damaging to Crane, who had a career to nurture, and little time, than to Twain, who had said what he had to say and was coasting on his fame.

Writing *The O'Ruddy* while devoid of any inspiration but the fiscal one, Crane claimed difficulty recalling enough of Ireland for his needs, although local color hardly mattered, for the carefree O'Ruddy departs from his homeland in the first episode of the story. But Cora had promised Pinker some typescript and wanted the pounds which he could only deliver if he had more than promises. Extravagantly, Crane one morning in October announced a holiday. "Edith has never been to Ireland. Let's go to Ireland." They packed for London en route to Holyhead. That evening there was a party for them at the Frewen town house. The next morning, Edith recalled,

we went to the station to take the train to the boat for Ireland, but found that we had had an old timetable and that the train had gone. No matter. It was fun to have another day in London. We missed that train three days in succession. It sounds as if we were all morons. But we were just happy, carefree country bumpkins who had lost the habit of catching trains. And each day and evening was full of more parties—lunches, teas, dinners. Everyone wanted to entertain the Cranes. Finally we reached Ireland and went from Cork to Ballydehob to Skibbereen to Skull to Bantry, ending in Glengarriff, staying at little country inns. We rode in low-back cars or in little trains which Stephen said leaped from crag to crag, and we made friends with people all along the way. We were to have gone to Killarney, but again we got homesick for Brede and the dots.

More likely, Crane was short of cash. At Brede he finished his first two chapters of the novel and sent them to Pinker. Then he put *The O'Ruddy* aside to "return to short stuff," as Cora put it, "which will bring in money at once."

During the summer and fall of 1899, Henry James had nourished his avuncular relationship with Crane. James would bicycle over the seven miles from Rye for a visit, or invite the Cranes to Lamb House for tea and literary gossip and shared concern over the way the war in South Africa with the Boers was going. He was privately appalled by the irregularity of the Crane union and preferred seeing his young protégé alone, even when Stephen made a game of a visit. According to one story, Crane would rein up outside Lamb House on one of his immense coach horses and, if the Master was not alone, alternately shock and amuse the company with his Bowery role, after which James would explain, "My young compatriot of genius. . . ." To Mrs Humphry Ward, who was once presiding over the tea service as Stevie came and went, he apologized, "It's as if . . . oh, dear lady, it's as if you should find in a staid drawing-room on Beacon Hill or Washington Square or at an intimate reception at Washington a Cockney—oh, I admit of the greatest genius—but a Cockney still, costermonger from Whitechapel. And, oh heavens, received, surrounded and adulated . . . by, ah, the choicest, the loveliest, the most sympathetic and, ah, the most ornamental. . . ."

Cora had hardly moved into Brede Place when she sent a note to James announcing their arrival in the area, but he was about to leave for Italy. By the time he returned, the Cranes were fixtures in Brede, and in August James had come to the benefit garden party for the Brede church, where Stephen in straw hat and white flannels carried pots of plants to purchasers' carriages, and Cora (who had substantial experience in making use of discards) ran a rummage booth. Vernall, the English-Swiss cook at Brede, baked doughnuts on which the portly James doted, and a photograph survives of the bald and bearded Master munching one of them in the rectory garden. Receiving the snapshot from Cora, James wrote her, accurately, "I look as if I had swallowed a wasp, or a penny toy. And I tried to look so beautiful. . . ."

James had sent Cora fifty pounds to support the children of Frederic's irregular family, and knowing that the "young barbarians" were regularly about Brede, he offered to her the hope that they were at play "far from Crane's laboratory." He was sincerely interested in Crane's work although Ford's story that James had once sent over a sheaf of his manuscripts for Stephen to look over seems unlikely.*

---

* The story was that one afternoon after a night of poker, Crane led a party of unshaven friends to Rye, where they refreshed themselves at a tavern before visiting James. When someone there observed that Lamb House was not open

While their attitudes toward life and their concepts of literary impressionism were different, they respected each other's achievements, and "what he is going to be" was important to James. Characteristically, he presented the younger writer with a copy of his *In the Cage* with an elaborate inscription—in French. Lending it to a friend, Crane confided, "I got horribly tired half way through and just reeled along through the rest. You will like some of it a lot. But I do not think that this girl in the [telegrapher's] cage is exactly an underclass clerk in love with a 'man about town.' Women think more directly than he lets this girl think. But notice the writing in the fourth and fifth chapters when he has really got started."

Although James once complained to a visitor at Lamb House that he was outraged by house guests at Brede who regarded Cora "as a kind of superior servant who ought to be delighted to be up at all hours to do some eggs in a chafing dish and find a bottle of wine for them," he himself allegedly carted curious visiting ladies to Brede, unannounced, and Cora would improvise a lunch. James was different. According to Edith Ritchie's testimony, he felt like a part of the family—a sort of bachelor uncle. When he would visit, there would be impromptu entertainment. Cora would say, "Now, let's have a concert!" And Edith would pick up the puppies and sing, while the animals howled in accompaniment. Or they would go into the huge kitchen, with its open fire by which the servants gathered, and Cora would announce, "Stephen wants some music." With combs and tissue paper, and Stephen conducting with a toasting fork, the Brede orchestra would provide a raucous concert to amuse James.

For the monster house party at year's end, the Master was present only in spirit. It was not his kind of social event. As it was, the party took place only because Stephen was unable to escape the twin burdens of his deteriorating lungs and the writings he owed to London publishers. "I am getting serious about the Transvaal," Crane had written Pinker in mid-September. "See if you can work it up." Cora, in a panic, intervened with Pinker, telling him that Stephen's health was not up to the war in South Africa—and it was not. He would

---

to strangers (which he was sure the ruffians were), Crane assured him, "Oh, sire, I know that the duel is not practised in this country, but I am prepared to waive that for your benefit." James, he announced, had sent him some manuscripts for his opinion and he was on his way to return one of them.

ride out to the railway station seated astride one of the two Kentish horses pulling their all-purpose wagon, and appear to be thriving under country life; but chronic malaria, unadmitted tuberculosis, and his grinding writing regimen were wearing him down. *The Whilomville Stories* (as they were titled in book form) were frail but clever; the *Great Battles* sketches were competent but without flair; his Cuban war tales, completed in August as *Wounds in the Rain,* were keenly observed pieces but did not experiment beyond the creative limits of *The Red Badge;* the ironically realistic magazine stories were more limited as he struggled for material out of his experience. Once he even turned a dream about a fire at Brede (there had been two, one of them almost catastrophic) into a tale, "Manacled," after practicing crawling down a corridor, his hands bound, to see how long it would take. *The O'Ruddy,* despite all the pressures to complete it, languished, although in letters to Pinker, Cora remained necessarily optimistic, for the Cranes were mired in Pinker's debt for advances he could no longer secure from publishers. A hero of literature, Pinker risked his solvency on some of the great writers of his time, but finally had to write Stephen, "I confess you are becoming most alarming. You telegraphed on Friday for £20; Mrs Crane, on Monday, makes it £50; today comes your letter making it £150, and I very much fear your agent must be a millionaire if he is to satisfy your necessities a week hence, at this rate. Seriously, you pinch me rather tightly."

Ignoring all the danger signals, Crane determined to usher the old year out and welcome in the year 1900 in a fashion befitting the Baron of Brede. "We of Brede Place," he wrote author H. B. Marriott-Watson on November 15, "are giving a free play to the villagers at Christmas time in the school-house, and I have written some awful rubbish which our friends will on that night speak out to the parish. But to make the thing historic I have hit upon a plan of making the programmes choice by printing thereon a terrible list of authors of the comedy and to that end I have asked Henry James, Robert Barr, Joseph Conrad, A. E. W. Mason, H. G. Wells, Edwin Pugh, George Gissing, Rider Haggard and yourself to write a mere word—any word [such as] 'it,' 'they,' 'you,'—any word and thus identify themselves with this crime."

The work and preparations for the event were the equivalent in energy expenditure, perhaps, to the production of a novel, or at the least to a volume of short fiction. But Stephen was either banking on some miraculously materialized best-seller or on intimations of mortality he alone sensed would solve all his problems. Guests were asked to bring their own bedding, and Cora invited nearly forty of them, renting iron bedsteads from the local hospital and setting up dormitories which separated most married couples in the icy, unfurnished rooms. The limited indoor sanitary facilities, primitive as they were, were available only through the female quarters. "Consequently," H. G. Wells recalled, "the wintry countryside the next morning was dotted with wandering, melancholy, pre-occupied men-guests. Anyhow there were good open fires in the great fire-places. . . ."

On December 28 at 7:45 P.M., despite heavy rains, winter lightning, and muddy roads, the play was performed in the old Brede schoolhouse, with an audience of local folk and Crane's guests, the house party having begun the night before. Mason—an experienced actor—was the ghost as well as the stage manager, and the cast of characters was a parody of fiction by the collective authors. The play escaped the London critics, but the *Sussex Express* managed a review which identified the performers as "the Brede Place house party, assisted by a few friends," and noted that "Mr Stephen Crane paid all the expenses in producing the play." The *Manchester Guardian* reported that it was a "remarkable piece of literary patchwork" which had been allowed "to waste its sweetness on the Sussex air" rather than appear in print or on the West End stage, "so devoid of good plays. . . . The expense of scenery could hardly be an objection, for both acts passed in the same locality—an 'empty room in Brede place.' " Obviously the writer had read the names of "a string of our most popular novelists" on the program and not seen the script, which was public school foolery at best. The Brede ghost, in the year 1950, is shown to be still terrifying tourists; the songs which convulsed the audience (as with "Three Little Maids from Rye") were obvious adaptations of familiar favorites; and the characters (such as Peter Quint Prodmore Moreau—references to James's and Wells's fiction) were broad parodies of the collective authors' own work. At the close, a grand chorus and dance of ghost and tourists, accompanied on the piano by Mrs H. G. Wells, closed the performance to loud applause, and—noted the *Sussex Express*—the audience sang "For they are jolly good people," the crucial words being altered "in consideration of the ladies among those acting."

For the Cranes at Brede the "ghost" house party on the twenty-ninth was a last hurrah, with flaming plum puddings, roast turkey with stuffed chestnuts, and champagne on a menu as extraordinary as the setting. Great candles burned in sconces improvised for the occasion by the Brede blacksmith, and whole tree trunks were ablaze in the great open fireplaces. The guests danced into the morning, slept until noon, breakfasted on bacon and eggs, American sweet potatoes, and beer—and were then induced by Crane to try their hands at American-style poker, which none took seriously, chattering through his futile instruction. "In any decent saloon in America," he complained, giving up uphappily, "you'd be shot for talking like that at poker."

To Wells it was a "sulky" reaction. Crane "was profoundly weary and ill, if I had been wise enough to see it. . . . He was essentially the helpless artist; he wasn't master of his party; he wasn't master of his home; his life was altogether out of control. . . . Sensation and expression—and with him it had been well nigh perfect expression—was the supreme joy of his life and the justification of existence for him. And here he was, in a medley of impulsive disproportionate expenditure, being pursued by the worthy Pinker with enquiries of when he could 'deliver copy'. . . ."

Once most of the visitors had departed, Stephen collapsed with a lung hemorrhage, fainting against the shoulder of one of the remaining guests. The bit of blood was nothing, he said on opening his eyes; he didn't want anyone to "bother" about it. But Cora told Wells, who remembered the tuberculosis he had survived as a younger man and knew otherwise. It was not yet dawn, and a cold drizzle was falling, but Wells, taking a bicycle, pedaled through the winter night, on dark lanes he did not know, to fetch a doctor in Rye.

"The truth is that Cuba Libre just about liberated me from this base blue world," Crane had confided to a friend in September. "The clockwork is juggling badly." To another in November he was "just a dry twig on the edge of the bonfire." And after the attack he seemed to recover rapidly. On New Year's Eve at Brede, he lifted his glass in a toast to his friend Mark Barr: "Let us drink to the twentieth century—in spite of your objection, Mark." Barr had insisted that 1900 was the last year of the old century, not the first year of the new one. But Crane could not wait a year. He also had to write, even from bed, for the money situation was worse than desperate; yet he still had enough pride in his work to get out of bed and go with Cora to London on January 20 to retrieve from Pinker two *Great Battles* sketches forwarded the day before (and mostly written, as well as researched, by Kate Lyon) because he had decided that they weren't good enough.

To Cora, the grateful Kate expressed confidence that Stephen would recover. God, she added, would be good to Cora, who had been so good to others. And she apologized for not having the Battle of Solferino further along, but would "heave away at it like mad." Lippincott had asked for two additional pieces "in order to make a more presentable volume," and Kate needed to know whether Stephen was "well enough to go over what I write? Do you mean me to work it up in a *finished* state for the magazine?" Clearly Kate was ghostwriting for Crane, and in the next few months Cora—who typed the manuscripts anyway, and had some writing ability—would be touching up other pieces, and even completing some of them. But Crane was still up to writing his usual desperate letters, although much of the gloomy mail he received was kept from him by Cora. He begged Pinker to furnish one hundred pounds by February 12 and to wire ahead whether it were possible to do so, but ambiguously, "because my post-master is my grocer." (As were those of all the other merchants in the area, his bills to Brede Place were long overdue.) Pressing Crane to complete *The O'Ruddy,* Pinker received in return only the query as to whether it would be wise to abandon "my lucrative short story game for this long thing which doesn't pay (much) until the end." By then he was pressing ahead with further chapters of *The O'Ruddy,* which Pinker was still calling "the romance," since Crane, writing hastily under the pressure of financial panic and premonitions of mortality, had not worried yet about such trivialities as a title. By the end of February he was nearly forty thousand words into the novel, inventing picaresque adventures for his hero as he went along.

The novel—Crane's proposed gamble at a popular success—was originally conceived to buy him time and tranquility to produce a work of real literary art. He now realized that he would never have either. The final appeal to Pinker was on March 31. Cora was away. That weekend, while reaching down to pat his dogs during lunch, Stephen felt his mouth fill up with blood. Although he had forbidden summoning Cora, the housekeeper wired for her return, and Cora—who would settle for nothing less than the most eminent lung specialist—sent for a fashionable society physician recommended by her London friends. It made no difference that Dr J. T. Maclagen was useless, since Stephen's case was hopeless. Like Dr Skinner of Rye, whom Wells had fetched at the time of the house party, Maclagen was guardedly optimistic, announcing that the right lung was entirely unaffected. For the opinion, and the physician's trip, with a nurse, by train to Brede, Cora had to find fifty pounds. Off went a request to Pinker, noting that the fee was worth it since Maclagen was encouraging, and adding—dropping her caution—"If Mr Crane should die I have notes of end of novel so it could be finished & no one will lose. . . ."

Through April Stephen seemed to be pulling through the crisis, and Dr Skinner even pronounced the affliction to be "only superficial," which Cora knew could not be so, since on the twenty-fifth she kept from Stephen a lugubriously witty Wells letter. He'd bet "an even halo," he wrote, "that haemorrhages aren't the way you will take out of this terrestial Tumult. From any point of view it's a bloody way of dying. . . . And confound it! What business have you in the Valley? It isn't midday yet and Your Day's Work, handsomely started I admit, is still only practically started."

An advance arrived from Lippincott on *Great Battles of the World* as a result of Cora's writing Pinker that Stephen was up to completing it, and she began planning to take Stephen away to the seaside, although friends recommended a cure at Davos in the Swiss Alps or the German "Nordracht treatment" at a Black Forest clinic. But while Stephen languished, Cora extravagantly dissipated the money on restoration activity at Brede, shutting out of her mind the certainty that it would be lost to her in a matter of months, if not weeks. Some of Cora's erratic behavior at the end is suggested in the last tale Stephen worked on, and which she herself polished afterward for publication. In "The Squire's Madness" the squire is not sure whether it is he or his wife who is really ill: "Night and day his wife watched Linton. He would awaken in the night to find her face close to his own, her eyes burning with feverish anxiety." A London brain specialist finally tells him: *"It is your wife who is mad! Mad as a Hatter!"*

According to Ford Madox Ford, Henry James's suffering for the dying boy (he was only twenty-eight) was acute. James's novel *The Sacred Fount* may have derived some of its poignancy—it was being written during Crane's last months—from, as Leon Edel describes it, "the vision the novelist had of the way in which Crane was visibly dying while Cora thrived, seemingly unaware of the tragedy being lived under her roof. It was an old theme with James—the way in which men and women prey on one another." (In the novel a country-house party is a major event, and Mrs Brissenden, who has married a man much younger than herself, drains his youth while she regains her own. James, from Rye, had watched it happen, and the theme, noted long before in his notebooks, gained immediacy from his association with the Cranes, bringing the dormant idea closer to the writing stage.) James spoke to Ford of "my young compatriot of genius" who was "of the most charming sensitiveness . . . so truly gifted . . . so very lovable." James then "was forever considering devices for Crane's comfort. He telegraphed Wanamaker's [in New York] for a whole collection of [presumably tinned] New England delicacies from pumpkin pie to apple butter and sausage meat and clams and soft shell crabs and minced meat and . . . everything thinkable, so that the poor lad should know once more and finally those fierce joys. Then new perplexities devastated him. Perhaps the taste of those far-off eats might cause Stevie to be homesick and hasten his end." It was a typical Ford invention, since nothing could possibly have arrived from America in time to make a difference, but suggested James's real concern, and the likelihood of some pathetically futile Jamesian gestures in Crane's waning weeks.

At the end Cora insisted upon a useless and expensive expedition to Badenweiler in the Black Forest, and James, unable to see Stephen off at Dover because of the unexpected arrival of page proofs which, as always, demanded instant attention, sent Cora fifty pounds, begging her to "dedicate it to whatever service it might best render my stricken friend. It meagerly represents my tender benediction to him." Moreton Frewen, to whom Crane owed a year's rent, raised one hundred pounds, and settled some of Stephen's local debts through his harassed solicitor, Alfred Plant, in Gray's Inn, while Associated Press London correspondent Walter Goode cabled Andrew Carnegie, who sent fifty. Ill and without funds, Conrad agonized over missing Stephen at Brede, but spent twenty minutes with him at the Lord Warden Hotel near the Admiralty Pier while the channel steamer awaited a calmer sea. Cora had managed to get Stephen there not only with a doctor and two nurses, but also with his niece Helen, the Brede Place butler, and their dog, Sponge. His wasted face shocked Conrad, who attempted to put on, he wrote John Galsworthy, "jolly manners." Robert Barr, arriving on May 19, three days after Conrad, gave in to Stephen's plea that he finish *The O'Ruddy,* 65,000 words done, with the manuscript halted at chapter 25. "He was too ill for me to refuse," Barr wrote a friend. "I don't know what to do about the matter, for I could never work up someone else's ideas.* Even your vivid imagination could hardly conjecture anything more ghastly than the dying man, lying by an open window overlooking the English channel, relating in a sepulchral whisper the comic situations of his humorous hero so that I might take up the thread of his story." He would get better in the *Schwarzwald,* Barr assured Crane without conviction, and they would take some convalescent rambles together. Since Cora was nearby, Stephen said, faintly, "I'll look forward to that," but he winked as if to say, Barr wrote, "You damned humbug, you know I'll take no more rambles in this world." Then, with Cora apparently distracted momentarily, he added, "Robert, when you come to the hedge—that we must all go over—it isn't bad. You feel sleepy—and—you don't care. Just a little dreamy curiosity—which world you're really in—that's all."

Wells saw him the day before debarkation and remembered his friend

lying still and comfortably wrapped about before an open window and the calm and spacious sea. If you would figure him as I saw him, you

---

* Barr did complete the novel, which was published in 1903.

must think of him as a face of a type very typically American, long and spare, with very straight hair and straight features and long, quiet hands and hollow eyes, moving slowly, smiling and speaking slowly, with that deliberate New Jersey manner he had, and lapsing from speech again into a quiet contemplation of his ancient enemy. For it was the sea that had taken his strength, the same sea that now shone, level waters beyond level waters, with here and there a minute, shining ship, warm and tranquil beneath the tranquil evening sky. Yet I felt scarcely a suspicion then that this was a last meeting. One might have seen it all, perhaps. He was thin and gaunt and wasted, too weak for more than a remembered jest and a greeting and good wishes. It did not seem to me in any way credible that he would reach his refuge in the Black Forest only to die at the journey's end.

At horrendous expense Cora chartered a private carriage on the train to convey the entourage to Basel and then, in the waning days of May, to Badenweiler. Rallying there briefly, Crane finally titled the unfinished novel with his hero's name and whispered suggestions of incidents with which Robert Barr might conclude *The O'Ruddy.* Cora took down the nearly incoherent dictation in a notebook. In the first days of June, Stephen's fever rose and muddled his mind further. "He lives over everything in dreams and talks aloud constantly," Cora wrote Frewen. "It is too awful to hear him try to change places in the 'Open Boat.'"

At three in the morning of June 5—"the same sinister hour which carried away our friend Frederic nineteen months before," as Barr put it—with his dog, Sponge, still at his side, Crane died. Cora cabled Frewen (who had rushed an additional twenty-five pounds), and the once and future squire of Brede went to Lamb House with the news. "What a brutal needless extinction—what an unmitigated, unredeemed catastrophe!" James wrote Cora. "I think of him with such a sense of possibilities & powers! Not that one would have drawn out long these last cruel weeks——! But you have need of all your courage. I doubt not it will be all at your service. Shall you come back—for any time at all—to Brede Place? You will of course hate to—but it occurs to me you may have things to do there, or possessions to collect. What a strange, pathetic, memorable chapter his short—so troubled, yet also so peaceful—passage there!" At midnight the same day, Barr and several other friends sat in the darkness at Brede, contemplating Crane and Frederic. Crane had possessed, Barr felt, "something of the old-time recklessness which used to gather in the ancient literary taverns of London. I always fancied that Edgar Allan Poe revisited the earth as Stephen Crane, trying again, succeeding again, failing again, and dying ten years sooner than he did on the other occasion of his stay on earth." At Brede, he reported, "We tried to lure back the ghost of Frederic into that house of ghosts, and to our company, thinking that if reappearing were ever possible, so strenuous a man as Harold would somehow shoulder his way past the guards, but he made no sign. I wonder if the less insistent Stephen will suggest some ingenious method by which the two can pass the barrier. I can imagine Harold cursing on the other side, and welcoming the more subtle assistance of his finely fibred friend."

The doomed search for health left Cora a thousand pounds in debt. On additional borrowed money she took Stephen's body on the *Bremen,* via England, to New York for the funeral. Nearly a month later, in widow's weeds, she sailed back to England, taking lodgings at the end of July at 47 Gower Street in Bloomsbury. Leaving Cora only with Stephen's manuscripts (which she soon lost to his family, as she had no legal rights), vans removed the vestiges of the Cranes from Brede Place.

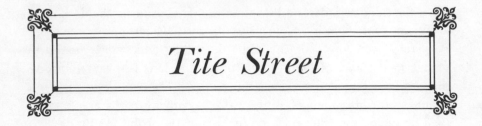

CHAPTER VI

Tite Street

Most of us are proud to be Americans. I am . . . and in spite of all the exasperating snubs we are made to suffer from ignorant [American] officials there are mighty few of us, I am glad to say —and you know—who would exchange his birthright for any number of official [foreign] distinctions, no matter how much easier things would thereby be made for those of us who live here. . . .

—Edwin Abbey to John Hay, January 1, 1899

WHEN James A. McNeill Whistler ended his self-exile in Venice in the early 1880s, following his bout with bankruptcy, he returned to his beloved Chelsea, and leased 13 Tite Street, "next door to myself," as he put it. It was as close as he could get to the White House, which he had built as house and studio before the Ruskin trial, and which he had lost when his court costs were beyond his means, despite his having won his libel action. (He had been awarded a farthing in damages.) By 1894 he had moved several times, exchanged a mistress for a wife, and was borrowing his old studio (now renumbered from 13 to 31) occasionally from its new tenant, John Singer Sargent.

At the turn of the old century, Tite Street, to artists what Harley Street was to physicians, seemed almost an American enclave. Oscar Wilde, who had dominated it in the early nineties, was gone by 1895, but at the lower end of the street, at 32, would live Romaine God-

dard Brooks, from Philadelphia by way of Capri, who would afterward interrupt her lesbian involvements and her portraiture in the
Whistler manner (which style she took as far as it could go) for a
stormy affair with Gabriele d'Annunzio. At 42, where the street
ended, and angled into truncated Dilke Street, which ran parallel to
the Embankment only a few steps to the south, would live Edwin
Austin Abbey, like Sargent a Royal Academician, and like his American neighbors also of Philadelphia parentage. Other American artists
lived nearby, such as Sir James Jebusa Shannon, who was considered
by some to rival Sargent as a portraitist. Only Philadelphia artist
Joseph Pennell lived remote from Chelsea, in a small house in Buckingham Street, below the Strand near Charing Cross.

Tite Street to the north, where it met the Queen's Road, was
dominated on Sargent's side by the hospital buildings of a small children's clinic;* beyond it, once his needs and income made it useful,
Sargent would acquire number 33, which adjoined 31, and have a
doorway built to connect the ground floors of both houses. There he
worked mornings at the rolltop desk along the dining room wall, entertained at lunch, and climbed the carpeted circular stairway to his
studio at two to await the first of his sitters. He had become the most
sought-after portraitist of his day, and in 1894, at thirty-eight, his
black beard beginning to be flecked with gray, he had been elected an
associate member by the Royal Academy. Sargent's pictures were
frankly portraits, unlike Whistler's "arrangements," which used a
person as focus for a design, but he often brushed onto his canvas
more about a personality than was ordinarily allowed in a fashionable painting. As a result the *New York Times* marveled at the
Academy's decision in "passing over painters of the orthodox academic routine to elect revolutionaries like John S. Sargent. . . . In
their present fit they might be quite capable of electing even J. M.
Whistler if they did not feel certain he would laugh at them."

Although Sargent had not even seen America until he was twenty,
in 1876, much of his early impetus as an artist would come from
across the Atlantic. Born in Florence because his mother—Mary
Newbold Singer of Philadelphia—preferred living in Italy or on the

---

* Replaced now, with its front on Royal Hospital (formerly Queen's) Road, by
the incongruous architecture of the Army Museum.

French Riviera on the substantial half-yearly remittances she extracted from her wealthy family, he was the son of a physician who
surrendered his profession and his purpose in life to raise a family of
leisured cosmopolites. Johnny Sargent would learn from the example
and never let a social-climbing wife—or any other kind of wife—
sever him from his purpose. Never having to worry about starving in
a Parisian garret, since he could sell his work, he set about unhur-
riedly learning how to paint. By 1883 he had developed a reputation
for portraiture, in one case because he had deliberately set out to do
a dramatic canvas, in the other because American diplomat Henry
White, soon to be moved to London, had a wealthy wife who wanted
to be painted by the up-and-coming young American whose work she
was beginning to notice and admire. The dramatic coup had been his
icily elegant and Whistlerian portrait in profile of Madame Judith
Gautreau, the Louisiana-born wife of a Parisian banker. The result
was a bold work which had become a scandal at the 1884 Salon,
attacked as "ugly" and "cadaverous." But after it, Sargent was known.
His portrait of Margaret Stuyvesant Rutherfurd White was elegant
and conventional. Charmed with it, she introduced him to visiting
Americans who would be potential subjects, and to an American
novelist resident in London who came to Paris to write occasional art
columns for English and American papers. Through Henry James,
Sargent would learn about London. And he would learn more from
Edwin Abbey, who painted and drew in the country but often borrowed studios in London—including Sargent's—until he had his own
town house on Tite Street. Abbey, Sargent, and James all enjoyed
rural life at Broadway—an ironic name to the three Yankees—the
Cotswolds village in the vale of Evesham where Abbey shared a
house with another artist, Frank Millet.

As much as Henry James could ever unbend, he did so with the
Abbeys, when the artist married a young woman from Vassar and
moved to Morgan Hill in Gloucestershire. James treasured the new-
laid eggs he brought back with him to London so much that he had
a special padded box made, to hold twenty-six eggs, which trans-
ported the precious commodity weekly even when he could not visit
in person; and his letters in acknowledgment were filled with elaborate and punctilious Jamesian courtesies. He treasured sharing con-

versation under their "ancestral beeches," and declared that their fresh breakfast eggs were "the brightest blessing of my sombre life." When the Abbeys had business in Boston which took them away for some months, James appealed on their return that until he could visit, "don't let your American gossip grow stale—or, above all, leak away."

Two years after Sargent, in 1896, Abbey at forty-three would become an Academician, and—perhaps even more significantly—an honorary M.A. at Yale—if, read the citation, he could "be present to receive it." Abbey's "genius as an illustrator, principally of Shakespeare and English songs and tales, is inseparable," it went on, "from the power which enables him in imagination to produce life in past times. . . . But this power would be inadequate were it not allied with cultivation of a high order and patient researches." With the art of illustration now nearly moribund, except in children's books, it is difficult to appreciate Abbey's ability to so evoke the past, but his contemporaries of a preelectronic age recognized it, and he became the first artist Yale had ever recognized by an honorary degree—this in days before degree inflation had produced a deluge of cheap doctorates. He journeyed to New Haven to acquire the precious sheepskin.

Election to the Royal Academy was highly unusual for an American, but not unheard of.* With the associateship came certain very English obligations, among them the custom that one make courtesy calls on elder Academicians. After a few such calls, Sargent reflected that it was curious, following years of detesting an artist's work, to find that he was a delightful fellow. It was an observation Whistler could never have made, but Sargent had not been frustrated and vilified at every step along the way. When he had left France at twenty-

---

* Of the five Americans who became Academicians before Sargent, George Boughton, a contemporary and friend of Whistler, was of English birth, as was the little-remembered Charles Robert Leslie, although his parents were American (barely—since he was born in 1794). John Singleton Copley was born in Boston when it was still part of the Massachusetts colony, and Benjamin West was born in Philadelphia when Pennsylvania was still British. Only the romantic landscape painter Washington Allston was American by both parentage and birth, if one can consider birth in South Carolina in 1779 as conferring American identity.

eight, he knew few people in England other than Henry James and a handful of American expatriate artists. What had kept him going, personally and professionally, until he had established himself, was his American contacts. Not only did he paint Americans residing or visiting abroad; he created a demand for his portraits that led Max Beerbohm to caricature a queue of elegant ladies waiting their turns in front of 31 Tite Street while Sargent looked out his front window to survey the press of business.

Contributing to the pressures on his time was the beginning of a new professional direction. The trustees of the new Boston Public Library had decided to decorate the building with murals and statuary. Augustus St Gaudens, despite his name an American living in Paris, had been entrusted with the statuary. Sargent, Abbey, and their French friend Puvis de Chavannes were offered the mural commissions, and the American artists went to Boston to survey the undertaking. It would be a long, difficult project, Sargent had realized, but the challenge fired him, and he agreed to decorate the corridor which met the principal staircase. It was eighty-four feet long, twenty-three feet wide, and twenty-six feet from floor to vaulted ceiling. He was to have a free hand and thirty thousand dollars to do the corridor and an additional wall. It would take him twenty-six years and drain his imaginative and intellectual resources.

There was too much work to do in too little time, he realized, realistically, at the start, and he suggested bringing in Whistler to undertake a large panel. Since Charles McKim, the architect (with Stanford White), and Samuel Abbott, a library trustee, were planning to be in Paris, Whistler offered to meet with them and Sargent for dinner at Foyot's to discuss the project. "Now one of three things will happen," Sargent had warned the others, "and I don't know which. Either he will be as silent as the grave, or outrageously vituperative, or the most charming dinner companion you've ever met." Whistler turned out to be in good humor and, flattered by the deference paid him, was anxious to find out what location he would be offered. The dinner was so great a success that the men never settled anything; but a second dinner was arranged, after which, when the table was cleared, Whistler enthusiastically drew on the white tablecloth a tentative idea for a great peacock fifteen feet high. His companions watched, and departed literally and figuratively in the greatest good spirits. Then the personnel at Foyot's put the cloth in the wash, and nothing further came of the mural. When Whistler returned to London he became occupied with other and easier things, chief among them the acquisition of American gold for work long completed but only then becoming marketable.

Americans, Whistler observed happily, were determined "to pour California into my lap," and not long afterward he was prophesying to London printmaker Tom Way that "now I fancy I see fortune looming on the horizon!—and I might really be rich! Who knows!" Chief reason was a magnificently mustached and fortyish bachelor from Detroit, Charles L. Freer, a manufacturer of railroad cars who had made sufficient millions to be able to leave much of his day-to-day work to others and indulge a passion for travel and for Oriental art. Things Oriental led eventually to Whistler, especially after Freer read of the prestigious sale to the government of France of the *Mother* portrait, which had languished since the early 1870s. Soon Freer was attempting to acquire every etching and lithograph Whistler had done, and had arranged to buy at least one copy of every new etching Whistler turned out, at an average (for the new ones) of four guineas each. And as a careful businessman Freer made sure that he had had the import duty on each exempted by a consular invoice upon which Whistler attested that he was an American artist "residing temporarily abroad."

Before long Freer also purchased a *Harmony in Blue and Gold* and three pastels and watercolors—for the staggering price then of thirteen thousand guineas. It was worth taking the trouble to complete Freer's consular invoices. For Whistler they meant freedom from care for the first time in his life, and as such prospects mounted, his wife, Trixie, suggested a house in Paris. Away from the press of increasing London publicity, perhaps he could return to serious work.

Whistler's stay in his elegant little house and garden at 110 Rue de Bac would be busy but brief, and crowded with American visitors. For Trixie they meant more than money in the Whistler purse. In Paris her husband visited his French artistic and literary friends without her, although in London she had long been part of Chelsea artistic life. Upper Bohemia in Paris was mostly a man's world, and

Trixie, besides, knew little French and had no interest in learning more than was necessary, even employing English servants. While work on their house went on, she absorbed herself in its decoration. It was intended to be the residence for the rest of their lives. Yet for Christmas, Whistler told Stéphane Mallarmé, "we return to the fogs." He had been invited to show a work at the opening exhibition of the Grafton Galleries, and had borrowed his own *Arrangement in Black, No. 5* from Lady Meux. A London newspaper featured a drawing of the top-hatted gentlemen and gowned ladies entering the "Large Room" for the private view while off to one side was an inset drawing of two ladies and another top-hatted gentleman carefully scrutinizing a full-length portrait of a woman. The caption was "Looking at the Whistler." It was an index of how far he had come in a once-hostile London.

While he visited his Parisian literary and artistic acquaintances, most of his own visitors—but for very close French friends like Helleu, Gandara, Montesquiou, and Mallarmé—were Englishmen and Americans. The younger generation of painters, and the older generation of collectors, sought him out on his Sundays; but almost never Frenchmen, who traditionally cultivated massive disinterest in foreigners, however prestigious. The garden at 110 Rue de Bac was a mecca for Americans. Henry James went to tea with the Whistlers "in their queer little garden-house . . . where the only furniture is the paint on the walls and the smile on the lady's broad face." At least one gathering there—early in 1894—would put American literature in its debt. William Dean Howells had come to visit his son, who was at the École des Beaux Arts, and in Whistler's garden he seemed untouched by the gaiety. Sensing his brooding but not realizing the reason—that Howells had just been summoned home from Paris, beautiful in the spring, by news that his father was dying—young Jonathan Sturges came over to commiserate, and Howells, having been affected by Europe in a way he could hardly express, put his hand on his compatriot's shoulder and said, "Oh, you are young, you are young—be glad of it: be glad of it and *live*. Live all you can: it's a mistake not to. It doesn't so much matter what you do—but live. This place makes it all come over me. I see it now. I haven't done so —and now I'm old. It's too late. It has gone past me—I've lost it. You have time. You are young. Live!"

Sturges—crippled but stoical about his problems—first kept the incident to himself; then when deeply unhappy over his own unlived life, he emotionally confided in his close friend Henry James. James recorded it in his notebook, adding, "I amplify and improve a bit, but that was the tone. It touches me—I can see him—I can hear him. Immediately . . . it suggests a little situation." Eventually the drama of the aging American in Paris, called home to reluctant duty and forgoing a life he might have preferred, became *The Ambassadors* (1903).

Although the artist-figure in the novel, the American sculptor Gloriani, had appeared earlier in James's *Roderick Hudson,* and was based largely on William Wetmore Story, in the new novel, born in the Rue du Bac, he takes on aspects of Whistler. Lambert Strether, who turns to Little Bilham in Gloriani's garden and passionately urges him not to miss life, sees in Gloriani's own artistic, worldly, even sexual success the "terrible life" he had quietly envied. The "great Gloriani" is "at home on Sunday afternoons," and there "fewer bores were to be met than elsewhere." He has a "queer old garden" in Paris in Whistler's district, the Faubourg St Germain, attached to "an old noble house" and "of decoration delicate and rare." As James later wrote his publisher, he "could easily focus the setting" in the "charming old garden attached to the house of a friend." In *The Ambassadors* the garden lives.

In the middle nineties, there were only two men in England associated with the creative arts whom one might call "Master." Both were Americans—James and Whistler. James's attitude toward Whistler's work by then had shifted. His compatriot seemed no longer a poseur who used a sense of theater to conceal the shallowness of his talents: he was a great artist. Although James had derided Whistler for nearly twenty years, on viewing a portrait of Sir Henry Irving as Philip of Spain (in Tennyson's play) he now stood apart from his conveniently forgotten earlier self,

in wonder reintensified at the attitude of a stupid generation toward an art and a taste so rare. Wonder is perhaps, after all, not the word to use, for how *should* a stupid generation . . . with a faculty trained to coarser notions, recognize in Mr. Whistler's work one of the finest of all distillations of the artistic intelligence? To turn from his picture to the rest of the show—which, of course, I admit, is not a collection of masterpieces—is to drop from the world of distinction, of perception, of beauty and mystery and perpetuity, into—well, a very ordinary place. And yet the effect of Whistler at his best is exactly to give to the place he hangs in—or perhaps I should say to the person he hangs for—something of the sense, of the illusion, of a great museum.

James said nothing of the painter who so carefully balanced forms and tones, and who was so careful to give abstract titles to his land-scapes and portraits. He had accepted Whistler on Jamesian grounds —as bringing artistic intelligence to characterization.

James had little difficulty in reconciling himself to Edwin Abbey's work, as Abbey had always been a close friend. When his *Holy Grail* frieze for the Boston Library had been completed in 1894, Abbey had exhibited it at his own expense in London before it was shipped to America, with a preface to the exhibition brochure vetted by Henry James. Work on the huge painting, each half ninety feet of life-sized figures based on studies in chalk, charcoal, and oils over four years, and involving scaffolding, stretchers, costumes, armor, casts, models, and other paraphernalia, and requiring research trips abroad, had practically ended Abbey's income from black-and-white illustration, and brought him only $7,000 (£1,400), out of which he had to pay his expenses and live his life. When the Abbeys sailed for New York and Boston with the first half of the frieze, they were £1,600 in debt. Less than a year later they were in the black, thanks to sales and com-missions the *Grail* exhibition had inspired. When Abbey was paid for the second half on its completion in 1901, he was already a wealthy man.

On returning from America, the Abbeys went to visit the Whis-tlers in Paris. Whistler was one of the supreme etchers, and Abbey, who had done drawings to illustrate Goldsmith's *Deserted Village,* perhaps the triumph of his black-and-white art, was exploring the idea of making copperplates of them through a Parisian firm. He was also interested in seeing Puvis de Chavannes, whose decorations for the library project were nearly completed. It would be their last visit to Whistler on the other side of the Channel.

In December 1894 Whistler locked the studio at the Rue Notre Dame des Champs and the house and garden off the Rue du Bac, and returned with Trixie to London. Willie Whistler, the painter's brother, had long before left the United States to set up a surgical practice on Wimpole Street. He confirmed Jimmy's worst fears. Trixie was suffering from incurable stomach cancer. She was not told, but the two years of her agony, spent partly in Lyme Regis, where Trixie was miserable in her loneliness, and in hotel rooms in London —Whistler kept insisting that she would be better and that they would return soon to Paris—were confused ones for him. He worked at his art when he could, and when Trixie did not need him he would visit old friends such as Sargent or the Pennells for comfort, his grumpy disposition exacerbated by his new problems. "We paid for the privilege," Elizabeth Pennell wrote, "by the loss of some of our friends who, for one reason or another, cultivated a wholesome fear of Whistler. Men who had been most constant in dropping in, dropped in no longer. . . . More than one would have run miles to escape the chance encounter, trembling with apprehension when in a desperate visit they seemed to court it, and often the several doors opening into our little hall served as important a part in preventing a meeting between Whistler and the enemy as the doors in the old-fashioned farce played in the husband and wife game of hide and seek."

Whistler thought again about consulting specialists in New York, but "the vast far-offness" of America dissuaded him. Instead, to "please" Trixie he rented space at 8 Fitzroy Street, after first trying to work at Walter Sickert's, then at Sargent's, studio. It was one flight up a ramshackle glass-roofed passage at the back of the house, and large enough for any conceivable need, but he was too busy shifting living quarters and tending Trixie to spend many hours there.

From each new address there was evidence of Whistler's continuing efforts to work amid disorganization and chaos. Sometimes so exhausted that he would fall asleep over the lithographic stone, he was still too restless to go to bed, finally dozing by midmorning, then going out on artistic business. He realized that there was no hope, although he and Trixie pretended otherwise to each other. G. P. Jacomb-Hood, once his neighbor in Tite Street, remembered "the misery and pathos of his sitting beside his wife's sofa, holding her hand while she bravely tried to cheer him with banter and gossip." To J. J. Cowan, whose portrait, *The Grey Man,* had been untouched for fifteen months, Whistler almost confessed the worst on April 4, writing from the hotel that Trixie's illness had made his life "one long anxiety and terror," and that for nearly two years he had hidden the fact: his "one thought" had been her care. "And so we have wandered, . . . going from town to country, and from doctor to doctor. Living in hotels, and leaving behind us the beautiful place you know so well in Paris—and the studio in which we both passed so many hours!" The "pilgrimage for health" had canceled all else, and Whistler could not speak in the first person singular about it— "all sense of time and ambition was lost—we were ill—and the sun had gone out of our sky!" Yet he still clutched at the impossible, "At last however there is hope . . . [that] all will be well. . . ."

Rather than hope, there was only another pilgrimage, this time to still-rural Hampstead Heath, where Whistler had rented a cottage from Canon Barnett, a local clergyman. He was able to joke about the hilly surroundings that it was "like living on the top of a landscape," but to Walter Sickert he wrote, again eschewing the first person singular, "We are very, very bad." Soon he was seen wearing one black and one brown shoe, the ultimate citadel—his fastidiousness—breaking down. On May 10, 1896, Sydney Pawling encountered him running across the heath, a wild expression on his face. Alarmed, Pawling stopped Whistler, who cried out, "Don't speak! Don't speak! It is terrible." And he raced on. Trixie had died.

Burial was at Chiswick Cemetery. The Sunday afternoon following the funeral, Whistler appeared at Buckingham Street to ask Elizabeth Pennell to go with him to the National Gallery, where he showed her the canvases Trixie loved, standing through a long silence before Tintoretto's *Milky Way*, which had been her favorite. There was none of the usual talk about pictures, and Trixie's name was never mentioned.

To his "dear kind friends" the Abbeys, who had sent a letter of condolence, Whistler wrote brokenly of how much he was touched, and added of his loss, "You have seen us in our home and can understand that, alone, I am but a forlorn reminder of the brightness that charmed you and all who came to us!" Trixie had wanted him to make a drawing or lithograph of Abbey, he recalled, and he would still do it, he vowed. It would never even be begun, and the Abbeys never would remind him of it.

188

The Pennells saw more and more of Whistler as he withdrew into the shell of his loneliness. He had asked his wife's young sister Rosalind Birnie Philip, whom he had made his ward and heir, to reopen the Rue du Bac flat and maintain it for him, but he went instead to William Heinemann's flat in Whitehall Court, where he remained for much of the next two years. Only when the publisher was gone on business did he move temporarily elsewhere, going to Garland's Hotel, or on drawing expeditions, or across the Channel to the Rue du Bac. The much younger Heinemann was good medicine for Whistler. His fashionable flat overlooked the Embankment; his dinner parties overflowed with celebrities, gossip, and good wine; and the Pennells lived nearby. Whistler would often arrive at Buckingham Street without even warning of his coming, sometimes arriving with an unsent wire in his pocket.

Although intermittently ill, Whistler traveled across the Channel on his own business at any opportunity, painter Anthony Ludovici once finding him in Paris "laid up with an influenza cold, wrapped in flannel, inhaling eucalyptus from a steaming jug." Commuting between Paris and London, he kept the Rue Notre Dame des Champs studio, but most of his work was being done in Fitzroy Street, where he painted portraits of rich American men and poor Cockney girls, and harangued visitors about the brief American war with Spain, then in progress. It was "a wonderful and beautiful war," he said. "The Spanish were gentlemen." There was reciprocity, too, he thought, describing to whoever would listen his version of the aftermath of a sea battle when a Spanish admiral was fished up out of his sinking vessel and brought to the deck of an American warship looking like —like—and Whistler paused to probe for a suitable description— "well, for all the world like a clod of cotton-wool pulled out of an ink bottle, and was received by everyone on board with all the pomp and ceremony due to his position, as if he had just stepped on board to inspect his own ship." His pockets were full of newspaper clippings about the battles, which he dragged out at London dinner parties and analyzed as "I, a West Point man."

Heinemann's loyalties to his difficult friend prompted him to suggest that Whistler permit an authorized biography. First Heinemann suggested W. E. Henley as author, and then Charles Whibley, but Whistler objected to both, finally agreeing to Joseph Pennell early in 1900. The Pennells then began recording the Master's table talk openly, probing him for details of his life on each visit to Buckingham Street. But he was much more talkative about the Boer War, and about foreign intervention in China.

"Here are these people, thousands of years older in civilization than we," he said at a dinner party in July 1900, "with a religion thousands of years older than ours, and our missionaries go out there and tell them who God is! It is simply preposterous, you know, that for what Europe and America consider a question of honor, one blue pot should be risked." A guest at the table, Captain Charles M. Hunter—a West Pointer—brought Whistler up to date on the Academy, including the information that the cadets now played intercollegiate football. Whistler was disgusted. "They should hold themselves apart and not allow the other colleges and universities to dispute with them for a ball kicked round the field—it is beneath the dignity of officers of the United States."

Not forgetting his years defending his art against what he considered to be British blindness and stupidity, and the admiration in which he basked on each visit to Holland, he was fervently pro-Boer, and applauded each dispatch which made the Empire seem blundering and foolish. General Buller's incompetence amused Whistler, and he was delighted by Buller's announcement that he had made the enemy respect his rear. When he was told of the general's boast that on one occasion he had retreated without losing a man, a flag, or a cannon, he added, "Yes, or a minute." He enjoyed repeating the rejoinder to a man exhorting an audience that the cream of the British army had gone to South Africa—"whipped cream." The Boers were defying the English: it was enough to win his praise. Yet the jests were fewer than ever before. As Joseph Pennell put it, Whistler was "suddenly grown old and thin and shrunken and sad."

He was often too ill in his rooms at Garland's Hotel to visit the Fitzroy Street studio, and made a Mediterranean voyage to look for sunshine and new settings. It was not a success. Early in 1901, while Queen Victoria's passing was being mourned throughout the Empire, Whistler was shivering in Corsica. But he survived well enough to work through the summer at Fitzroy Street; determined now to spend the rest of his working days in London, he made plans to give up his expensive and redundant quarters in Paris.

In October, Whistler returned to France, closing the studio, the stairs of which he could no longer climb, and selling the house in which his ground-floor quarters were too damp for him to live. In London he moved to Tallant's Hotel, in North Audley Street, where he was again ill in the now-chronic way which made friends realize his deterioration. He could still joke about it: "In this room, sir," the landlady had said as recommendation, "Lord Ralph Kerr died." "I told her," Whistler said, "what I wanted was a room to live in!"

Although keeping his historically distinguished room, sometimes he stayed with his mother-in-law and Rosalind in the house acquired at 36 Tite Street. In December he went to Bath with them to escape the London winter, and when spring came he returned to the Thames, leasing 72 Cheyne Walk from architect C. R. Ashbee, and having "the ladies" move in with him. The house stood on the site of a riverfront fish shop which Whistler had once lithographed, and had a ground-floor studio at the back. Two flights up was the drawing room, where (in glass cases) Whistler displayed his still-beloved blue-and-white china. Except that it returned him to his favorite part of London, the choice was a curious one. Almost all the windows opening on the river were so small and high that little of the Thames could be seen, and the bedrooms were three flights up, a struggle.

He hardly went out anymore, but prospective patrons eager to visit him came by, one of them a New York gambler, Richard A. Canfield, whom Whistler began painting in April 1902. Like Freer, Canfield had no shortage of cash, and sent Whistler an advance of five hundred pounds on the portrait, adding to it in April a further check "for pictures not completed," which was returned by Whistler with a note, once Canfield had begun sitting: "You have seen that the work is all absorbing—and indeed I myself find the difficulties in the brush quite sufficient in themselves, without allowing them to become complicated with anything distantly resembling responsibility of any kind!"

Sometimes he would leave his new flat and, leaning heavily on his cane, now a sturdy stick to replace the stylishly thin wand he had once brandished, walk slowly, almost ghostlike, along his old haunts on Tite Street and Cheyne Walk (which imperceptibly changed into Queen's Road), passing homes in which he once had lived, or visited when Rossetti and Wilde were in their heyday, or looked out of to paint as the fog curled around the bridges and banks and boats on the Thames. Often he would spend all of his Sunday at Abbey's house at the foot of Tite Street. Arriving in the morning, he would follow Abbey to the studio after lunch, seat himself in a comfortable chair to watch Abbey work, and fall asleep. The arrival of such guests for tea as Henry James would awaken him, and refreshed, he would add to the chatter some flashes of his vintage repartee, and linger on until dinner, which he was easily persuaded to share. Then he would call for his cane and trudge back to 72 Cheyne Walk, although one evening Mark Twain stopped by, and the two aging wits sat talking in Abbey's studio until dawn.

In May, Whistler began a portrait of the long-faced, bearded Freer, lunched with the visiting Rodin—who offended him by not asking to see his pictures—and found a new cause for distress. Ashbee had begun building a new house next door to the one he had leased to Whistler. It was "knock, knock, knock all day long." He became nervous and irritable, and when his new studio became impossible, he referred the matter to his patient solicitor, William Webb. The doctor warned him that the agitation was too much for his heart, and Freer, who dined with him at Cheyne Walk on June 17, suggested relaxation in Holland. But at the Hôtel des Indes in The Hague he became critically ill. Freer called a local doctor, and Whistler survived, but during the scare he made a new will. When he left Holland feebly in mid-September, it was to return to 72 Cheyne Walk, and to the continued sounds of hammering and sawing. The stairs to the bedroom at the top of the house were too much for him, and he was moved, along with his Empire bed, to a small ground-floor room adjoining the studio and looking out onto the street, where the clatter of traffic added to the noises of carpenters and bricklayers.

Whistler now realized that he would never leave London again. He went out little, but received visitors to the studio, with the watchful Miss Birnie Philip, Mrs Whibley, or Mrs Birnie Philip sitting apart but present to caution visitors when Whistler seemed overtired. It created an additional sense of strain and near-imprisonment, both in Whistler and in his visitors, for there were subjects which could not be discussed before the ladies. Still his friends came, although Whistler spent much of the day sleeping in an easy chair after sleepless nights, and often dozed, too, at the dinner table, or amid conversation with his guests. When his head drooped they dutifully waited, then withdrew.

The studio and bedroom were littered in the fashion of a sickroom. The Pennells recalled that once Whistler insisted to them that even in his most difficult days he had been the dandy: "If I had only an old rag to cover me I would wear it with such neatness and propriety and the utmost distinction!" Now he shuffled about forlornly in a substitute for the dressing gown he no longer owned. His clothes hung on him, and because he was cold he often wore an old brown furlined overcoat, now gone shabby, over a white nightshirt, black trousers, and a short black coat, a far cry from his former dapper dress; while his hair, once primped and curled, was now thin and flat.

His spirits usually rose when he had cause for indignation, but Elizabeth Pennell found him looking "frightful" and agitated over the news that Count Montesquiou had sold his portrait by Whistler for 75,000 francs. "I painted it for a mere nothing . . . and it was arranged between gentlemen." Worse still, it was bought by another friend, Richard Canfield, who eventually gambled his money on thirty-four Whistlers. The Master had hoped that the *Montesquiou,* at least, would go eventually to the Louvre, but there was nothing he could say publicly. Then he found a new source for rancor. In America, Elbert Hubbard's *Roycroft Press* had published a pamphlet, "A Little Journey to the Home of Whistler." "Really," he told the Pennells, "with this book I can be amused—I have to laugh. I don't know how many people have taken my name in print, and, you know, usually I am furious. But the intimate tone of this is something quite new. What would my dear Mummy—don't you know, as you see her with her folded hands at the Luxembourg—have said to this story of my father's courtship? And our stay in Russia—our arrival in London—why, the account of my mother and me coming to Chelsea and finding lodgings makes you almost see us—wanderers—bundles at the end of long sticks over our shoulders—arriving footsore and weary at the hour of sunset. Amazing!" On January 2, 1903, he responded sarcastically to Hubbard, "I congratulate you. The book contains several things I never knew before." Other recognition was more acceptable. Late in the month, D. S. MacColl came as an emissary from Glasgow University to inquire whether Whistler would accept an honorary doctorate if one were offered. He agreed, and the official invitation came in March, but Whistler had to accept the degree in absentia. The farthest he now traveled was a drive in Heinemann's auto along the Embankment, heavily swathed in blankets, and even then the eyes which once sparkled at the sight of the Thames usually closed in sleep after ten minutes.

Through the autumn, Whistler puttered about on good days, examining the accumulations from his Paris studio, and when his strength permitted that winter, he went through his canvases and prints, sorting and destroying—preparing for the end, whether or not he consciously acknowledged it. John Lavery arrived one day to discover a stack of large canvases against a wall, their backs turned, and the fireplace full of ashes. Realizing that Lavery knew what had gone into the fire, Whistler remarked, "To destroy is to exist, you know." While Lavery was still there Whistler had a "bad turn," and Lavery helped him to his bed, Whistler struggling for breath. When he was able to sit up again he said, understanding the situation, "I don't like this at all, Lavery, not at all." They both understood.

While Whistler clearly was failing further, Freer and Canfield vied with each other for whatever of the Master's work appeared available. As Whistler was unwilling to sell flawed or unfinished works, and was too weak to do much more painting, it meant finding owners willing to part with their pictures, and Canfield, who had already pried away the *Montesquiou,* went to see Graham Robertson, offering him £1,000 for his *Rosa Corder.* Robertson refused, and Canfield doubled his offer. This time Robertson agreed. Canfield, telling the story to the Pennells, sputtered, "Damned fool! I would have offered five thousand. . . ." On the first of March, Whistler telegraphed to the Pennells to come to see the

Rosa Corder for the last time. He had cleaned it, and it was to be shipped to New York the next day, along with lesser work. Freer, who arrived again from Detroit in the spring, quickly added to his Whistlers, buying from the Cheyne Walk stock nine lithographs, nine watercolors, two pastels, one oil, seven sketches in ink, and two in pencil, for a total of £1,363 7s., the artist again signing the ironic customs declaration which lowered the import duty:

I, James McNeill Whistler, do hereby certify that I am a Citizen of the United States of America, and by profession an artist; that my place of permanent residence in the United States is ——; and that I departed from the United States of America on or about the —— day of ——, that I have not given up, and that it is not my intention to give up, my residence in the United States, and that it is my purpose to return ultimately to the United States. . . .

The duty on imported works of art, although reduced when created by "resident" Americans, was a Tite Street obsession. "What am I, that I should raise my little peep?" Edwin Abbey had written to his friend John Hay, then secretary of state, not long before. "One of a small class of expatriated American citizens," he answered his own question,

who is taxed by his grateful country for sending his "things" home, instead of disposing of them here. I have sometimes wondered how it can be legal to discriminate against artists in this way. The members of other learned professions are let off—and I wonder whether the amount we are taxed, however troublesome and vexatious it is to us, really benefits those men very greatly who prompted Congress to impose a duty upon our work. If ever there was a learned profession ours is one, and one it takes a long time to learn, too—I doubt if anyone ever got it "good and learned"—and, as a rule, the reason we stay here is because we are students, and not, as I have heard, because it is cheap (which I have yet to discover). In the instructions to the Consul in Rome, the U.S. Treasurer spoke of us as having our "places of business" abroad. I wonder if he knew what he meant by that. I suppose he would call the Vatican, or the South Kensington Museum, a "place of business."

Most of us are proud to be Americans. I am . . . and in spite of all the exasperating snubs we are made to suffer from ignorant officials there are mighty few of us, I am glad to say—and you know—who would exchange his birthright for any number of official distinctions, no matter how much easier things would thereby be made for those of us who live here; and I do not think we should be fined for this sentiment, as though we were a disgrace to our country, either. As you know, many things would be made easier for us, as students—or even members of society—if we were subjects of foreign sovereigns. All sort of privileges, for instance, are accorded the *pensionnaires* of the foreign academies at Rome which our boys of the American School find very difficult of attainment —and simply because they have no official position. . . . I'm afraid that most of the knowledge of art students at the disposal of our Consuls and even Ministers is gathered from a perusal of *Trilby.*

In 1908 Abbey was still campaigning for a reform his nation was reluctant to provide, for as long as art was classified as a luxury there was little outcry to rescind a tax on it, for whatever reason. To Myron Pierce, the secretary of the American Free Art League, a lobbying group, he reiterated his concerns that his country was not interested in "an atmosphere of art" which was "the breath of life to the artist," and was leaving the choice of what art works would enter the country to Parisian dealers who would send what was salable. The lack of a climate for art had kept Abbey in London as it had drawn other painters and writers across the Atlantic, away from even the cultural centers of the burgeoning nation. Sargent had, for the most part, solved the problem by the late nineties. He would paint Americans on his trips to America. Six sittings would do it, and he would pocket anywhere from five to ten thousand dollars for a finished canvas.* His portraits seldom crossed the ocean.

So busy that he was forced to turn down more commissions than he accepted, Sargent constantly raised his price to discourage sitters, but the higher fee only increased his cachet. He acquired a large rubber stamp with the letters DAMN to vent his feelings on unwanted mail as he sat at his high rolltop desk. Prospective subjects worried about how to behave as they sat for the great man, and one went to Henry James for advice. To Mrs Mahlon Sands, one of the most elegant Americans resident in London, and a talented artist herself, he advocated "self-surrender to the artist"—leaving Sargent

* His minimum fee at the turn of the century was 1,000 guineas, then about $5,200.

alone and asking no questions, trusting him in "his variations, his mysteries and circumgyrations and idiosyncrasies." The sitter was involved in what was nearly a religious experience, James suggested. "You are outside of it altogether. . . . It's *his* affair—yours is only to be as difficult for him [to paint] as possible; and the more difficult you are, the more the artist . . . will be condemned to worry over you, repainting, revolutionizing, till he, in a rage of ambition and admiration, arrives at the thing that satisfies him and that enshrines and perpetuates you."

There was less and less of Whistler in Sargent's portraiture as he painted a swath through London society. He was still evoking character as astutely as before, but Whistler's economy of detail and setting was unappealing to Sargent's moneyed sitters, who wanted to be planted firmly in their comfortable backgrounds. Besides, as Jacques-Émile Blanche, one of Sargent's painter friends, put it, "Covering a surface with forms and lines in a definite pattern was beyond Sargent's powers; he invoked the aid of the dressmaker and the florist and filled in holes with the help of pieces of furniture; satin and velvet flowed in cascades, cushions bulged like Zeppelins on sofas, azaleas moved from vases to urns, and arum lilies added a white note to a park-like background." Whistler would have been content with the white note, but his old Tite Street studio was now a different kind of workshop. Yet he might have been proud to claim as his own the masterly portrait of Asher Wertheimer (1898), who owned a gallery on New Bond Street, in which the black-coated art dealer, brandishing his cigar, looms from the blackness, exuding success and power, and a panache rare in Sargent's men. Sargent enjoyed visiting the family mansion on Connaught Place, where he was a warm friend and fees were not discussed, and through 1905 painted the whole Wertheimer family. Nine of the twelve portraits were left by the dealer to the Tate Gallery. Henry Adams, who saw the canvas at Tite Street before it was exhibited, observed with his usual anti-Semitic sneer, "Sargent has just completed another Jew, Wertheimer, a worse crucifixion than history tells of." Through the blinders of his bias, the sweep and the verve of Sargent's conception had escaped him.

Sensing that there was no chance to lure Sargent, now stout and florid with prosperity, Edward VII, as his coronation loomed, selected the scholarly Abbey to do the official canvas of the event. There was no diplomatic way that he could refuse the honor—and obligation—and *Punch* noted that it was appropriate, given the setting for the ceremony, that its representation would be by a painter named Abbey. Some French correspondent, it added, would very likely record that the task "was entrusted to one of the clergé du Cathédral, M. l'Abbê de Westminster." Recording the scene on a fifteen-by-nine-foot canvas to be crowded with dozens if not hundreds of people was, for a muralist, a problem in compression, and the artist sat in the Abbey before, during, and after the coronation to get the setting right. When, late in 1902, he had sittings with the principals, one of them, the future George V—then Prince of Wales —surprised Abbey by questioning him about Sargent's income. The prince assumed that one of the portraitist's closest friends and neighbors would know the answer to a question apparently much discussed in London. Abbey confessed that he didn't know. "Do you suppose it's ten thousand pounds?" asked the prince.

"More likely twenty thousand," said Abbey.

"My God!" said the heir to the greatest empire in the world; "I wish I had twenty thousand pounds a year."

By the middle of 1903 Whistler no longer came to visit in Tite Street. Recurrent pneumonia, coupled with heart disease, made it even more difficult for him to shuffle about, even on the ground-floor level of the house. Elizabeth Pennell called on July 1, and the maid let her in, but communicated Miss Birnie Philip's warning that the visit should be brief, for Whistler was tired. "He was in bed, distinctly worse, with a curious vague look in his eyes, all the life gone out of them. He said nothing, and seemed almost in a stupor, though he must have been listening, for every now and then he interrupted to ask, 'What's that?' " Critic Theodore Duret came from Paris, and found Whistler only able to stare at him dumbly. During a second visit Whistler struggled again to talk, showed him some of the etchings of recent years which had been lying about, and appeared glad to have his friend recall the old days. But speech came with difficulty. Duret was overcome with emotion and left, trying to blink his eyes clear.

On Friday, July 17, Charles Freer went off to Cheyne Walk to take Whistler for a drive, as he had done the day before, when Whistler had seemed better, in the midst of a new rally. By the time Freer had arrived, at half past three, Whistler, who had taken a sudden turn for the worse after his lunch, was dead at sixty-nine.

A few years earlier, when one of his long-time adversaries died, Whistler had lamented that he hardly had a close enemy left in London. The truth of the paradox had been demonstrated first at Chelsea Old Church and then at the graveyard at Chiswick where he had been buried. Police were at hand to restrain the crowd, but there was no crowd. The small squat-steepled church by the Thames where Whistler had dutifully taken his mother a generation earlier had been less than half full, and few followed, by cab and carriage, to the graveside, where a clergyman mumbled rapidly through the service. Barely a dozen old friends had remained, and with them several women—including the two sisters of his late wife and an elderly lady who kept in the background and was suspected to be his loyal but cast-off model and mistress of thirty-six years before, Jo Hiffernan, the *White Girl* of his famous early canvas. With her was a tall man who was not her child but Whistler's, "an infidelity to Jo," as he had once put it.

There were only two wreaths, one a gilded laurel creation that Whistler would have deplored, and a single primrose for each official mourner to drop into the grave after the coffin was lowered. Among the pallbearers had been Abbey, Sargent, and Pennell, and it was Pennell who directed the great Whistler memorial exhibition in London in 1905, beginning almost immediately after the obsequies to flush out paintings, etchings, drawings, and prints from Germany, France, and Austria as well as England and Scotland. He supervised the hanging, the invitation list, the formal ceremony opened by Rodin, the visit of the King and Queen. Alexandra fell to his charge, and because she was deaf, her questions were so loud that they could be heard throughout the galleries. "And what are these?" the Queen asked, looking at the little drawings on wood made by Whistler with Trixie's assistance, but never engraved. Pennell explained elaborately, with the pride of personal ownership of the rarities. "And what do you propose to do with them?" she continued, with what Pennell thought was an obvious interest in their acquisition.

"Keep them, ma'am," he retorted, while hearts in the hushed gallery skipped a beat. Saying nothing, Alexandra went on.

"You have kept the blocks but you have lost a knighthood," he was told afterward. Court etiquette, someone said, required him to respond, "They are yours, ma'am!" A Whistler missionary so zealous that he was rapped by *Daily Chronicle* editor W. J. Fisher, for whom he wrote a weekly column, "You really must contrive to keep Whistler out of your notices a little more," Pennell was unlikely to give up any Whistleriana, even to the Queen.

He had become the crankiest of critics. He pushed his causes relentlessly, and unsparingly castigated those contemporaries he disliked. Although he had praised Abbey earlier for treating illustration as a branch of art, and even prefaced a catalogue of an exhibition of Abbey's pastels at the Fine Art Society in 1895,* in the new century he seemed to view his fellow Philadelphian as an apostate from the kind of art Pennell felt that Abbey should be doing. "What you say about Abbey," Fisher had to warn him after a *Daily Chronicle* column, "—whether right or wrong—is certainly in bad taste." In another case the editor warned that Pennell's comments were "quite needlessly sarcastic," and urged him, "Do try to be sympathetic where a dead man is concerned—or one who will be dead when the notice is printed."

Pennell even strayed from art to write about the Gordon-Bennett automobile race, always promoting the new and the innovative, as could be seen in the excitement his pen-and-ink art

---

* Pennell wrote of the forty-eight pastels, which included scenes from such plays as *She Stoops to Conquer* and *The Rivals,* not only of Abbey's "perfect command of material," but of "the perfect grace, the exquisite refinement, which he throws around every subject he touches. Simple as are the means he uses, and direct as is the treatment, the result is substantial, solid and real. . . . In every one of these pictures there is the most perfect sense of movement, the most perfect feeling that the next moment the trees will sway or the clouds will pass, and what is shadow will be sunshine, and where the light sparkles will be quiet shade. . . . What other painter is there who makes one feel that plays are real? When did Sir Anthony Absolute and Sir Lucius O'Trigger swagger so pompously? And when upon the stage was David so humble or Bob Acres so fine? . . . There is no parade of these things. There they are. And yet when you come to look at them, they are put down with a touch, but that is right. How can one write about works that are altogether beautiful?"

could give to architecture, industry, and engineering—such as the Panama Canal drawings he would do as the ambitious American project got under way. As for the automobile, Fisher cautioned him, "What I want least of all is to adopt the attitude that the road is made for the motor, and that riders and drivers and all kinds of ignorant pedestrians must shift for themselves. Of course I know you hold that view privately, but it will be quite useless your attempting to get it into the 'Chronicle.' I simply will not have it. I am anxious to do nothing to discourage motoring, and I do not at all object to this road race, although it seems to me a rather futile proceeding. So if you favour me with anything more on the subject you must be studiously moderate, and you must bear in mind that the motor is not master of our roads. Otherwise, I am afraid you will have to direct your contributions to another channel." Even at that, Fisher was more flexible than his successor. When Fisher retired in 1904, Pennell was quickly sacked, and afterward given only occasional critical assignments.

That the anglophilic Abbey was actually proposed for a knighthood would have infuriated Pennell, had he known it. The genial and scholarly Abbey, growing stocky with age, and depending more and more on his rimless glasses; owning a country house and a town house, and devotedly playing cricket; trimming his mustache carefully and parting his hair rigidly down the middle, and dressing in soberly vested suits, was the opposite to the Yankee Pennell. (So was Sargent, who some people thought resembled General Kitchener.) The slender Pennell, whose whitening beard and mustache were ragged, and who affected the large cravats of the prosperous Left Bank artist, loved his view of London from his studio, from Charing Cross Bridge to St Paul's; but he and Elizabeth were unyieldingly American, even to naming their cat "William Penn"— and when Pennell was slated for jury duty he rushed to his solicitor, George Radford, to demand that, as an American, he be removed from the panel. Impossible, said Radford, who had patiently borne much from the litigious Pennell; he had lived in England (by then) for twenty-seven years, and after ten any resident was a potential juryman.

That Americans were ineligible for knighthood (without giving up their citizenship) was lost on the King, who proposed to his prime minister, Sir Henry Campbell-Bannerman, that Abbey and Sargent (both R.A.'s, he observed) be knighted, one for painting the coronation picture, the other as "the most distinguished portrait painter in England." A feeler went to each, and each declined. Sargent wrote to Sir Henry that he deeply appreciated being considered for "the high honor to which you refer," but that he held "it is one to which I have no right to aspire as I am not one of His Majesty's Subjects but an American citizen."

Abbey found himself knighted in the press in any case. Like Whistler, he was first the subject of another of Elbert Hubbard's wildly fallacious *Little Journeys* pamphlets, which among other inventions endowed the childless artist and his wife Gertrude with "a goodly brood of little Abbeys." Then J. Walter McSpadden, in *Famous Painters of America,* borrowed much of his misinformation from Hubbard and added, "From a printer's 'devil' . . . to a knighthood from the King is surely a long step." It was one which Abbey never took.

Without relinquishing his English resident status, Abbey was turning more and more toward America and things American. The Boston Library murals had given him great cachet, just as his appointment as official coronation artist had added to his R.A. laurels. On a visit to Philadelphia to receive an honorary doctorate from the University of Pennsylvania, he was visited by Joseph Huston, the architect of the new Pennsylvania state capitol building in Harrisburg, and urged to do murals for the rotunda of its dome. It was Abbey's native state, and again he found a commission difficult to refuse. A celebrity now in the United States, he visited his old friend John Hay and was taken to the White House to meet the President, Theodore Roosevelt. Once Lincoln's private secretary, Hay had achieved the nation's highest appointive offices and represented the cream of American intellectual life. Even the presidency was, if only by the accident of an assassin's pistol, in the hands of a man who loved literature and enjoyed the company of writers, although he was deaf to most music and blind to most art. But the arbiters of taste in America, as Abbey realized, still largely lived in the philistine world of the late President William McKinley.

The next year it would be Sargent who would stop at the White House on a trip to the States, and who would visit with Hay. After an obligatory stay with art patroness Mrs Jack Gardner at Fenway Court, where she had set up a studio for him, he, too, was the guest of Theodore Roosevelt, to paint the presidential portrait. (His willingness to do it was even the subject of a congratulatory editorial in the *New York Times*.)

The White House was a dull place for a painter. Sargent was left to himself, and filled the time by doing small landscapes of the grounds, and keeping out of the way of the small Roosevelt children and their friends. After lunch the President posed, on a stair landing, grasping the glass-topped newel post. It was not his idea of a proper setting, but Sargent had rejected all the familiar rooms with their colorful names because the light was wrong and there was nothing presidential to pose against. Grasping the post lent a sense of vigor, of muscularity, he thought, to Roosevelt's stance. Sargent took advantage of it, under pressure because the President had difficulty holding still, and kept up a commentary with his retinue, who determinedly conducted the business of the Executive Office while Sargent searched for subtle character nuances. After five sessions he declared himself finished, although he was not very proud of his work. He was determined to have no more of presidential portraiture.

At McKim's urging, Sargent also painted Hay, in his house on H Street, and then went on to Philadelphia to acquire his own honorary doctorate, returning to Washington to paint one of the two other men who received doctorates with him at the University of Pennsylvania, Roosevelt's close friend General Leonard Wood, whose fencing sessions with the advocate of the vigorous life had been curtailed by Sargent's work on the President. (The other doctoral recipient was a Princeton professor, Woodrow Wilson.)

Before leaving Washington, Sargent stopped by to see Henry Adams, a veteran of so many years in London. Adams thought he saw vast changes in his old friend. "Sargent is stodgy!" he reported in a letter. ". . . I can understand how an American catches English manners; and how they do catch English minds! Especially how they do keep such in these days when the English mind is no longer good form even in England. The generation of Harry James and John

Sargent is already as fossil as the buffalo." What Henry Adams had failed to understand was that his friend, now that he had painted Roosevelt and Hay, was indirectly asking whether Adams wanted his own portrait done before Sargent, who was tiring of that trade, gave it up altogether. The dialogue, evasive on one side and obscure on the other, went nowhere. The painter went off to Boston to see McKim and Mrs Jack, and then returned to his London routine.

The portrait of Hay would be a milestone, his final dignity. He was personally closer to Sargent's neighbor Abbey, but Ned Abbey practiced a different art. Hay would soon be ailing and, in his last illness, finally go for a futile "cure" to Bad Nauheim in 1905. From there he wrote to Abbey realistically, "Getting sick and dying is not nearly so serious a matter as it is to lose sight and touch of one's friends in the process." In London in June for a few days, the secretary of state and former minister to England declined all invitations except one to lunch with the Abbeys at Tite Street. After lunch he asked if he could see what work was in progress in the studio, and Abbey offered to have him carried up the stairs. Hay refused, making his way slowly and in pain and losing himself briefly in the Harrisburg decorations, the drawings for the Shakespeare tragedies (Abbey had already done 132 drawings for the comedies), and a nearly finished ten-foot canvas, *Columbus in the New World.* Abbey would never see him again.

Back again in London, Abbey worked furiously on the Harrisburg murals, and began work on panels for the American church in Paris, somehow squeezing in a week at Morgan Hall to play cricket with his friends as well as time at Tyneside and other industrial locales to research settings for the capitol decorations. There were to be four large circular panels, representing Law, Art, Science, and Religion. Each was to have a nine-foot central figure and an inscription. For Law he chose a statement by Alexander Hamilton: "Justice is the end of Government." His statement on religion came from Latimer, who wrote that a monk's cowl did not make one religious, but rather "Justice, Righteousness and Well-doing." For a scientific quotation he went, improbably, to an inscription on the Egyptian temple of Isis: "I am what is, what hath been, what shall be—My veil hath been disclosed by none. The fruit which I have brought forth is this—

the Sun is born." Searching for a motto for Art he went to Henry
James, who replied, typically,

You must positively (for the locality) have an English thing, and a
very good and weighty, and if possible (though not imperatively?)
prose thing, in spite of the fact that there is nothing the *greater* English
writers have delivered themselves upon so little as Art. Look into Ruskin
and he's all about Nature—splendidly often, but *loathing* Art. And I
have been hunting Emerson this evening—with the consequent conviction that he hadn't a notion of what it is. Browning had, and there may
be something in him, but he is in general fearfully unquotable, and was
always speaking in some particular dramatic sense. I was haunted by the
memory of something in Shakespeare, but find it's only the scrap out of
Winter's Tale (Perdita):

> . . . this is an art
> Which doth mend nature—change it rather;
> But the art itself is nature.

I think that would be excellent, almost, for any reference to the Art your
depicted labours represent; but not for your figure and circle (besides
being too short). You want something large and majestic, and not too
philosophic . . . I doubt if there *be* any at all grand English *definition*
—there is only perhaps some sufficiently ample *image.* Your creature
trampled upon—I don't know what he could better be than a small
simulacrum of ——.

Here is, after all, a small thing out of Emerson's *Essays*—but I am
omitting half a sentence that spoils it. "Art is the need to create; but in
its essence immense and universal, it is impatient of working with lame
or tied hands. Nothing less than the creation of men and nature is its
end. . . ." Should you think of it you must make the image in her hand,
not a model of the Parthenon, but of a small and exquisite human
(male) figure, and as form she ought to be "trampling" on something
that symbolises the Void and the Vague—or *standing* on *all* plastic
material! (a ball of putty!) But give me a little more time, as I say.

Eventually Abbey located a motto himself, in his own library at
Morgan Hall, a statement by Plotinus that began with the premise
that Art "deals with things forever incapable of definition. . . ."

Mural work created needs for more space. When the end of his
lease for his country house at Fairford loomed, rather than renew

it he began looking for larger and more remote quarters, often going out in his Daimler with Henry James to examine homes advertised in *Country Life*. Abbey enjoyed strenuous work and strenuous leisure. "There are no holidays in my trade," he said. "It is always in the back of one's head, no matter what one is doing." (The artistic effect was always in the back of his mind, as when he visited Trinity College, Cambridge, for chapel service and observed of the singing of the undergraduates that "the effect of the whole thing would be enhanced if they washed their surplices oftener.") James loved automobile travel but never felt he could afford such luxury himself. After several expeditions in which they saw much of the countryside but no suitable houses, he recommended that the best solution for the Abbeys was "just to keep on quietly with Morgan Hall, Chelsea Lodge, the motor—*and* Henry James."

Overwork by then was beginning to tell on Abbey, who felt sufficiently "dambad" to consult his physician, Sir William Osler, and go to bed. Osler and James both agreed that Abbey needed to put all work aside, James advising, as the Abbeys made plans to spend the summer of 1906 at the seaside and in the Tyrol:

. . . Ned's indisposition, of which I heard something . . . interests me not less, and I hope with all my heart *that,* too, is exorcised. . . . It is too long a stretch of work—of work at high pressure. *Slow down,* put on the brakes, stop at every station, and visit the refreshment room. That is all you want—more buns and ginger-beer and *Tit-Bits* (at the newsstand), and less mere steaming ahead. I do hope this system is *already* showing good results. I didn't write, as I was moved to . . . because I have long since learned that the cloud of enquiring letters in cases of Modern Illness add a new terror to the state alike of Patient and Nurse. . . . Keep it up—I mean the keeping of it *down* (the fever of creation and the storm and stress of the studio). Above all, don't worry—everything arranges itself. I pat Edwin very affectionately and healingly and smoothingly on the back and dream of the day when I may see you again.

Just after Whistler's death, Romaine Goddard Brooks, of the Philadelphia Goddards, had moved into No. 32 Tite Street, opposite Sargent's house, having purchased her freedom from homosexual English writer John Ellingham Brooks in Capri for an annuity of three hundred pounds a year. (Earlier in Rome a fey young English archaeologist had confided to her that he had recognized his own orientation after falling in love with the marble head of a Greek boy he had unearthed in an excavation, and she confessed to having loved the photograph of a dead nun she had found in her convent school.) Twenty-nine, wealthy, with a model's face and figure, and bisexual, although leaning toward lesbianism, she had tired of her brief marriage of convenience and wanted to practice portraiture in the place where it seemed to be done best. Brooks was superfluous.

She had learned about artistic London from Whistler's patron, Charles Freer, in Paris. Freer had taken her to dinner and then to a music hall, but was aware that he had established no rapport with the elegant but severe young expatriate. Perplexed at her boredom but not discouraged, he told her tales of Whistler and Chelsea, and invited her to leave with him for England, where he would take her on "a sentimental trip up the Thames," after which they would go to America. Her response was to ask to be driven back to her hotel.

She then went to England on her own. Money was no problem—she had inherited what remained of the Goddard fortune in Philadelphia from her mad, spendthrift mother two years earlier—and the Tite Street house was decorated with antique wainscoting and filled with Jacobean furniture. A tall, oaken easel was moved in, and a supply of paints and brushes, and servants were hired. But the Romaine Brooks who occupied the house was soon unrecognizable as the slender young woman who had taken the lease. She had cut off her long hair and now dressed in male sporting and leisure attire she had purchased—to find her size—in a London shop for boys. Denizens of Tite Street may not have been sure what manner of man or woman lived there unless the servants talked.

One of them, who otherwise might have, did not last long. Romaine had imported him from Italy. Giovanni, her "boy-of-all-work," was the son of her gardener, and wore, at her insistence, a *marinaio*'s garb of dark blue blouse and trousers with red sash and knotted scarf. But he longed to be a proper English butler, and acquired clothes which seemed appropriate but which made the short, swarthy adolescent look like a caricature of his ideal. Romaine said nothing until another servant reported that Giovanni had been observed in his room kissing a photograph and crying out, *"La mia signora! La mia signora!"* It proved to be a stolen portrait of his mistress, who quickly found a place for him in a small Italian restaurant.

In Whistler's milieu in part because she wanted to paint like him, and to view the external world through his lens, she hired models and quietly painted in her version of his manner, writing in a memoir that she "wondered at the magic subtlety of his tones but thought his 'symphonies' lacked corresponding subtlety of expression." The early results were frustrating. One canvas was "still another melancholy self-expression: a young man with head bowed over a pink tie, and evidently in the last throes of dejection." But it was accepted for an exhibition, and she persevered.

What she learned from the Whistler manner was to paint her figures against a subdued light, flattening them out, and to use tones natural to the fog-shrouded Chelsea Embankment. Instead of the brilliant primary colors of the Mediterranean, blacks, whites, and grays now dominated her palette, and one striking canvas she produced was a mannish figure in black riding habit and gray gloves looming over gray-green Chelsea rooftops and a ribbon of river and of Battersea beyond. A black hat shaded the face above the bridge of the nose, and only a narrow border of white cuffs and white shirtfront and open collar above a forceful, almost spectral, face lit the picture. It was the painter's icy self-portrait.

Painting in the severe but evocative Whistler style, she had no use for Sargent, and no interest in his lush mannerisms. She never bothered to meet him. It is possible that the shy Sargent never knew who his neighbor across the street was. But she became close to Beardsley's one time friend Charles Conder, who painted delicate designs and was killing himself with absinthe, and to "Bosie" Douglas, who was trying to salvage a writing reputation from his liaison with Oscar Wilde. The women in her life in London, if any, are unknown. A sensitive portrait she titled *Maggie,* of a girl in pigtails and a red hat, is that of a young English girl she considered adopting. Probably John Brooks would have had to participate in the legalities, a consideration which made the move impossible.

Whistler had once gone to St Ives, on the Cornish coast, to paint, and a colony of artists persisted there. Late in 1904, Romaine took a small studio at St Ives, looking out over the opalescent sea, where she experimented in painting with a pervasive gray. When she came back to London, she saw nothing further for her there, personally or artistically. The back rooms of her house were constantly invaded by the sounds of doleful hymn singing from a chapel just beyond her small garden plot, while Tite Street resounded with the crying of sick children brought to the children's hospital which took up a part of the opposite side. The gloom oppressed her. Besides, she decided, to attract notice for her work she would have to take her acquired artistic signature of black, white, and gray to a setting in which it would be striking, and where she could live a less inhibited life. She emptied No. 32 Tite Street of its painting paraphernalia and moved to Paris.*

Another American lady remained in London to paint, the daughter of Henry James's great friend Mary Sands, who had entertained the Prince of Wales, Gladstone, and the Rothschilds at her great house in Portland Place and had been painted by Sargent. Ethel Sands, unlike her mother, was not a celebrated beauty. Her prominent teeth and a long face gave her a horsy look, but she painted with impeccable refinement. The elegant parties she gave at her Chelsea studio at 15 The Vale (and her country house at Newnington, near Oxford) left no room for doubt that it was her American dollars rather than her artist's income which made it possible for her to surround herself with beautiful people and beautiful things.

The great love of her life was Nan (nicknamed "Man") Hudson, another American expatriate painter, whom she had met in Paris in 1894 when she was twenty. The relationship was more emotional than sexual, but they remained together until Nan's death nearly sixty years later. Too young to become part of the Tite Street group, from which her mother's sudden death at forty-two, in 1896, separated her, she and Nan became involved with the Fitzroy Street set, working at first under the wing of Whistler's former protégé Walter Sickert, and gradually associating with the Blooms-

---

* There she lived in her upper-class lesbian Bohemia (but for a passionate heterosexual interlude in 1910–11 with flamboyant Italian hero Gabriele d'Annunzio) until 1970, when she died at ninety-six.

bury artists. In 1912 Ottoline Morrell would suggest that Lytton Strachey marry Miss Sands and thus acquire a hostess. Given Strachey's sexual predilections it would have been only a convenient domestic arrangement, but he was repelled by her "appreciative shiny teeth" and would have preferred marrying her house.

As the Edwardian decade lengthened, Sargent grew increasingly weary of the pressure of portraiture, which began to show in the unevenness of his results and his impatience with the routine. Society painting had meant so many compromises with his artistic aspirations that, however brilliant the effect promised to be, he was no longer interested in famous faces atop modish couture. Sometimes, still, the subject and the result pleased him, as when in 1905 Ena Wertheimer arrived in a sweeping cloak and plumed hat—like a ship in full sail, thought Sargent, who began a portrait to which he would give the title *A Vele Gonfie.* Visiting from America, veteran artist William Chase saw it after the plumed hat was painted in and exclaimed, "Wonderful, my dear fellow. Marvelous! You couldn't do it better! You mustn't touch it!"

"I'm going to scrape it out in the morning," said Sargent, sounding like Whistler.

On another visit to Tite Street, Chase was shown a large, unfinished portrait of the lushly beautiful Countess of Warwick with her son. "I've simply got to finish that damn thing," he complained. "The boy keeps getting older and the woman keeps getting younger." And when another visitor to the studio poked about among unsold canvases and asked if Sargent would sell any of them, he growled, "I need them around to console me for the rotten stuff I am doing."

Once an adventure, crowding Tite Street and the surrounding streets, even narrow Paradise Walk and Swan Walk, with waiting carriages, and now with belching motorcars, "Show Sunday" had become to Sargent a disagreeable and outmoded tradition. Each artist felt obligated then to exhibit the work he had selected to send to the Royal Academy. If there were portraits among the canvases destined for Burlington House, the subjects and their families and friends came to call. Lady Randolph Churchill looked forward to it and Henry James was certain to be there although, he claimed, "I loathe the general practice." It was a day for insincere praise and undisguised backbiting, as critics, subjects, friends, and enemies vied for the appropriate things to say.

Not only was the event harrowing for Sargent, despite his immense reputation, he found (as his biographer Charles Merrill Mount has noted) that the succession of elegant ladies and noble gentlemen who pressed him for portraits no longer interested him. He did not need their fees, and he resented the time they took from his work on murals. "Collectively they had not the intellectual energy to motivate a fly. When he took brush in hand it did not move with all the old vigor." As he wrote in 1907 to one lady for whom he had already done other family portraits, he had been "working at my Boston Library [murals] all winter and refused all portraits for a year past, but there are arrears to accomplish. . . ." He refused one appeal for what he was now calling a "paw-treet" with "Ask me to paint your gates, your fences, your barns, which I should gladly do, but NOT THE HUMAN FACE."

He had always loved travel, and now would spend half the year away—if not in the States, in Italy, Greece, Spain, or even Egypt, under the winter sun. Offered even larger sums than ever to do people in oils, he preferred landscapes and watercolors and did not care if they were salable or not.* It was a matter of national significance. Max Beerbohm wrote in the *Saturday Review* that "Mr. Sargent, who has excelled in depicting the restlessness of great ladies on priceless sofas, is said to have decided that he can do it no more. There is on view at this moment, as an earnest of his resolve, a portrait by him of a naked hermit in a desert . . ., undisturbed even by the urban complexity and velocity of Sargentine technique."

Involved in his own work, he did not keep up with the new generation of artists, and was unwilling to lend his support to Roger Fry's Post-Impressionist Exhibition at the Grafton Galleries late in 1910. And to evade the grind of doing multiple sittings for large portraits he had adopted a new stratagem. Rather than refuse each portrait commission, he suggested (in cases where he liked the people or felt it was important to offer an alternative) that he make a charcoal drawing. In 1908 he did only seven portraits in oils and in 1909 only three.

---

* After his death a sale of 237 pictures at Christie's brought £170,000.

His reluctance only fired those who wanted what might be the last Sargent portrait. In Philadelphia, friends of Dr J. William White, who wanted to present a likeness of him to the medical school of the University of Pennsylvania, pleaded that they had gotten up a subscription in order for Sargent to paint his eminent old friend. He gave in, writing White that his face haunted the artist's sleepless nights, "invoking the savage grin in the name of friendship to hurl me back to the damned abyss of portraiture, out of which it has taken me two years to scramble." Early in 1909, when the question of length remained unsettled, and White was about to sail for London, Sargent cabled, "Prefer death to three-quarter length."

The picture was not a success. White, who had become sun-burned on shipboard, was to sit in his crimson doctoral robes. The result startled Henry James, who had gone to Tite Street to see the result, which Sargent rationalized would protect him from further portrait applications. "It will suit my purpose better to let people think that this is my present style than to make a plea for extenuating circumstances."

Abbey, too, had resisted doing more of what had made him famous, conserving his energies for major mural work, not only the Harrisburg project but another for a building in his native city. Publisher Edward Bok wanted a design for the new Curtis Building in Philadelphia. With his panels for the collar of the capitol dome already in place, and other work for the structure well along, Abbey agreed to show Bok what might be done. In 1908 Bok crossed the Atlantic and agreed on a single canvas, fifty feet by thirteen feet, *The Grove of Academe,* based on a design done years before on a small wooden panel, and a price of fifty thousand dollars. Early in 1909, to make studies for the commission, Abbey visited Greece, coming back to begin work on his "Plato picture" and envying "the beautiful things" Sargent, who had been in Corfu, had done there. Abbey's neoclassic turn after years of pen-and-ink work had satisfied him more than it did the critics, and after a new book praised his old work at the expense of the new, he wrote to a friend, "I shall stick to what I set out to do, in spite of fashion. I *must* see how my way is coming out. . . . I see miles farther than I can do, and if

I ever learn how to refine what I have laboriously learned and un-learned I shall be content. I shall have to be, I suppose. We usually know how we should have played the ball that got us out—after the event." He went back to his huge historical and allegorical studies for Harrisburg, one thirty-five feet square, and another—for the ceiling of the dome—a twenty-four-foot circle. Then he took time out to play a game of cricket against an eleven of musicians; and he put some of his American dollars into a new automobile. "The idea of your new noiseless Daimler," Henry James wrote Mrs Abbey, "solicits more powerfully than I can say, and do—oh, *do!*—take me [on] two or three such interesting spins as all your country makes possible! . . . Pardon my greedy frankness; it isn't that I love ——— and ——— less, but that I love you and Daimler (with Ned squeezed in between us) more!"

On May 6, 1910, Edward VII died. While Abbey had painted him in his regal glory, messengers were hurriedly dispatched to Tite Street to ask Sargent to do for the dead king what he would not do in life. He went immediately to Windsor to sit at the bier and do a charcoal portrait. "Edward in death," writes C. M. Mount of the drawing, "was hardly more than his mother's long nose and some whiskers." Sargent did his best and was quietly ushered out.

It was then the turn of Joseph Pennell, who was, since Abbey's withdrawal, the foremost active pen-and-ink illustrator active in England. As Elizabeth told the story, from the day of the King's death until after the funeral on May 26, "Our front door was besieged by newspaper, messenger and telegraph boys. The post-man came heavy-laden. The *Daily Chronicle,* the *Illustrated London News, The Times* clamoured for drawings, and the journalist in him, long quiescent, awoke as of old. He would not have sought the work, he had done with this sort of illustration, but when it fell to him uninvited, he plunged into it with his accustomed go and vigour." His journalistic daring resulted in a photographic ac-curacy where cameras were forbidden. "Only I could have done what I did," he boasted of his scoops. To draw the lying-in-state for the *Daily Chronicle* (for fifty pounds) he got into Westminster Hall, where no artists were allowed, by posing as a workman, and made his drawing beforehand. Then, when the press was admitted, he added the attendant figures to his already finished setting and rushed it off to the newspaper while other artists were still struggling. For the funeral procession for the *Illustrated London News* he used his friendship with politician John Burns to get onto a roof in Whitehall the day before and capture the scene with his usual architectural fidelity. Then, when the cortege went by, all he had to do was add the coffin-laden gun carriage, the King's horse, his dog, and the mounted figures. It ran as a full page, and Pennell reveled in his success.

Pennell had needed a success. Despite his indefatigable traveling on illustration assignments for publishers and his constant pushing forward to manage the American sections of international exhibitions, he was a frustrated man. His kind of art was giving way to the camera, as—with the rare exception—had his kind of journalism. His and Elizabeth's Whistler biography had turned into a nightmare of litigation—as Rosalind Birnie Philip disputed their claim to write an "authorized" life—until George Radford had won the day for them in Chancery. And even then the published book—a monumental effort at documentation—was sniped at by critics as too reverential. But the worst blow to the crusty, increasingly conservative Pennell had been the America he saw changing with each visit, as immigration from the south and east of Europe had flooded his favorite cities with alien cultures and alien tongues. In his unhappiness with change, he became even more bigoted than Henry Adams. To John van Dyke in New York he complained, "Illustration as an art is virtually dead—so the story of it should be told—and how long we shall have to endure the 'picture' made in German or Polish or Yiddish by a camera or a fluke—I don't know. . . ."

In mid-1910 he was in Chicago, complaining again to van Dyke about his loneliness amid the alien masses:

Mr. Pork Packer and 2,916,418 and ½ jews, niggers, slovaks, dagos, irish, sicilians, scandinavians and one supposed native American—preserved in a bottle in a freak museum—make up the population of hustle —village—where there are no signs on the streets which are made of mud and filth, where the English tongue in Irish mouths is rarely heard—the American language never—all others all the time—where palaces of a sort blossom in a lopsided row called a "bulleyvar"—where O Lor everything that ever was said agin the place is gospel—and not the half has been told—anything said in its favour is a dam lie.

If this is a fair specimen of the West may I never see it—if these are "the plain people"—Gosh!!

England—and even France—looked better. He went back gratefully to London.

In the first days of 1911, Abbey finally made the drawing for his new bookplate. He was planning to move to Woodcote, in Hampshire, where his new country home would have a magnificent library to house his collection. He was also working on an eight-foot-high portrait in oils of his wife, as a present for Woodcote, and she already looked proud in it, blonde hair piled high and broad, bared shoulders gleaming above a long black gown. He was too busy, he told Lord Carlisle, to do a panel of the lying-in-state of Edward VII for the Houses of Parliament. And he was.

In April he ordered a large canvas, fifty feet by thirteen feet, to be delivered to Tite Street, to place upon it the design he had now worked out for his Philadelphia mural. Then there was the spring Private View at the Academy, and in May a dinner for the Artists' Cricket Club, of which he was president, was held at Chelsea Lodge. But he was suffering increasingly from exhaustion, and Sir William Osler, consulting with another specialist, recommended exploratory surgery. "It can't be that!" Abbey said. "I have so much work to do, and I feel so capable of doing it!" Dr White, of Sargent's portrait, now retired, was summoned from Philadelphia, and with Osler and two other specialists performed the surgery on June 25. There was nothing they could do. Cancer had spread to the liver. It would be a matter of weeks. Bedfast, Abbey thought his recovery had been slowed by the heat, unusual for London. Soon his letters had to be dictated to his wife. Ten days before the end, as he finally understood it would be, he asked to have his bed carried up to the second-floor studio, where he could see his *Valley Forge,* now ready to be sent to Harrisburg, his *Columbus,* ready all but for some touches to the beach where the sea came in, and the designs for other works now ready for their panels. In the last days of July he sank into a coma. On the first day of August, at fifty-nine, he died.

"I can only wonder," Henry James consoled Gertrude Abbey, "at the cruelty and perverseness of his extinction—to say nothing of his suffering. The tenderness of my affection for him abides with me." But, he added, his friend had done what there was in the world for him to do. "He had *had* it, he hadn't missed it: he had sat at the full feast and had manfully, splendidly, lived."

Whatever of the unfinished work could be completed was executed by a former assistant, Ernest Board, under the direction of John Sargent, who for a time spent more hours on the other side of Tite Street than on his own, going over areas of canvas with his own brush where he thought it useful. And he posed Abbey's friend Lord Northbourne as the final foreground figure in the group of signers of the Declaration of Independence, so that canvas, too, could go to America. Then Tite Street became a much stiller place.

CHAPTER VII

Lamb House

Let it suffer the wrong of being crudely hinted as my desire earnestly, tenderly, intelligently to admonish you, while you are young . . . , in favour of the American subject. There it is round you. Don't pass it by—the immediate, the real, the only, the yours. . . . Profit, be warned, by my awful example of exile and ignorance. . . .

—Henry James to Edith Wharton, in 1904

ON SEPTEMBER 16, 1897, Henry James received a telegram from Rye, offering him first refusal on a lease which had seemed, since the idea had first occurred to him, little more than a dream. He had summered at Rye the year before, happy to be away from the city. Despite the twenty good years of his residence in London, it was also the place where a succession of professional failures had soured his outlook, culminating with the first night of *Guy Domville* at the St James's Theatre early in 1895.

No literary activity was more financially rewarding than the box-office success of a play. *Guy Domville,* James had hoped, would make his fortune as well as his popular reputation as a playwright. Wary of first nights, he had come in at the stage door only at the curtain, and above the muffled sounds of applause had heard the hoped-for cries of "Author! Author!" He had no idea that the shouts were derisory.

Stepping forward for his bows, James was greeted by a cacophony of catcalls and jeers. It was less an audience at a play, he wrote his brother William, "than a cage of beasts at some infernal zoo." According to Enid Bagnold, James "fled from the stalls to wander, broken, about London. So Ethel Sands told me—who went that night with him."

The play had closed the next month, to be replaced by Oscar Wilde's most successful comedy, *The Importance of Being Earnest*. James swore to his notebook that he would never be so humiliated again. He would return to his métier, the novel. "I take up my *own* pen again—the pen of all my old unforgettable efforts and sacred struggles. To myself—today—I need say no more. Large and full and high the future still opens. It is now indeed that I may do the work of my life. And I will." In his middle fifties he was beginning again.

One of the Cinque Ports, Rye in the Middle Ages had been at the edge of the Channel. The water had withdrawn, and Rye resembled an Italian hill town with its steep cobbled streets and its houses clustered about the town's part-Norman St Mary's Church, with its square tower. When James's rental arrangement for the summer months ended in August 1896, and his writing was still going well, he was reluctant to leave. Finding another temporary house, the old Vicarage, he again moved his papers, books, bicycle, servants, bird, and dog, and worked contentedly in the shabbier, smaller garden, while the pears yellowed in the September sun. It was not up to Point Hill, he wrote his brother William, "but this little corner of the land endears itself to me—and the peace of the country is a balm."

On one of his excursions to relax himself for work, he came upon a red-brick Georgian house at the bend in West Street where it curved toward the church. Not a chance reconnaissance, it had resulted from his seeing a drawing of it made by his friend Edward Warren. At the ironmonger's, he used the excuse of a small purchase to inquire whether Lamb House might possibly become vacant, and left his name and London address.

For the summer of 1897 neither Point Hill nor the Vicarage were available. James reluctantly divided his time between hotels in Bournemouth and Torquay, then returned to his fourth floor at 34

De Vere Gardens to find that the ironmonger in Rye had remembered him. The owner of Lamb House, Arthur Bellingham, had decided to try his luck in the Klondike gold rush, and was emigrating to Canada. James could have a twenty-one-year lease for seventy pounds a year. He took it, writing Arthur Benson that he marveled at his own optimism: "One would think I was your age!" But King George (I, rather than II, as James thought) had slept there and it promised to be the May-to-October retreat from London he had always wanted. Soon Edward Warren reported that he had seen in the local solicitor's office a book which indicated (erroneously) that the first two Georges had both been entertained at Lamb House. "Two Georges!" James exulted to Warren. "I thought that in the rent I was only paying for one and getting him extraordinarily cheap. But this is a bargain indeed. . . ."

Lamb House was good for James's writing. Although there was quick rail access to London, he could work relatively undisturbed, continuing the process of recovery from his disappointments of the mid-nineties, and the depression which had accompanied them. He gave up his De Vere Gardens lease, and for fifty pounds a year took rooms at the Reform Club for occasional visits and for refuge in winter. Always in a panic over finances, he counted himself happy over the new situation. Electric lighting had not yet come to Rye, and he needed his bedroom candle, but despite his relatively grand style, living was inexpensive. Even with his bibulous servant couple, the Smiths, moved from London, and an added gardener as well as—a little later—a housemaid and an all-purpose boy, he could still afford the luxury of a "typewriter" to whom to dictate directly onto the machine; and the Remington itself, too cumbrous to move back and forth easily to London, almost assured that he would be spending most of his creative days in the place where it sat, which for years would be Rye.

He had taken in, he wrote William, "a great deal of pecuniary sail." He had also acquired nearly an acre of garden in which to read and write on the many more sunny days than he had known in twenty-two years of London. But with the first house that was ever his own came the hazards and inconveniences. Furnishing and refurbishing was not for him the easy task it had been for the Cranes, who came to Brede Place with almost nothing, and improvised with anything cheap and secondhand. James moved thousands of books from London, as well as portraits of family and friends, and pictures by Du Maurier, Whistler, and Burne-Jones. Lamb House was to be a place, he wrote Arthur Benson, "as I may, when pressed by the pinch of need, retire to with a certain shrunken decency and wither away in—in a fairly cleanly and pleasantly melancholy manner—towards the tomb."

James was turning out copy as if the tomb were close at hand, and he had much left to do. William MacAlpine had sufficient typing to do to keep him down from London for days at a time, but even there James decided to economize. A female typewriter would cost half, he knew, and after MacAlpine was found more rewarding employment, Mary Weld took over the machine in 1901. It was Miss Weld who finished *The Ambassadors* and began the next novel, both of which would show a new, more confident James. Even physically it was a different James who now came up on the train to London. He had shaved his beard, which had made him look, in Sargent's portrait reproduced in the *Yellow Book,* like a sea captain on shore leave, and he now looked more Mediterranean, like a cardinal in an influential Vatican post.

For thirty years James had been writing fiction which had represented Americans as morally superior to Europeans. Daisy Miller, Caroline Spencer, Christopher Newman, and Isabel Archer had been victims of the moral corruption of Europe. Events had made him look across the Atlantic less nostalgically, and identify more with the view from London. The Venezuela affair had almost made him return his American passport, and the Spanish-American War had made him "want to curl up more closely in this old world corner," yet he regarded the war to put down the Boers as necessary, for things "really had to be taken in hand." The leisured, sophisticated London society he knew, and its counterparts in Paris or Florence or Rome, now seemed vital in shoring civilization against creeping vulgarity and dullness. As Clarence King wrote to John Hay about their friend, "Whenever he describes the periphery, as anywhere over one cab-fare from his dear Piccadilly, there is a nervous, almost nostalgic, cutting and running for the better quarters of the town. Even when talking of Blackwell or Hampstead, you feel that he looks a little askance, that he wants to go home; and you positively know that before going into these gruesome and out-of-way parts of the town, he gathers up a few unmistakeably good invitations and buttons them in his inner pocket, so that there should be no mistaking the social position of his corpse if violence befell him."

His four major novels at the turn of the century—*The Sacred Fount* (1901), *The Wings of the Dove* (1902), *The Ambassadors* (1903), and *The Golden Bowl* (1904)—display James at the culmination of his powers. He had made his peace with European values, and even evidenced it in the demonstrative nature of his close friendships with a series of young men who often evoked a more than avuncular emotion in him. It was largely a paper passion, limited to effusive letters and an occasional touch of the hand or press of the shoulder. But through it James was able to release himself from the need to end his novels with the usual renunciation of physical love; and even when there is such a gesture, it is clear that James's heart is not in it. Thus in *The Ambassadors,* Lambert Strether, sent from Woollett, Massachusetts, to rescue the scion of an industrial fortune, Chad Newsome, from the clutches of Mme Vionnet, is entranced by the lady and convinced of her love for Chad. Also, he has himself been drawn to a charming Europeanized American, Maria Gostrey, and she to him, but James has him back out and return—reluctantly—to America, Strether feeling that it would be wrong to get anything for himself out of the mission he has deliberately aborted. Despite the concession, James, it is clear, is no longer on the side of renunciation.

The plot—the belated maturation of Strether's consciousness—had been worked out with labyrinthian subtlety, despite James's oral method of composition, and the reader for *Harper's* in New York had been worried about its suitability for American magazine serialization. "It is subjective," he wrote cautiously, "fold within fold of a complex mental web, in which the reader is lost if his much-wearied attention falters." He did not advise acceptance, and closed his report with "We ought to do better." But James would not adulterate his art to satisfy a publisher used to yesterday's fictional techniques. Ultimately (1902–3) it was serialized in the *North American Review.*

Taking dictation was to Miss Weld like accompanying a singer on the piano. She would arrive at ten each morning and type while the Master paced back and forth, narrating his lines. At lunchtime he was finished with dictation, but for Miss Weld there were sheaves of pages to be repeatedly retyped, as James spent other hours in revising, "a building of the prose page," as Leon Edel describes it, "by a process of accretion." James could also work on more than one thing more easily than before, and not tire as easily, because the physical strain of longhand was now limited only to his most personal correspondence. As a result he could work not only on long fiction but also on short pieces, and even—for the money—on a biography, *William Wetmore Story and His Friends* (1903).

For James, Story's life encapsulated the experience of the American artist who depended upon American markets. A Boston sculptor, Story had chosen to live and work in Italy, and James had the opportunity to work out, using another subject than himself and another art than his own, the price of expatriation upon an artist's work. A lawyer who was determined to live his life as an artist in a place where artists were a more meaningful part of life than in America, Story became prosperous selling his narrative sculpture to American businessmen in Rome eager to carry home a piece of "art." But he never became more than an amateur, and as James, writing on commission for Houghton Mifflin in Boston, delicately put that truth, Story was "so restlessly, sincerely aesthetic and yet, constitutionally, so little insistent."

Houghton Mifflin's editors tried to get James to do another biography, one of poet and critic James Russell Lowell, who had been American minister to Great Britain, but James had had enough of trying to apply a creative imagination to one life he felt was unsuited for biography. There must be, he wrote in declining, "an intrinsic richness of matter. If a man has a quiet life, but a great mind, one may do something with him; as one may also do something with him if he has a small mind and great adventures. But when he has had neither adventures nor intellectual, spiritual, or whatever inward history, then one's case is hard." He went back to fiction, and began *The Golden Bowl.*

At sixty James was flourishing. Although he complained of his solitude in Rye, he was working hard and well. His finances were adequate, for his small legacy from his sister Alice (rents on American properties) was a cushion against any literary dry spell. More than ever he was a popular guest, although his conversation seemed to have taken on even more of his habitual dictating manner than he realized. There was even a dramatic element in his hesitations, playwright Alfred Sutro thought. "One had to wait a long time for the thought to be expressed; one watched the process of its germination and development; but when it came one felt that it had been tremendously worth waiting for. . . . He talked as if every sentence had been carefully rehearsed; every semicolon, every comma, was in exactly the right place, and his rounded periods dropped to the floor and bounced about like tiny rubber balls."

One episode at the time, nevertheless, left him nearly speechless. At sixty he was as confirmed a bachelor as any gossip column could have imagined, yet a young American woman from Kentucky, plump and red-haired, would be erroneously associated with him as the original of his Milly Theale in *The Wings of the Dove* and as the woman with whom the Hearst press had him "deeply in love." Emilie Grigsby was one of the more unfortunate by-products of his friendship with the Harlands, who had her at their at-homes, along with other expatriate Americans. Earlier, in New York, elderly Chicago traction magnate Charles Yerkes had established her in a Park Avenue mansion. When he fled accusations of wholesale bribery and established himself in London, Miss Grigsby, then twenty-three, followed. Yerkes quickly involved himself with a syndicate expanding the London underground rail system, and while he sailed close to bankruptcy, Miss Grigsby prudently pursued social success and pocketed Yerkes's pounds.

James was embarrassed when she referred to him as an intimate friend who had utilized her as model for his heroines, yet he *had* met her several times, and had committed the error of atoning for his refusals of her many invitations by paying a formal ten-minute call upon her at the Savoy. The returns in gossip made all of Miss Grigsby's machinations worthwhile. Still, she would never appear in a James novel. Yerkes, who died, broken, in 1905, as he was trying to divorce his wife in order to marry Miss Grigsby, would, however, inspire Theodore Dreiser's *The Titan,* in which Emilie Grigsby becomes "Berenice Fleming." With the money from Yerkes that she had squirreled away, she established herself as a *grande dame* in Mayfair, still uncomfortably close to James. Not until 1906 would the rumors connecting her with him fade.

Although James was not pleased by the innuendo about late-blooming virility, his next novel, *The Golden Bowl,* demonstrated more passion—consummated rather than renounced—than any earlier novel, hovering—doubly—on the edge of incest, perhaps a metaphor (or an evasion) of other varieties of forbidden love. Maggie Verver, a young American heiress who had become mother-less at ten, has a suffocatingly close relationship with her father, Adam—a name hardly chosen at random. Enigmatic in his Yankee innocence, he has accumulated wealth, and spends it luxuriously in his English paradise without any indication of need to oversee its vague American origin. His daughter's marriage to an impoverished but elegant Italian, Prince Amerigo—another heavily freighted name —is arranged via mutual friends. One of them, Charlotte Stant, a striking American woman of small means but infinite determination, has been the prince's mistress. She returns to London for the wed-ding and asks the prince's assistance in buying Maggie a wedding present. No present is purchased—it is a ruse to see him alone—but at a shop in Bloomsbury, Charlotte is attracted to, and puts aside, a gilded crystal bowl. It has a flaw. If there is a weak place, says the prince, it will split—"On lines and by laws of its own."

Princess Maggie's marriage is in just such danger. Charlotte has come back to reclaim Amerigo, and does, despite the marriage. Her task is made easy, for she is put in Adam Verver's path to divert him from his daughter, who remains her father's dearest possession. Having become "a domestic resource" to him, Charlotte is wooed and wed by the forty-seven-year-old widower. He collects things, and adds her in much the way he has collected Prince Amerigo's antique title and lineage for Maggie and the future little *principesso.* But Charlotte, now the mistress of a town house in Eaton Square and an estate in the country, remains, too, the mistress of the man who is now her stepson-in-law.

Maggie, at first, is blind to the deception because she is still so emotionally close to her father* and she remains a grown-up child.

---

* There is a suggestion of John Morgan Richards—father of Pearl Craigie—in Adam Verver. Both were wealthy Americans with splendid town houses and country homes, acquisitive tastes, and daughters for whom they sought titles purchasable by marriage. Also, the father-daughter relationship was an intense

The situation gives the adulterous couple their opportunities, for to the prince and to Charlotte, the continued happiness of father and daughter is claimed as their sacred trust—their pious rationalization not to end the affair but only to keep it secret. But the forbidden passion cannot persist, although coping with it provides Maggie with her sentimental education.

With her knowledge comes power. If her father finds out, the millions which the prince has married are gone, and Charlotte's life of sophisticated ease is over. The prince is an ardent anglophile and Charlotte has made no secret of her love for London and her distaste for her own country. "She hates America," says her confidante, Mrs Assingham. "There was no place for her there—she didn't fit in. She wasn't in sympathy—no more were the people she saw." One had to be "blessedly an American," James has Charlotte think about appreciating a cool August morning in London—"as indeed you had to be blessedly an American for all sorts of things: so long as you hadn't, blessedly or not, to remain in America." But Maggie has come, accidentally, into possession of the golden bowl—and the guilty secret. She connives at the bowl's "accidental" destruction before the shocked eyes of Amerigo. It breaks into three pieces and before long each of the principals possesses at least some fragment of the disquieting secret. Verver decides at Maggie's discreet urging to return to America, an act which would rescue both marriages. In a tense confrontation with Maggie (who already knows), Charlotte breaks the paralyzing news as if it is her own will. "Our real life isn't here," she explains with feigned assurance. As James remembered from Ecclesiastes, "Or ever the silver cord be loosed, or the golden bowl be broken, or the pitcher be broken at the fountain, or the wheel broken at the cistern. Then shall the dust return to the earth as it was: and the spirit shall return unto God who gave it."

Nothing can really be as it was. No attempt is made by Maggie to repair the golden bowl. It was flawed, and is best forgotten, like lies—and like the strategic lies to protect the earlier lies. All the

---

one, "John Oliver Hobbes" openly detesting her mother and adoring her father. It is obvious from *The Wings of the Dove* that James had already been thinking about the family at Lancaster Gate.

Verver belongings are packed for shipment to America, and Maggie's father and his wife arrive at Portland Place for a parting tea with the prince and princess. Maggie arranges it stylishly, ostentatiously taking her father aside for a private farewell so that the separated lovers can have their brief parting. Charlotte handles her side coolly, making a proud occasion of her exile to her own country. And James closes the narrative, with its brilliant but labyrinthian circumlocutions, with a scene in which Maggie determinedly prevents Prince Amerigo from unburdening himself with a confession. As long as the subject remains closed to Amerigo, she will be mistress in her own house, for without confession there can be no forgiveness. Everything, the prince understands—for he has said it earlier—"is terrible in the heart of man." And woman.

The novel would be James's last completed long fiction, and in many ways it restated his familiar themes; but in its sexual dimension it had an emotional urgency unknown to his earlier work. And it had much to imply about James's own increasing nostalgia for his country. Charlotte is punished for her slights to America not by being forbidden it, but by what was, on the novelist's part, nearly deportation. Whether James realized it or not, he was thinking of going home.

In November 1903, when he was nearing the end of writing *The Golden Bowl,* James accompanied Mrs John La Farge and her daughter to the Tilbury docks along the Thames to see them off to America. When he returned to Rye, he was, according to Ford Madox Ford, "singularly excited, bringing out a great many unusually uncompleted sentences." James had gone aboard the ship, the *Minnehaha,* and had experienced such a strong feeling that he should be sailing, too, that he claimed afterward that only the lack of a heavy overcoat for the voyage, and an extra bunk in the ladies' cabin, had kept him from joining them across the Atlantic. He offered his good-byes and fled out through the "encumbered tubular passages" and then along the docks in the "grimy fog," "never stopping till I clutched at something that was going back to London."

He had no end of reasons for returning. He had been away for twenty years. Now he wanted to discuss with American publishers his idea for a collected edition of his works, and he wanted to see for himself what had happened to his country before—as he wrote

Howells—"senile decay sets in." But it was more than that, he confided. "I *want* to come, quite pathetically and tragically—it is a passion of nostalgia." He could write a book of impressions to finance
the trip, he told his brother, but William warned him that "many
features of our national life" would inspire "physical loathing." The
literary business, he urged, could be handled by an agent.

Nohing could have been calculated to intrigue James more. He
needed new literary material, which meant new experience. The altered America might not be to his liking, but he wanted to see it. He
wanted "to see everything," he wrote to William, "I want to see the
Country, scarcely a bit New York and Boston, but intensely the
Middle and Far West and California and the South." To do so he
overcame his concerns about lecturing, having learned that fees of
$150 or $200 were likely. And he further financed the adventure by
accepting an offer from Harper's to serialize his American impressions in magazines and make a book of them afterward.

Learning of the impending trip, Joseph Pennell offered to do illustrations for the volume of travel essays he predicted would emerge
from the trip, but James, who had already agreed to the book,
feigned uncertainty. It was not inconceivable, he wrote Pennell, that
once he were there he might be eager to produce some travel impressions, yet he would have to be there to be sure the inspiration would
come. There would be further discussion on the subject, but James
was disinclined to have his impressions compete with the hard architectural reality of Pennell's line.

His chief interest before sailing, in any case, had to be to confirm
his complicated itinerary and arrange for what he would take and
what he would leave behind. He bought a new steamer trunk, and
saw his London tailor. And he arranged for the rental of Lamb
House at five pounds a week, to include not only the property but
"the servants, the forks and spoons, and house linen and books, and
in short everything that is in the house. . . ." Five pounds would
just cover the wages of the five servants, but James was more interested in the character of the occupant and the care of Lamb House
than a profit. Miss Weld was to find other hourly employment while
James was away. Before he returned, she would find a husband.
Someone else would have to type the American impressions.

James crossed on the North German Lloyd liner *Wilhelm II*. He had last seen New York in 1883. It was August 30, 1904, when the ship anchored in New York Harbor at Hoboken. He was forty when he had left what was a provincial but burgeoning city. He was now past sixty, and the skyline of New York in early morning looked like a "broken hair-comb turned up." The twenty years of his country's life he had missed had been a time of explosive growth, dominated by two symbols he could see from the deck: the tall buildings that had changed the face of the city and the immigrants from Europe—many new arrivals were in steerage on the *Wilhelm II*—who had changed the nature of the population. He came expecting to be a "repentant absentee," but what he saw, from the start, made him yearn for London.

At his summer home at Deal Beach, New Jersey, the head of Harper's, Colonel George Harvey, entertained James at dinner. There was another guest—and Harper author—the white-haired, white-suited Samuel Clemens. Explaining his delay in departing for his brother's home in Chocorua, New Hampshire, James wrote him, "Poor dear old Mark Twain beguiles the session on the deep piazza." It had been four years since the two had met in London. The choice of adjectives reflected James's sympathy: Olivia Clemens had died several months earlier in Florence, after a long illness, and wit came less readily to the tired and depressed Clemens, then living in a hotel on lower Fifth Avenue.

A train took James to New England, where he remained until the summer heat had broken. Final proofs of *The Golden Bowl* had been sent to him there, giving him occupation. Then he walked the once-familiar streets of Boston and Cambridge, and visited Concord and Salem. Once he asked his way of a young man who turned out to be an Armenian immigrant; on looking for the "House of the Seven Gables," he asked directions of another who proved to be newly landed from Italy.

Like Joseph Pennell, James was appalled by the consequences of immigration. The American melting pot—especially what he saw of it in New York—had destroyed the Anglo-Saxon homogeneity of language and culture he had known; and the poverty of the new and unassimilated population had led to swarming ghettos and a sense of alienation which only accented the prevailing impermanence. While his senses recoiled from the smells and the sounds, he realized reluctantly that the "great fact" was that as new as the immigrants were to America, "they were *at home,* really more at home, at the end of ther few weeks or months or their year or two, than they had ever in their lives been before."

Stirred by what he had already seen, he wrote Colonel Harvey on October 21, "I am moved inwardly to believe that I shall be able not only to write the best book (of social and pictorial and as it were, human observation) ever devoted to this country, but one of the best—or why 'drag in' one *of,* why not say frankly *the* Best?—ever devoted to any country at all." And to his agent he wrote that he wanted to do "a really artistic and valuable book," not one knocked off in war correspondent fashion, written "on his knee or his hat."

Soon James wandered through lower Manhattan looking for familiar sights in the Fourteenth Street neighborhood where he had lived as a boy. He felt haunted by a sense of dispossession. "It takes an endless amount of history to make even a little tradition," he later wrote in *The American Scene,* "and an endless amount of tradition to make even a little taste, and an endless amount of taste, by the same token, to make even a little tranquility." He found it wanting everywhere he went, but most of all in New York, to which he gave nearly half his eventual book.

Looking for the house of his boyhood, he found it gone. So was the large brownstone church across the street. He had watched it being built and had seen it consecrated. It had "vanished as utterly as the Assyrian Empire." At least in Boston he had found the house in Ashburton Place where he had written some of his early fiction, but the cycle of dispossession reappeared there too. When he returned for another look a few weeks later it was gone, to make way for something bigger, "the new landmarks crushing the old quite as violent children stamp on snails and catterpillars." America, with all its energy and wealth, he concluded, "doesn't believe in itself. . . . Its mission would appear to be . . . to gild the temporary with its gold. . . ." And he found the symbol of such glorification of the temporary to be the American hotel, the home of the transitory guest, and in the Waldorf-Astoria he saw "a social order in positively stable equilibrium," created by the "American genius for organization."

American architecture regularly disappointed him. The many-windowed skyscrapers of New York appalled him with their vulgarity and sameness, and the great new Boston Library, which housed the "so brave decorative designs" of Abbey and Sargent which he had watched develop in London, was—apart from a splendid staircase—"mere chambers of familiarity and resonance." Still, he rationalized weakly, the decorated public places in Italy served the "graceful common life," and "Was it not splendid . . . to see, in Boston, such large provision made for the amusement of children on rainy afternoons?"

After Boston, New York, and Philadelphia, James was the guest of Henry Adams in his house on Lafayette Square in Washington. John Hay lived next door, and the White House was only a short walk across the square. President Theodore Roosevelt, who had privately called James "a miserable little snob," invited him to dinner and a diplomatic reception. In his published impressions James wrote only of the "rich sense of the past" which the Executive Mansion still reflected, but of his encounter with the booming, energetic President he discreetly said nothing. To a friend, James described Roosevelt as "the mere monstrous embodiment of unprecedented and resounding noise."

His tour of the South took James through the remnants of slave-era opulence to the luxury of Palm Beach, "a void furnished at the most with velvet air." Still undeveloped by tourism and coastal sprawl, Florida was, he wrote his wealthy friend Mrs Cadwalader Jones, "a fearful fraud—a ton of dreary jungle and swamp and misery of flat forest monotony to an ounce or two of little coast perching-place—a few feet wide between the jungle and the sea." After ten days in the sun he returned by Pullman (a "rushing hotel") to Philadelphia and New York. His book would go no farther, although he had material for a second volume in his trip west. He seemed to have little desire to relive it on the typewritten page, closing with his despairing reverie on the train north from Florida. "Is the gem of anything finely human," he asked, "of anything agreeably or successfully social, supposably planted in conditions of such endless stretching and such boundless spreading as shall appear finally to minister but to the triumph of the superficial and the apotheosis of the raw?" He was even more bitter about what had replaced the dispossessed "painted savages." The strident skyscrapers and ugly slums and ravaged countryside were wounds which had "caused the face of the land to bleed," and the "pretended message of civilization" was "brag" and "cynicism." Harper's dropped the section from the 1907 American edition.

The problems for the publisher were that James had written in a style not easily accessible to the average reader, and—despite his toning down his real feelings—had been bleak rather than uplifting about the possibilities of his country. Even some of the better things he had said privately (amid the pessimism) failed to turn up in his pages. To his novelist friend in England, W. E. Norris, for example, he had written that December, "New York is appalling, fantastically charmless and elaborately dire; but Boston has quality and convenience, and now that one sees American life in the longer piece one profits by many of its great ingenuities." Some of the praise as well as the blame escaped the text.

The late winter was especially harsh. When James set out by train for St Louis and Chicago to deliver his lecture on the novel, "The Lesson of Balzac," he watched miles of snow recede past his window. He found the Middle West featureless—"a single boundless empty platitude." At each lecture stop he would read his address standing, one hand in a pocket, the other available to turn the loose sheets of typed paper. Talking in a low key, he would not alter his standard opening to fit the geography or the guest list, instead offering in his first line a rationalization for not doing so: "I have found it necessary, at the eleventh hour, to sacrifice to the terrible question of time a very beautiful and majestic approach that I had prepared to the subject on which I have the honor of addressing you."

In Chicago he boarded a Pullman for the West Coast, relieved to be free of the kind and good but "too boresome" people. For expenses he carried $1,350 of his earnings. To reach Los Angeles he endured three days and nights of "unspeakable alkali deserts," writing a friend on arrival that the country was "too *huge* simply, for any human convenience." But he went up and down the coastal cities— San Diego, Los Angeles, Monterey, San Francisco, Portland, and Seattle—meeting old literary acquaintances and making new ones, and even being refused a bill by the owner of St Dunstan's Hotel in

San Francisco, who considered it a privilege to have had so distinguished a guest. It had been an effort to get there, but the state rated high in the unwritten part of James's book of impressions. "Brave golden California," he noted, "more brave and golden for such possibilities, surely, than any other country under the sun!"

A long Pullman ride eastward brought him to New York via St Paul, Chicago, and Albany. Then it was time for a final circuit of New England, to revisit William, and to earn a few more lecturing dollars with the familiar speech, now even more in demand as his travels had turned him into a public figure. Letters to newspapers commented on his books as well as on the circumlocutions of his style, and there were jokes current in cultured circles about him— such as the story of the American lady who boasted that she could read Henry James "in the original." Inevitably he was asked to deliver a commencement address—and did so at Bryn Mawr College in May, lecturing also at Smith College and in Baltimore. There were last visits to friends, including one to William Dean Howells in Kittery Point, Maine; and just before James left New York his agent, J. B. Pinker, arrived from London to join him in discussions with Scribners about the definitive edition of the novels and stories.

On July 5, after ten months, he embarked on the Cunard Lines steamship *Ivernia* for the nine-day passage to Liverpool. On deck he began revising his first novel, *Roderick Hudson,* for the collected edition, but the voyage was not entirely a working one as also aboard were expatriate friends, returning, like James, from rare visits "home." One was the novelist "C. E. Raimond," actually Elizabeth Robins, a blue-eyed and beautiful Ibsenite actress still in her twenties when she played in a stage adaptation of James's *The American* in 1891. She had left Boston in 1888 after her young husband, George R. Parkes, despondent about his own acting career and their loveless marriage, had donned a suit of stage armor and drowned himself in the Charles. In London the widowed Mrs Parkes had returned to acting as Miss Robins, putting her excess energy into writing and suffragism, and even doing a play, *Votes for Women!* ("A Dramatic Tract in Three Acts"), which the Court Theatre in Sloane Square produced in 1907.

Too career-directed to intimidate James sexually, she developed into a close friend and frequent theater companion, the Master unwittingly becoming her "cover" for a secret affair with drama critic and Ibsen translator William Archer, who had a wife and son. She later transferred her affections no less covertly to John Masefield, another Court Theatre playwright and the future Poet Laureate. The stage door, she recalled, closed for her "with no slam. It closed quietly, gently, without bitterness, without even the decency of sharp regret." When there were no longer any new Ibsen roles to prepare, or any other acting work that appealed to her, she continued writing thesis-novels on euthanasia, prostitution, women's rights, and other subjects which might have embarrassed James had they been published under her own name while she was seen on his arm.*

Aboard the *Ivernia* she listened to James air the possibility of a new novel about the "New Americans" he had seen. "The theme was the immensely increased, the all-but-complete separation of the sexes in modern America. . . . So far, he said, as concerned men's intellectual life, so far as concerned all higher work and most real work of any kind, in every but one relation, a practical divorce between the sexes prevailed." Aware as was Miss Robins of the easy intellectual relations between the sexes in the London society he frequented, James considered the American way to be "a state of segregation beyond anything existing out of the Orient. His novel was to be called *The Chasm.*" He apparently never began it.

The date of a conversation James had with Logan Pearsall Smith is unknown, but its nature suggests that it might have happened on the return to Lamb House, as James was reviewing his American notes and putting them in order for his book. While walking in Romney Marsh, Pearsall Smith filled James's ears with invective about America until finally James protested. How could he speak so of his own country and countrymen? It was altogether shocking. Then James stopped, and turned full circle, surveying the quiet, unpeopled landscape. Reassured that they were alone, he put his hand on Pearsall Smith's shoulder. "My dear boy," he said, "I can't tell you how passionately I agree with you." But that level of reproach is never reached in *The American Scene,* although the tales with an American locale which he wrote afterward betray his sense of loss and disillusion.

* In March 1906 the identity of "C. E. Raimond" became known "by a mischance," and James offered to have his literary agent, Pinker, act in her behalf.

One of the stories, "Crapy Cornelia," seems to have had its title suggested in the "becraped, feminized world" James described in his American impressions after a visit to Charleston, South Carolina. His women, however, are New York types, and his hero explores the lower Manhattan of his young manhood, unhappy with the "gloss of new money" and the "frequent violence of transition" which characterizes the city. He misses "the pitch of history," and finds it only in such "little old New York objects" as were "things of his own past." In "The Jolly Corner" James fictionalized the search for his own past in a Manhattan house near Washington Square, written about earlier in his American notes. To it, an expatriate has come home. Spencer Brydon wonders what he might have been had he never left for London, and stalks the ghost of his would-be self. There were other stories, also set in the revisited land, of which the most interesting may be "A Round of Visits," in which Mark Montieth, returning to New York after ten years abroad, discovers that he has been robbed by one of his oldest friends. The betrayal is a secret sorrow that he wishes to confide to someone, but there is no one who seems, in his round of visits, to possess the requisite sympathy. New York itself rejects him at first, for the blinding snow—a "great white savage storm"—inhibits his mobility. Eventually he confronts the guilty friend, who shows no regret. Unassimilated wealth corrupted, and the world of new money was predatory and remorseless. As the constables close in, the friend shoots himself— not as the response to a code of conduct, but because he is trapped. The implicit message is clear: James felt that he had been robbed and betrayed: robbed of his own history—the only patrimony he really cared about—and betrayed by what change had wrought in America. The last fiction he published, it appeared in *English Review* in 1910.

Despite his disappointment with New York, much in James's collected works would celebrate the city, and he would spend most of his literary energies preparing the edition during the four years that followed his return. "I should particularly like to call it the New York Edition if that may pass for a general title of sufficient dignity and distinctness," he wrote Scribners, aware that what major sales he might count on would have to come from there—or from London. He had not, he explained, had the "opportunity of rendering that sort of homage" to his "native city." Only the works he wished to preserve were to be included, and only twenty-three volumes were projected. Fifteen would be needed for nine novels (six took two volumes each) and the remaining stories would be fit into eight volumes, James choosing only 66 of the 108 he had written until then. In the process he underestimated his wordage and had to concede a twenty-fourth volume, which he did grudgingly, having perceived, he wrote Scribners, "a certain harmonious physiognomy" in the original plan. What it was is unknown: Balzac had *begun* his collected edition with twenty-three volumes, which may have something to do with the choice.

Every line of prose had to be rewritten to reflect the Master's mature style. In addition there were substantive changes. The younger James never made much of physical intimacies, but in his later years he had tried to add heat to his love scenes. Now he sought to overcome earlier timidities, turning, for example, a kiss in *Portrait of a Lady* from a sentence to an entire paragraph. The problem was that the later Jamesian style was intended for late Jamesian characters, and in making what were sometimes wholesale changes —as in *The American* (1883)—he made characters who were incapable of the passions or the intellectual subtleties of *The Golden Bowl* less faithful to their original selves.

Also there were to be eighteen prefaces (second volumes of novels did not call for such treatment), elaborating upon his intentions and his points of view. James happily analyzed his technique, and explained—selectively—his sources of inspiration, elucidating what he felt critics had missed in his work. It was an opportunity he had waited for. As Pennell and Beardsley had learned, James was impatient of pictures accompanying his prose, and resented having imposed upon him magazine illustrations which did violence to the nuances of his words. Another opportunity now presented itself: each volume, in the tradition of collected editions, would have a frontispiece. James knew exactly how he wanted to acquire them. A young American photographer he knew, Alfred Langdon Coburn, had moved to London with his cousin, F. Holland Day, an independently wealthy American who had taken up the camera as a hobby.

James had met Coburn in New York in 1905 when the photographer was twenty-three and on an assignment for the *Century Magazine*. Coburn had paid two visits to London and had shown his work publicly, to the admiration of professionals as well as an accomplished amateur photographer, Bernard Shaw. For the catalogue of Coburn's Royal Photographic Society exhibition Shaw would write the preface, and he would also sit for Coburn's camera in the nude, in the pose of Rodin's *Thinker,* in 1906. Coburn also paid a visit to Lamb House in 1906, photographing a pensive profile of James, and getting instructions on the principles by which he was to secure what James called optical symbols—pictures which would enhance the text without commenting upon it. The Master had exact ideas—the portal of a particular hotel, street scenes with objects which would not be commonplace, a carriage entrance to a mansion, a theater façade, a particular statue in the Luxembourg Gardens, a *palazzino* in Venice, a Roman bridge.

When it came to London scenes, James insisted upon pointing the way to locations which were meaningful to him. He knew his London, Coburn wrote,

as few men have known it, in all its quaintness, its mystery, and its charm. He obviously enjoyed our search, for he wrote of the street scenery of London "yielding a rich harvest of treasures from the moment I held up to it, in my fellow artist's company, the light of our fond idea—the idea, that is, of the aspect of things or combinations of objects that might, by a latent virtue in it, speak of its connection with something in the book, and yet at the same time speak enough for its odd or interesting self." H.J. knew so perfectly what we should achieve, for after all it was *his* books we were illustrating. . . .

The afternoon that we went to St. John's Wood to photograph the little gateway and house which was to serve as the illustration for the second volume of *The Tragic Muse* was an unforgettable experience. It was a lovely afternoon, I remember, and H.J. was in his most festive mood. I was carefree because this time I did not have to hunt for the subject, for I had the most perfect and dependable guide, the creator and author himself. I had not even read *The Tragic Muse,* but I shared his enthusiasm when after considerable searching we came upon exactly the right subject. Where the house is located I do not now recall, it may in fact no longer exist, for so much of London has passed away into the domain of forgotten things; but in the photograph it is preserved, crystallised as a memento of what Henry James had meant it to be.

Now it was tea-time, and pleasantly fatigued by our exertions, now triumphantly rewarded, we looked for a teashop to refresh ourselves, but were only able to find a baker's shop. We descended on this and came out with Bath buns, which we thankfully devoured as we walked down the street.

Although not literally a photographer, I believe Henry James must have had sensitive plates in his brain on which to record his impressions! He always knew exactly what he wanted, although many of the pictures were but images in his mind and imagination, and what we did was to browse diligently until we found such a subject. . . .

The triumph of the exploration, and its culmination, was the evocative photograph of Portland Place which opens the last volume. Never a society photographer, since his private income made it unnecessary for him to be fashionable, Coburn was able to experiment in technique, creating moody portraits and scenes which were often Whistlerian in impact. In the preface to *The Golden Bowl*, James wrote that for it,

nothing would so nobly serve as some generalized vision of Portland Place. Both our limit and the very extent of our occasion, however, lay in the fact that unlike wanton designers, we had not to "create" but simply to recognize—recognize, that is, with the last fineness. The thing was to induce the vision of Portland Place to generalize itself. This is precisely, however, the fashion after which the prodigious city, as I have called it, does on occasion meet halfway those forms of intelligence of it that *it* recognizes. All of which means that at a given moment the great Philistine vista would itself perform a miracle, would become interesting for a splendid atmospheric hour, as only London knows how, and that our business would be to understand.

The photograph of several lonely horse-drawn cabs in the vastness of Portland Place on the late afternoon of a foggy day has become almost the symbol of the Victorian twilight, its mood captured by two Americans, one young and one old, exploring the city for exactly that image. London always ended, James wrote, by "giving one absolutely everything one asks."

One of the results of the re-explorations of the city was renewed interest in what he had described to Edmund Gosse, just before sailing to America, as "a romantical-psychological-pictorial-social" book about London, with his observations radiating out concentrically from Westminster. His surviving notebook beginning in late 1907 records his attempts to "catch *on* to . . . the feeling *for,* about, what is being (even so poorly) attempted for the greater greatness of poor dear old London; the kind of affectionate sense of property, the sentimental *stake* in it," but nothing came of it. The work on the collected edition, and its prefaces, proved too demanding and he had little energy left for anything else. By then—late in 1907—the first volumes had begun to be released in New York, with the last finally published in 1909.

By the end James was exhausted and impatient, and regretted having begun the wearying grind at all, for sales were dismal and reviews meager. The first annual American royalty check was for $211 and the second was for $596.71. Eight years after the titles had appeared, he wrote to Edmund Gosse of his frustrations. The *New York Edition* had been, from point of view of profit, "practically a complete failure." He was realizing about £25 a year from Macmillan in London, and "very little more" from Scribners. "I remain at my age," he confessed, "and after my long career, utterly, insurmountably, unsaleable. . . . The edition . . . has never had the least intelligent critical justice done it—or any sort of critical attention at all paid it—and the artistic problem involved in my scheme was a deep and exquisite one, and moreover was, as I held, very effectively solved. Only it took such time—*and* such taste—in other words such aesthetic light. No more commercially thankless job of the literary order was (Prefaces and all—*they* of a thanklessness!) accordingly ever achieved."

William James had warned his brother, in the bluntest of fraternal criticism, that his complex style would sink the venture. "You know," he wrote,

how opposed your whole "third manner" of execution is to the literary ideals which animate my crude and Orson-like breast, mine being to say a thing in one sentence as straight and explicit as it can be made, and then to drop it forever; yours being to avoid naming it straight, but by dint of breathing and sighing all round and round it, to arouse in the reader who may have had a similar perception already (Heaven help him if he hasn't!) the illusion of a solid object, made (like the "ghost" at the Polytechnic) wholly out of impalpable materials, air, and the prismatic inferences of light, ingeniously focussed by mirrors upon empty space. But you do it, that's the queerness! . . .

But it's the rummest method for one to employ systematically as you do nowadays; and you employ it at your peril. In this crowded and hurried reading age, pages that require such close attention remain unread and neglected. You can't skip a word if you are to get the effect, and 19 out of 20 worthy readers grow intolerant. The method seems perverse: "Say it *out,* for God's sake," they cry, "and have done with it." And so I say now, give us *one* thing in your older directer manner, just to show that in spite of your paradoxical success in this unheard-of method, you *can* still write according to accepted canons. Give us that interlude; and then continue like the "curiosity of literature" which you have become. . . .

At the time the collected edition was completed, Max Beerbohm, sensitive to James's objectives, inserted into a dramatic review the sort of response James never made to William:

To read (say) "The Golden Bowl" or "The Wings of the Dove" is like taking a long walk uphill, panting and perspiring and almost of a mind to turn back, until, when you look back and down, the country is magically expanded beneath your gaze, as you never saw it yet; so that you toil on gladly up the heights, for the larger prospects that will be waiting for you. I admit, you must be in good training. People often say "Oh, what a pity it is that dear Henry James won't write the sort books he *used* to write. Do you remember 'The Portrait of a Lady'?" etc., etc. I always hint to these people, as politely as possible, that an artist's business is not to keep pace with his admirers, and that their business is to keep pace, if possible, with *him;* and that, if they faint by the way, they will be safer in blaming themselves than in blaming *him.* Mr James, that very conscious and devoted artist, may be trusted, he especially, to have followed the right line of progress—to have got the logical development of his own peculiar gifts. . . .

Artistically, Beerbohm may have been on the side of the angels. From the standpoint of the publisher's accountant, what was true of the *New York Edition* was also, as James had confided to Gosse, true of all his work since 1900. Through 1914 none of his novels or collections of tales published after the turn of the century had paid back its advances. His modest life-style (for his class) was not in jeopardy, but he was feeling professionally frustrated and embarrassed. For his last seven books of fiction he had received £1,600 from his English publisher. They had earned a few shillings more than £672. It was also true of his American sales. Even *The American Scene* had earned in royalties, ten years after publication, £126 16s. 7d. less than his English advance and $1,234.69 less than his American advance. Fortunately, James had his small family income (about $3,500 a year), his trickle of royalties from earlier books, and his prepublication sales to magazines. And he also had, although he did not know it, Edith Wharton.

Living abroad, mostly in France, in a de facto separation from her husband, Teddy, whom she largely supported from family wealth, Mrs Wharton was busy finding herself artistically and emotionally. The wisest professional advice she had ever received had come from James, who fortunately knew her sister-in-law, Mary Cadwalader Jones. Despite his remark that he found a new novel to be the hardest thing to read—"Any is hard enough, but the hardest [are] from the innocent hands of young females, young American females perhaps above all"—James had read *The Valley of Decision,* and was sent by Mrs Jones, after a visit to Lamb House, the two volumes of Mrs Wharton's short stories. A long letter to the author followed, replete with superlatives, but concluding that while she was young and free and in command of her professional direction, she should drop subjects remote from her experience—as in the eighteenth-century Italian setting of *Valley of Decision*—"in favour of the American subject." He wrote from the experience of the expatriate whose subject matter becomes ever more distant: "There it is round you. Don't pass it by—the immediate, the real, the only, the yours, the novelist's that it waits for. Take hold of it and keep hold, and let it pull you where it will. . . ." She should profit—or be warned—he added, "by my awful example of exile and ignorance. You will say that *j'en parle à mon aise*—but I shall have paid for my ease, and I don't want you to pay (as much) for yours. . . . All the same, *Do New York!* The 1st-hand account is precious." The Jamesian counsel would be triumphantly fulfilled in *The House of Mirth.* Soon they would get to know each other on his visits to Paris and her visits to London and Lamb House.

One "lady" not welcome at Lamb House was Cora "Crane," whom James earlier had accepted out of love for Stephen. In the autumn of 1907 she was back in London, at 47 Gower Street, having fled Florida at the urging of the father of her new husband, Hammond McNeil, to prevent her testifying at a murder trial. He had shot and killed Harry Parker, the nineteen-year-old alleged lover of his wife, while Cora cowered out of the line of fire. McNeil, himself sixteen years younger than Cora (who was then forty-three), had been proprietor of a saloon in Jacksonville near her newest house of joy, the Court. Although her reputation had preceded her to London, the Frewens permitted her to visit at Brede Place, and the H. G. Wellses at Spade House in Sandgate. In Rye itself she could only take tea at the venerable Mermaid Inn and stroll down the cobbled street past Lamb House. James had written her curtly that a call there "will not find yours truly." By mid-December she and her companion, "Miss Hattie," the Court's housekeeper, were at sea en route home.

Before long McNeil, out of prison, sued Cora for divorce, complaining of abusive treatment, including beatings with a shoe; despite the new scandal she had another prospective husband in the wings, Ernest Budd, an impecunious real estate salesman who spent most of his money betting on horses and most of his time at the Court. His wife refused him a divorce and had him arrested at Cora's house for nonsupport. It was all too much for the aging former mistress of Brede. In January 1910 she suffered a stroke but had recovered enough by September 4 to go out into the hot Florida sun to help push an automobile out of the sand. She collapsed and died the same day. Her tombstone would identify her as Cora E. Crane.

James was only indirectly involved in Edith Wharton's discovery of her emotional self, which resulted from her observation of manners and morals among the inhabitants of the American expatriate world in which she moved, and her sexual awakening—at forty-five, in 1907—by the original of James's Merton Densher, Morton Fullerton, then a newspaperman in Paris. As an act of friendship she prepared, with Fullerton and under his name, a long, appreciative essay on the significance of James's collected edition, which was duly placed in the *Quarterly Review* (April 1910) and reprinted in America in *Living Age* (after *Scribner's Magazine* had turned it down). Then she used James to help her get a check for one hundred pounds indirectly to Fullerton through James's publisher, ostensibly as an advance for a book on Paris, so that Fullerton could recover incriminating letters from yet another woman whom he had dallied with but not married.

The conspiracy gave her still another idea. James was constantly worried about money, while Mrs Wharton's American properties and book royalties, despite a lavish life style, brought her more money than she could spend. She would take months investigating a way to get funds to James, just as she conspired with him over Fullerton.

William James and his wife, visiting at Lamb House in the spring of 1910, were unable to lift Henry out of despondency. He was depressed not only by professional frustrations—another fling at playwriting had been unsuccessful and his new novel, *The Ivory Tower,* had been laid aside—but by the obvious decline in his brother's health. William was on his way to Bad Nauheim for another hopeless "cure" for his heart ailment. Mrs Wharton offered her Panhard and chauffeur for long drives in the awakening countryside, and Lamb House was itself freshening in the spring mildness; but even the world outside had its auguries of gloom. In May, Edward VII died, and everywhere there was a sense that an era had ended, that the mood of expansive confidence that had pervaded England for a decade was fading. For the funeral and the mourning period all the theaters were closed, and James's play *The Outcry* would never open. Producer Charles Frohman forfeited one thousand dollars to the author, who accepted it as small consolation. An entry Alice James set down in her notebook at Lamb House that June tells everything: "William cannot walk and Henry cannot smile."

Somberly, James busied himself gathering his last stories into a volume to be called *The Finer Grain.* Scribners and Methuen had each agreed to advances, $1,000 from New York and £150 from London, and among the tales would be "The Velvet Glove," based upon Edith Wharton, who is its "Amy Evans" (she had been Edith Jones). What James did not know was that Mrs Wharton's velvet glove was then being used in his behalf, but the subterfuges would be, for her, long and exasperating.

For a fortnight in May, Alice James took Henry and her husband to the palatial, part-Elizabethan country house of John Singer Sargent's patroness and greatest admirer, Mrs Mary Hunter, Hill Hall, near Epping Forest. Sargent and others in whose company James usually warmed were of little effect. He had "dark and difficult days" in the "vast, wondrous, sympathetic house," he confided to a friend. "I am unfit for society." A trip to Switzerland did neither brother any good, and they returned to Lamb House, with James determined to accompany William and Alice to America, although he was having heart trouble himself as well as gout, and had consulted Sir William Osler. "I eat, I walk, I *almost* sleep," he wrote Edith Wharton.

On August 12 the three Jameses sailed on the *Empress of Britain* for Quebec, accompanied by the Lamb House jack-of-all-trades, Burgess Noakes. William's son Harry met them and took them to Chocorua, where William, who had suffered through the placid voyage, and the journey to New Hampshire, died on August 26. His brother's grief and helplessness were profound. It was as if he had suffered, he wrote Edith Wharton, a "mutilation." But he stayed on, moving back with William's family to their home on Irving Street in Cambridge. He did some writing, pored over proofs of *The Finer Grain,* and wandered about the streets of Boston, which seemed now empty. "This is a hard country to love," he wrote John Sargent's sister Emily. And to novelist Rhoda Broughton, also in London, he complained of "the tedium of vast wastes of homesickness here. . . . Better fifty years of fogland—where indeed I have, alas, almost *had* my fifty years."

Tended by Burgess Noakes, he avoided all publicity and accepted few invitations. When the "Devastating Angel," as he teasingly called Edith Wharton, arrived for a fortnight in America, he went to visit her at her New York hotel, but he remained a private person until he accepted an honorary degree from Harvard in the spring of 1911—"with deference to William's memory." He spent hours talking shop with William Dean Howells, and—with the "Devastating Angel" back again—visited her home in Lenox, Massachusetts, "The Mount," which she was considering selling, to cut her ties completely with America. By then it was early summer, and James was palpably miserable. Without her realizing that James had already booked passage to London, she arranged for him to sail from Boston almost immediately. "Good God, what a woman—what a woman!" he exclaimed to his friend George Abbot James. "She does not even scruple to project me in a naked flight across the Atlantic." On July 30 he sailed on the *Mauretania,* as he originally planned. He had been in America for nearly a year.

The Reform Club had been James's London retreat almost as long as he had lived in Lamb House. When he returned he sought to expand his base in London. "I find," he wrote a friend from Lamb House, "that since my illness, long and dismal, of 1910, I can't stand lonely hibernation here, where for several years I have had too much of it. Miles of pavement and lamp light are good for me; but for 4 or 5 or even 6 months of the year . . . , my little old house here is as dear to me as ever." However, the club did not permit women in the rooms, and his typist, Theodora Bosanquet, who was willing to return to work for him in London as well as at Lamb House, needed a place in which to take her dictation. As James put it, the need to express himself "on the old Remingtonese terms" required "a seat and temple for the Remington and its priestess. . . ."

Happily, Miss Bosanquet's flat at No. 10 Lawrence Street in Chelsea had two unneeded rooms at the end, with a separate entrance. James rented them and began what would be his memorial to his brother, *A Small Boy and Others,* the beginning volume of his memoirs, pacing up and down, resonantly "sounding out the periods," and reliving his past. He did not settle into Lamb House again until the following June, when he had already begun his second volume, *Notes of a Son and Brother.* With a five-hundred-pound advance from both his publishers for each volume, he felt able to put away fiction until the tasks were accomplished.

Just before sailing, James had learned that the companion of so many of his days in London and Rye, Jonathan Sturges, had died in England. The crippled but good-humored Sturges had been but one of the Master's young disciples, a number of them Americans, who were no longer young and were being replaced by others in James's affections as Time had scattered them. His once-young American friends were, among other things, his entrée into worlds he shrank from penetrating. Sturges, in and out of a nursing home in Wimpole

Street and perhaps the most frequent guest at Lamb House, had been devoted to Whistler, and was to James "a little body-blighted intelligence—a little frustrate universal curiosity—and [with] a little pathetic Jack-the-Giant Killer's soul." Out of New York and Dartmouth, and financially (if in no other way) comfortable, Sturges, twenty years younger, was James's household "demon," a fascinating companion who wrote much but published little, and was—James wrote cryptically to Henrietta Ruebell—"saturated with London, and with all sorts of contrasted elements of it, to which he has given himself up. Handicapped, crippled, invalidical, he has yet made his way there in a wondrous fashion, and knows nine thousand people, of most of whom I've never heard. So he's amusing, and to him (as I'm very fond of him), I make sacrifices. But they *are* sacrifices."

Illness and frustration sometimes caused a darker side of the "demon's" personality to break through the shell of his stoicism. It only increased his hold upon the Master—if one is to believe a Ford Madox Ford recollection in which Sturges is clearly James's unidentified guest at Lamb House. "I have attended," Ford claimed,

at conversations between him and a queer tiny being who lay as if crumpled up on the stately sofa in James's magnificent panelled room in Lamb House—conversations that made the tall wax candles seem to me to waver in their sockets and the skin of my forehead and hands to prickle with sweat. I am in these things rather squeamish; I sometimes wish I was not, but it is so and I can't help it. I don't wish to leave the impression that these conversations were carried on for purposes of lewd stimulation or irreverent ribaldry. They occurred as part of the necessary pursuit of that knowledge that permitted James to give his reader the "sense of evil." . . . And I dare say they freed him from the almost universal proneness of Anglo-Saxon writers to indulge in their works in a continually intrusive fumbling in placket-holes as Sterne called it, or in the lugubrious occupation of composing libidinous Limericks. James would utter his racy "Ho-ho-ho's" and roll his fine eyes whilst talking to his curious little friend, but they were not a whit more racy and his eyes did not roll any more than they did when he was asking a housemaid or a parson's wife for advice as to the advisability of employing a Lady's Help, or than when he was recounting urbane anecdotes at tea on his lawn to the Ladies So-and-So and So-and-So. It was all in the day's work.

Exactly what may have been his intimate conviction as to, say, what should be the proper relation of the sexes, I don't profess to know. That he demanded from the more fortunate characters in his books a certain urbanity of behaviour as long as that behaviour took place in the public eye, his books are there to prove. . . .

Logan Pearsall Smith also had a fund of lurid anecdotes for James, and also, with far less cause, affected a life of semi-invalidism, bringing with him from his house in St Leonard's Terrace, Chelsea, or his farmhouse in Hampshire, dark curtains to shut out the bedroom light, and a special hard pillow. If he talked after nine o'clock he would suffer from insomnia, he claimed, but James would write from Lamb House such lines as "Logan Pearsall Smith was just with me for 36 hours—and the tide of gossip between us rose high, he being a great master of that effect." His pose of invalidism always involved his hot-water bottle and his umbrella, and fear of getting his feet wet, but at least vicariously his interests ran to sex, from the lubricious to the unspeakable. "I was never one of those / Who wrote songs about the rose," he confessed. But his friend at Lamb House was cautious about indulging such curiosities. When Forrest Reid, in his twenties, innocently sent James a copy of his novel *The Garden God,* an idyll of schoolboy friendship which included a languorous bathing scene in which the hero persuades his companion to pose naked for him among the rocks, James was appalled, and sent Reid (according to E. M. Forster's biographer P. N. Furbank) "an exceedingly frosty letter."

To listen to the talk of another semi-invalid, Howard Sturgis, James usually had to travel to Queen's Acre—"Qu'Acre" to intimates—Sturgis's Georgian mansion on the edge of Windsor Great Park. He was the son of American banker Russell Sturgis, whose wealth, but not whose drive, he had inherited. After Eton and Cambridge, he had settled into Victorian domesticity with a younger companion, William Haynes Smith—who ran the household—and occupied his time with his writing, his guests, his dogs, and his embroidery. He also enjoyed visiting the grander country houses for which his inherited American dollars would not have sufficed to pay the kitchen staff. One day he and James, with Ethel Sands and Ottoline Morrell, were invited to lunch with Miss Alice Rothschild, who had been a friend of Ethel Sands's mother. It was an occasion to see priceless works of art so guarded from human contact that as they moved through the silent rooms and corridors, marshaled by Miss Rothschild, Ottoline was warned "not to touch" when her hand rested for a moment on a table. In the oppressive hothouse environment she felt as if she were

moving in the interior of a Louis XIV clock that would cease ticking if I stepped off the drugget that was laid across each room. A breath of criticism was indeed cried into my ear by Henry James; his basilisk gaze had absorbed the company of seven-foot-high footmen that waited on us, the hothouse flowers and the dish of enormous white strawberries that were in front of the plates. He looked up at the footmen, he looked down on the strawberries. "Murder and rapine," he said, "would be preferable to this."

So inhuman was the atmosphere of this private museum that none of us were directed to the place which is after all so necessary a provision even in a museum. When Howard Sturgis suggested asking one of the young giants where it was to be found, Henry James threw up his arms and said to him, "Howard dear, what I thought was an Elysian dream you have made into a physiological fact."

There were few physiological facts in Sturgis's fiction. He wrote fastidiously, finishing only three novels, and claiming that to occupy his hands while he conversed—he disliked smoking—he needed his crocheting needle. "Howdie," said his cousin George Santayana, was the "last and permanent baby" of Sturgis's widowed mother, and matured into "a perfect young lady of the Victorian type." Mustached and prematurely white-haired, the handsome Sturgis had written an Eton-based novel, *Tim,* about a romantic affair ("passing the love of women") between a sensitive boy and an elder, more conventional friend which ended with the mawkishly depicted death of the boy. A second novel, *All That Was Possible,* used the old-fashioned form of a series of letters, and concerned the attempts of a discarded mistress to live a new life in what proves to be the intolerant country.

James thought it was good enough to encourage Sturgis to try again, which he did, in a long and lovingly written novel, *Belchamber,* the hero of which suggested its author. A young English marquis marries despite his passive nature, flattered at the interest an attractive young woman has shown in him. Once she has his title and money, she acquires a series of lovers; thus, although she never consummates the marriage, she soon provides her husband with an heir, and he is strangely satisfied, bestowing on the infant all the affection of the most devoted father, and otherwise remaining in his inner world until poetic justice overtakes the principals. "Bring your book and read it aloud!" James wrote Sturgis on inviting him to Lamb House in 1903.

When Sturgis visited, he left his galleys for James, who observed that he was prepared to "pass" the novel except for one major qualm. Because Sturgis had made his hero a member of the upper nobility, "there are whole masses of Marquisate things and items, a multitude of inherent detail in his existence, which isn't open to the painter *de gaieté de coeur.* . . ." Open especially to an American, James was implying, even to one so closely identified with England. Later he added his concern that the hero was "all passive and nullity," and complained surprisingly that there wasn't a word about his physiology. Sturgis considered the details of the Master's criticism and announced that he would not permit the novel to be published. Then "Howdie" had to be reassured, and James painfully insisted that since no one else was likely to recognize the "esoteric" flaws he had seen, the novel would "be the joy of thousands of people. . . ." Reaction to *Belchamber* was tepid when it was finally published in 1906: critics thought that Sturgis had wasted his gifts on a disagreeable subject. But it remains worth reading for its sardonic wit, reminiscent of Sturgis's table talk, rather than for its curious bleakness, reminiscent of his strange—although luxurious—life.

The squire of Qu'Acre published nothing more, although he wrote a story, "The China Pot," about a great writer who so demolished the work of a younger man that the disciple takes his own life. In a scene at the burial, the elder author and a friend wonder what had motivated the suicide, for their dead companion had everything to live for, from youth and good looks to intellect and wealth. To the great man the death is "amazing, mysterious and inexplicable." But the other "could see that he knew as well as I did, and that he knew that I knew." James would have understood.

One of James's younger friends was an American sculptor who lived most of his life in Italy. Henrik Anderson constructed massive

Punch toasts Mark Twain, 1907.

Coburn's portrait photograph
of Mark Twain in London.

Alvin Langdon Coburn's evocation of
Victorian London: Portland Place
in winter twilight.

A study of Bret Harte, 1893.

Pearl Craigie, who took the
nom de plume John Oliver Hobbes.

The last photograph of Stephen Crane, 1900.

Henry Harland by Max Beerbohm.

The Coroner reading last week's depositions to Mrs. Mills.   Mrs. Mills, the Christian scientist.   Dr. Brown.

Mr. Stokes (Harold Frederic's executor.)   Dr. Freyberger, specialist.   Miss Frederic.   Miss Kate Lyon.

Harold Frederic in 1898.

Miss Kate Lyon and Mrs. Mills in court.

Sketches of principals
at "Kate Frederic's" trial after
Harold Frederic's death.

Edwin Abbey's portrait by
Sir W. Q. Orchardson.

Romaine Brooks's *Self Portrait*.

Brown and Gold: Self Portrait
by Whistler, 1900.

Caricature of Joseph Pennell in
the style of Whistler by Beerbohm.

Beerbohm's "The Queue outside Mr Sargent's,"
where society ladies lined up to have their portraits painted.

Portrait photograph of
Jennifer Churchill, c. 1895.

Jacob Epstein's *Rock Drill*.

Henry James at seventy
in a portrait by Sargent.

Ezra Pound
photographed by
Alvin Langdon Coburn
in 1913.

Oscar Wilde's tomb sculpted by Jacob Epstein.

Robert Frost in 1913.

A pen-and-ink sketch of T. S. Eliot
by Wyndham Lewis.

and vaguely expressive nudes, often in the form of fountains, to the massive indifference of purchasers. The painfully repressed Master once had written Anderson passionate letters which were vicarious embraces. As the Edwardian decade waned, their reunions were fewer, and the elder man's disappointment in the artist's inability to live up to the excessive vision was unhidden. And there were new and younger men attracted to James's orbit, no longer American in origin—Percy Lubbock, Jocelyn Persse (whose letters from James have the fervid intensity of the early correspondence with Andersen), and the worshipful Hugh Walpole, who would make a name for himself as a popular novelist, and in doing so shamelessly culti-vate the Master. The relationships with the younger men, which James would describe to each as "exquisite," contained on the aging James's side, at least, a sort of love, but what it actually was in each case is unknown. In his later years, Walpole told Stephen Spender "that he had once offered himself to the Master and that James had said, 'I can't, I can't.' " It may have been true, too, of some others.

In 1911 Mrs Wharton was back in England, looking for ways to assist James financially, and, as usual, to indulge him in his passion for motoring, which she thought he denied himself needlessly with excuses about money, although he "took advantage, to the last drop of petrol, of the travelling capacity of any visitor's car." Her rem-iniscences of Henry James the automobilist are familiar, yet any pic-ture of the Master at Lamb House is incomplete without them, for James loved exploring and re-exploring the some counties, and on seating himself in Mrs Wharton's car he would become

as jubilant as a child. Everything pleased him—the easy locomotion (which often cradled him into a brief nap), the bosky softness of the landscape, the discovery of towns and villages hitherto beyond his range, the magic of ancient names, quaint or impressive, crabbed or melodious. These he would murmur over and over to himself in a low chant, finally creating characters to fit them, and sometimes whole families, with their domestic complications and matrimonial alliances, such as the Dymmes of Dymchurch, one of whom married a Sparkle, and was the mother of little Scintilla Dymme-Sparkle, subject of much mirth and many anec-dotes. Except during his naps, nothing escaped him, and I suppose no one ever felt more imaginatively, or with deeper poetic emotion, the beauty of sea and sky, the serenities of the landscape, the sober charm of villages, manor-houses and humble churches, and all the implications of that much-storied corner of England. . . .

On Mrs Wharton's visits to Qu'Acre she would usually stop first at Lamb House to take James along. The Master fancied himself to be an expert navigator, often misguiding the chauffeur on an exploratory detour, but the most absurd occasion of his getting the party lost occurred on a visit to Sturgis, when their automobile arrived in Windsor after dark on a rainy evening.

We must have been driven by a strange chauffeur—perhaps Cook was on a holiday; at any rate, having fallen into the lazy habit of trusting to him to know the way, I found myself at a loss to direct his substitute to the King's Road. While I was hesitating, and peering out into the darkness, James spied an ancient doddering man who had stopped in the rain to gaze at us. "Wait a moment, my dear—I'll ask him where we are"; and leaning out he signalled to the spectator.

"My good man, if you'll be good enough to come here, please; a little nearer—so," and as the old man came up: "My friend, to put it to you in two words, this lady and I have just arrived here from *Slough;* that is to say, to be more strictly accurate, we have recently *passed through* Slough on our way here, having actually motored to Windsor from Rye, which was our point of departure; and the darkness having overtaken us, we should be much obliged if you would tell us where we now are in relation, say, to the High Street, which, as you of course know, leads to the Castle, after leaving on the left hand the turn down to the railway station."

I was not surprised to have this extraordinary appeal met by silence, and a dazed expression on the old wrinkled face at the window; nor to have James go on: "In short" (his invariable prelude to a fresh series of explanatory ramifications), "in short, my good man, what I want to put to you in a word is this; supposing we have already (as I have reason to think we have) driven past the turn down to the railway station (which, in that case, by the way, would probably not have been on our left hand, but on our right), where are we now in relation to . . ."

"Oh, please," I interrupted, feeling myself utterly unable to sit through another parenthesis, "do ask him where the King's Road is."

"Ah—? The King's Road? Just so! Quite Right! Can you, as a matter of fact, my good man, tell us where, in relation to our present position, the King's Road exactly *is?*"

"Ye're in it," said the aged face at the window.

At Queen's Acre a cheerful lavishness of hospitality prevailed, while at Lamb House Mrs Wharton regularly observed "an anxious frugality . . . combined with the wish that the usually solitary guest (there were never, at most, more than two at a time) should not suffer too greatly from his or her supposed habits of luxury, and the privations imposed by the host's conviction that he was on the brink of ruin." Yet James, she realized, while haunted by the specter of impoverishment, was the most generous of men, and needed somehow to be drawn back into his old, gregarious ways, and to regain confidence in his fiscal stability.

First, she commissioned a charcoal drawing of him by Sargent, mainly a way to force him into sittings—and thus companionship—with his old friend. It did not go well, and neither James nor Mrs Wharton liked the result, although it now survives as part of the Royal Collection at Windsor. More automobile touring with James also proved unhelpful, especially as he continued complaining about how low his professional earnings were compared with her own. To funnel funds to him that he would accept, she began a quiet campaign to secure for him the Nobel Prize for literature. It had already been won by lesser writers. Kipling had received the lucrative award, worth then nearly eight thousand pounds, in 1907, and Mistral, Carducci, Echegeray, Björnsen, and Sully Prudhomme in other years. Through Howells, Gosse, and other statesmen of letters she had the Swedish Academy thoroughly briefed, but James was little translated, and—in his later manner—almost untranslatable; and, to a foreigner, he was almost invisible—more a private than a public figure, exactly as he preferred. The prize went to the Belgian Maurice Maeterlinck, author of *The Bluebird*.

Undeterred, Mrs Wharton remembered how she and James had funneled money to Fullerton. Secretly, she arranged with Charles Scribner, their mutual publisher, to divert dollars from her own royalties* to offer an advance to James to begin a major new novel

* In a note "for my biographer," which Edith Wharton jotted down fourteen years later, she recalled, apparently in error, "I gave Mr. Scribner this $8000 from the earnings of *The House of Mirth* to encourage H.J. to go on writing, as he was so despondent about his work. The result was successful and no one knew." But her biographer discovered that royalties from that novel of 1905 had been scant by 1913, and that the money very likely had come from the $15,000 ad-

of American life. J. B. Pinker had let it be known that James had indeed begun a new novel, *The Ivory Tower,* before his illnesses of 1910. "As the publishers of your definitive edition," Scribner wrote James, "we want another great novel to balance *The Golden Bowl* and round off the series of books in which you have developed the theory of composition set forth in your prefaces." They were prepared to pay him four thousand dollars on signing the contract, a similar sum on delivery of the manuscript, and a 20 percent royalty. Pinker advised acceptance, as James was delighted to do; and Pinker received, to Mrs Wharton's annoyance, 10 percent of her money as his agent's fee.

Edith Wharton was prepared to do more. The "royalty" deception had not been an adequate substitute for the Nobel Prize, yet a larger advance would have made James suspicious. The Master's seventieth birthday would occur in 1913. She wanted it to be the occasion for James's own countrymen to do something generous— perhaps to provide a sufficient purse for him to be able to afford his own automobile and chauffeur. In March she arranged for a letter, signed by William Dean Howells and herself, to be sent to thirty-nine American friends:

April 15th next is Henry James's 70th birthday.

His English friends and admirers have raised a fund to present him with a portrait. We believe that his American friends will be at least as eager to ask him to accept a gift commemorating this date.

In view of the shortness of time, such commemoration, we think, might most appropriately take the form of a sum of money (not less than $5000) for the purchase of a gift, the choice of which would be left to him. . . .

Letters—urging that the proposal "be kept *strictly confidential"* —were mailed to such literary and moneyed friends of James's as John Jay Chapman, Henry Adams, Mrs Jack Gardner, Dr S. Weir Mitchell, Charles Scribner, and George Vanderbilt. Unfortunately, one of the recipients, George Abbot James—no relative—informed

---

vance she had received from Appleton for *The Reef.* Thus Mrs Wharton "was using Scribners as a secret conveyor of money supplied to her by the house for which she was gradually abandoning Scribners" (R. W. B. Lewis, 1975).

Henry James's nephews, and one of them cabled Lamb House. A return cable plunged the sponsors into confusion: "Immense thanks for warning. Taking instant prohibitive action. Please express to individuals approached my horror. Money absolutely returned. Uncle." Howells quickly pulled out, sending Mrs Wharton what she described as "an ineffable letter . . . senile and querulous—*how* it explains his novels!" James himself wrote a letter that hurt her deeply. "There was nothing on earth I valued as much as his affection," she wrote a mutual friend, Cambridge don Gaillard Lapsley (another American). "I can never get over this."

By July she was well over the affair, and James was again writing to her in his teasingly grand manner. Her divorce had also become final, leaving her freer, and she returned to London determined to acquire property nearby on which to settle. "The eventful change in her life and even in her identity brought about by the divorce," her biographer R. W. B. Lewis writes, "had led inevitably to thoughts of a major change of place, and she was feeling more drawn to England all the time. She longed to hear English spoken on all sides for at least part of the year; she longed as well for quieter surroundings . . . [than] the noise and roar of Paris. . . ."

A property near Hill Hall, called Coopersale, eighteen miles north of London, was available. She went to inspect it with Bernhard Berenson and Walter Berry, who agreed that it was right for her. The house was set far back from the walls enclosing the land, and there were more than a hundred acres of landscaped gardens, orchards, woods, and a brook. Mrs Wharton decided, in a verb Howard Sturgis coined for the occasion, to "Cooperbuy," and made an offer of six thousand pounds. The estate agent decided that the amount was inadequate, and her intentions of being an English country dame hung fire while they haggled through the year. Finally she learned what the heavy income tax would be for her as a foreigner residing in England, and decided not to "Cooperbuy" after all. Instead she would look in from time to time, from Paris.

While Mrs Wharton's birthday scheme had fallen through, the English equivalent, organized by the half-American Edmund Gosse and such younger admirers as Percy Lubbock and Hugh Walpole, had gone on. James had again objected, but his confidante Lucy Clifford had told him that he was "cold, callous and ungracious," and he had given in. The English strategy had been more subtle. No one was permitted to subscribe more than five pounds, and nearly three hundred people subscribed. The author of *The Golden Bowl* was to be presented with a gilded silver bowl of Charles II vintage, with the balance to be offered as honorarium to John Sargent to do a birthday portrait. Sargent refused to take any money, and suggested that it be used to commission a bust by a young sculptor, Derwent Wood; James agreed to sit for the portrait by his friend, provided that it would go to the National Gallery in London if it wanted the canvas, or to the Metropolitan Museum in New York if the country of his adoption was not interested. Then he sat, during the spring of 1913, in bow tie and striped waistcoat, for one of Sargent's most sensitive canvases.

Friends like Jocelyn Persse and the young actress Ruth Draper, newly arrived in London from America, would visit the Tite Street studio to distract James while Sargent painted. The result, James wrote Rhoda Broughton, was "Sargent at his very best and poor old H.J. not at his worst; in short a living breathing likeness and a masterpiece of painting. I am really quite ashamed to admire it so much and so loudly. . . ." He was truly embarrassed about his open admiration for the picture since he was not only admiring his friend's work but admiring himself.

Acknowledging his English friends' "brave gifts and benedictions," James had a letter printed to send to all the signatories.* "I was drawn to London long years ago," he wrote, "by the sense, felt from still earlier, of all the interest and association I should find here, and I now see how my faith was to sink deeper foundations than I could presume ever to measure—how my justification was both stoutly to grow and wisely to wait. . . ."

In December Sargent opened 33 Tite Street for three days for a special showing to the donors (whose money he had not accepted for himself), to give James a further opportunity to thank his friends

* Including Bennett, Galsworthy, Shaw, Kipling, Wells, Gosse, and other luminaries, as well as such younger friends as Arthur Benson, Pearsall Smith, Virginia Woolf, Rupert Brooke, and Hugh Walpole.

and preen beside his portrait. The event was a great success, but earlier in the year it appeared as if there might be no celebration at all. At his flat in London not long before his birthday—he had moved from the Reform Club to 21 Carlyle Mansions, a "Chelsea perch" overlooking the Thames, near the Albert Bridge, that January—he had fainted. With his history of heart trouble he was worried, but his doctor was reassuring, and James had returned to Lamb House for the warmer months as planned. Still, he knew that he had to restrict further what remained of his life. "Time, awful Time"— as he wrote Hugh Walpole—was intervening, but at Lamb House that summer, after he had finished sitting for Sargent in London, the sun shone and he expanded happily among his visitors and put the last touches to *Notes of a Son and Brother*. He was well aware that both tradition and realism suggested that one wrote one's memoirs when one had said all that was to be said in other forms, and that doing so was also a profound bow to mortality. His sister-in-law had pressed him to return to Boston and Cambridge for another long stay, and he had declined. "Dearest Alice," he wrote, "I could come back to America (could be carried back on a stretcher) to die—but never, never to live."

CHAPTER VIII

Church Walk

I am that terrible thing,
*   the product of American culture,*
Or rather that product improved
*   by considerable care and attention.*
. . . Behold the the that I am;
. . . London's last foible in poets.

—Ezra Pound in "Redondillas" (1911)

ON OCTOBER 8, 1908, Ezra Pound arrived in London, his baggage consisting mainly of copies of *A Lume Spento,** the thin volume of verse he had published at his own expense in Venice. He had three pounds and knew no one. America at the time, he later said, "was still a colony of London so far as culture was concerned. . . . The only way I could educate the educatable minority in the United States was to come to London." By his twenty-third birthday, at the end of the month, he was living at Miss Withey's boardinghouse at 8 Duchess Street, Portland Place, where he had stayed for a week in 1906, on a European holiday which followed the award of his M.A. at the University of Pennsylvania.

For the academic year 1906–7 he had existed upon a fellowship in Romance languages. It paid him a stipend of five hundred dol-

---

* *With Tapers Quenched.*

lars (in eight installments) and made him financially independent—since he lived at home with his parents in Philadelphia. He had decided, however, not to go on for a doctorate. "I have spatted with nearly everybody [there]," he wrote a friend. There was little more chance that he would get along in an even more rigid academic situation, but he accepted a teaching job at Wabash College, a small Presbyterian college in Indiana. Within a month he knew he had made a mistake. He disliked the work, the people, the atmosphere. Even the "effete East" now seemed attractive.

When not correcting papers, he wrote in his spare time, and contemplated marriage with Miss Mary Moore of Trenton, New Jersey, whom he had met the previous summer, before his move to the Midwest. Since Crawfordsville proved stultifying, he had "a crying need," he confided, for "merely degenerate decadent civilization." At Wabash he was already considered as the local representative of the decadence, having visited London and Paris; but his reputation was confirmed when a young "lady-gent impersonator" from a traveling burlesque show was stranded in town without a penny, and Pound, who had encountered her while walking through a snowstorm to mail a letter, put her up for the night. The maiden ladies who had let his rooms were less sympathetic, and telephoned the college authorities the next morning.

In January 1908, after four months, the academic career of Ezra Pound was over. So was his romance with Mary Moore, who had found distance a strain upon the affections, and had become engaged to a more accessible beau. There was nothing to keep him home, and his father—Homer Pound was an official at the United States Mint in Philadelphia—was willing to stake him to some writing time abroad. In February the young poet and scholar landed in Gibraltar with eighty dollars in his pocket. He had fifteen left when he began looking for ways to survive in London.

Chance helped. It was not a very auspicious connection, but a travel agent in Philadelphia had given him, with his ticket, a note to a man at Covent Garden Market who somehow "persuaded the London Polytechnic to let me give a course of lectures. . . ." Pound was unknown, but he had an M.A. and a "published book." He was authorized to deliver a "short course" on the development of literature in "Southern Europe" in January and February, which if successful in drawing auditors would lead to a more elaborate series the following autumn. With something to work toward, he rented a room at 48 Langham Street, next door to a pub and close to the Polytechnic. Besides, it was only a penny bus ride to the British Museum, his newest university, where one had, in the great domed Reading Room, not only the largest collection of books in the English-speaking world, but heat, light, a desk, free pens and blotting paper, and lavatories limited to "casual ablutions."

At 81 Mortimer Street, nearby, were the printers Pollock & Co. There, in December, Pound had one hundred copies of a twenty-eight-page pamphlet of sixteen poems published, shrewdly entitled *A Quinzaine for This Yule*. With Christmas close at hand, the ls. 6d. edition sold out, and Pound arranged with a real publisher—Elkin Mathews, of *Yellow Book* memory—for a second printing. In a few months in London he had published his "second book," become a Polytechnic lecturer (and seen leaflets issued advertising him), and come to the attention of a leading spirit in English publishing. He was, as "Sandalphon," one of the poems in the new collection claimed, "causing the works to speak. . . ."

There is no record of Pound's reconnoitering London to search out the literary luminaries of the age. He had not arrived with romantic dreams but rather with the drive to be known himself and to make a difference in the way literature was written and read. For that purpose Elkin Mathews was the kind of person it was necessary to meet. The English writing he admired, after Robert Browning and Dante Gabriel Rossetti, was that associated with the nineties, much of which Mathews published. *Fin de siècle* was not yet a spent force. Although Ernest Dowson (whose "Cynara" he had been "drunk with") and Lionel Johnson and Aubrey Beardsley had died young, some nineties writers were more influential than in the heady days of the *Yellow Book* and the *Savoy,* particularly William Butler Yeats, who, despite his involvement with Irish matters, had become a towering presence in English poetry.

Pound had arrived without romantic susceptibilities, unlike Van Wyck Brooks, who had come from Harvard the year before at twenty-one, and was awed, when "responding to a knock at my grimy

Soho door one day, I confronted a footman in livery on the landing outside." For a while, although Brooks worked doggedly in the British Museum, where "grizzled old men in threadbare morning coats . . . dozed behind piles of ponderous books and stealthily drew from their pockets papers full of crumbs," London was for the future critic "a kind of play that I found rewarding only when I saw it across the footlights. . . . Shaw, for one, who reminded me of the Etruscan warrior in the Museum of New York, for he had, with his grey beard, the muscles of a boy. Many times I heard him speak, an aging man springing from his chair with youth in every gesture and sally of the voice. I often saw Chesterton's bushy head, and one day in St. Martin's Lane I encountered J. M. Barrie, pipe in mouth, with his deep black eyes and bright red necktie. He was turning down an alley to the stage-door of the theatre where *What Every Woman Knows* was about to open. Then at the British Museum I stood beside a familar face that said to the young man at the desk, 'Any books for Ellis?'—and I was surprised when the young man asked 'What initial?' and the man with the beard was obliged to answer 'H.' For I had instantly recognized Havelock Ellis."

Brooks returned to America on the saloon deck a year later, a gesture to convince himself, perhaps, that he had accomplished much since his crossing to England in steerage. He had in fact written and published an "unripe little book" (so he would call it) and had been gainfully if not excitingly employed in a press-cutting agency; he may have wondered whether he would have been farther ahead had he remained in Cambridge and returned to Harvard. In New York he managed to find a job with the magazine *The World's Work,* which did not last long, but in the process he managed to meet the publisher Mitchell Kennerley, who was willing to bring out Brooks's *The Wine of the Puritans,* not because of its success in London—it had none—but because Sisley's had hundreds of sets of unbound sheets to sell. The price had to be a bargain, since Brooks had absorbed half the printing cost to get the book published.

For the American edition Kennerley purchased and bound two hundred copies, launching the author modestly—almost imperceptibly—in New York. Ironically, Brooks's argument in *The Wine of the Puritans* was that the American artist should sacrifice himself in

America. In his return from London to make his way frustratingly on his own side of the Atlantic, he was living his message.

On a later stay in London as a critic with an emerging reputation, he saw a copy of his first book at an open-air bookstall, exposed in the sixpenny box, "where I had observed it many times with the rain bespattering it so that the gilt on the cover grew dimmer and dimmer." When it sank to the penny bin, he rescued the book.

Years after, Brooks recalled that "AE" (the Irish poet George W. Russell) had told him "that one should never try to meet celebrated persons, that in the end one inevitably met the persons whom one was intended to meet, the persons whom one truly had a reason for knowing." So Pound discovered, for in quick order after Mathews he met the influential Ford Madox Ford and Mrs Olivia Shakespear, a lady who would lead him not only to Yeats but to her daughter.

At his cheap room in Langham Street, Pound "wrote [himself] into a state of exhaustion doing five chapters [of a "damn bad novel"] at one sitting, arose the next day, filled [more] reams and then stuck." He burned the manuscript, then went back to writing his Polytechnic lectures and several poems which paralleled the lectures. For his course he was researching the songs and ballads of the troubadour tradition. One evening in the "Turkish Coffee" café in Soho, he had been angered by overhearing "a certain sort of cheap irreverence which was new to me. I had lain awake most of the night. I got up rather late in the morning and started for the British Museum with the first four lines [of a poem] in my head. I wrote the rest of the poem at a sitting at the left side of the Reading Room, with scarcely any erasures." After lunch, unable to work further, he went off to Fleet Street, hoping to sell the poem, "for I began to realise that for the first time in my life, I had written something that 'everyone could understand' and I wanted it to go to the people." "I try not to repeat myself," he later told Malcolm Cowley. "Having written this ballad about Christ, I had only to write similar ballads about James, Matthew, Mark, Luke and John and my fortune was made." Yet he was claiming a virtue from which he was not tempted. Only the *Evening Standard* was even willing to consider "The Ballad of the Goodly Fere," and it turned the poem down. A vigorous monologue in the Old English tradition (*fere* is Anglo-Saxon for *comrade*), the ballad related, from the standpoint of Simon Zealotes, the story of the life and death of a tough, stubborn Jesus, "the goodliest fere o' all." Ford Madox Ford would eventually publish it.

A more direct by-product of Pound's preparations for the lecture series was his even more vigorous "Sestina: Altaforte." Altaforte was the castle of the warlike Provençal poet Bertrans de Born, whom Dante had consigned to hell as a stirrer-up of strife. The poet, who in Pound's lines considers peace womanish and foul, and the clash of swords the only worthwhile music, had proved almost impossible to translate. "Then it occurred to me that I . . . wanted the curious involution and recurrence of the Sestina. I knew more or less of the arrangement, I wrote the first strophe [beginning, "Damn it all! This our South stinks peace."] and then went to the British Museum to make sure of the right order of the permutations. . . . I did the rest of the poem at a sitting." Technically, Pound thought much later, it was one of his best efforts.

Both poems came too late for his next small book, *Personae.* He had taken the manuscript to Vigo Street, where he recalled Mathews as asking whether the poet "cared to contribute to the costs of publishing"—not an unusual request in the case of an unknown writer, particularly a poet. "I've got a shilling in my clothes, if that's any use to you," said Pound. "Oh, well," sighed Mathews, "I rather want to publish 'em anyhow."

The most valuable new friend after Mathews proved to be Mrs Shakespear, who invited him to tea at her home at 12 Brunswick Gardens, Kensington. The fortyish wife of a prosperous solicitor, and a minor novelist herself—she published six novels between 1894 and 1910—she was "the most charming woman in London," Pound wrote his mother. A cousin of the late Lionel Johnson, whose poetry Pound admired, as well as a friend of W. B. Yeats, Mrs Shakespear —the "Diana Vernon" of his memoirs—was the very benefactor who, in the nineties, had relieved Yeats of the burden of his virginity. Now she had a daughter, Dorothy, who at first merely sat quietly on a low stool near the fireplace and listened to the excitable, red-haired young poet; but her mother apparently had other ideas for her. Mrs Shakespear decided to purchase tickets for Pound's lecture series for herself and for Dorothy, and Pound would be paying many more visits to Brunswick Gardens.

Through Mathews and the writers he published, and the Shake-

spears and the writers they knew, Pound quickly made useful contacts. Mathews took him to a writers' club which met once a month
at the United Arts Club in St James's Street, and included Bernard
Shaw and Hilaire Belloc. It was useful to get close enough to the
great men of letters to discover that they were real people, and
Pound quickly shed any residual timidity he had toward his elders
and "betters." At Mathews's bookshop in Vigo Street, a meeting
place for young writers, he became friendly with two young poets
and critics, Frank Flint and T. E. Hulme. Soon Flint, whom Pound
entertained in his tiny room, where the bed took up most of the
space, reviewed the sixty-six pages of *Personae* in A. R. Orage's lively
and eccentric *New Age,* and Orage would eventually invite Pound
to contribute to the weekly. Flint's review was not especially well
written, the poet explained to his father on forwarding the clipping
that spring, but it would be good advertising. Pound, Flint had written, was "a rebel against all conventions but sanity," and despite his
indebtednesses to medieval poets, to Browning, and to the nineties,
his work could be accepted as poetry "without reference to the
sources of raw material. . . . This book is as tufted with beauty
as the bole of an old elm tree with green shoots. . . ."

Personae was widely noticed, with praise for its energy and its
eloquence, and objections to its perversities, to its borrowings from
the past, and to its projection of the poet as "artistic malcontent." He
made, said one critic, "a lively din." The pattern of a lifetime was
already forming, and Pound, realizing his métier, junked a vast
prose-and-verse sequence and the libretto for an opera. The title of
his next collection of verse, *Exultations,* published later in 1909 by
Mathews, would reflect his feelings about the pace of his progress in
London.

To his friend William Carlos Williams, an amateur poet from
Rutherford, New Jersey, then studying medicine at the University of
Pennsylvania, Pound wrote on February 3, "Am by way of falling
into the crowd that does things here. London, deah old Lundon, is
the place for poesy." He urged Williams to "come across" and
broaden his mind. Pound was certain that he was broadening his own
mind. Until he had settled in England there were no American poets
he could regard except with contempt. "From this side of the Atlan-

tic," he wrote in a half-dozen pages of reconsideration, "I am for the first time able to read Whitman." Now Pound saw him, despite his flaws, as America's only poet, a true "forbear" although "his tricks are not yet my tricks." The authentic Pound voice was already struggling to be heard. "I honour him, for he prophesied me. . . ."

One magazine which reviewed *Personae* was a new publication on the lookout for the new, managed in disorganized fashion by the pale, portly Ford Madox Ford from chaotic rooms at 84 Holland Park Avenue in Kensington. The *English Review* published Pound's "Goodly Fere" and "Sestina," and Ford invited the poet to parties at Holland Park Avenue where writers produced *bouts-rimés* for a prize of authentic bay leaves. Pound turned up "wearing one earring," Violet Hunt remembered, "which was considered very scandalous. . . . Dollie Radford won the first prize and . . . Hilaire Belloc won the second prize. . . ."

Ford admired the sharpness of the young poet's mind, and would be of immense value to him. Anyone in literary London whom Pound had not yet met, and who he thought might be useful to know as he lay siege to the remnants of Victorianism, Ford professed to know, and usually did. "Fordie," Pound would later write in his *Cantos* (74), "who wrote of giants. . . ." Besides, Pound remembered elsewhere, "It was POSSIBLE to discuss a serious idea with him." When Ford first met Pound, he wrote, with his usual ease of hyperbole, in a volume of memoirs, the poet's "Philadelphia accent was comprehensible if disconcerting; . . . he was astonishingly meagre and agile. He threw himself alarmingly into frail chairs, devoured enormous quantities of your pastry, fixed his pince-nez firmly on his nose, drew out a manuscript from his pocket . . . and looking down his nose would chuckle like Mephistopheles and read you a translation from Arnaut Daniel. The only part of the *Albade* that you would understand would be the refrain: *Ah me, the darn, the darn it comes too sune!*"

It may have been "Fordie" who recommended that the poet move to more respectable quarters, and during the summer of 1909 Pound seems to have tried both Brook Green and Hammersmith, but the bus fare to the British Museum was thruppence. In addition, Ford as well as the Shakespears lived in Kensington. Emboldened by prospects of success when, in July, he had been promised payment for a full series of Polytechnic lectures, Pound moved to a first-floor room—eight shillings a week—at 10 Church Walk, a cul-de-sac of small houses off Kensington High Street near St Mary Abbots Church. He had an iron bedstead, a mahogany washstand with a lid to enable it to be used as a desk, and a low cupboard upon which to pile books. There were even chairs, including one which converted to an extra bed. He could now reciprocate T. E. Hulme's invitations to his rooms in Frith Street, Soho, where young writers and critics gathered to argue about how English poetry could be renewed.

Again Pound ebulliently described his exploits to William Carlos Williams, in the process offering Williams little hope that one could succeed in literature from a small town in New Jersey. Williams had, at his own expense, printed a tiny pamphlet of his poems and mailed a copy to Church Walk. "Great art it is not," Pound replied. "Poetic it is, but there are innumerable poetic volumes poured out here in Gomorrah." And he set Williams a syllabus for his improvement as a writer, recommending, in a short lecture for unfortunates within reach of libraries, but not London, some deep reading in Yeats, Browning, Francis Thompson, Swinburne, and Rossetti. Then, in a less than optimistic appraisal of his friend's potential, he suggested the names of Margaret Sackville, Rosamund Watson, and Ernest Rhys, so that Williams could "learn what the people of the second rank can do. . . . You are out of touch." As for himself, Pound confessed that he had "sinned in nearly every possible way, even the ways I most condemn. I have printed too much. I have been praised by the greatest living poet. I am . . . become suddenly somewhat of a success. . . . There is no town like London to make one feel the vanity of all art except the highest. To make one disbelieve in all but the most careful and conservative presentation of one's stuff. I have sinned deeply against the doctrine I preach." He would continue to do so. Americans were not expected to behave as Englishmen, although Bret Harte had blended imperceptibly into the London scene, as would T. S. Eliot. Pound's pose, by degrees, became the man, and was working to his advantage. As Rupert Brooke already was describing Pound to a friend on reading *Personae*, he was "the most modern of modern poets." Four years later, in his *Cantos,*

Pound devoted line after line to the persons and places and episodes of the Church Walk years, which were

. . . our London,
my London, your London.

Pound's Sunday and Monday literary evenings took him into the near past as well as into contemporary London. He reserved Sunday evenings for visits to Victor Plarr, librarian of the Royal College of Surgeons, who in the 1890s had been a member of the Rhymers' Club with Johnson, Symons, and Yeats. He began visiting "Old Billyum" himself (Yeats was forty-four), frequenting the poet's Monday evenings at his flat, hung with Pre-Raphaelite pictures, above a cobbler's shop in Woburn Buildings (now Woburn Walk) near Euston Station. Yeats was impressed, writing Lady Gregory in December 1909 about "this queer creature . . . who has become really a great authority on the Troubadours [and] has I think got closer to the right sort of music for poetry. . . ." That remark would have pleased, and even more emboldened, Pound had he known it, for his aim was less to promote Ezra Pound than to propagate new standards for verse. The Tennysonian fuzziness he saw as an inheritance from the Romantics he despised had substituted prettiness for precision. He wanted to synthesize a new, living tradition based on what he saw as the best of the European past. Behind his increasing theatrics was a sense of mission, but the zealous stridency with which he urged the overhaul of contemporary poetics would alienate, one by one, his closest allies. Pound would claim in 1934 that the vocabulary of English verse, until he set out to renew it, had been "a horrible agglomerate compost, not minted, most of it not even baked, all legato, a doughy mess of third-hand Keats, Wordsworth, heaven knows what, fourth-hand Elizabethan sonority blunted, half-melted, lumpy." He wanted distinct, unslurred syllables heard again in the language. At the start he compelled his London acquaintances, even those he put off by the swagger and conceit with which he concealed his beginner's role, by practicing in his own verse what he was preaching wherever he found an audience of intellectuals—that poetry needed the hardness, the edge, the tautness of good prose, and the precise word or image, regardless of its origin, whether English or alien. He had large ambitions and was content to be misunderstood at first, as long as it was clear that he was being heard. And he was being heard even in *Punch,* which parodied him as "the new Montana (USA) poet, Mr. Ezekiel Ton, who is the most remarkable thing in poetry since Robert Browning."

No. 84 Holland Park Avenue, where Madox Ford edited his *English Review* from a flat above a fishmonger's shop, was close to Church Walk, and Pound visited often, meeting such other "discoveries" of Ford's as D. H. Lawrence, as well as such established writers as Galsworthy, Wells, and W. H. Hudson. With Elkin Mathews willing to publish yet another sheaf of poems, Pound added his *English Review* work and other recent verse to a selection from his earlier collections (fourteen of the twenty-seven poems were new) and offered Mathews *Exultations* in August. A month later it was on its way to the printer. He was also eager to see his new Polytechnic lectures, a projected twenty-one of them, running into 1910, published as a book, and began preparing them as *The Spirit of Romance.* The ideal publisher was J. M. Dent, for whom Ernest Rhys edited the *Everyman Library,* and Rhys invited Pound to an evening of poetry reading at his house in Hermitage Lane.

At the reading later that evening, Pound, unimpressed by the efforts of the others, asked whether anyone objected to his "having the roof taken off the house." Since no one did, he declaimed his "Ballad of the Goodly Fere," Rhys remembered, "like Henry Irving with an American accent." Ford, who had arranged the introduction, had come with D. H. Lawrence, then a schoolmaster in Croydon. Yeats and Pound had also been invited to supper before the others arrived. Yeats, who enjoyed a monologue, dominated the dinner table with a dissertation on bringing poetry and music together, and Pound, either bored with hearing his views at second hand or eager to draw some attention to himself, took one of the tulips decorating the table and munched it, petal by petal. Too absorbed in himself to notice, Yeats went on. Too well bred to notice, the others ignored the demonstration. Pound then went on to eat the remainder of the tulips—a Noble-Savage-from-America performance he would repeat at other houses and among other guests, as the memoir literature of the time attests. He was determined to be different and to be noticed, although the much-remarked affectation of an earring was a short-lived phenomenon. The Shakespears had invited Arthur Symons to tea to meet Pound, and Symons had come with an American writer-friend, Agnes Tobin. When Symons presented Mrs Shakespear with a single red rose, Pound apparently asked whether there was something for him also, and Miss Tobin as a joke presented him with one of her turquoise earrings. For a while Pound wore it.

Having impressed Rhys, Pound acquired a contract from E. J. Dent in September 1909 for a book based on his lectures on the troubadour and Tuscan poets. Not until a month later did he have a specimen chapter ready for use in securing an American publisher, who would be E. P. Dutton in New York. It took his fifth book to finally break through the barrier of American indifference.

Exultations had appeared at half a crown that October. "It is quite safe to say," wrote the anonymous reviewer in the *Observer,* "that few new poets have so quickly become known to literary London." Nevertheless, although critics found his work extraordinary, agreement ceased there. His sometime friend Frank Flint, who, in the *Spectator,* had been compared unfavorably as a poet to Pound, in *New Age* condemned even the generally admired "Goodly Fere" as "a jargon which, I believe, is supposed to be Old English." Belittling the poet's use of foreign languages, especially in titles, Flint explained, "Mr. Pound is an American, and a hotch-potch of picturesqueness, made up of divers elements—in literature, words from divers tongues—is the American idea of beauty." Still, he concluded, Pound had proved in his *Personae* and *Exultations* "that the old devices of regular metrical beat and regular rhyming are worn out. . . ." Yet *Exultations* was the triumph of his first manner. In it he proved himself master of his material. Bookish though his inspiration was, he had worked a kind of alchemy upon his Italian and Provençal and other medieval sources in "Sestina: Altaforte," "Ballad of the Goodly Fere," "Peire Vidal Old," "Sestina for Ysolt," "On His Own Face in a Glass," and a half-dozen other poems that still glitter with energy. Pound was even learning from his excesses as he published the poems. Some of the verse in *Exultations* would become leaner and more compact in later revisions.

One may suspect that the poet's regular shipment of press clip-

pings as well as books to his parents in Philadelphia had something
to do with the occasional allowance he was still receiving from
Homer Pound. Whatever the reason, the correspondence remained
warm on both sides except when he was offered professional advice.
When his mother suggested that he devote himself to an American
theme—perhaps an epic of the American West—he replied that
Whitman, who had tried to let the nation speak through him in epi-
cal fashion, was now of interest only as "ethnology." He was an
ocean away from America because "praise from Yeats or appreciation from a circle that have listened to Swinburne reading his own
verse are . . . rather preferable to competing with . . . Beecham
Pills for American celebrity." Yet he was acquiring some American
celebrity, aside from the material Homer Pound was constantly feed-
ing the Philadelphia newspapers, which itself proved useful. Picking
up a story in the *Philadelphia Evening Bulletin,* the *Boston Herald*
wrote of Pound's discovery in England, where—as a "mere youth"
of twenty-four—he was delivering lectures at the Polytechnic, had
already published four books of verse, and was "his own most un-
sparing critic, having destroyed the manuscripts of two novels and
three hundred sonnets."

The fun which *Punch* had with his name was "something of a
guaranty of fame" to the *Literary Digest;* and soon Floyd Dell and
H. L. Mencken would be reviewing American editions of his work.
In London, meanwhile, he received a curious bit of celebrity shortly
after the usually stodgy *Fortnightly Review* purchased one of his
poems that November. In a letter to the *Saturday Review* on November 27, the much-traveled R. B. Cunninghame Graham, a stylist in
words himself, wrote, "I observe with pleasure that our best writers
—as Conrad, Hudson, Galsworthy, George Moore, Henry James, and
Ezra Pound—are devoting themselves more and more to short pieces,
and in them doing some of their finest work." Ironically, the testa-
ment to modern English writing included only one writer—Galsworthy—native to England. Conrad came from Poland, Hudson was
born in Argentina of American parents, Moore was born in Ireland,
and James and Pound, of course, were Americans.

The celebrated lectures were not going well. Pound blamed the
poor attendance on fog, and was thinking about an escape route once

the final chapter of *The Spirit of Romance* would be completed in February. He would "drift home" for the summer to make some needed money. But William Carlos Williams arrived at Church Walk early in March, and Pound set about, in his all-purpose fur-lined overcoat and broad-brimmed hat that made his silhouette familiar, to show him "the wonders of our dusky and marvellous city," which were, primarily, Mrs Shakespear and Dorothy, and W. B. Yeats. One evening they went to a Yeats lecture at the Adelphi Club, where Williams had to sit alone, Pound joining "his crowd" elsewhere in the hall. Presiding, Williams recalled, was that pillar of the literary establishment, Edmund Gosse.

I was fascinated by the proceedings, listening closely to what was being said. The hour was drawing to a close when Yeats began to speak of those young men, Lionel Johnson among them, who had been consistently denied an audience in England though in his opinion they well merited it and more.

What was there left for them to do, then, but to live the decadent lives they did? What else, neglected as they found themselves to be, but drunkenness, lechery or immorality of whatever other sort?

He got no further, for Sir Edmund, to everyone's consternation, at that point banged the palm of his right hand down on a "teacher's bell" on the table beside him. Yeats was taken aback, but after a moment's hesitation went on or tried to go on with what he was saying. Again Sir Edmund rudely whammed his bell—and again Yeats tried to continue. But when it happened the third time, Gosse, red in the face and Yeats equally so, the poet was forced to sit down and the lecture came to an end. My own face was crimson and my temples near to bursting but I had not been able to get to my feet and protest.

"Why didn't *you?*" some of the ladies were saying to Ezra. "Why didn't you say something for your friend? None of you was up to it. You let him browbeat you—without a protest."

The Ezra Pound reputation for combativeness had not held up. Pound would not jeopardize his chances for success. Defending a valuable friend and ally by antagonizing one of the leading literary statesmen in London was something the poet who had translated the feisty Bertrans de Born would not risk. He was, of course, not alone. No one else had opposed Gosse either.

During another evening in London the two went to a restaurant in Pound's price range where he ordered, for two, a cheap and filling risotto and an inexpensive bottle of wine. Williams ate hungrily while his host "looked boldly about him, wriggling in his chair, turning to examine the faces about him in his bold way." When they had both finished, and got up to leave, Williams took his friend's heavy coat from the rack to help him slip into it, and Pound "turned on me, laying me out in no uncertain way for my presumption, jerked the coat out of my hands and, presenting it to the waiter, made him hold it, as he scolded me, saying that one didn't do things that way in London. Angry now, I waited, gave my coat to the waiter to hold for me and as the whole restaurant smiled, we made our way to the street." Pound had learned the ways of London in other respects as well.

Despite such puzzling experiences, Williams found his week with "Ez" instructive. "It was an intense literary atmosphere, which though it was thrilling, every minute of it, was fatiguing in the extreme. I don't know how Ezra stood it; it would have killed me in a month. It seemed completely foreign to anything I desired. I was glad to get away." Yet London and "Ez" would continue to be useful, and Williams would owe his first published book of poetry to both. Through Pound, Williams would publish seven poems in the *Poetry Review* in 1912, and nineteen as a small book, *The Tempers,* issued by Elkin Mathews in 1913 after the poet put up fifty dollars of the publication costs. For the book, Pound even contributed a brief, deliberately cautious preface. He had his own London reputation to keep in mind. "God forbid that I should introduce Mr. Williams as a cosmic force," he began. ". . . Having said recently that no man now living in America writes anything that is of interest to the serious artist, my position is none the more easy." But Williams was "one compatriot to whom I could take without a lexicon . . . , some one who has apparently a common aim with me." Whether or not Williams agreed with that, the fact of London publication was a vital beginning.

After Williams sailed for home, Pound took the fifteen pounds he had received for three poems which had appeared in the *English Review* that January ("Fordie" was often late in payment) and went off to Italy via Paris. Olivia and Dorothy Shakespear had promised to join him in Italy, and Pound was enthusiastic about Lake Garda and the town of Desenzano, which perched "in proper Whistlerian fashion on the opposite ledge of the lake" from Verona, where he planned to stay. There news reached him that a Boston publisher was interested in bringing out an edition of his poems. Since it came as he was correcting proofs of *The Spirit of Romance,* and translating the poems of Dante's contemporary, Guido Cavalcanti, he was feeling a satisfaction about his professional progress which only increased when the Shakespears arrived and told him that Yeats had been saying "nice things" about him, describing Pound as a "solitary volcano" in London, a remark he passed on to his family in Philadelphia.

While on the train to Venice, where Dorothy Shakespear intended to do further watercolor landscapes, the trio were amused to overhear passengers sitting opposite speculating whether the young couple were affianced, or only brother and sister. For Dorothy the conversation could not have been better timed, for she had wondered about it herself. As for Pound, he was soon to get a letter from his and Williams's friend Hilda Doolittle, whom he had known since both were children, informing him that she was thinking of visiting Europe. With Williams they had once been an adolescent triangle. Now he had to reassess his feelings for Dorothy in the perspective of the imminent proximity of "H.D."—as she signed her still-unpublished poems. He hoped she would arrive before the middle of June, he wrote her, for he was crossing the Atlantic in the other direction, to visit his family, on June 15. He and Hilda would see much of each other later, as poets.

Pound was in New York and Philadelphia until the following February, making notes, in Henry James fashion, about how different America appeared after being abroad; calling upon the poet's father, painter John Butler Yeats, who lived in a Manhattan rooming house; arranging for publication of some of his poems, one in the *Philadelphia Sunday School Times* (which brought a welcome fifty dollars); visiting Williams at his parents' home in Rutherford, New Jersey (once accompanied by H.D., who was back); meeting manuscript collector and patron of the arts John Quinn at his law office in New York.

Pound was impressed by the vigor of the country, and by how

high the brightly lit office buildings had risen in the few years he had been away; but he was not eager to remain. Since he could not persuade Williams, who wanted to practice medicine at home, to enlarge his mind in London, on his trips to Rutherford Pound left books to give his friend access to appropriate literary inspiration. On one visit it was Metastasio's *Varie Poesie,* which provided Williams with the format for his *Kora in Hell;* another time it was a book of Spanish lyrical poems, four of which Williams (whose mother was Puerto Rican) adapted for the book Pound would help him publish in London; a third was Quevedo's *El Perro la Calentura,* which Williams and his mother would translate jointly twenty years later and also reuse in other forms. But as Pound wrote the next year, "If a man's work requires him to live in exile, let him live in exile, let him suffer (or enjoy) his exile gladly." His last visit to Williams was on February 13, 1911. On February 22, the day he sailed from New York, he wrote his father that he knew he would have less physical comfort abroad, but that his future lay on the other side of the Atlantic. Not for twenty-eight years would he see his country again.

For A. R. Orage's *New Age,* which would pay him two pounds a week for several years, Pound would quarry two series of articles from his American experience, the philosophical *Patria Mia* in 1912 and the more political *America: Chances and Remedies* in 1913. Even before that, the *New Age* published his "I Gather the Limbs of Osiris," a series of essays which appeared in twelve parts between November 1911 and February 1912. He was also publishing poetry copiously, with some of the verse as well as the prose conceived or written in America and awaiting its opportunity. It was not his purpose, he declared in *Patria Mia,* to find fault with his country. It was the essence of democracy "that each man should look after his own sort of affairs," as opposed to the "patent brands of sociology" he saw experimented with in England, which proposed that every man "should look after everybody else's affairs." But he did think that America needed, and would have, an intellectual awakening, to free it from the tyranny of its "highly respected and very decrepit magazines."

It is well known that in the year of grace 1870 Jehovah appeared to Messrs. Harper and Co. and to the editors of "The Century," "The

Atlantic," and certain others, and spake thus: "The style of 1870 is the final and divine revelation. Keep things always just as they are now." And they, being earnest, God-fearing men, did abide by the words of the Almighty, and great credit and honour accrued unto them, for had they not divine warrant!

And if you do not believe me, open a number of "Harpers" for 1888 and one for 1908. And I defy you to find any difference, save on the page where the date is. . . .

It is cheering to reflect that America accepted Whitman when he was properly introduced by William Michael Rossetti, and not before then.

And when I add that there is no man now living in America whose art in letters is of the slightest interest to me, I am held for paradoxical. And the answer to that is, that there is practically no one in America who knows good work from bad—no such person, I mean, who is part of the system for circulation.

Regardless of place, Pound admitted, art and prosperity were incompatible for magazines which had to maintain their circulation, but gentility in literature was irreconcilable with art. In his own time, he noted, America had given to the world two men who produced masterworks, Whistler and James, and both had to escape America. As a result of the disputes over James's style, Americans failed to realize that "much of the real work of the world is done, and done almost solely by such quiet and persistent diagnoses as his are. This core of his work is not limited by America, yet no one has better understood the charm of all that is fine in American life, the uprights, or, so to speak, the piles that are driven deep, and through the sort of floating bog of our national confusion." Just as he took delight in James's novels, he "gathered . . . more courage for living" from Whistler's paintings than from the Panama Canal (then under construction) or any other expression of American energy, for Whistler was

a man, born American, with all our forces of confusion within him, who has contrived to keep order in his work, who has attained the highest mastery, and this not by a natural facility, but by constant labour and searching. . . .

The man's life struggle was set before one. He had tried all means, he had spared himself nothing, he had struggled in one direction until he had either achieved or found it inadequate for his expression.

273

After he had achieved a thing, he never repeated. There were many struggles for the ultimate nocturnes. . . .*

What Whistler has proved once and for all, is that being born an American does not eternally damn a man or prevent him from the ultimate and highest achievement in the arts.

And no man before him had proved this. And he proved it over many a hindrance and over many baffled attempts. He is, with Abraham Lincoln, the beginning of our Great Tradition. . . .

He would write a poem in 1912 celebrating Whistler as "our first great," an artist who experimented in many directions and gave him "heart to play the game." "To Whistler, American" saw the painter in Pound's own image as unsure, trying one style after another, stretching and tampering with his medium:

> You had your searches, your uncertainties,
> And this is good to know—for us, I mean,
> Who bear the brunt of our America
> And try to wrench her impulse into art.

From Church Walk, Pound—in England, as he now thought, to stay—increased his efforts to reshape English writing. And through T. E. Hulme, he began to focus also upon art. Hulme had discovered an intense young sculptor, Henri Gaudier,† from whom he bought little works to help him eke out a living. Through Gaudier at the Frith Street Tuesday evenings (there were also meetings at a nearby restaurant on Thursdays) Hulme and Pound encountered a stocky, powerfully built New York sculptor who had been struggling in London since 1905, Jacob Epstein. As Frank Flint recalled as early as 1913, in reviewing a new Ezra Pound book, those evenings in Soho "were not dull always: there were generally some six or seven of us—T. E. Hulme, Ezra Pound, Edward Storer, T. D. FitzGerald, myself, Miss Florence Farr, F. W. Tancred; at times the sculptor Epstein would come; Mr Pound himself did not join us until the third evening, and he may have forgotten or have been unaware of the excitement with which the diners on the other side of our screen

---

* Which Pound saw at the Tate Gallery in 1912.
† Gaudier-Brzeska after he added the name of the much older woman with whom he was living, Sophie Brzeska.

heard him declaim the 'Sestina: Altaforte,' now in *Exultations;* how the table shook and the decanters and cutlery vibrated in resonance with his voice! I do not think that that evening was dull. However, the outcome of those meetings was three or four books of verse. . . ."

Already thirty, Epstein by 1911 had fully committed himself to England, having become a British subject in 1907; and he had weathered one controversy over his work and was about to find himself in another. He had done, Bernard Shaw wrote Robert Ross, who ran the Carfax Gallery (in which G.B.S. had shares), "amazing drawings of human creatures like withered trees embracing," and wanted to exhibit them. When Shaw, realizing how poor Epstein was, "advised him to get commissions for busts of railway directors," the sculptor "repudiated me with such utter scorn that I relented and promised to ask you to look at his portfolio. It is a case of helpless genius in the first blaze of youth. . . ."

In the spring of 1907 Epstein had received a commission to decorate the new British Medical Association building in the Strand. Since it was his first major commission, he asked too little to do the eighteen larger-than-life figures to go in niches around the building. In fourteen months of toil he had finished the work and was five hundred pounds in debt. Even worse, the nude figures, representing Man and Woman from birth to old age, and in the Greek and Renaissance tradition, seemed to inspire public disturbances, especially after the National Vigilance Society protested them, and the *Evening Standard* declared piously that "they are a form of statuary which no careful father would wish his daughter or no discriminating young man his fiancée, to see. . . ." Passengers on top of open buses in the Strand stood up at Agar Street to get a better view, and at night the statuary was defaced. *The Times* attacked the silly prudery, and Epstein defended his work in the *British Medical Journal* as embodying in sculpture "the great primal facts of man and woman." The protests to the London County Council eventually faded, and Epstein found himself famous—although without further work. "A[n American] chemist named Fels," he remembered, heard that he was in debt because of the Strand statues, and appeared one day with five hundred pounds. Epstein put his broad-brimmed working hat back on—it looked as if it had come from the Spanish-American War—and rolled up his sleeves.

Robert Ross had not forgotten him, but Epstein did not hear of his commission to carve a tomb for Oscar Wilde's grave in Paris—Ross was Wilde's executor—until friends called to congratulate him. Secrecy had been maintained, even from the sculptor, to prevent others from hindering the plan. It took some time for Epstein to create a design he thought appropriate, after which he bought a twenty-ton monolith from a Derbyshire quarry and had it hauled to his studio on Cheyne Walk, near Tite Street, where crowds gathered to watch its transition into a monument. The great carving was still in progress when Pound first met his compatriot. "I wish he would wash," Pound wrote his mother, "but I believe Michael Angelo *never* did, so I suppose it's part of the tradition."

He got on well with "Yakob," who was as articulate and opinionated as Pound, and began publishing critiques about Epstein, who shared his interest in pure form. For Epstein the interest in abstraction was short-lived, although he acknowledged that he had profited from "the discipline of simplification of forms, unity of design, and co-ordination of masses." Some of that simplification came from his increasing interest in the carvings he saw in the British Museum from Mexico, Egypt, Africa, and New Guinea, and Robert Ross would receive a note from a friend expressing relief that the "greater part" of the Wilde tomb had been accomplished before Epstein's "Neo Papuan enthusiasm had been born," although he conceded that the result was "not unworthy."

Epstein had already been rejected for membership by the hidebound Royal Society of British Sculptors—a predictable reaction to the creator of one of the few contemporary masterpieces in stone. Dominated by a winged angel which echoed some of Hulme's aesthetic theories, the work suggested the great Assyrian winged bulls, and the Egyptian sarcophagi, which Epstein found in the British Museum, but at the Père Lachaise cemetery Epstein found that the only interest the tomb had for the authorities was that the angel had clearly defined sexual organs. These were ordered concealed by a tarpaulin and guarded by a gendarme. Protests from artists and writers multiplied, but the French insisted that the indecency be removed or covered. Epstein refused, but Ross, to the sculptor's dismay, gave in and had a bronze plaque affixed to the angel's genitals. In a night raid of poets and artists, the bronze codpiece was removed. Again the authorities covered the offending angel with tarpaulin. Epstein continued to be frustrated, but famous, and his misanthropy increased. Yet his freedom as an artist might have been even more limited, he realized, in New York.

One result of the Hulme-Pound association was Epstein's temporary enthusiasm for machinery, and in 1913 when he bought a secondhand pneumatic drill, he decided to integrate it with a sculpted figure. Like the language Pound wanted used in poetry, it was to be hard, austere, dynamic. "The planes of Mr. Epstein's work," Pound would write, "seem to sink away from their outline with a curious determination and swiftness." Epstein's *Rock Drill on Machine Base,* mounted, on the drill itself, made an object ten feet high, "a machine-like robot, visored, menacing, and carrying within itself its progeny, protectively ensconced." It was, Epstein thought, "the armed, sinister figure of today and tomorrow." When he exhibited the demonic sculpture on the drill and tripod of supporting legs, the enthusiastic Gaudier-Brzeska took Pound to see it. The poet, Epstein remembered, immediately "started expatiating on the work. Gaudier-Brzeska turned on him and snapped, 'Shut up, you understand nothing!' " But Pound understood enough to know that he was in the presence of an augury of the future. In 1952, still adding to the major work of his later years, he titled *Cantos* 85–95 "Section: Rock-Drill de los Cantares," recalling the sculpture which he had not seen for thirty-six years and which had actually been so radically modified—the sculpture having been separated from the drill—that it was no longer the object Pound remembered. No matter: *"Rock Drill,"* he told an interviewer, "was intended to imply the necessary resistance in getting a certain main thesis across—hammering. . . . One is held up by the low percentage of reason which seems to operate in human affairs. . . ."

The Pound-Epstein relationship, like most of Pound's London friendships, would not last. Pound demanded too much acquiescence from his peers. "Fordie" and "Uncle Billyum" were his elders, a fact which permitted at worst an awkward harmony. His friendship with John Gould Fletcher was more typical. Fletcher, a Harvard dropout who came to England on a family inheritance to write poetry, had been captured by the possibilities of London even before he arrived, and recalled walking down the Strand wondering how such an alien as he could hope to conquer London, to batter down the walls of the Pall Mall clubs and achieve "the authoritative anonymity" of *The Times Literary Supplement* ("which Pound affected to despise each week"). Born in 1886, Fletcher was in his mid-twenties when he met Pound, having escaped the indefatigable American during his first four years in London through a stubborn self-isolation which had freed him to produce pages of verse while leaving him almost friendless and unknown. Desperately lonely, he had sought out the Fabians, but politics, even of the intellectual variety, failed to interest him, and all he elicited from the experience was the advice of A. R. Orage to abandon the Romantics and read Whitman. As with Pound, it had taken a residence in London to acquaint him with his compatriot, who had not been highly regarded within the hallowed halls of Harvard.

Although he would leave his expensive but kitchenless Adelphi Terrace flat (just below the Strand), with its sweeping view of the Thames, only to look for a place to have a meal or a park bench upon which to perch while he read his latest volume of French verse, as the winter of 1912 approached he had become determined to move to Paris. There he could stuff French poetry into his overcoat pockets with far less strain. Yet he could not leave having proved to his sisters—his surviving family—that his years in London were wasted. Having heard that there were publishers in London "not averse to publishing small books of verse, if they were only paid to do so," and possessing enough manuscript poems to fill a large volume, he decided on a different strategy. Dividing his verses into five small books to be published under five different imprints, he sent them off, some to venerable and fussy firms, others to vulnerable and tolerant publishers.

John Murray quickly declined, with thanks. The firm had published Lord Byron. It did not recognize in Fletcher his successor. Grant Richards haggled for the last penny yet was glad to have the work. Erskine Macdonald "was astonishingly cheap, but so unbusinesslike in detail as to cast a doubt on his probity." Constable was surprisingly cooperative, because a young editor, Michael Sadleir, new to their staff, was interested. The new firm of Max Goschen was managed by a young man named Douglas Goldring, a protégé of Ford Hueffer, and charged him "astonishingly little." He was also the only publisher who later advertised after publication.

All of the books* would emerge in a single month—May 1913. But by the end of that month Fletcher had given up on London, closed his flat, and gone to Paris, where there were several American poets he knew. Only two critics, he would recall, had given him notices that were neither contemptuous nor condescending: A. R. Orage and Edward Thomas. Still, Paris would prove even less hospitable, and he was soon back in London. In both cities Fletcher would encounter Pound, and his memories, although vivid, are very likely discolored by their almost immediate dislike of each other. Pound was

a man of about my own age and height, dressed in a brown velvet coat, a shirt open at the neck and no necktie, and pearl-gray trousers. His fine-chiseled, forward-jutting features were set off by a rounded mass of fiery curly red hair and a beard and mustache similarly red and curly, trimmed to a point. Gray-blue penetrating eyes, shielded by pince-nez, peered at the world behind high-projecting cheek-bones; and a high-pitched, shrill, almost feminine voice provided strange contrast to the pugnacious virility of the poet's general aspect. He had, I soon saw, slender feminine hands, which, as he talked, he fluttered to and fro. His body was almost equally mobile, jumping and twisting in its chair, with a backward jerk of the head, as he emphasized each point. . . .

I discovered him to be as baffling a bundle of contradictions as any man whom I had ever known. Internationally Bohemian in aspect, he yet preserved marked far-western ways of speech and a frank, open democracy of manners. Hating the academicians of England, he yet laid claims to be a great scholar in early Provençal, Italian, and Latin. Keen follower of the *dernier cri* in art and letters, his own poetry was often deliberately archaic to a degree that repelled me. In short, he was a walking paradox, a pioneer in the last great wave of American expatriates who, like myself, had turned from the West to the East and had come abroad . . . bent on submitting their own rule and untaught native impulses to the task of assimilating and, if possible, surpassing the traditional achievements of Europe.

---

* *The Book of Nature* (Constable), *The Dominant City* (Goschen), *Fools' Gold* (Goschen), *Fire and Wine* (Richards), *Visions of the Evening* (Macdonald).

So desperately in need of literary friends "as to be ready to accept anyone who was American, literary, and like myself, an expatriate," Fletcher hung on in London because it was the place where Pound lived. "Here was an American who, by using his wits, had succeeded in the attempt in which I, a more well-to-do man, had lamentably failed; and he had succeeded, through sheer resourcefulness and courage, in keeping himself before the British public."

Early in 1911, when Ford Madox Ford had lost financial control of the *English Review,* Fletcher had tried to invest his small income in it, "feeling that the proprietorship of so distinguished a periodical would be the best means of establishing my name and reputation among the literary circles of London." When he was unable to acquire the *Review,* he put the idea aside, but Pound was aware of the offer, and proposed another use for Fletcher's money. Since his return from America, Pound had become acquainted with two English-women, Harriet Shaw Weaver and Dora Marsden, who were running a radical feminist weekly, the *Freewoman.* Miss Weaver, a shy, thirtyish intellectual with Quaker sympathies who had inherited a modest income, believed that her money was tainted by usury and thus not to be spent for her own promotion or comfort, and suppressed any notice of her generosities. Yet Pound knew, and his later preoccupation with usury as the root of all modern evil may have had its beginnings in the scrupulous Harriet Weaver, who had been financing the paper as a means of publishing the writings of Miss Marsden, a Theosophy-minded libertarian and the *Freewoman*'s editor. Dora Marsden's writings, according to Fletcher, "consisted only of four or five weekly pages of abstruse philosophical comment on feminist psychology and the need for liberation from all conventions and traditions." The remainder had to be filled with whatever could be found, often contributions from amateur writers belonging to the Women's Social and Political Union. For the first two issues that assignment went to a young assistant editor, Cicily Fairfield, who wrote under the name of Rebecca West. After a quarrel with the proprietors, she left, and Miss Weaver went off to Church Walk to talk to Pound, whom she had met before and who seemed to her to know everyone who wrote, to enlist his help. Pound agreed to conduct a literary department, although he privately thought that women's demand for the vote was a useless thing, as democracy was a sham and more untrained voters casting ballots would not improve matters.

Not content to start small, he wrote to Henry James for a contribution to the journal, now rebaptized at Pound's urging *New Freewoman*. They had met a few months earlier and, Pound wrote his family in Philadelphia, "glared at one another across the same carpet." A month later they met again at the home of a mutual friend, Mrs Dilke, for lunch, after which Pound was to lecture in her "swank drawingroom" for a fee provided by James's friend Maurice Hewlett. Pound now liked James "more on further acquaintance." They discussed America. "It is strange," James pontificated, to Pound's agreement, "how all taint of arts or letters seems to shun that continent." The Master's "wonderful conversation" was a high point for Pound. Although they were too far apart in ideas and lifestyles for any intimacy, he remembered vividly

the massive head, the slow uplift of the hand, *gli occhi onesti e tardi,* the long sentences piling themselves up in elaborate phrase after phrase, the lightning incision, the pauses, the slightly shaking admonitory gesture with its "wu-a-wait a little, wait a little, something will come"; blague and benignity and the weight of so many years' careful, incessant labour of minute observation always there to enrich the talk. I had heard it but seldom, yet it is all unforgettable.

In the *Pisan Cantos,* Pound recalled James trying to escape from a bore:

Mr James shielding himself with Mrs Hawkesby as it were a bowl shielding itself with a walking stick as he manoeuvred his way toward the door.

And he remembered, too, how another apostle of high culture was

holding dear H. J.
(Mr. James, Henry) literally by the button-hole . . .
in those so consecrated surroundings
(a garden in the Temple, no less)
and saying, *for once,* the right thing
namely: "Cher maître"
to his chequed waistcoat. . . .

Evading the risk of association with a journal so radically titled
—he had been embarrassed by another compatriot's journal, the
Yellow Book, years before—James responded that he had "no
charming little pieces on hand that might be suitable for a journal
calling itself the *New Freewoman,*" and warned Pound to be careful
lest he end up a "Bondsman." Since Pound knew he would have to
pay contributors if he were to acquire anything up to his standard,
he suggested to Fletcher that he put up a small sum each month for
that purpose, and that Pound, of course, would as literary editor
print anything which the useful Fletcher cared to furnish. His pride
stung by the implication that it was the only way he could break into
print, but bullied into opening his checkbook, he agreed to supply
some money, on the condition that his name not appear in the
journal. He would grumble privately that Pound had touched him
for money for *New Freewoman* with indiscreet haste, but in the interests of literature Pound rarely felt that he had time for discretion.
And to Fletcher, desperate for recognition, Pound's professed connections, and willingness to look over Fletcher's manuscripts, appeared worth the price.

Pound's comments on *Irradiations* (the improvisational style,
hinted at in the title, came from Post-Impressionist art and the Ni-
jinsky ballet) remain among Fletcher's papers at his home-state University of Arkansas. On legal-size white sheets Pound marked words
which were "cheap" or "commonplace," assonances which appeared
too obvious, and suggestions for omission. "How can a mosaic be
palpitant?" he would ask. Fletcher would receive many such school-
masterly responses to his work, and stubbornly would not accept
many of them, leaving their literary relations a series of crises and
Fletcher less of a poet than he might have been. Eventually he would
offer his verse to *New Freewoman,* after Pound, dissatisfied with the
title, and its suggestion of a single-subject journal, had convinced
Miss Weaver, who was still happily subsidizing the printing costs,
to adopt the challenging title of the *Egoist.* As the *Egoist,* it would
acquire, Fletcher recalled, "a certain acclaim among the more literate;
though I must confess that I never discovered anyone capable of pe-
rusing regularly the philosophical essays by Miss Marsden on the
front pages."

Pound was fast becoming an impresario of letters in London. The June 1912 issue of Harold Monro's magazine, *Poetry Review,* mentioned "a new school of English poetry still at present very small and under the formidable direction of Ezra Pound." The "school" was his device to launch Hilda Doolittle into London literary life. H.D. had followed up his invitation. William Carlos Williams had not. He was even getting married in the hinterlands of New Jersey, and sent Pound an invitation complete to ticket imprinted "Please present this card at the church." Before putting it in an envelope and mailing it back to Williams, Pound scrawled on it, "Dear Bill, I regret that I will be unable to comply with the above request. Will you act for me in the matter?"

The tall, blonde H.D.—Pound had called her "Dryad" when they were adolescents—was a willing pupil and moved easily among Pound's literary friends, quickly becoming close to the ruddy, burly Richard Aldington, who at nineteen (in 1912) was his youngest recruit and six years younger than Miss Doolittle. Age meant little. Ezra Pound himself was both younger and older than all the others, even younger than a crusty New Hampshire farmer, nearing forty, who had come to England to write poetry. He was a greater risk, but Pound would sponsor Robert Frost too.

An event four thousand miles away in Chicago gave Pound his new opportunities as literary impresario. Harriet Monroe, fifty and looking for a literary cause, was launching a new magazine, *Poetry,* and could count upon enough money to keep it going. Once ambitious for a personal literary career, she had written a blank-verse tragedy, *Valeria,* which Henry Harland had praised, and which she published privately in 1892. The convent-educated daughter of a prominent lawyer, she had connections among the Chicago wealthy but supported herself during her middle years through lecturing and critical journalism, having come to notice because her ode recited at the opening of the World Columbian Exposition in Chicago in 1892 and printed in the program of the event had been reprinted by the *New York World* without her permission. She had sued for violation of copyright and in 1894 won a judgment of five thousand dollars, as much money as any American poet had derived from a poem.

Chicago, Edgar Lee Masters later wrote her, was a difficult place in which to be a poet. "Well, what was Chicago then as an inspiration to the muse? There was no market for anything and no interest in it after you did it." *Poetry* was her device to change that, and in London in the summer of 1910 while Pound was in America, she hunted for material and ideas before resuming what would be a trip around the world. Elkin Mathews sold her *Personae* and *Exultations,* explaining that the author was a young American genius, and she remembered "breathing the books' perfume on the long Siberian journey. . . . The impassioned beauty of his poems—their strange new insinuating rhythms, their half-interval cadences, the Debussy-like under-tones—seemed to come out of the air, from some presence disembodied, impassioned, tense and sure.

> As bright white drops upon a leaden sea,
> Grant so my songs to this grey folk may be!

said the poet in his opening 'Grace Before Song'; and the poems that followed had the crystal clarity and iridescent dream of dew-drops in the morning sun. As Mr. Mathews had said, they were 'pure poetry,' with no dusty alloy of baser motive than the sheer command of the muse." Back in Chicago she wrote to ask Pound to contribute. He replied, stating his ideological terms:

Can you teach the American poet that poetry *is* an *art,* an art with a technique, with media, an art that must be in constant flux, a constant change of manner, if it is to live? Can you teach him that it is not a pentametric echo of the sociological dogma printed in last year's magazines? . . . Are you for American poetry or for poetry? The latter is more important, but it is important that America should boost the former. . . . The glory of any nation is to produce art that can be exported without disgrace to its origin.

Impressed, Miss Monroe published, along with Pound's "To Whistler, American," an announcement in the inaugural number (October 1912): "Mr. Ezra Pound, the young Philadelphia poet whose recent distinguished success in London led to wide recognition in his own country, authorizes the statement that at present such of his poetic work as receives magazine publication in America will appear exclusively in *Poetry*." In the second issue (November 1912) there were already poems placed by Pound as well as a second announcement—that he had "consented to act as foreign correspondent of *Poetry,* keeping readers informed of the present interests of the art in England, France and elsewhere."

Much of what Pound had learned about French verse had come from Fletcher's defense of his methods in *Irradiations,* in which he had cited new techniques and new "schools" from Paris. His interest aroused, Pound borrowed an armful of books, and soon published in the *New Age* a series of notes titled "The Approach to Paris." Fletcher was outraged. The principles and practice were not his literary property, but he had lived with both, and Pound had learned from *him.* They argued, and Pound, who had done what Fletcher in any case would have been too diffident to accomplish, promised to press *Irradiations* into *Poetry,* and Fletcher felt ashamed of his outburst.

Doing as he vowed to do, Pound did send Fletcher's verses to Miss Monroe, writing realistically that he did not expect her "to use the full sequence," but urged her to "hack out ten or a dozen pages" because "if you don't print a fairish gob of him, you don't do him justice or stir up the reader's ire and attention." It was a mischievous way to suggest that here was something to make the reader take notice, but there was no international code of practice about promoting poets.

Pound's first poems for *Poetry* other than his own were three by Richard Aldington (November) and three by Hilda Doolittle (January). With Aldington's work was a note by Pound that the writer was "a young British poet, one of the 'Imagistes,' a group of ardent Hellenists who are pursuing interesting experiments in *vers libre;* trying to attain in English certain subtleties of cadence of the kind which Mallarmé and his followers have studied in France. . . ." Part of it was true. Both Aldington and H.D. were scholars in Greek, and Aldington claimed to have arrived at *vers libre* by imitating "a chorus in the *Hippolytus* of Euripides." Pound had even told him on seeing his first poems, "I don't think you need any help from me." But he did need help—as did H.D.—in getting published. And the "Imagist" movement was created, not very seriously, Pound claimed later, to get H.D.'s poems "a hearing without its being necessary for her to publish a whole book. It began certainly in Church

Walk with H.D., Richard and myself." Actually the movement began over tea at a shop nearby, Aldington remembered:

I have no exact memory of what was said at this bun-shop meeting, but
I do remember that H.D. looked very much pleased by the praise Ezra
generously gave her poems. I didn't like his insistence that the poems
should be signed "H.D. Imagist," because it sounded a little ridiculous.
And I think H.D. disliked it too. But Ezra was a bit of a czar in a small
but irritating way, and he had the bulge on us, because it was only
through him that we could get our poems into Harriet Monroe's *Poetry,*
and nobody else at that time would look at them. (My impression is
that even so Ezra had to bully Miss Monroe to get her to accept this
"new" poetry.) So we had to give in.*

Urging H.D.'s poems on Miss Monroe, Pound had written:
"This is the sort of American stuff that I can show here and in
Paris without its being ridiculed. Objective—no slither; direct—no
excessive use of adjectives, no metaphors that won't permit examination. It's straight talk, straight as the Greek! And it was only by
persistence that I got to see it at all." On publication an accompanying note identified "H.D. *Imagiste*" as "an American lady resident
abroad, whose identity is unknown to the editor." As far as Harriet
Monroe was concerned, it was true. And the strategy worked. The
mystery evoked about the writer helped sell her later work, and her
lyrics, with their vivid, concrete imagery, upheld Pound's contention
—in an essay in the same issue of *Poetry*—that the *"Imagistes"*
were characterized by precision and economy in expression as opposed to the "numerous and unassembled writers who busy themselves with dull and interminable effusions." The March issue followed up Pound's campaign with a Pound-ghosted "interview" with
an Imagist by Frank Flint, which intimated the gathering strength
of a real movement. But as Pound had confessed in *Poetry* two
months before, "To belong to a school does not in the least mean
that one writes poetry to a theory. . . . A school exists when two
or three young men agree, more or less, to call certain things
good. . . ."

Eventually Pound would put together a collection of poems

---

* At the same time William Carlos Williams was complaining to Harriet Monroe
about the power of "the divine Ezra" to "bludgeon" her into publishing the work
he wanted to see in print.

which met the vague technical requirements of Imagism. At first he proposed that he, H.D., and Aldington publish a joint book of poems. "H.D. and I were in favour of this, because it seemed the sort of thing the three musketeers would have done. But Ezra soon changed his mind. He gravely pointed out to us that he was internationally famous while we were miserable unknowns, and that consequently the whole attention of the world's press would go to his poems and ours would not even be noticed." Then an opportunity arose. For the first number of a periodical to be called the *Glebe,* he shipped to New York, under the title *Des Imagistes: An Anthology,* a sheaf of twenty-three poems by the three "founders," five by F. S. Flint, and one from each of seven other contributors— Skipwith Cannell, Amy Lowell, William Carlos Williams, John Cournos (all Americans), Ford Madox Ford, Allen Upward, and James Joyce. There were delays in publication. By the time it appeared in the summer of 1914 the contributors—if they had anything in common before—were beginning to part company, and Amy Lowell, from both Boston and London, was busy taking control of the very flexible movement. "Why, I too, am an Imagiste!" she had allegedly exclaimed on reading H.D.'s verse in *Poetry.* Later the wealthy and domineering Miss Lowell, Pound would complain, was turning "Imagism" into "a democratic beer garden."

One noncontributor to *Des Imagistes* had been John Gould Fletcher, whom Pound had pressured unsuccessfully. Fletcher saw the collection as a response to Edward Marsh's *Georgian Poetry* anthologies, which Pound considered as perpetuating the effete quality of English verse. Meeting H.D. in Church Walk at Pound's urging (she and Aldington had married and moved to a flat close to Pound), Fletcher denied that he belonged to any school. "Richard and I," she said, evading mention of Ezra, "are very keen on this idea of an anthology of all the writers who don't belong to the Georgians." But *his* poetry, he insisted, wouldn't fit. "It is shambling, grotesque, formless. . . . In fact, compared with your poetry, it's like . . . a dinosaur in the Parthenon." Their laughter defused the tension. But Fletcher would have been trapped in the citadel of his integrity even if he had been a better poet. He did not know how to advertise himself. Pound did.

Far from Church Walk, across the Thames in Southwark, lived

one of the transitory Imagists, John Cournos, whose rooms, Pound claimed, were the farthest east of Cursitor Street he traveled for years.* Cournos, although born in the Russian Pale to which Jews were largely restricted, had emigrated to Philadelphia as a boy, then moved to London in his twenties to risk a career as a writer. For Pound the Philadelphia connection was magnetic, and Cournos, although more a journalist than a critic, was a possible ally. His first sight of London, in June 1912, had exhilarated him. Even a walk down Tottenham Court Road had been suffused with romance. Settling south of the Thames in a tiny thoroughfare just off Elephant and Castle, Cournos paid his landlord nineteen shillings a week for his rooms and his meals—a great sum to earn by his pen, as it was nearly five American dollars—and lived among the ghosts of Chaucer, Bunyan, Massinger, and Goldsmith.

One way to both make connections and sell copy, he knew, was to interview the illustrious for the American papers in New York, Philadelphia, and Boston with which he had associations. H. G. Wells and Gordon Craig quickly provided him with material. Artists needed to advertise their wares. Through Craig he met Pound, who to Cournos was "one of the kindest men who ever lived" and "made no effort, as some do, to conceal the fact. American poets in London found a patron in him, and he insinuated his poetic gospel into them. He was a stickler for technique, and he had the uncanny gift of taking some one else's poem and pulling it together by the simple process of cutting things out and changing a word here and there. He was a remarkable corrective for sloppiness. In very modest circumstances himself, he would rise heaven and earth to help any fellow artist in need. On one occasion he came to me and asked me among others to write a letter to the proper authorities petitioning them to allow Harry Kemp, charged with being a stowaway, to stay in England, for he understood that Kemp pleaded a desire to see the picture galleries. He had no use for Kemp as a poet, but he could not see a fellow mortal denied such simple aesthetic privileges without doing something to have them granted."

Through Pound, Cournos met Ford, Yeats, and Hulme, and

* Cursitor Street, just off Chancery Lane, was the location of Orage's *New Age* office.

began to frequent Church Walk. "One day I called at his room. He was pounding away on a typewriter, and did not look up as I entered. He said, 'I'll talk to you in a minute. I'm doing a 240-line poem to show that it can't be done!' He had at this time the theory that only in a short poem could the perfection of finality be obtained. And of course if he couldn't do a 240-line poem, no one else could! This was long before he undertook to do his *Cantos.* Another day, again, I came in upon him as he was typing his duel challenge to Lascelles Abercrombie. . . ."

The proposal to the gentle Abercrombie, one of the leading Georgian poets, was in the feisty tradition of Bertrans de Born—and Whistler. Abercrombie—small, shy, and bespectacled—had written in one of the literary weeklies that young poets should abandon barren realism and study Wordsworth. Long an admirer of *The Gentle Art of Making Enemies,* Pound composed a response which lacked only the signature of the barbed butterfly to be Whistlerian.

Dear Mr. Abercrombie:
Stupidity carried beyond a certain point becomes a public menace. I hereby challenge you to a duel, to be fought at the earliest moment that is suited to your convenience. My seconds will wait upon you in due course.

Yours sincerely,
Ezra Pound

When a friend told him that Pound was an expert fencer, the mild Abercrombie was terrified. Then, realizing that the challenged party had the privilege of choosing the weapons, he accepted, and proposed that they bombard each other with unsold copies of their own books. Pound, for once, was both indignant and helpless. It was Abercrombie's finest hour.

Encouraging Cournos, Pound told him after reading his literary and art criticism that he "had a chance of occupying the place that Arthur Symons once occupied. . . . " It was overly generous, and probably misdirected Cournos, who was surviving on translations from the Russian while working on a book on American artists, and actually finishing chapters on William M. Chase and J. S. Sargent. "Delightful," Pound wrote confidently in the margins on one page.

"The only possible way of presenting Chase." While researching the book in 1913, Cournos went to talk to Jacob Epstein. "I saw Epstein living with his wife in an attic of the Poetry Bookshop, in a room barely big enough to contain the bed and with a roof so sloping that you could scarcely stand up. But he was belligerently independent, and he would not allow any one to patronize him. Though he lived in great poverty in this little attic he had a ramshackle barn as a studio not many yards away, and in this studio he had valuable chunks of unworked marble and priceless finished statues."

On the night of the first London performance of Igor Stravinsky's *Le Sacre du Printemps* (July 11, 1913), an event which, like the Post-Impressionist Show in 1910, hammered another nail into the coffin of tradition in the arts, there was controversy among the denizens of Harold Monro's attic. To Epstein's strange new vision had been added Stravinsky's, and a copy of Epstein's *Christ* in Monro's living room downstairs "had to be rescued hastily and indiscriminately from his opponents and exponents alike, and I from the sister of an eminent British novelist . . . , who was threatening Stravinsky in my unworthy person with her umbrella."

It was Cournos who brought another sculptor, the ragged and poor Gaudier-Brzeska, to Church Walk one day to hear Pound read his poems. Leaving, Gaudier was pleased because Pound had dared to use the word *piss*—and Cournos reported the reaction to the poet. Pound was delighted, but confided that he had used another and quite innocent word which had a similar sound. But it reflected the need to be, or at least appear to be, outrageously rebellious, and soon Pound would pick up the suggestion and insert *merde* into a poem. Cautious then, even in his rebellion, he put his scatology into French.

Soon after, Gaudier agreed to work on a head of Pound, possibly hoping that through Pound's influence some of Sophie Brzeska's stories could be sold, and that Pound might even purchase *Stags,* a work in heavily veined alabaster he had praised. But Pound, after provoking the emotional Sophie by suggesting that women had no need for emancipation, since they could dominate men without any new laws, confided to Gaudier that his critical clout did not extend to unmarketable fiction. Further, he was only interested in his bust, having already invested more than he could afford in small sculptures, and Gaudier was soon complaining to Sophie about Pound's sittings for the work which would become *Hieratic Head,* "I've just about had enough of him. He comes and stays for hours without speaking."

During the winter of 1913–14, Pound's mind was more on creating a market for his newly minted Imagistic movement, which he had announced prematurely as a counterweight to the Georgians. If necessary, he would expand his definition of *Imagisme* to encompass new adherents, and one of the unlikeliest of poets to be classified as such was James Joyce, who had no idea that he was an *Imagiste* when he sent a copy of one of his unsalable poems to Yeats. Pound at the time was spending several months with Yeats at Stone Cottage, Coleman's Hatch, in Sussex, acting as the great man's secretary, in the process of which he continued his efforts to drag Yeats out of his beloved 1890s. That December the name of an obscure teacher of English—and author—in Trieste, with whom Yeats corresponded, came up. Pound, warming to the story of a great literary genius living in poverty and obscurity in Italy, reacted with an encouraging letter, offering to help Joyce place his work in English magazines which paid a little or not at all (but had "slight advertising value"), and in American ones which paid "top rates." It was the first time, he confided (except for French authors, as he had connections with the *Mercure de France*), that he had written to a writer outside his own "circle of acquaintance." He was *"bonae voluntatis,"* and had no idea whether he could be of any use. "From what W.B.Y. says I imagine we have a hate or two in common; but that is a very problematical bond or introduction. . . ."

In return, Joyce detailed to Pound the saga of his frustrations in getting his book of short stories, *Dubliners,* printed, but before it arrived, forwarded from Church Walk, Yeats turned up a copy of Joyce's unpublished poem "I Hear an Army." Pound immediately declared Joyce an Imagist, and wrote to him offering to use it in *Des Imagistes* and even to pay for it. Encouraged, Joyce mailed not only a copy of *Dubliners* but the first chapter of *A Portrait of the Artist as a Young Man.*

He wasn't supposed to know much about prose, Pound wrote, acknowledging the arrival of the packet, but he thought the novel was "damn fine stuff." For him the joy of creating a work of art was no greater than that of discovering a new creative talent. He pressed the *Egoist* into taking Joyce up, and that interest in *Dubliners* forced the hand of Grant Richards, who finally agreed to print it; while Dora Marsden and Harriet Weaver began publishing *Portrait* in installments,* with their deadlines pushing Joyce into finishing the novel. He was finally launched.

The Ezra Pound impact was pervasive. He seemed to be sponsoring, or editing, or contributing to, or translating, or adapting, or advising, in every corner of literary London, yet finding time to write essays and polemics (he titled one collection in 1913 with the fencing term *Ripostes*) and poems. He was tenacious when there was a talent to be nurtured. While working with Yeats and initiating his sponsorship of Joyce, he found time to again urge William Carlos Williams to return to England for the sake of his art. That Williams was married, and in medical practice, and that his wife's pregnancy was past term, was no more worth a thought to Pound than was his silent "improvement" of a senior poet's lines —as had happened to Yeats. Having induced Yeats to offer some of his verse to Harriet Monroe, Pound then changed the wording in three places before sending the pages to *Poetry*. Yeats had asked him only to check the punctuation, and was outraged at the impudence. That Pound was sequestered with him that winter in Sussex indicated the extent of Yeats's forgiveness, and willingness to accept further advice. He had even accepted one of Pound's changes at the time, altered the punctuation in the second case to overcome the weakness Pound had discovered, and in the third rewritten the passage. Pride forbade accepting all of the energetic young poet's emendations.

During the fall and winter of 1913–14, Pound read to Yeats (who preferred Browning, William Morris, and Doughty's *Dawn in Britain*) at Stone Cottage, took down his dictation, and became the elder poet's literary mentor, possessing the persuasive advantage of the monopoly of Yeats's time. He convinced Yeats to turn the fractious manuscript of *The Player Queen* from tragedy to comedy,

---

* In the issue in which the first segment appeared (March 16, 1914) Pound also placed Williams's long poem "The Wanderer."

and recommended that he eliminate Victorian abstractions from his verse. Agreeing to the experiment, Yeats asked Pound to point out the offending language, and was amazed at how many words were marked for purging. But Yeats's newer verse became more spare, and more effective.

Pound had also become the literary executor for the Oriental scholar Ernest Fenollosa, having impressed his widow, and Yeats was excited by what Pound was digging out about the traditional Japanese Noh drama. Pound had begun publishing his adaptations of Fenollosa's translations and transcriptions of Chinese and Japanese poetry and plays, and was instrumental in the revival of interest in Noh, including Yeats's own experiments in the form. In bringing a consideration of Japanese and Chinese literary values to the aesthetics of English poetry, Pound very likely saw himself anew as another Whistler, who had brought Japanese concepts and techniques to English art. The obtuseness and hostility of hidebound English critics had never caused Whistler to put down his brush, and he had eventually altered not only the way artists drew, but the way people saw. The lesson there kept Pound going.

"Ezra never shrinks from work," Yeats wrote Lady Gregory. "A learned companion and a pleasant one, he is full of the Middle Ages and helps me get back to the more definite and concrete, away from modern abstractions; to talk over a poem with him is like getting you to put a sentence into dialect. All becomes clear and natural. Yet in his own work he is very uncertain, often very bad though very interesting sometimes. He spoils himself by too many experiments and has more sound principles than taste." But Yeats was grateful. When Pound finally married Dorothy Shakespear in 1914, "Uncle Billyum" offered Stone Cottage for their honeymoon retreat.*

With marriage suddenly in prospect, Pound carried on his literary business with increased vigor, instructing Harriet Monroe on how to run *Poetry;* publishing in the *Egoist* and the *New Age;* acting as literary scout for Willard Huntington Wright's well-financed new magazine in New York, the *Smart Set,* whose curmudgeonly literary

---

* "How will you keep her?" H. H. Shakespear asked the impecunious Pound when the poet had solicited Dorothy's hand. Having received payment for a piece of writing so recently that he had just cashed the check, Pound withdrew a handful of banknotes from his pocket and said, "But look! I have money here!"

editor was H. L. Mencken;* operating as literary impresario for a
dozen London friends (and the distant William Carlos Williams
and James Joyce); and beginning a feud with the newest of the
Imagists, the imperious Amy Lowell. Determined, at forty-nine, to
bring her own writing into harmony with modern trends in all the
arts—she was learning about Fauré and Satie, but was baffled by
Picasso and Cubism—she had been especially fascinated by what
Poetry's obviously brilliant foreign correspondent had been writing.
Having decided that she was an incipient Imagist, she had sailed
for London in the summer of 1913 with a letter of introduction to
Pound from Miss Monroe.

Taking a top-floor suite at the Berkeley Hotel with a view
across Piccadilly to Green Park, she gave an elaborate dinner party
for Pound and his impecunious friends—Hilda Doolittle, Richard
Aldington, and John Gould Fletcher—not realizing that in one room
she had snared all the authentic Imagists and then some. Short and
stout and an incessant cigar smoker—a habit that seemed at odds
with her old-fashioned, high-collared but expensive clothes and her
schoolmarmish manner—she appeared remote from any poetic type
Pound had encountered, but she knew what she wanted, and fired
knowledgeable questions at him.

Pound launched into involved explanations, bringing in Fenollosa's theories about Chinese ideograms and Japanese plays, referring
to Italian and Provençal poetic practices, and drawing other recondite
and abstruse allusions. Finally he quoted as an example of Imagism
his own "In a Station of the Metro"—which he had ruthlessly pared
down from thirty lines to two:

> The apparition of these faces in the crowd;
> Petals on a wet, black bough.

Miss Lowell would write her own equivalent in "A London Thoroughfare, 2 A.M." The first two of its six brief lines would be

> They have watered the street,
> It shines in the glare of lamps. . . .

* While Mencken, a young Baltimorean, would become famous under his own
name, Wright would be better known as "S. S. Van Dine," creator of the erudite
detective Philo Vance.

"He is the oddest youth," Miss Lowell wrote a friend, "clever, fearfully conceited, &, at the same time, excessively thin-skinned; and I imagine that never, since the days of Wilde, have such garments been seen in the streets of London." Pound often did seem to dress in costume rather than in clothes, making the most in self-advertising out of his small means. At times the effects were even accidental. Alvin Langdon Coburn had gone to Church Walk in October 1913 to take a photograph of Pound, to be used in his next collection of poems, and found the author, recovering from an attack of jaundice, in a dressing gown. Coburn set up his camera anyway, and produced a portrait which Dorothy Shakespear's father described as resembling "a sinister but very brilliant Italian." Pound, too, thought it had a Renaissance effect, and Mrs Langley, his landlady (could she have known his "Goodly Fere"?), said, "I hope you won't be offended, sir, but, eh, it *is* rather like the good man of Nazareth, isn't it, sir?" Said Yeats: "That'll sell the book."

When Fletcher had first met Pound he had been struck by the air of the dandy—pearl-buttoned velvet coat, fawn trousers, a loose-flowing dark cape, sombrero, and silver-topped Malacca cane. But the unposed Ezra Pound revealed that the uniform of successful bohemian artist "merely concealed a state of poverty bordering upon indigence." What Amy Lowell saw was very likely the bohemian uniform, now showing a bit more evidence of wear. In the interest of larger goals, however, she could overlook anything, and at her dinner and after, as she made the rounds of publishers, editors, and poets, she seemed to Pound to be a valuable ally. He offered to place her newest poem, "The Garden"—written just before she had sailed—in the *Imagist* anthology. Without all the explanations, she had been an Imagist after all, apparently a result of exposure to precept and example in *Poetry*. Having made new friends among the younger American poets, and having been accepted into the sacred circle, she booked passage home in August. She had already made herself memorable within the poetry establishment. At a hushed, respectful reading of his verses by Rupert Brooke, the young lion of literary London in 1913, she had broken the silence from her conspicuous place in the back row with a contralto "Louder, please!"

Although the Imagist school was still presumably safe from

being absorbed into Amygism, Pound restlessly involved himself with the promotion of still another, and more rebellious, movement. Through Gaudier he had met a brilliant young artist and writer, Wyndham Lewis, who had rented two floors of a house in Blooms-bury and established what he called the Rebel Art Centre. Born in 1882 (on his father's yacht) to an upstate New York family which lived on both sides of the Atlantic when he was a child, Percy Wyndham Lewis did not become a permanent Londoner until his parents separated when he was eleven. After living with his mother in a succession of suburbs, he went to public school. Last in his class at Rugby, he had gone on to study painting at the Slade School of Art, where, although he was good at it, he was known, because of his other interests, as "Lewis the poet."

Following some bohemian years, mostly in Paris, Lewis began writing, as he told J. B. Pinker, whom he wanted as his agent, "simply to make money." First there was a preposterous would-be thriller in which an American gang kidnaps someone impersonating, for another gang, a Cockney woman who, unknown to herself but not to the conspirators, has inherited a million pounds. Pinker thought it had no money value and Lewis took the manuscript back, confessing that it was "a lesson showing the futility of potboiling for me." (*Khan and Company* was not published until 1978, and then under a title Lewis had not intended, *Mrs. Dukes' Million.*) His next effort was better—the stories collected as *The Wild Body* in 1909—but by then "Lewis the poet" was developing the drawing techniques leading toward abstraction which he had picked up in France.

By the time he became friendly with Pound, he was pronouncing the art and writing around him in London to be flabby, exhibitionistic pap. Through his Rebel Art Centre he planned to wage war on contemporary culture. It would provide a focus for like-minded artists, while its lectures, demonstrations, and exhibitions would bring his "objectivist" brand of modernism to the public in the most energetic manner possible. And there was, of course, to be a peri-odical—the organ of the revolution. Marinetti had come from Italy with his machine-age doctrine of Futurism, and Picasso and others had put Cubism on the London map. Borrowing from both and,

Pound thought, from Imagism, Lewis had christened his movement Vorticism. The VORTEX—it would be referred to by the founders in large block capitals—was never clearly defined, but suggested hard, concrete images and an energetic outspokenness. The organ of the doctrine, it was promised, would furnish a clear manifesto. Meanwhile Pound's *Egoist* essay of February 16 on Gaudier and Epstein furnished a preview. Humanity had proved "unbearably stupid," he wrote belligerently; it had refused to be led into the future by its prophets, the artistic community. "The artist has been at peace with his oppressors long enough. He has dabbled in democracy and he is done with that folly. . . . The aristocracy of entail and of title is decayed, the aristocracy of commerce is decaying, the aristocracy of the arts is ready again for its service . . . and we who are the heirs of the witch-doctor and the voodoo, we artists who have been so long the despised are about to take over control." The aggressiveness that was characteristically Pound's had been rapierlike, in the image of Whistler. Wyndham Lewis even thought Pound was a bit old-fashioned. The new explosiveness seemed borrowed from Lewis's rhetoric; the organ of Vorticism would even be christened *Blast.* An announcement of its forthcoming and still unnamed first issue, then in preparation by Lewis and Pound, appeared in the *Egoist* of April 15, 1914, headlined "End of Christian Era."

Despite the taunt in the advertisement, the wedding of Ezra Pound and Dorothy Shakespear took place, quietly and circumspectly, five days later at the church of St Mary Abbots. According to the marriage register, Pound was twenty-eight and Dorothy twenty-seven. Among the half-dozen wedding guests, all members of the bride's family, was a young relative by marriage, Miss Bertha Georgie Hyde-Lees, twenty-two, who had musical and literary ambitions, and confessed to an interest in the occult. A few years later she would marry a fiftyish friend of both the bride and groom and replace Pound as presiding influence. The friend was W. B. Yeats.

Shortly before the wedding Pound relinquished his tiny room at 10 Church Walk—John Cournos took it—and moved to a small flat around the corner at 5 Holland Place Chambers. With him went his newest and most treasured possession, a clavichord built for him by Arnold Dolmetsch with a motto inscribed inside the lid: *Plus fait Douceur que Violence*. Despite Pound's myriad activities and publications, his income was less than modest—one reason for the delay in a marriage that had appeared to his friends to have been inevitable for years. Yet he spent what was for him a fortune to buy an instrument on which he could barely pick out a tune, the symbol of the love he and the maker (to whom he later paid homage in the *Cantos*) shared for music "back before Mozart or Purcell, . . . [in] tones clear as brown amber. . . ." Pound saw a relationship between the music of the clavichord era and his literary politics, writing a few years later that "music was vorticist in the Bach-Mozart period before it went off into romance and sentiment and description." In rejecting what he would call in 1938 "the slop of the damned XIX century," he spurned not only the music and other arts of the bourgeois century but the political and economic system which underlay them. Few things, however, could be as far removed from each other as the Dolmetsch clavichord, with its gentle inscription, and the future organ of Vorticism.

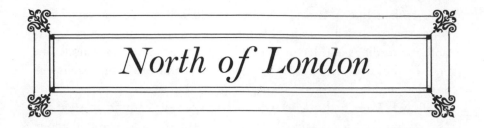

North of London

And Ezra Pound, the stormy petrel, I must tell you more about him. . . . He has found me and sent a fierce article to Chicago denouncing a country that neglects fellows like me. I am afraid he overdid it. . . .

—Robert Frost to John T. Bartlett, April 1913

EARLY ON THE MORNING of January 8, 1913, the tenant of the Bungalow, Reynolds Road, Beaconsfield, took the Great Western Railroad for the short ride into the city. He was living, he had happily written a friend, within a mile or two of the place where Milton completed *Paradise Lost,* no farther than that from the country churchyard where Gray lay buried, and "within as many rods as furlongs of the house where Chesterton tries truth to see if it won't prove as true upside down as it does right side up. To London town what is it but a run? Indeed when I leave writing this . . . I shall be able to see the not very distinct lights of London flaring like a dreary dawn."

At 35 Devonshire Street, only a five-minute walk from the British Museum, its advertisement claimed, Harold Monro's Poetry Bookshop was opening. At the refurbished eighteenth-century house, in a narrow, slumlike thoroughfare, the crisply mustached Monro, who looked like a Guards officer, would sell books of verse few other shops carried, publish his poetry magazine, make space available for readings and lectures, and let rooms upstairs "at a moderate rate to those in sympathy with our aims, who are temporarily in London, and care to avail themselves of our hospitality."

Robert Frost had not seen the advertisement. "I used to steal off to London for an occasional day," he recalled, "and wander about the streets." He found himself on that dark winter morning "pausing before the window of a shop where a clerk was arranging volumes of current poetry. A notice announced the opening, that night. . . . I went in and asked if I might return for the evening." The shop assistant told him that it was an invitation-only affair, but that he might try.

In the evening the narrow shop was crowded for the opening formalities, and Frost had to watch from a seat on the stairs leading to the balcony. There a round-faced young man with glasses tried to make conversation through the jumble of voices.

"American?"

"Yes. How'd you know?"

"Shoes. Writing?"

"Yes."

"Poetry?"

"I accept the omen."

"You should know your fellow countryman, Ezra Pound."

"I've never heard of him."

"Well, if you ever meet him, you won't be foolish enough to say that to his face!"

Frost explained that he never paid much attention to literary gossip and read few magazines. Frank Flint offered to let Pound know of Frost's existence, and led him to a shelf on which Flint's own book of poetry was displayed. Prudently, Frost bought a copy of *In the Net of the Stars*. Flint had also let it be known that he was a critic.

Following up the introduction, Frost, from Beaconsfield, wrote his new friend a letter full of flattering phrases about Flint's verse. He had frankly enjoyed that evening at the bookshop, he confided, having seldom been in company "in which I hadn't to be ashamed of having written verse. Perhaps it will help you understand my state of mind if I tell you that I have lived for the most part in villages where it were better that a millstone were hanged about your neck than that you should own yourself a minor poet."

Even given Frost's need to cultivate Flint's interest with some exaggeration of his previous condition, that earlier state, for someone who aspired to recognition as a poet, had been grim. At thirty-eight in the spring of 1912, having eked out an existence in New Hampshire as a teacher and as a farmer, he was still nowhere as published writer. His solution was to give up teaching at the school in Plymouth, which paid little, and to sell the farm. The proceeds, and an eight-hundred-dollar annuity under terms of his grand-father's will, would permit him time either to find himself as a poet or to establish that he was not one. He had published few of his verses. He was hardly noticed, he told Susan Ward, even among the versifiers whose work was filler material in magazines, and one journal had been holding a poem of his unprinted for three years. "I may be too old to write the song I once dreamed about . . . ," he worried to her, but he was going to try. "If there is any virtue in Location—but don't think I think there is. I know where the poetry must come from if it comes."

Although his friend John Bartlett had moved to British Columbia, Frost had rejected Canada for England, and afterward was de-liberately fuzzy about the reasons, perhaps because there was a virtue in location after all. Despite the romantic aura about a "Spirit of Place," what was more important was the opportunity the place afforded. One might *write* poetry on Vancouver Island or in Derry, New Hampshire, but one *published* poetry in places like London. Still, Elinor Frost had urged her husband, both later said, to live under a thatched roof for a while—which meant the English country-side. He didn't go for the literary life, he insisted ever afterward, "but we could live cheaper there. The six of us went to England, and we stayed there for three years for thirty-six hundred dollars, fare and everything. We lived poor, but we had a little garden, . . . and we had some chickens." Nothing drew them to England, he wrote an inquirer in 1938, but "the cheapness of peasant life over there and the distance it would put between us and our worried relatives. . . . We went there to be poor in peace and to live a few years for nothing but my writings." Yet in 1957 he identified his motives for an Edinburgh newspaper as "I wanted to visit the cradle of lyric poetry—and also to live under a thatch."

Whatever the real reason, in August 1912 they settled on trying the London suburbs, and sailed from Boston to Glasgow, with all of their bedclothes, two rugs, Elinor's rocking chair and Robert's Morris chair, and some books and pictures, but with no letter of introduction to anyone. After the long trip by rail from Scotland they arrived in London in early September, and spent a week in a hotel, exploring the city and looking for a place to stay. Quickly they found their way to the theater, where they saw Shaw's long-running comedy on feminism, *Fanny's First Play;* paid thruppence for their first copy of *The Times,* applied for an admission card to the British Museum Reading Room, and went to a public meeting (the best free entertainment in London) where Frost "heard G. B. Shaw tease the Suffragettes . . . till they didn't know whether he had come to help (as advertised) or hinder them. . . ."

To find a place to live, Frost went to the offices of *T. P.'s Weekly,* which had a "Country Walks" column. The writer had sounded as if he knew the suburban areas in which Frost was interested, and turned out to be a genial former policeman who was delighted to guide the Frosts about. The first few properties were unsatisfactory, but in the Beaconsfield area of Buckinghamshire, the last cottage on the right-hand curve of Reynolds Road was available, although at a steeper rent than the Frosts had anticipated. They took it anyway. For the equivalent of $150 they bought enough furniture to fill their five rooms, and hung the key on the nail. The children—Lesley, the oldest, was thirteen—were placed in local schools, and Frost settled down to serious writing.

His first idea was ambitious. He would write a novel about the conflict between two New Hampshire farm workers, one just out of college and the other a veteran of the soil. After beginning the first chapter unsatisfactorily, he thought of turning the subject into a play, but could not find appropriate situations in which to dramatize the tensions between the two points of view. He put it aside, and since he seldom threw anything potentially useful away, converted the material into a poem, "From Plane to Plane," which was not published until 1947 in *Steeple Hill*. For Frost there was seldom any connection between time of writing and date of publication. Sometimes a poem would appear fresh from the pen; more often years—sometimes decades—would elapse before he found an appropriate place for a poem he had frugally preserved, and the scrambled chronology would confuse critics unaware of his methods.

Next he tried a lyric which was his reaction to the attractive strangeness of the Buckinghamshire countryside, in which the poet sat on a gate in a soft rain and felt a trace of salt in the breeze because in England one was "never far from sailing." Again Frost was dissatisfied, and put aside the verses. (They would not be published until 1944.) It was obvious that he was not ready to write about England, yet beginning again remote from the sources of his earlier writing made him weigh the batch of poetry—twenty years of it—which he had brought with him. In the evening lamplight he spread the pages out on the floor near the fireplace to see whether any shape or theme might unify some of them into a book. A few went into the fire as not worth saving. Rejecting chronology, although he could not escape recognizing many poems as young works, he eliminated, too, the most obvious thematic approach—it would mean using the love lyrics he wrote to and for Elinor during their courtship and since their marriage (troubled though it often was). Neither he nor his wife was prepared, as reticent Yankees, for the intensity of self-revelation inevitable in such a sequence. Still, he told a prospective biographer years later, "I saw . . . that I had one book written and all I had to do was throw it into shape to make it mean me."

He arranged a sequence of thirty-two poems which traversed the seasons as well as moods from despair and withdrawal to aspiration and affirmation, and linked them, in a curiously old-fashioned way. Under each title on the table of contents pages he placed a brief, ironic gloss which established relationships he wanted the reader to perceive. From Longfellow's "My Lost Youth" he took a title: *A Boy's Will*. Lesley typed clean copies on their old Blickensderfer machine.

"I hadn't the shadow of a hope," he confided in the 1920s, "that

I would find a publisher in any country for many years. I couldn't afford to set my heart on getting published if I was going to be happy in my writing. Nevertheless I resolved to have a shot or two at the publishers." But he didn't know any. "I decided to take them to the policeman-columnist—my only friend. I hadn't met anybody yet. I thought he might know about smaller publishers. It didn't even occur to me to go to the bigger ones." The "Country Walks" man examined the pages and announced, "Little books like that cost the author about fifteen pounds." Frost declared in proper New Hampshire spirit that he would never publish a book at his own expense. The ex-policeman then proposed Elkin Mathews, but Frost was sure that Mathews would exact a fee. Then the name of David Nutt came up, and Frost recalled that he had seen the Nutt imprint on a volume of W. E. Henley's verses. It was enough. He found the offices at 6 Bloomsbury Street, close to the British Museum, and made an appointment.

Returning with his typescript, he was shown into an office where sat a small, sad woman "dressed all in black, as if she had just risen from the sea." When Frost looked puzzled she said in a French-accented voice, "I will speak for David Nutt." What Frost did not know was that both David Nutt and his son Alfred were dead, and that the woman in weeds was Alfred Nutt's widow. The atmosphere was melancholy and mysterious, but Frost felt that he had no choice but to leave his book. In a few days, he was assured, she would let him know the decision of the firm.

A few days later the postman dropped a letter from Mrs Nutt at Reynolds Road, written in an awkward English that could only have disturbed the poet about the prospects of his book in her hands. She was interested in bringing out his poems on a royalty basis, she wrote on October 26, but could not put "a cut and dry proposal" before him yet, as she wanted to think about the most suitable form to give the book. On his next visit to London, Frost called on her to discuss terms, and was too innocent of publishing to object to a clause which gave the firm of David Nutt the first option to publish his next four books of poetry or prose. It may have even been good to think that one had a publisher far into the indefinite future. "I suppose I ought to be proud to be so much in demand," he wrote Thomas Mosher in America: "the embarrassment is so novel in my experience. But won't it seem traitorously un-American to have all my first work come out over here?"*

Quickly he put his delicacies behind him, writing a New Hampshire friend that since he had settled in Beaconsfield he had been versifying "like a pawing horse let go." Now when he asked himself, in the words of the old song, "Oh, why left I my home, Why did I cross the deep," he had to confess that it had been to write prose rather than verse (the aborted novel). That flirtation with unreality had ended. He was ready to promote himself as a poet, and at the time of his encountering the Poetry Bookshop he needed only that kind of accident to begin his campaign.

Frost's follow-up letter to Frank Flint had ensured that Ezra Pound would hear of him. By the end of January there was a printed calling card from Church Walk. "At home—sometimes" was all Pound wrote. It was meant as a friendly gesture suggesting a visit, but there was too much arrogance in the curt message for Frost. "I didn't like that very well," he recalled. He preferred to wait until his call would appear unhurried, and very likely used the time to locate and read some of Pound's work. It was already March when he decided to go down to London. In Kensington he took Pound's card from his vest pocket and hunted for the right address in the narrow alley alongside the graveyard. Responding to the knock, Pound invited the caller in, and came to the door in his dressing gown: he had been interrupted while taking a bath in a shallow tub he usually concealed under the bed.

Eleven years older than Pound, the neatly suited, sandy-haired Frost looked younger than his years and nothing like a gnarled New England farmer. No respecter of age anyway, Pound, wasting little time on familiarities, scolded Frost for wasting precious weeks in answering his card. A literary career, after all, hung in the balance. "Flint tells me," Pound went on, "[that] you have a book."

"I ought to have," said Frost.

* According to notes in a fair copy of *A Boy's Will* which Frost made in 1951 for Clifton Waller Barrett (collection University of Virginia Library), after Mrs Nutt he showed the manuscript to publisher William Heinemann, who "objected to my quotations without quotation marks" in "Love and a Question" and "Into My Own." If true, Frost was exploring alternatives before putting himself irreversibly into Mrs Nutt's hands.

"You haven't seen it?"

No, said Frost, but he assumed that bound copies might now be ready for reviewers. He had already read proofs.

"What do you say we go and get a copy?"

Since it was difficult to say no to Pound, the pair walked to Bloomsbury, where Pound demanded a review copy. "Didn't show it to me—put it in his pocket," Frost remembered. "We went back to his room." There he was directed to keep busy while Pound read, looking up at one point to ask, "You don't mind our liking this?"

"Oh, go ahead and like it," said Frost.

What Pound had liked was a short poem, "Neglect," which Frost explained, more dramatically than accurately, referred to how he had been deprived of legacies by his Frost grandfather and his Uncle Elihu, and how his grandfather had mistreated him by sending him out, he hoped to die, on the bleak Derry farm. Actually his grandfather had bought the New Hampshire farm for him on the condition that he live there at least ten years, which to the transplanted Philadelphian Ezra Pound may have seemed much like a death sentence anyway. Soon Pound laughed at something he read, and Frost indicated that he knew where that was. Before long Pound looked up again and said, "You'd better run along home, I'm going to review it." Frost had never even touched—and hardly seen—the pebble-grained binding of his first book. Puzzled by what had happened, he found his way back to Beaconsfield without a copy of *A Boy's Will* but with an invitation to meet Yeats and with presentation copies of Pound's *Personae* and *Ripostes*.

Within a few days Pound was writing to Harriet Monroe's assistant at *Poetry,* Alice Corbin, "Have just discovered another Amur'k'n. VURRY Amur'k'n, with, I think, the seeds of grace. Have reviewed an advance copy of his book, but have run it out too long. Will send it as soon as I've tried to condense it—also some of his stuff if it isn't all in the book." When he sent the review to Miss Monroe, he added, "Sorry I can't work this review down to any smaller dimensions! However, it can't be helped. Yes it can. I've done the job better than I thought I could. And it's our second scoop,* for I only found the man by accident and I think I've about

* The Bengali poet Tagore was Pound's first "scoop," just before Tagore had been awarded the Nobel Prize for literature.

the only copy of the book that has left the shop. . . . I think we should print this notice at once as we ought to be first and some of the reviewers here are sure to make fuss enough to get quoted in N.Y."

Receiving the messages early in April, Harriet Monroe confessed that before Pound had pushed them, *Poetry* had rejected some of Frost's verses. Now they were interested. "Alice says *mea culpa* about Frost," she wrote. "For we find him among our returns and it was done while I was in New York. She has the grit to stand up, however, and say if it was returned it deserved it, or at least those particular poems did. You can apologize for us and say we are very contrite and would like some more some day." On April 22 Pound replied diplomatically that he didn't doubt that what was sent was bad, but that Frost had also done "good things," and "whoever rejected 'em will go to hell along with *Harper's* and *The Atlantic*." After his "declaration of glory," Pound predicted, there would be public demand for Frost's writings, and he would personally pick the best of the unpublished work to offer to *Poetry*.

Not quite that much power over his new discovery was left to Pound after he had shown a carbon copy of his review to Frost. "There is another [new] personality in the realm of verse," he began, "another American, found, as usual, on this side of the water, by an English publisher long known as a lover of good letters. David Nutt publishes at his own expense *A Boy's Will*, by Robert Frost, the latter having long been scorned by the 'great American editors.' It is the old story." Frost had mixed feelings about such praise. To upbraid American publishers would only create resistance to his work later, he worried.* But the worst was yet to come. Later in the review Pound explored the personal note in Frost's poetry, and came to the story he had been told about "Neglect," which was, he explained, written to the poet's wife "when his grandfather and uncle had disinherited him of a comfortable

---

* Eager to separate himself from the image of disgruntled expatriate, Frost used his first American opportunity to issue a disclaimer. The book review section of the *New York Times* of August 8, 1915, quoted him as explaining "that his book of poems was published first in England merely by accident. He happened to be in that country when it occurred to him that he had enough manuscripts to make a book. The collection of poems was accepted quickly and gladly by the first publisher to whom he showed it. . . ."

fortune and left him in poverty because he was a useless poet instead of a money-getter."

The story was exactly right for Pound's acerbities about materialist values, but the exposure, let alone its inaccuracies (for which Pound was not responsible), struck horror into the reticent New England hearts of both Frosts. Elinor even wept. Yet Pound remembered Frost's saying—"I don't know whether it is his own or whether it is a gem he collected"—that a summary of his prayers might be "Oh God, pay attention to *me*." God did not reside at 10 Church Walk, although he did seem to have a surrogate there. "I'm afraid he overdid it," Robert wrote John Bartlett. It was too late to stop Ezra Pound from booming Frost in his way, and he followed up his review by telling Frost that Yeats had declared *A Boy's Will* to be "the best poetry written in America for a long time."

Soon Frost was a guest at Yeats's flat on one of his Monday evenings, meeting some of the London literary establishment and listening skeptically to tales of ghosts and fairies and other occult phenomena with which his host was preoccupied. Frost found the crush as well as the conversation not to his liking, and returned only once, as he was now making other acquaintances through Pound and through the interest generated by his book. There was less time for the lonely quiet of Beaconsfield, where Frost would write seated in his favorite chair, brought in a crate from Derry, on a wooden shelf removed from a closet and placed across the chair arms. He and Pound and other friends dined out together in London, talking of poets and poetry and the future, with Pound embarrassingly unpredictable as usual. In one restaurant he gave a demonstration of jujitsu. "Wasn't ready for him at all," Frost remembered. "I was just as strong as he was. He said, 'I'll show you. Stand up. Stand up.' So I stood up, gave him my hand. He grabbed my wrist, tipped over backwards and threw me over his head. . . . Everybody in the restaurant stood up. . . ." Dining again with Frost, and disgusted with the triviality of the conversation of two literary ladies he had wanted Frost to meet, he rose from his chair, knocking it over, and walked out, telling his friend, "I leave these ladies to you!"

The first London notices of Frost's book appeared early in April; additional ones would turn up into September. Some were short and unenthusiastic, but Flint (after noting "faults of diction here and there") praised "the direct observation of the object and immediate correlation with the emotion" as well as Frost's "ear for silences." Norman Douglas, who had taken Ford's place at the *English Review,* saw the poems as images of "things really heard and seen" and as echoing "that *inevitable* response to nature which is the hallmark of true lyric feeling." In London the *Academy* and the *Nation* welcomed him as a true poet, and the *Dial* became the second home review (after Pound's in the May *Poetry*) to note Frost's work, observing that his poetic world was one in which "passion has been stilled and the soul grown quiet. . . . His songs give us the sort of pleasure that we have in those of the *Shropshire Lad* of A. E. Housman." It was a perceptive aside, for Housman's influence had been pervasive since 1895, even among poets who claimed to dislike the melancholy lyrics and ballads of the *Lad.* Pound even parodied a Housman theme in such verses Frost may have known as

> The bird sits on the hawthorn tree
> But he dies also, presently.
> Some lads get hung, and some get shot.
> Woeful is this human lot.

Much later in life Frost did not conceal his contempt for the cynical Housman, whom he called an "ignorant" poet, but the derision hid some apparent indebtedness. Like Housman's inverted Arcadia, Frost's bucolic New England camouflaged a cruel world, and there are clear and very likely unconscious echoes of *A Shropshire Lad* in lines of Frost's so familiar as to seem wholly derived from his personal sense of place. His commerce with the English poetic tradition was undervalued by early critics who saw in him only a Yankee philosophical rustic, but he knew the minor as well as the major poets—"Stopping by Woods," for example, echoes Thomas Beddoes as well as the second lyric of *Shropshire Lad*—and it was no accident that he had come to the land of Palgrave's *Golden Treasury.*

The year 1913 had proven an *annis mirabilis* for American poets in London, especially for first books. In addition to Frost's *A Boy's Will* there had been John Gould Fletcher's carefully contrived five volumes and William Carlos Williams's *The Tempers*. There was also Ezra Pound's *Ripostes*. Frost made a point of praising *Ripostes* and the earlier *Personae,* and Pound said, brushing them aside, "If you value them. . . . But it's all old stuff. I shall not go back to it." Frost himself kept a pile of "old stuff" he hoped to combine with new writing for another book, and such easy discarding of one's work because one might change fashions in verse as readily as one might change fashions in neckties disturbed him. He was already discouraged because his book was only a small *succès d'estime,* and he suffered as well from periods of homesickness, as was inevitable from his comparative isolation in Beaconsfield.

In July, Elinor Frost wrote to Sidney Cox in New Hampshire that the children did not like England as well as America, "though London seems a wonderful and fascinating place to them. Sometimes I have wished that we had taken lodgings in the city itself instead of a house so far out, as the life there would have been exciting for us all. . . ." But she rationalized that it was healthier to be away from the foggy, smoky city, and that Beaconsfield was beautiful in the later spring and summer. Elinor and the children, who did not have Frost's literary opportunities for travel to London and London friends, and usually saw the city as a glow in the sky at evening, concealed their own unhappiness as much as possible, although there were some marital quarrels precipitated by his apparent selfishness in making the family bear the burden of his literary ambitions, and by long-standing religious differences.* Even his yearning for home increased when he began recognizing Americans in London by their box-toed boots. "I'm a Yank from Yankville," he wrote a friend.

Uncertainty about his future helped create more and more distance between Frost and his eager mentor. In his rush to be first with his discovery, Pound had precipitated the alienation. He had

---

* Elinor, a militant atheist (she was "flatfooted against God," Frost once confided to a friend), regularly challenged the conservative theology Frost concealed behind a poetic façade of wit and irony and hints of skepticism.

been, Frost said later, "so quick and kind," but the trouble lay in Pound's "haste to speak of my poetry before anyone—anyone before him or beside him. . . . I have always felt grateful to Ezra for the start he tried to give me. He continued generous, he reviewed me justly, even after we'd acutely quarrelled and disagreed, as we did in a very short time." But Frost resented being put aside by Pound as much as he was angry at being helped in Pound's manner. He was being bullied, he wrote Thomas Mosher. "The fact that he discovered me gives him the right to see that I live up to his good opinion of me. He says I must write something much more like *vers libre* or he will let me perish of neglect. He really threatens." Yet one must read into Frost's letter his own desire to manufacture a persona as well as Pound's eagerness to mold his new "find" into his own kind of poet. Further, what Frost did not confide was that while he was struggling to escape Pound's domination, he was also jealous of the attentions paid to the newly married H.D. and Richard Aldington, whose work Pound was praising and promoting far in excess of anything he was doing for Frost. Mosher, a small publisher in Maine, was a pipeline to other publishing media, and Frost was quickly learning that one had to manipulate as well as cultivate such powers. Thus to a biographer in his later years Frost recalled that Pound

tried to, he asked me to join the little group of Imagistes who shortened one another's poetry: F. S. Flint, T. E. Hulme, H.D. and Richard Aldington. The poets were interesting. Flint, especially, became a friend I have kept to this day. But I had to work alone. Pound, to illustrate what it should be, took a poem of mine, said: "You've done it in fifty words. I've shortened it to forty-eight." I answered, "And spoiled my metre, my idiom and idea."

Knowing that he had created a personal form which gave him freedom to develop his material effectively—particularly the blank-verse dramatic monologues which he intended to emphasize in his next collection—Frost resisted Pound's imperious generosity and elected to remain outside the clan. It was easy to do so since Mrs Nutt was eager for another book, and the first had already introduced Frost, as he put it in a letter to an American friend, "to other people who write."

One product of the developing tension was a free-verse parody which, on July 6, 1913, he sent to Frank Flint but which Frost was unwilling to publish in his lifetime.

> My nose is out of joint
> For my father-in-letters—
> My father mind you—
> Has been brought to bed of another poet,
> And I am not nine months old.
> It is twins this time
> And they came into the world prodigiously united in wedlock.
> (Don't try to visualize this.)
> Already they have written their first poems in vers libre
> And sold it [them] within twenty-four hours.
> My father-in-letters was the affluent American buyer—
> There was no one to bid against him. . . .

"You are in awe of that great intellect. . . . ," Frost accused Flint. "You saw me first but you had to pass me over for him to discover." Flint tried to dissuade him from an open break with the useful Pound, but the result was another poem, more in Pound's idiom, and disparaging his intervention:

> . . . I took your words at their face value
> I accepted your words like an encyclical letter
> It did not matter
> At worst they were good medicine
> I made my stand elsewhere
> I did not ask you to unsay them.
> I was willing to take anything you said from you
> If I might be permitted to hug the illusion
> That you liked my poetry
> And liked it for the right reason.
>
> You reviewed me,
> And I was not sure—
> I was afraid it was not artis[ti]cally done.
> I decided I couldnt use it to impress my friends
> Much less my enemies.
> But in as much [as] it was praise I was grateful
> For praise I do love.

I suspected though that in praising me
You were not concerned so much with my desert
As with your power
That you praised me arbitrarily
And took credit to yourself
In demonstrating that you could thrust anything
    upon the world
Were it never so humble. . . .

Flint saw nothing to be gained by goading Pound, and hoped that Frost would keep the satirical verses to himself. "You know I think his bark is much worse than his bite," Flint wrote, "and that much that seems offensive to us externally is merely external and a kind of outer defense—a mask." But Frost, according to his authorized but unworshipful biographer, Lawrance Thompson, wanted "to achieve the comfort of superiority" by accumulating evidence that his compatriot had abused him rather than accomplished "more than anyone else to make Frost's literary start in London successful." There was a dark, moody side to the poet that was largely kept private, encountered only by his embattled wife and a few close friends to whom he unburdened himself of unattractive feelings which would have exploded the public image he was carefully building. Having worked up so much resentment toward Pound which he could not release at Pound himself, he let it go at other friends who had kindly invited the Frost family to holiday with them in Scotland. The Gardners, he wrote uncharitably to John Bartlett, were a couple he had met at the Poetry Bookshop on his memorable first visit, who "hunt lions and they picked me up cheap as a sort of bargain before I was as yet made." What troubled him most, according to Thompson, "was that whenever someone praised him for his best, actual or possible, he was reminded of his worst. Guilt was always quick to waylay him. . . ." He had, Frost told Bartlett in 1927, an "Indian vindictiveness. Really I am awful there. I am worse than you know." Although he could recognize the weakness in himself, he was seldom able to control it, as he confided to a pocket notebook he bought in England: "Evil clings so to all our acts that even when we not only mean but achieve our prettiest, bravest, noblest, best, we are often a scourge even to those we do not hate. Our sincerest prayers are no more than groans that this should be so."

The acceptance of *A Boy's Will* had breached the dam of Frost's poetic reticence. In Beaconsfield dramatic monologues and dialogues had burst forth to supplement what he had carried across the Atlantic, so that by the time Mrs Nutt was preparing to list his book in her spring (1913) catalogue, Frost was prepared with a provisional title for a second book, which she duly listed as forthcoming —*Farm Servants, and Other People.* On his own copy Frost crossed it out and wrote above it *New England Hill Folk.* He would find still other titles before he had copy to deliver to Mrs Nutt, but was pleased with the way his work was going. To add to three dramatic narratives (the best of them "The Death of the Hired Man") and a lyric ("The Good Hours") he had written on the farm in Derry, he had drafts of new work in various stages, some of which would appear in the second book. One new effort was a Christmas poem ("Good Relief") which he began on the train after shopping for presents for the children. Others were the products of nostalgia and distance, meditative poems which remain among his most memorable work—"Birches," "Mending Wall," and "After Apple Picking."

In 1936, at a reading, Frost told his listeners, "I wrote the poem 'Mending Wall' thinking of the old wall that I hadn't mended in several years and which must be in terrible condition. I wrote that poem in England when I was very homesick for my old wall in New England. Now I'll read another which I wrote while I was a little homesick: 'Birches.'" But he also claimed, his memory mellowed by time, "I wrote whole poems of two hundred lines at a sitting. I believe I was not over two hours with 'Home Burial.' It stands in print as it was in the first draft." Frost hid many of his traces, but surviving work sheets suggest that he was busier than that at his shelf-board desk in Beaconsfield. And he would never write better, although some of the evidence would not be in the new book. "Birches," for example, written early in 1914 when he was tramping the muddy yard at the bungalow in Beaconsfield, and recalling the crystalline winters at the Derry farm, was put aside.

To Thomas Mosher on October 24, 1913, Frost announced that the title of the new book was the only part of it not ready.

He had rejected more than a dozen possibilities, including *New England Eclogues* and *New Englanders,* but one night after everyone else had gone to bed, he paced the dining room in the cottage and remembered the Boston newspaper which geographically categorized properties advertised for sale by such vague terms as "North of Boston." His English friends warned him of confusion: there was a Boston in Lincolnshire; but Frost was thinking more about the book's potential at home, and Mrs Nutt was satisfied.

Although Ezra Pound realized that his relations with Frost were becoming tenuous, he was determined to make his compatriot's voice heard in America, and asked him for something "new" which he could place in *Poetry.* Harriet Monroe had assured Pound of acceptance this time, and Frost, knowing that he had failed with *Poetry* on his own, produced a substantial poem for Pound—"The Death of the Hired Man." With malice aforethought, Frost did not identify the work as dating back to Derry and 1905-6, and Pound wrote his father (and similarly to others) that Frost had "done a 'Death of the Farm Hand' since the book that is to my mind better than anything in it. I shall have that in the *Smart Set* or in *Poetry* before long." At Church Walk, when John Gould Fletcher came calling, Pound picked up a typewritten manuscript from the table and read "Death of the Hired Man" aloud "to the last syllable with every mark of admiration." Although he applauded the "championing of another outcast American," Fletcher was puzzled by Pound's hearty approval of poetry so unlike his own and with "not inconsiderable echoes of Wordsworth, whom Pound valiantly despised, and of the still hated Georgians." What Fletcher failed to realize (because Pound did not admire Fletcher's confessedly "clangorous, unrealistic, metaphorical, and confusedly rhetorical" verse) was that his friend recognized poetry of a high order, whether or not it fit his formulations. Eventually, too, Pound hoped, he could harness that talent to produce poetry closer to his own specifications.

Two facts that seemed to Pound to make the *Smart Set* a better American platform from which to launch Frost were that Willard Huntington Wright's magazine paid better, and that it issued from New York. Then Frost discovered where the poem was sent. He became puritanically indignant and demanded that Pound withdraw it. Pound refused, and the estrangement between the two seemed complete; but to Pound's dismay, he was unable, despite his prodding, to get *Smart Set* to print "Hired Man." Things like that, wrote Wright, were a dime a dozen, and he had just published another poem about a hired man by the Ohio tramp-poet Harry Kemp.

Pound was furious. He had briefly befriended Kemp in London, and had even intervened with the American minister, Walter Hines Page. But Kemp's "pseudo-Masefieldian poem" had been "written in a stilted, pseudo-literary language, with all sorts of floridities and worn-out ornaments," Pound charged, and he used the incident to repeat his assertion that the typical American editor had "resolutely shut his mind against serious American writing."

"I am out with Pound pretty much altogether," Frost wrote Thomas Mosher that October. ". . . I count myself well out, however. Pound is an incredible ass and he hurts more than he helps. . . ." For Frost it was a safe move. Pound would remain loyal anyway—despite the rebuffs, he would publish some influential praise of *North of Boston*—and some of the contacts made through the Poetry Bookshop were beginning to be useful. One was Wilfrid Wilson Gibson, who belied his Cambridge education in popular balladlike verse narratives of life in the mines, the factories, the slums. Gibson even recorded Frost's visit metrically in "The First Meeting," where there is a knock on the door of his "London garret" above Harold Monro's bookshop:

> A stranger, an American, called Frost,
> Had turned up, and would like to have a word
> With me. I put my manuscript aside. . . .
> It wasn't long before the two of us
> Were chatting in a close companionship;
> And I had lost the last shred of regret
> That I'd been interrupted in the business
> Of my comparatively inconsequent work;
> As I sat listening to Frost's racy speech
> And relishing his pithy commentaries
> On this and that. And when, too soon he rose
> To leave, I gladly took from him a sheaf

Of verse he, diffidently, handed me;
Saying he'd be obliged if I would bother
To look it through, and let him have a word
Of what I thought of it. . . .

Gibson would review *North of Boston* in the (London) *Book-man*. He also introduced Frost to Lascelles ("rhymes with *tassels*," Frost would say) Abercrombie, one of the acknowledged leaders of the Georgian poets, and a man who was actually living "under thatch" in Gloucestershire, as Frost had long dreamed of doing. Gibson planned a similar life-style—as soon as he could marry Harold Monro's secretary and take her with him. Elated, Frost talked of joining them, if he could sublease his house. "I give you fair warning," he wrote Mosher on October 28, "I am going to have my moderate success in these islands." The younger Georgian poets had adopted him, and the elder ones had been kind. Laurence Binyon had even invited him to lunch with the new Poet Laureate, Robert Bridges, he crowed. "These Englishmen are very charming. I begin to think I shall stay with them till I'm deported."

Fortunately for Frost, although not for the family, a lessee for the Reynolds Road cottage was difficult to find. For the children it meant continuing at the Beaconsfield school, to which Lesley and Irma went with such resentment at the backward teaching methods that they were finally withdrawn. (Carol and Marjorie had been tutored by Elinor almost from the start.) It meant more work for their mother, who now had to teach all four children as well as tend to every other domestic chore. Yet remaining in proximity to London through the fall and winter made it possible for Frost to meet additional Georgians, among them poet Ralph Hodgson and critic Edward Thomas, who he discovered had reviewed *A Boy's Will* anonymously (and favorably) in Chesterton's *New Weekly*. It was Hodgson who brought Thomas and Frost together over coffee at St George's Restaurant in London, and Thomas would become his closest friend in England, with significant consequences for both men. Another acquaintance who became a friend was Harold Monro, to whom he sold two poems for *Poetry and Drama*. The price agreed upon was that when the Frosts were ready to move and were between houses, they could spend a week in two furnished rooms above the shop. Also, Pound purchased a poem, "The Housekeeper," for the *Egoist* and arranged for sale of "The Code" to *Poetry,* both of which Frost agreed to despite their falling out. Yet Frost would write, meanly, to Mosher on January 20, 1914. "*Poetry* (Chicago) hasn't done anything but foster Pound and a few free-verse friends." But he confessed that he would like any money he could get from magazines. "One has to live and eat," he said, and sold the four poems from the new book.

Mrs Nutt disagreed, rebuking him that January for publishing any poetry in magazines during the term of his agreement with her, afterward punishing him for breach of contract by refusing to pay him royalties due from *North of Boston.* Only in America would he escape her grasp, but she had proved useful even in her French-peasant tight-fistedness, putting him between the covers of the books which established him. What he soon discovered, however, was that she also forbade him to enter into any arrangements with American publishers. That was her right as well. Even there, however, her tough stance with publishers in New York would later pay off for Frost.

In the first weeks of spring the Frosts packed their belongings, closed the cottage in Beaconsfield—in his unhappiness with the delays it had become "The Bunghole" to Frost—and moved temporarily to London. Their neighbor across the hall above the Poetry Bookshop, Frost wrote a friend in America, was "Epstein, the futurist sculptor, the New York Polish Jew, whose mind runs strangely on the subject of generation, [and] whose work is such a stumbling block to the staid and Victorianly but who in spite of all is reckoned one of the greatest living geniuses." The week in the city was to be a special treat for the children, whose homesickness was not allayed by Frost's assurances that once he had published another book in London—not *North of Boston* but a third collection for which he was assembling poems and ideas—they would take a boat back to America. The family was dismayed. The taste of London from their roost above the bookshop, Elinor and the children feared, might be their last experience of civilization for months or even years. The prospect of Gloucestershire now seemed like indefinite exile within exile, for there was yet no third book, nor was there any sign that one was about to materialize.

A week of smoke and grime made a difference. As their train took them through the fresh green of early April from the town of Gloucester to the hamlet of Dymock, the family became increasingly elated. The meadows were covered with yellow daffodils, and the fields in which cattle and sheep grazed were turning deep green. Unseen in the distance, the Severn wound its way toward Wales.

Abercrombie and the Gibsons awaited them at the Dymock station with two large carriages which deposited the Frosts and their baggage at the Gallows, just below the village of Ryton. Named for the hanging of a deer poacher on the site centuries before, the Gallows was Abercrombie's cottage—actually two cottages joined—on the lush farmlands and woodlands of the current Lord Beauchamp. Distant as it was from London, the Gallows had become a center of Georgian poetry activity, from which Abercrombie produced a locally printed quarterly, *New Numbers,* and from which the Frosts went house hunting.

Little Iddens, a boxlike five-room cottage of black timber and whitened bricks, just over the Herefordshire border south of Ledbury, and two miles from the former nailmaker's shop which was now the Gibson house, was available for an annual rental of ten pounds. It did not have a thatched roof, but it did have leaded windows and other evidences of its sixteenth-century origin, including primitive kitchen facilities and an iron pump outside the shed. Also a cider barrel. They were in cider country, Frost wrote Sidney Cox in May. Although they had approved neither of making it nor of drinking it while on the farm in New Hampshire, now— Frost explained—they had to keep cider for guests and hired help or they would have neither visitors nor hired hands. And they sampled it themselves, "adding drink to cigarette smoking in the record of our sins. Even Elinor gets drawn in since the only kind of ladies we know over here are all smokers." Elinor may have needed the new sins to help her endure the new austerities. For Frost the compensations were the inspiration of the idyllic scenery and the closeness of new cronies. For Elinor the combined difficulties

of living conditions, of entertaining her husband's friends, and of
tutoring the children left her on the edge of what she admitted in
letters home to be "complete nervous prostration." But one of the
new friends, she contended, was worth the price.

Edward Thomas had been their first visitor from London, bringing with him his teenage son and daughter, Mervyn and Bronwen.
A sensitive critic and essayist who was barely able to survive on his
writing earnings, Thomas was despondent about his professional
future, and poured out his problems to Frost as they wandered
through the countryside which Thomas, a Welshman, knew well.
He admired Frost's verse, and thought it often captured his own
dark moods, and they talked of how Thomas was planning to
present *North of Boston* in the notice of it he was writing for
Ford's *English Review*. He had long known the Georgian poets new
to Frost—Abercrombie, Gibson, Walter de la Mare, Rupert Brooke,
Gordon Bottomley—but had never considered himself one of them.
To Frost that was Thomas's greatest professional mistake. He pointed
to Thomas's *The Pursuit of Spring* and told him to rewrite it as verse
in the same cadences. His poetry "declared itself in verse form,"
Frost urged, and the lessons seemed to take hold in Thomas's review of *North of Boston,* which began, "This is one of the most
revolutionary books of modern times, but one of the quietest and
least aggressive." Frost's poems, he explained, lacked the exaggeration of rhetoric and seemed even to lack poetic intensity, as their
medium was common speech. "Yet almost all of these poems are
beautiful. They depend not at all on objects commonly admitted to
be beautiful: neither have they merely a homely beauty, but are often
grand, sometimes magical. Many, if not most, of the separate lines
and separate sentences are plain and, in themselves, nothing. But
they are bound together and made elements of beauty by a calm
eagerness of emotion."

In understanding Frost, Thomas better understood himself. To
extricate Thomas from the "heap of his own work in prose he was
buried alive under," Frost cajoled him into realizing that he owed
it to himself to take his chances in verse. "You are a poet, or you
are nothing," Frost would tell him; and gradually, as their friendship deepened through the year, Thomas's reluctance to express him-

self in verse was broken. "One may as well write poems," he wrote Eleanor Farjeon, who typed for him, about his "delight in the new freedom." To her sister Leona after Thomas's first long visit, Elinor Frost wrote, "Rob and I think everything of him. He is quite the most admirable and lovable man we have ever known." Frost afterward called him the only brother he ever had.

North of Boston was released by Mrs Nutt in May 1914, with its first review five guarded, anonymous sentences in *The Times Literary Supplement*. It was an improvement: *A Boy's Will* had received only two. But Frost's new connections began to pay off thereafter. Ezra Pound asked for several review copies, planning to go all out for Frost, despite the coolness between them. "Your damfool publisher," Pound wrote him, "has not sent me review copies of your new book—nor has she sent one—so far as I know—to [Ford] Hueffer." John Cournos offered to send stories about the book's expected favorable reception in London to American papers, and Frost guided his hand by telling him which poems and lines were best to quote. There were some doubts, he told Cournos, that certain tones meant to survive on paper as well as in the ear would really be effective. "They'll probably last as long as the finer meanings of words," he was sure. "And if they don't last more than a few hundred years that will be long enough for me—much longer than I can hope to be read."

Before long Frost's English friends were in print about *North of Boston*, mostly in the then traditional anonymous reviews which concealed the extent of their involvement. In the *Nation* Abercrombie compared Frost's "shy and elusive" simplicity to Theocritus, and saw a "queer, dry, yet cordial, humor" present along with the loneliness and tragedy. In the *Outlook* Ford wrote amusingly and unknowledgeably about the differences between farming in Pennsylvania and New England, describing Pennsylvania farming as primarily a matter of chasing the sheep out of the corn field before retiring to eat watermelon, while in unfertile, harsh New England the climate and soil made farmers provincial, cranky, and often a little mad. But Ford, pushed by Pound to write something which would boost Frost, was influential and at least interesting to read, and in the end advised that the poet's verse was so queer and harsh and unmusical that even people who disliked poetry would enjoy his effects. To Cournos that July, Frost would observe that he had just read Ford's article "and I like every word of it. What more could anyone ask for a while?"

Wilfrid Wilson Gibson contributed a review to *Bookman* that July, calling *North of Boston,* in "its starkness, its nakedness of all poetical fripperies," the "most challenging book of verse that has been published for some time." That month, too, perhaps under the pressure of favorable notices which had already appeared and which were known to be forthcoming (such as Thomas's in August and Harold Monro's in September), *The Times Literary Supplement* produced a second and longer review, concluding that poetry "burns up out of" Frost's verse, "—as when a faint wind breathes upon smouldering cinders." Frost was now well launched. American reviews—such as Pound's "Modern Georgics" in *Poetry* and Amy Lowell's praise in the *New Republic*—would consolidate his reputation. To Frost's discomfort, Pound would again observe that it was "a sinister thing that so American . . . a talent as that of Robert Frost should have to be exported before it can find due encouragement and recognition." And it was a welcome change, he added, to have a writer discover humor in things as they are, for "one is godforsakenly tired of the post-Bret-Hartian, post-Mark-Twainian humorist." Amy Lowell, knowing that Pound had been using Frost as his example in attacking the timidity of American publishers, would make sure to observe that *North of London* "was by an American living in England so its publication on the other side of the Atlantic came about quite naturally, and was no reflection on the perspicacity of our publishers at home."

By August 7, before either review appeared, Florence Holt, wife of the New York publisher, was writing to Frost admiringly of *North of Boston.* The Henry Holt firm, after some hard bargaining by Mrs Nutt, would be Frost's American publisher for the rest of his long life. From Beaconsfield and from Ledbury, Frost had abetted, although not orchestrated, the glowing reviews which had announced the emergence of a major poet, and in the process he made the discovery of how one could manipulate and control one's public image. The relationship with Pound had shown him, too, how vital it was to conceal from one's potential critics any information, whether false or factual, which might distort a picture of the poet which was to become as carefully composed as his best poems. Frost had not only perfected his art as a poet but learned the arts of literary politics and public relations which would make his name synonymous with poetry in America.

Earlier in the summer Abercrombie and Gibson had been involved in booming Frost beyond the critical columns. A second volume of *Georgian Poetry* was being planned by Edward Marsh, along with Abercrombie and Gibson. For the first volume they had sought two poems by Pound which he refused to release as he wanted their first book appearance to be in one of his own. Now Frost came up. Marsh was eager to include Ford's "On Heaven," which Abercrombie called "slop, but . . . certainly by far the best specimen of the slop-pail school that I have come across." But Marsh, he acknowledged, was "master of the feast," and could do as he liked. Still, he urged, "If you do put Hueffer in, I think . . . that you certainly ought to put Frost in too. . . . Frost, at his best, is far more genuinely and deeply original, much more beautiful and interesting, and however experimental, is firm, finely proportioned and intellectually constructed—the very opposite of slop." Ford solved part of the problem by refusing to be bedfellow with the Georgians, and Marsh as editor then decided that Frost was "not British and therefore ineligible." The decision saved him from being classified in a way that might have been an obstacle to acceptance in America.

For the month of August, at Frost's insistence, Edward Thomas rented a cottage "three meadows away" from Little Iddens, as he would write in his essay "This England." The children knew each other, and both families looked forward to the time when they could live as one. In London it was a hectic summer. In the rolling green countryside just east of Wales, the turmoil was hardly noticed, as Frost and Thomas bicycled and walked and talked and ignored the outside world. As they pushed their bikes up a hill side by side one day, Frost, commenting on Thomas as a critic, guessed that his friend "hadn't been proved wrong so many times in his first judgment of new poets." Thomas stopped him: "Not so very many times?" And he demanded to have any cases whatever cited where he had been wrong. Frost had only tried to draw him out, to reinforce his uncertain sense of his own worth. "Two or three times I stopped him short like that with the way I put something. He was great fun." But Thomas disapproved of Frost's laziness as an outdoorsman. The American had been a farmer, not an explorer. "He would have liked me better," Frost mused, "if I had walked further with him. He wanted me to want to walk in[to] Wales."

That midsummer, Thomas wrote, without mentioning his friend by name, he would spend most of his waking hours with Frost, while "all day the rooks in the wheatfields were cawing a deep sweet caw, in alternating choirs or all together." His routine that hot and rainless August was that

once or twice or three times a day I used to cross the meadows, the gate, and the two stiles. . . . There, at another stile, the path ceased. . . . The little house of whitened bricks and black timbers lay a few yards up the road. . . .

How easy it was to spend a morning or afternoon in walking over to this house, stopping to talk to whoever was about for a few minutes, and then strolling with my friend, nearly regardless of footpaths, in a long hoop, so as to end either at his house or my lodging. It was mostly orchard and grass, gently up and down. . . .

If talk dwindled in the traversing of a big field, the pause at gate or stile braced it again. Often we prolonged the pause, whether we actually sat or not, and we talked—of flowers, childhood, Shakespeare, women, England . . . —or we looked at a far horizon. . . .

Whatever road or lane we took, once in every quarter of a mile we came to a farmhouse . . . under the trees stood a thatched cottage, sending up a thin blue smoke against the foliage, and casting a faint light out from one square window and open door. It was cheerful and mysterious too. No man of any nation accustomed to houses but must have longed for his home at the sight, or have suffered for lacking one, or have dreamed that this was it. . . .

Alone, Frost sat under a plum tree and wrote "To Earthward," of living "on air / That crossed me from sweet things. . . ." With Thomas and a Gloucester solicitor who was an amateur botanist, John Haines, he walked into the evening to grope by the light of a

match for a rare spleenwort fern by a bridge over the Leadon, or—
as Haines remembered—"climbed May Hill with its dish-cover shape
and clump of firs on top and the widest view in the West Midlands
for all its mere thousand feet." And he remembered, too, "the
bread and cheese we used to eat in the tiny pub at its foot, the
walk in the Leadon Valley by the Ketford Mill during which
[Frost] and his children astounded me by the ease with which they
jerked stones across to the further bank, and the unusual flowers
of that valley, the Ladies Tresses, the Little Teasel, the Spreading
Campanula, loveliest of harebells, and the queer things that grew
in the salt springs that burst out of the Leadon by the Hunting
Bridge belonging aright to the sea." Comparing the wild flowers
with their equivalents in New England, Frost would be pleased when
he found a link to home. He was especially fond of a poem in which
Edward Thomas would combine his bent for fancy with his love for
flowers:

> If I should ever by chance grow rich
> I'll buy Codham, Cockridden, and Childerditch,
> Roses, Pyrgo, and Lapwater,
> And let them all to my elder daughter.
>
> The rent I shall ask of her will be only
> Each year's first violets, white and lonely,
> The first primroses and orchises—
> She must find them before I do, that is.
> But if she finds a blossom on furze,
> Without rent they shall all for ever be hers,
> Whenever I am sufficiently rich:
> Codham, Cockridden, and Childerditch
> Roses, Pyrgo, and Lapwater,—
> I shall give them all to my elder daughter.

The friends would refresh themselves at out-of-they-way inns
for bread and cheese and cider—or sometimes perry, the local Dymock drink, the fermented juice of the perry pear. And they would
argue about poetry. As Thomas later reconstructed it,

> The sun used to shine when we two walked
> Slowly together, paused and started

> Again, and sometimes mused, sometimes talked
> As either pleased, and cheerfully parted
> Each night. We never disagreed
> Which gate to rest on. . . .

Once, making their way back after a long walk into the Malvern hills, crossing fields and hedges already dripping with evening dew, and watching the mist rising around them, they found themselves in a penumbra of phosphorescence, sometimes called foxfire,

> And we stood in it softly circled round
> From all divison time or foe can bring
> In a relation of elected friends.

The experience, remembered long after, was recaptured in Frost's poem "Iris by Night."

In London there were suffragette riots and threats of strikes, and people worried over the imminence of war. Even as distant as Thomas and Frost were from London newspapers, Thomas would later write, "We turned from men or poetry / To rumours of the war remote. . . ." A month before he had left for Herefordshire there had been an assassination in a remote town in Bosnia, Sarajevo. Through July there were ultimatums issued, and across Europe troops mobilized. In London, John Cournos's nights were interrupted by a recurring dream that he was back in Philadelphia and had an excruciating need to get back to London. "Up and down Chestnut Street I ran—up and down looking for a ticket office and not being able to find one. I would waken bathed in perspiration." In the Café Royal a pretty suffragette he knew "drew a little whip from her bosom to show me. She had been using it that afternoon on a hostile crowd, forcing it to make way for women speakers. . . . There was a dynamism in the air fraught with the sense of dire things to come." He went with Pound to one of Yeats's Mondays, and remembered leaving the calm, candlelit rooms on an "omniously quiet evening" in the company of a young Georgian poet who had visited Frost at Little Iddens, Rupert Brooke. "The handsome poet scarcely said a word during the long walk; there was about him an air of troubled brooding."

Cournos saw artillery passing through Piccadilly Circus, and listened to pacifist orators in Hyde Park. At Trafalgar Square he saw "the living equestrian figure" of the onetime soldier of fortune Robert Cunninghame Graham standing on the steps of the Nelson column exhorting a silent crowd to oppose war. But after the Germans had poured into Belgium, and France had declared war, pacifism would become unpopular. By August 4 England was also officially at war. To Cournos, Frost wrote from Little Iddens that he was thinking of him "in these hot times. I don't suppose you are going to run away to America. I'm not. I am too much committed."

Up from London came Rupert Brooke, just before his enlistment, to stay with the Gibsons and to help Abercrombie wrap and mail what each thought would be the last issue of *New Numbers*. In the city Brooke had reacted to the confused but generous enthusiasm with which the English had greeted the decision to intervene on behalf of the Belgians and the French with a sonnet which began, "Now God be thanked Who has matched us with His hour. . . ." Now he and his compatriots gathered with the Frosts in the quiet of the whitewashed living room of the Old Nailshop, amid piles of freshly inked magazines. "In the lamplight," Gibson remembered in a poem,

> We talked and laughed; but, for the most part, listened
> While Robert Frost kept on and on and on,
> In his slow New England fashion, for our delight,
> Holding us with shrewd turns and racy quips,
> And the rare twinkle of his grave blue eyes.
> We sat there in the lamplight, while the day
> Died from the rose-latticed casements, and the plovers
> Called over the low meadows, till the owls
> Answered them from the elms, we sat and talked—
>
> Now, a quick flash from Abercrombie, now,
> A murmured dry half-heard aside from Thomas;
> Now, a clear laughing word from Brooke; and then
> Again Frost's rich and ripe philosophy,
> That had the body and tang of good draught cider
> And poured as clear a stream. . . .

To his American friend Sidney Cox, Frost wrote, "You must think I have . . . gone to war for the country that has made me a poet. My obligation is not quite as deep as that." He was too old, and a father of four, he pointed out; yet he knew that he "might decide that I ought to fight the Germans simply because I know I should be afraid to." Edward Thomas, a family man of thirty-six, was already talking in such terms. Besides, war was only helpful for writers of propaganda, and Frost was not that kind of poet. It was an "ill wind," he confided to Cox. "It ends for the time being the thought of publishing any more books. Our game is up."

CHAPTER X

Bedford Place
to Booking Office

. . . Go to Pound. Show him your poems.

—Conrad Aiken to T. S. Eliot in 1914

ON MARCH 10, 1914, the *Rokeby Venus* by Velázquez was assaulted in the National Gallery by an ax-wielding suffragette, Mary Richardson, as a protest against public indifference. Women had knocked in vain, she declared in court, against the doors of government. Although security was increased at each of London's major art galleries, two months later—early in May—no one paid any attention to an elderly white-haired woman who was carefully studying the Sargent portrait of Henry James in the Royal Academy spring exhibition at Burlington House. Suddenly she removed a meat cleaver from her purple cloak and swung at the canvas. Before she could be seized, James's head, mouth, and shoulder had sustained ugly gashes, and the floor was littered with broken glass.

At the police station the woman gave her name as Mary Wood. She had not heard of James or Sargent until she read about the value of the picture in her newspaper. It had nothing to do with the painter's conservative opinions nor with the novelist's professed distaste for female militancy, which James had satirized as early as 1886 in *The Bostonians*. "I have tried to destroy a valuable picture," Mrs Wood announced in police court later that day, "because I wish to show the public that they have no security for their property, nor for their art treasures, until women are given their political freedom."

Rushed to Burlington House, Sargent examined the damage and announced that he could restore the canvas; rushed to jail, Mrs Wood went on a hunger strike and after a few days was released. Hundreds of letters arrived at James's London flat, and he wrote to a sympathetic female friend that he felt personally "scalped and disfigured, but you will be glad to know that I seem to be pronounced curable." To William Dean Howells he was less diplomatic. "Those ladies really outrage humanity, and the public patience has to me a very imbecile side." But he was satisfied by Sargent's skilled restoration work. Before the end of the month the portrait was hanging again—under guard.

To most correspondents the seventy-year-old James apologized for using the "cold-blooded form" of dictation to respond, and pleaded "deep wells of unwellness." But despite such protestations he offered to come to tea at the Pennells, and to bring with him his young niece from Boston, Margaret James. It was while walking with Miss Peggy in Chelsea one afternoon that James encountered a couple whose faces were familiar; and he introduced to Peggy the newly wed Dorothy and Ezra Pound. Politely, they then exchanged some small talk. With the incident at Burlington House fresh, Pound almost certainly did not remind James of his sarcastic refusal to write for the *New Freewoman*. James, however, wanted to ask Pound a question, and motioned the two women to walk ahead of them, Dorothy Pound then hearing the question put to her husband, in the Master's deliberate phrasing, "Is she a compatriot?"

Dorothy Shakespear Pound was not a compatriot. Despite Ezra Pound's compulsion to promote American writers, most of his difficulties with people were with Americans—Fletcher, Frost, Lowell, Williams, even James—and often with writers whose work he admired. As a result he was mired in long-distance arguments with

Harriet Monroe, which he could not understand, about the poets he boomed. Having pressed a Ford poem upon her, he had to defend himself from the charge of liking only "importations." That was nonsense, he wrote back on May 23. Most of the writers whose work he urged upon *Poetry* were Americans. "Are you going to call people foreigners the minute they care enough about their art to travel in order to perfect it? Are the only American poets to be those too lazy to study or travel, or too cowardly to know what perfection means?" Pound seemed more and more to bristle with outrage, venting some of it indirectly upon Miss Monroe in letters to Amy Lowell, whom he was courting for a subsidy for the *Egoist.* If she would open her capacious purse, Pound suggested, she could run the paper—or any paper she liked—from Boston, while he and Ford "and anybody [else] you've a mind to pay for" would do the actual work in London, the work presumably being to foster the kind of poetry to which Pound thought he had converted her. Yet despite the appearance then of *Des Imagistes* in America, where it was widely reviewed, Pound had already turned the corner into Vorticism and had more revolutionary concepts to promote in Wyndham Lewis's forthcoming *Blast.*

On June 23, Miss Lowell and her maid and chauffeur—the last in his maroon livery to match her automobile—sailed from Boston en route to Liverpool and London. They were at sea when the ship's wireless picked up news of the assassination at Sarajevo. At the Berkeley in London, Amy Lowell, unperturbed, again set up headquarters and arranged for tickets to the entire repertoire of the visiting Russian Ballet, including Stravinsky's *Petroushka* and *Le Sacre du Printemps.* Then she began planning to see publishers and poets, and to host a grand *Imagiste* dinner.

In London, news vendors' placards screamed scare headlines about war preparations on the Continent, but otherwise there was business as usual. At the Poetry Bookshop Miss Lowell purchased a copy of *North of Boston,* and read it through the same evening, until, she recalled, "I was saturated with the atmosphere of the New Hampshire hills; and when I went to the window and looked out at the moon, it was not Piccadilly that I saw before my windows, but Monadnock. . . ." It was her duty, she decided, to bring Robert

Frost to the attention of American publishers. At the office of George Macmillan she bargained to have her own new book, then in press, made available in England, and came away with a distribution agreement. It had helped to have become identified as an *Imagiste* certified by Ezra Pound.

Despite forebodings from the Continent, Henry James left London for Lamb House in mid-July. His niece, and nephew Alex, were still with him; Edith Wharton had left for Paris again after a strenuous London schedule, and the West End theater had been disappointing, notably a "deplorably platitudinous" dramatization of an Arnold Bennett novel, and a "rotten" comedy by Shaw, "shallow," "vapid," "vulgar," and "senseless." His impression of *Pygmalion,* he told Hugh Walpole, was "one of the blackest." But he had been somewhat more perceptive in two articles he had been invited to do that spring for the prestigious *Times Literary Supplement* on "The Younger Generation" of English writers. Taking his assignment literally, James mentioned no American writers, but would have been hard-pressed to find many young novelists (he fixed only upon writers of fiction) he had read. His first article, in fact, was devoted to Conrad, Hewlett, Galsworthy, Wells, and Bennett, the youngest of whom was forty-seven. They did not have, he confessed, anticipating the subjects of his second article, "quite perhaps the early bloom of Mr Hugh Walpole, Mr Gilbert Cannan, Mr Compton Mackenzie and Mr D. H. Lawrence."

"Who is D. H. Lawrence? Who, you think, would interest me?" he had asked his friend Walpole; and his agent Pinker had recommended Mackenzie, who had recently published *Sinister Street*. At Lamb House, invigorated by Channel breezes, he expected to do some serious writing. There was that novel for which he had accepted the largest advance in his career.

There would be no Lamb House or Berkeley Hotel that summer for another arrival from Boston, the young Savannah-born poet Conrad Aiken. Arriving with letters of introduction to Rupert Brooke, Edward Thomas, and Ezra Pound, but with little money (it would be the story of his life), he would look for a lodging house near the Poetry Bookshop and the British Museum, and find one in down-at-the-heels Bedford Place. Not quite twenty-four,

Aiken had twice escaped Harvard to travel on the Continent and in England in search of poets and poetry, and several of his early poems had English settings, notably "Leicester Square" (later, "Parasite"), about a prostitute who falls in love with a client. Already married, and with a child, he had seized the opportunity of his wife's visit to her parents in the last months of her second pregnancy to return to London, where—by correspondence—he knew Harold Monro. Aiken was known, as well, to Ezra Pound, about whom he protested the year before to Harriet Monroe. Pound, he had complained, was using *Poetry* "egotistically," to give expression to his own personality and propagandize for his own coterie. Aiken used words like *highhanded* and *autocratic* to describe how Pound was abusing "his self-created position of authority," and noted that one would not realize, from Pound's pronouncements in Miss Monroe's magazine, that "as a matter of fact, England is teeming with poetry." She had not printed the letter.

Every month in Massachusetts had been a month away from the place where poetry was happening. On June 2, 1914, Aiken had written to a friend that since his wife and child had gone to his parents-in-law, "I think I will be happier if I waste no time in getting to London. There I shall do as much work as I can, and as much selling and self-advertising; in fact I am hoping to obtain an opportunity of reading some of my works aloud at the Poetry Bookshop . . . , as I am taking letters [with me] and already know by correspondence the Prince of the Place." With him would be copies of two poems by a Harvard friend then just off to study on the Continent. Officially, Thomas Stearns Eliot was to use his Sheldon traveling fellowship at Merton College, Oxford, to study Aristotle under Harold Joachim, a disciple of F. H. Bradley, on whom Eliot was writing a doctoral thesis, but first he intended to participate in Marburg University's summer program for foreign students. As his proxy, Aiken carried "the typescript of *Prufrock,* typed by its author with meticulous care on a Blickensderfer which produced only italics, and *La Figlia che Piange* ["Stand on the highest pavement of the stair . . ."], neither of which I was able to sell."

Introduced by Rupert Brooke at a "poetry squash" in Devonshire Street, Aiken offered Monro "The Love Song of J. Alfred

Prufrock" for *Poetry and Drama*. Monro soon returned it, saying that it was "absolutely insane, or words to that effect. . . . Later, at a party, during a discussion of symbolism with H.M. and Flint, and thinking of the pertinence of 'La Figlia,' a copy of which was in my pocket, I produced it, only to have Harold thrust it back at me, with the remark, 'O I can't be bothered with this.' He so obviously thought I was seizing the opportunity for showing something of my own that I put things right the next day by sending it to him, with Eliot's address in Germany and—of course that too was rejected." Aiken filed the poems away for a later campaign, and shifted his emphasis to his own needs, going to see Ezra Pound, who served him "tea, not so exquisitely, among his beautiful Gaudiers." The right contacts, Pound assured him, were the most crucial part of the literary game. "And for Pound it *was* a game, a super-chess game. . . . For example, this was the summer of the famous *Blast* dinner for the Vorticists. . . . Pound sent me a card, . . . naming the place and date, and saying, rather peremptorily, 'I think you had better take this in.' This put my back up. I had no intention then, or ever after, of joining any group or movement, and I therefore sidestepped the Vorticists just as I sidestepped both the Imagists and the Amygists. I didn't attend the dinner, for which in a way I'm now sorry, and Pound never forgot or forgave. Nineteen years later, in an angry letter from Italy about some review I'd written which began: 'Jesus Gawd Aiken, you poor blithering ass,' he concluded by saying: 'I've never forgotten that you wouldn't go to the *Blast* dinner.' "

Late in going on sale, *Blast* finally justified months of noisy advertising by its gaudy appearance on June 20. John Lane, its publisher, had a long memory. Any nightmares he had about the reaction to the modest sacrileges of Henry Harland's *Yellow Book* must have been magnified by what he saw in Wyndham Lewis's copy for the first issue of *Blast*. Lewis had wanted to promote his ideas for the visual arts and had the encouragement of Gaudier, but it had become apparent that more text was needed to carry the message. Even Pound's poems, Lewis felt, were not up to the "radical purism of the visual contents," but Pound "cheered things up a little by a couple of 'fresh' lines: namely 'The twitching of two abdominal muscles / Cannot be a lasting Nirvana.' John Lane . . . asked me to come and see him, and I was obliged to allow him to black out those two lines. Happily the black bars laid across them by the printer were transparent. This helped the sales."

It was essential to be belligerently offensive "against the discipline of the universe." To Lewis the body, which imprisoned the intellect, the only vigorous part of man, was itself incarcerated in the grotesque prison of the world. Self, he wrote sardonically in his unactable play *The Enemy of the Stars,* published in *Blast,* "is the one piece of property all communities have agreed it is illegal to possess. . . . Self is the ancient race. . . . Self is the race that lost." Self-consciously artistic, he sought repellent imagery, writing of rats and exposed viscera and darkness and death, and describing portentously two figures which "sat, two grubby shadows, unvaccinated as yet by the moon's lymph, sickened by the immense vague infections of night." Even more than England, America had to be regarded with distaste. It was the future gone wrong. "Geography doesn't interest me," says Hanp in Lewis's play. "America is geography."

Pound, laboring to be as extreme as Lewis, saw himself in *Blast* as a "creator agonistes," dedicated to use the artist's superior and violent intelligence to wrest beauty from a reluctant and inchoate world. The modern world, he argued, in a manifesto in *Blast,* was the result "almost entirely" of "Anglo-Saxon genius," a determination which suggested erroneously that he had little use for the Japanese and Chinese art he had acquired from Fenollosa, or the Italian and Provençal poetry which had inspired much of his best early work. Upholders of the traditional culture in a violent Pound poem, "Salutation the Third," were "fungus" and "gangrene," supported by Jewish money and hostile to "true poets." He would not go to an early death to please the "detesters of Beauty," he screamed in lines peppered with words in capitals and dripping with hate:

> HERE is the taste of my BOOT,
> CARESS it, lick off the BLACKING.

Despite all his entrepreneurship and all his apparent influence in the cause of belles lettres, Pound barely eked out a living in his little flat in Kensington. Unequal distribution of income, he concluded logically, was the cancer in the body of civilization, forcing meretricious artists to serve the mob. "This rabble, this multitude," he wrote in a piece to be printed in *Poetry* later in the year, ". . . does not create the great artist. They are aimless and drifting without him." *Blast* would arrest the drift, he and Lewis announced; but their prefascist posturings, essentially conservative rather than revolutionary, would fill only two issues of *Blast,* after which it would expire of lack of interest on the part of a world transfixed by greater violence than that of the printed word.

In the usually hospitable *New Age,* A. R. Orage found Lewis's surreal *Enemy of the Stars* to be "extraordinary," but had nothing good to say for the rest. Lewis was the only authentic Vorticist. Even Ezra Pound seemed an imitator. But Pound was too busy to confide whether he cared, writing in the *Egoist* under his pseudonym, Bastien von Helmholtz, of "that picturesque relic," the House of Lords, and reviewing the Grant Richards edition of Joyce's *Dubliners.* In the same issue of the *Egoist* Richard Aldington (who had signed the Vorticist manifesto) reviewed the first *Blast,* declaring —at least partly tongue in cheek—that Pound's contributions were unworthy of him because he was too gentle a man to pen satire. "I cannot help thinking," he concluded, probably to Pound's dismay, "that all this enormous arrogance and petulance and fierceness are a . . . wearisome pose." Aldington and H.D. were moving more toward the safer Amy Lowell. It was safe to antagonize Pound gently, and Aldington did more of it in a series of parodies he called "Penultimate Poetry." One pseudo-Poundian lyric was titled "Altruism":

> Come my song,
> Let us praise ourselves;
> I doubt if the smug will do it for us.
> The smug who possess all the rest of the universe.

The *Blast* inaugural dinner was held on July 15 at the Dieudonné Restaurant in Ryder Street, just east of St James's Street, below Piccadilly. It was a distinctly unrevolutionary setting, the occasion for self-congratulatory speeches and bold display of the 9½-by-12-

inch magazine, which resembled a pink telephone book. Only the shabby, scrubby-bearded Gaudier-Brzeska looked appropriately rebellious.

Fashionable London was curious enough about *Blast* to want to view the new oddity and its editor. According to Lewis, "the luncheon and dinner-tables of Mayfair were turned into show-booths. For a few months I was on constant exhibition. . . . Coronetted envelopes showered into my letter-box. . . . It was extremely instructive. As a result of these sociable activities I did not sell a single picture, it is superfluous to say. But it was an object-lesson in the attitude of what remained of aristocratic life in England to the arts I practised." What he saw went into his mordant novel *Tarr,* which he began writing that summer.

Two evenings after the *Blast* inaugural there was another and grander feast, with many of the same guests and in the same restaurant—Amy Lowell's *"Imagiste"* dinner. Ford, who had managed a quarrel with Miss Lowell at the earlier affair, was nevertheless back on July 17 to announce loudly that he had no idea what an *Imagiste* was and that he suspected no one else did either. "Anyhow," he recalled, "it was a disagreeable occasion—evil passions, evil people, bad, flashy cooking in an underground haunt of pre-'14 smartness," hosted by a "monstrously fat, monstrously moneyed, disagreeably intelligent" woman he did not identify directly in his 1919 *English Review* account, since Amy Lowell might have gone to the law. The band in the cave played; the obese American woman "leant monstrously sideways" while she devoured the bad food "with gluttony and nonchalance" and listened to speeches directed, Ford claimed, at her "breeches pockets." And John Gould Fletcher had his copy of *Des Imagistes* signed by each of the contributors present.

Miss Lowell had written to John Cournos that she "liked Russians," and had him to the *Imagiste* dinner. The added place created a problem. With the Aldingtons, the Pounds, Cournos, Fletcher, Flint, Gaudier, the Hueffers (which meant not only Ford, but Violet Hunt, who called herself Mrs Hueffer), Allen Upward, and Amy Lowell's companion Ada Russell, there would have been thirteen. The waiters made up a side table for Fletcher and Violet

Hunt, which warded off any catastrophe, and everyone but Ford delivered jolly speeches, including the shy Gaudier. What was at first veiled—since it was Ezra Pound who had invited Miss Lowell to the *Blast* dinner—was the widening breach between the two. As soon as she had arrived in London, she later told Harriet Monroe, Pound had asked her for five thousand dollars a year to run a magazine. "Like many people of no incomes," she explained, "Ezra does not know the difference between thousands and millions, and thinks that anyone who knows where to look for next week's dinners, is a millionaire, and therefore [he] lost his temper with me completely . . . and he accused me of being unwilling to give any money towards art."

Instead, she had suggested that the *Imagiste* anthology become an annual, on the order of *Georgian Poetry,* to "enable us, by constant iteration, to make some impression upon the reading public." The Aldingtons, and several others included in *Des Imagistes,* were already enthusiastic, she said. "Ezra was annoyed. He accused me of trying to make myself editor instead of him, and finally tried a little blackmailing." The "blackmailing" was only an impulsive gesture typical of Pound. He wanted nothing for himself but would agree to join the group only if Miss Lowell would obligate herself to give two hundred dollars a year to an indigent poet—apparently any indigent poet. She would not be "intimidated into buying anything," she insisted.

At the dinner Pound began exacting his revenge. Slipping out of his seat while Gaudier, in his broken English, argued about Greek sculpture with Aldington, he returned (according to Fletcher) "flushed and disheveled, bearing upon his head a large tin bathtub, of the old-fashioned, round-edged variety, to the amazement and consternation of all present." It had probably come from the old hotel upstairs, and whether the waiters who followed him were doing so out of curiosity or to keep track of hotel property, they clustered by the restaurant entrance to watch what Pound intended to do with the tub.

Carefully depositing it on the floor next to Miss Lowell, he "swept back the dank, disheveled locks from his forehead and addressed the gathering." Henceforth, he announced, there would be a new school of poetry, no longer *Imagiste,* but *Nageiste.* The bath-tub might be taken as its symbol. Miss Lowell had inaugurated the newest fashion with her poem "In a Garden," included in *Des Imagistes,* but which concluded with the line "Night, and the water, and you in your whiteness, bathing." Hence the appropriate-ness of the symbol.

Everyone laughed nervously, and Miss Lowell announced that Ezra had to have his little joke, and that she was personally glad to have had the interruption, since it ended the squabbling between Gaudier and Aldington, which seemed to her to have nothing to do with poetry. As hostess she thanked her guests for coming, and hoped that whether as *Imagiste* or as *Nageiste* the new movement would prosper.

Pound's practical joke, however, was only the beginning of his campaign to pry the *Imagiste* tag away from the formidable woman who had kidnapped his followers and adopted his movement. (Al-dington called the dinner a "Boston Tea Party for Ezra.") He would like to see, he explained to Miss Lowell, *Imagisme* "retain some sort of a meaning. . . . I should like it to stand for hard light, clear edges." Instead, he worried, democratization of standards would lead to "splay-footed" and "sentimental" writing. By early August he was suggesting that she identify her proposed anthology by the only bond he saw among the potential contributors, and call it *Vers Libre.* She refused. Pound then went to his friends and demanded that they choose between the two. Aldington, H.D., Fletcher, Flint, and D. H. Lawrence chose the sponsor who had the resources to finance the publication herself, if need be. Feeling betrayed, Pound contemptuously renamed the new movement *Amygisme.* To "save Ezra's feelings," Miss Lowell confided to Harriet Monroe, the new collaborators would explain in a preface that Pound had abandoned them for artistic reasons, because of a dif-ference of opinion in their interpretations of *Imagisme;* and in a grand gesture she wrote a poem about their row, "Astigmatism," dedicated "To Ezra Pound with Much Friendship and Admiration and Some Differences of Opinion." In it the Poet, who owned a fine ebony walking stick which was the sum of his aesthetic ex-perience,

> A work of art and a weapon,
> A delight and a defence,

wandered among the world's flowers, beheading daisies with his cane, then gillyflowers, dahlias, and other blooms, angry with them because they were not roses, and leaving behind him "destruction and waste places." All that remained to him were the colors which danced on his cane in the firelight.

> But these things were dead,
> Only the candle-light made them seem to move.
> "It is a pity there were no roses," said the Poet. . . .

In private she had harsher words:

Ezra has always thought of life as a grand game of bluff. He never has learned the wisdom of Lincoln's famous adage about "not being able to fool all the people all the time." Advertising is all very well, but one must have some goods to deliver, and the goods must be up to the advertising of them. Now that Ezra has ceased to be a youthful phenomenon he must take his place in the steady march by which young men of talent gain to a real reputation, and he finds himself falling back at every step, and this naturally makes him exceedingly bitter. He is very brilliant, but he does not work enough, and his work lacks the quality of soul, which, I am more and more fain to believe, no great work can ever be without. . . .

As summer waned, she continued her attempts to placate Pound, inviting him, with Dorothy, to private dinners at her hotel, and suggesting compromises, but he remained aloof from her projects. Once, when he announced that he would not go to the railroad late at night to greet his parents, who were arriving from Philadelphia to meet the daughter-in-law they had not yet seen, Miss Lowell offered to go instead in her Pierce-Arrow touring car. Pound decided to go alone.* In her large private dining room at the Berkeley, on July 30, she entertained, without Pound to oversee, Frieda and D. H. Lawrence and Richard Aldington and H.D., while Austrian waiters—already called to the colors at home—set out an elaborate table to the accompaniment of traffic noises below. Aldington opened

---

* Beaming with parental pride, Pound's Philadelphia father would tell Londoners about his erudite son, "That kid knows *everything!*"

340

a window to look out into Piccadilly and the park. At the corner of the Ritz opposite was a newsstand with a bold placard: "Germany and Russia at War, Official." As he watched, news vendors rushed by shouting hoarsely "Extra!" and "Special Edition!" A bundle was tossed to a man tending a newspaper kiosk. Aldington watched him open the poster which came with it: "British Army Mobilised."*

The next day Miss Lowell and Mrs Russell left hurriedly by automobile for Dorchester, to make good on a previously postponed invitation to tea with Thomas Hardy. An intermittent drizzle was followed by a steady downpour; yet each time the rain slackened Miss Lowell insisted on lowering the top of their Pierce-Arrow. When they arrived at Max Gate they were drenched and bedraggled, and the stuffed bird on Miss Lowell's hat had peeled completely off. The Hardys were amused and hospitable. The hours seemed too short when the ladies departed for Bath, en route to London.

Newspaper headlines in Bath made them hurry on. In London Miss Lowell immediately arranged to have her automobile crated and shipped home, to prevent it from being commandeered, and set about finding passage for herself. That night people marched down Piccadilly waving flags and shouting support for the Belgians and French, singing the *Marseillaise* and shouting, "We want war! We want war!" It sounded, she wrote Harriet Monroe, "savage, abominable." And there was no passage to be had to America. She was in a panic. Feeling trapped, she raged at a bobby on his beat and at the crowds massed in the streets, indignant that the police had done nothing to help her make her way to her hotel. "Don't they know I'm Amy Lowell?" she screamed, and when back inside the safety of the Berkeley she lit one of her long cigars and paced up and down her suite. "And it was this month that my book of poems was coming out here!" she claimed erroneously to herself and Ada Russell. "What attention will it get with this going on? What has happened to England? Why don't they stop the war?" She was a Lowell of Boston, but that fact was of no use in London,

---

* War headlines undoubtedly were being utilized to hawk newspapers, but Aldington's reconstruction of the event was more dramatic than accurate. Russia had indeed mobilized on July 30, which inevitably led the next day to Austrian and German mobilization. War followed a day later, on August 1.

except to Ford, who had adopted the name for the timid antihero of his ironic and subtle new novel, who would be a Lowell—of Philadelphia.*

Also on August 3, Conrad Aiken, diverted from literary talk and from "the tedious necessities of sex" by the imminence of war (he found fidelity to an absent spouse unimportant), watched the crowd of Germans milling about their embassy trying to find a way home, and was smuggled into Parliament by a friend (who was Keir Hardie's secretary) to listen to the debate on the declaration of war, "the inconclusive fragments of excited talk." Afterward he went to Gray's Inn, where Rupert Brooke lived, to exorcise what he had heard by playing a Bach Brandenburg Concerto. German music would soon be suspect in England.

But the sound of that excitement from the city, the feeling of that mounting tremor, was disturbingly perceptible even there, high up among the plane trees: and . . . by the next day there could no longer be the shadow of a doubt of it. The whole city had been seized by a kind of madness, a crowd frenzy, in its way comparable, but with a different intent, to that, so many years after, of the time of jubilee. The crowds coalesced, amalgamated, like an animal force forming itself instinctively out of its constituent cells, in a passionate need for union and direction: and once thus united, poured themselves, now to the Mall, to sweep up to Buckingham Palace, where the prolonged cheers brought out the little figures on the high stone balcony, and again to Whitehall and down to Downing Street, and, without knowing it, past the spot where their dead, their own countless dead, and themselves among them, were to be commemorated. The crowds dissipated, broke up in fatigue, fell away in remnants, shredded out into side streets, only then to rejoin, reform, renew their vitality out of new elements, new recruits: cars were commandeered: taxis were swarmed upon, the roofs climbed: flags waved: all day and late into the evening that human sea grew wilder, beat higher against the city's walls, as if in a kind of terrible joy, a dance of death. [Aiken] had himself many times gone back to the house in Bedford Place to rest, only then to find that the excitement made it impossible to stay in, he must go and see it again, join it again, it was irresistible.

* In its first part, serialized in *Blast* (1914), *The Saddest Story*—to be *The Good Soldier* in book publication in 1915—the narrator on his first appearance is a Lowell, whether by design or printer's error. He becomes a Dowell in the text of the book.

On a holiday from the termagant of an older woman John Gould Fletcher was then living with, and whom he would disastrously but loyally marry after her divorce,* Fletcher rushed back from Italy just as frontiers were closing. The exhausting trip to the Channel coast, by frequently halting trains, would take a week.

John Cournos walked by Parliament, where there had been people standing for two days in nearly dead silence, to see happy hysteria replace the long waiting. On he walked, down the Mall.

"Shall we eat German sassingers?" shouted a cockney in front of Buckingham Palace.

"No-o-h. . . ." came the drawn-out reply from the mob.

"What shall we do to those Germans?"

"We'll cut their gizzards out!"

"Gizzards? We'll cut their _____ out!" A guffaw.

"Where's Kaiser Bill goin' to 'ave 'is Christmas dinner?"

"In the Tower! We'll stuff his turkey for him, we will!"

"Hear! Hear!"

Sporadically, here and there, the crowd broke into song:

> *"Rule, Britannia! Britannia rules the waves!*
> *Britons never, never, never shall be slaves!"*

Passing a barracks, I saw men in the yard embracing one another and dancing in twos and threes—madly and wildly.

Down Whitehall a crowd pursued Winston Churchill's open carriage, lustily cheering. An open taxi passed by with a girl standing on the seat, a union jack in her hand, which she waved energetically. Indifferent to modesty, she stood with leg lifted, foot on the hood, and shouted at the men who ran in the taxi's wake:

"On to Berlin, boys! On to Berlin!"

Thus it went on through the night while the newspaper boys ran in the streets. . . .

Through the darkness—midnight, August 4, had made the war official—the rumble of men and vehicles and military bands even

---

* Beginning in April 1914, Fletcher had begun to lead a double life, moving into Mrs Daisy Arbuthnot's house in suburban Sydenham when her complaisant husband moved out. Only an hour by train from his literary friends in London who knew little or nothing about his domestic life, he maintained his literary contacts and wrote verse with great energy, adding love poems to his lengthy "symphonies" and "London excursions." The idyll would not last, but he would be trapped in the relationship for two disastrous decades.

flooded Bloomsbury, "floating intermittently over the dusty lilacs in Russell Square and up against the Byzantine minarets of the Hotel Imperial," where only a few weeks before Conrad Aiken had lunched with Ezra Pound and a writer for a newly founded New York magazine, the *New Republic*—another young man from Harvard, Walter Lippmann. Pound seemed to know everyone, and literary-minded Americans had learned to look him up. But he had not yet met Aiken's Harvard friend Eliot, nor even seen his poetry.

In the summer of 1913, Pound had heard from Aiken that (as Pound would put it in an interview later) "there was a guy at Harvard doing funny stuff." Yet Aiken was clearly trying English contacts before offering Eliot into the hands of the resident American midwife of letters. At the time of his lunch with Pound and Lippmann, Aiken had not known that Marburg University was already so much in tumult over the assassination in Sarajevo and so filled with expectations of war that Eliot was trying to leave. Finally, via Rotterdam, he managed to get to London in the third week of August. Eliot had left Marburg even before the suitcase which Aiken had forwarded to him had arrived in Germany. The disruption of civilization which had cast him so abruptly adrift would leave its mark upon him all his creative life.

There was time before Eliot had to take up residence in the backwater of Oxford. Term at Merton College began in October. He chose to stay in crowded London; yet England, to a cosmopolitan young man who had already lived in France and in Germany, was clearly impossible, he complained to Aiken. "A people which is satisfied with such disgusting food *is not* civilized." For three years he had written almost no poetry, concentrating upon his doctoral work in philosophy, but from his bed-and-breakfast lodgings at 28 Bedford Place, near the British Museum and Russell Square, where the war did not seem to touch him at all, he made notes which became future poems. To his brother, Henry Ware Eliot, he wrote on September 8 of the life which animated Bloomsbury, of an old woman who had sung "The Rosary" for pennies, and a young house-maid chatting at the gate. In "Morning at the Window" he tried to recover the atmosphere of "rattling breakfast plates in basement kitchens," and of maids arriving down the "trampled edges of the street" and pausing "despondently" at each gate:

> The brown waves of fog toss up to me
> Twisted faces from the bottom of the street,
> And tear from a passer-by with muddy skirts
> An aimless smile that hovers in the air
> And vanishes along the level of the roofs.

According to his London notes as described by Lyndall Gordon, "He saw determined matrons in tailormade suits and ugly hats advance on Assyrian art in the British Museum and then fade beyond the Roman statuary. He saw a vulgar shopgirl in a department store, and her false teeth and the pencil stuck in her hair spoke to him of heated nights in second storey dance halls." The Bloomsbury area, which already encompassed the genteel, the shabby-genteel, and the decayed, would permanently enter the geography of his verse.

The world of the music halls would also invigorate his poetry, and it is apparent from it as well as from his published recollections that Eliot quickly began to frequent West End variety theaters —the Tivoli, the Oxford, the Holborn Empire, the Alhambra, the Coliseum, the Victoria Palace, the Palladium, the Pavilion, the Middlesex, all only a short walk from Bedford Place. His memoir of Marie Lloyd, written nine years later, just after *The Waste Land* was published, recalls her and Nellie Wallace and "Little Tich" with the vivid familiarity of the veteran observer. To appreciate the pathos and the comedy of Marie Lloyd's last great music-hall song, "One of the Ruins That Cromwell Knocked Abaht a Bit," Eliot explained, "one ought to know objects a middle-aged woman of the char woman class would carry in her bag; exactly how she would go through her bag in search of something; and exactly the tone of voice in which she would enumerate the objects she found in it. This was only part of the acting. . . ." It was the act she made famous in mid-1914, on her return from a tour of America, just as Eliot was settling briefly into London; and one can also hear anticipations of Eliot in such of her hits of the nineties as "Oh! Mr Porter."

The dominant middle classes, Eliot would declare in 1923, possessed no distinctive art form for the stage, and therefore no Marie Lloyd to express it. "The middle classes, in England as elsewhere, under democracy, are normally dependent upon the aristocracy, and the aristocracy are subordinate to the middle class, which is gradually absorbing and destroying them. The lower class still exists; but perhaps it will not exist for long. In the music-hall comedians they find the expression and dignity of their own lives; and this is not found in the most elaborate and expensive revue."

Eliot had also been prepared by his reading for the London that would emerge in his verse. Even Marie Lloyd—the saucy younger comedienne of 1894—had appeared on the stage of the Oxford in a Walter Sickert watercolor in the first number of Harland's *Yellow Book;* and Arthur Symons of the *Savoy,* in his own affectionate lyrics of the nineties, had been the bard of the London music hall as well as the bearer of Parisian Symbolism. "Our sympathies, I think," Eliot wrote in his last years, "went out to those who are known as the English poets of the nineties, who were all, with one exception, dead. . . . And Yeats himself had not found his personal speech; he was a late developer. . . . What the [other] poets of the nineties had bequeathed to us besides the tone of a few poems by Ernest Dowson, John Davidson, and Arthur Symons was the assurance that there was something to be learned from the French poets of the Symbolist Movement—and most of them were dead, too."

The W. E. Henley of the "In Hospital" and "London" sequences, whom Eliot failed to mention, was no less important to him than the John Davidson of "Thirty Bob a Week," who had appeared in Harland's *Yellow Book*. Henley's "In Hospital" literally described the patient anesthetized on the operating table, the street organ, the magic lantern, the sprinkled pavements and April in the city, all echoed in "Prufrock" and "Portrait of a Lady." In a preface to a selection of poems by John Davidson, Eliot would acknowledge his indebtedness to the author of *Fleet Street Eclogues, The Thames Embankment,* and *In the Isle of Dogs,* and in a broadcast in his later years he noted the "terrific impact" made upon him and its "very important place in the development of my own poetic technique." The very people and places of Eliot's poems through *The Waste Land,* as well as their atmosphere, seem foreshadowed in Davidson, in Dowson, in Symons and others of the *Yellow Book* years.

Although Eliot had expected to find Aiken at Bedford Place, his Cambridge crony was gone, and in the first frenzy of wartime no one was particularly interested in an outsider. As quickly as Aiken could book passage after Parliament had made the war official, he had left his lodging house to rejoin his family. But he had also left a laconic parting injunction to Eliot: "You go to Pound. Show him your poems." Eliot hesitated; he poked about London, read quietly, and kept to himself. Aiken had first shown him Pound's poetry in *Harvard Advocate* days, he remembered. "He showed me those little things of Elkin Mathews, *Exultations* and *Personae*. He said, 'This is up your street; you ought to like this.' Well, I didn't really. It seemed to me rather fancy old-fashioned romantic stuff. . . . I wasn't very impressed by it . . . though I now [he said in an interview when he was in his seventies] regard the work I saw then as very accomplished. . . ." He held back.

While many Americans crowded the steamship booking offices, the literary Yankees for the most part stayed. John Jay Chapman had actually arrived the day before the war began. From the Artillery Mansions Hotel, Boston critic Chapman wrote a letter to *The Times* which was published on August 5 as "An Appeal to Americans":

Sir—The Americans who have come from Germany during the past few days are the only people in England who have already experienced the awe-striking brutality of actual war. . . .

On reaching England we saw the smiling fields, men and women playing tennis—welcome everywhere, affection, comfort, the inexpressible relief of personal safety—the kind world again. Yet we were haunted by a terrible sentiment—namely, that England did not understand the depth of the Continental disturbance, or the size and nature of the convulsion. In any case England is wisely holding back and husbanding her power—it is all going to be needed. France now holds the fort of modern civilization; but the whole power of England is needed to buttress her.

As for America, our history and our policy force us to stand outside the conflict; though every American who understands the conditions will feel the appeal so strongly as to make him almost desire to enlist under the British Flag. That we cannot do. But one thing we can do—namely, we can use our personal power to explain this war to Americans at home,

to the millions of our fellow-citizens far away, who may think that this
is an ordinary European war with which we have little to do—a European
diplomatic imbroglio which will settle itself. The understanding sympathy of one hundred million Americans is no small power in European
affairs. It is for us through our influence at home to educate America. . . .

The day after it appeared he wrote home, "I have telegrams and
letters of congratulations on my *Times* letter—one from Henry
James, quite to my surprise as to his fiery approval." Two days later
he saw his son Victor off at Charing Cross station, en route to
France to enlist as a volunteer in the French Army. "I really envied
him a good deal," he noted.

Henry James's "fiery" reaction would have come as no surprise
to Chapman had he understood the depth of the Master's com-
mitment to England. When his faithful manservant Burgess Noakes
delayed his enlistment, "for fear of too much incommoding" James,
the Master gave signs, he told Edith Wharton, that he "had been
much expecting and even hoping for it," and afterward he wrote
solicitously to Private Noakes as if he were a son. (Mrs Wharton
sent him Frederick, one of her own servants, to help out temporarily.) To Howard Sturgis he wrote belligerently of the need to
defeat the "infamous autocrats." Edith Wharton, having come over
from Paris with Walter Berry—who used his influence to have her
car shipped from France for her convenience—and borrowed a house
at 25 Grosvenor Place, recalled James's cry as he emerged from
brooding in his cab, "My hands, I must wash them! My hands are
dripping with blood. All the way from Chelsea to Grosvenor Place
I have been bayoneting, my dear Edith, and hurling bombs and
ravishing and raping. It is my day-dream to squat down with King
George of England, with the President of the French Republic and
the Czar of Russia, on the Emperor William's belly, until we squeeze
out of it the last irrevocable drops of bitter retribution."

Looking in at Qu'Acre, Mrs Wharton found Howard Sturgis "in
an intensely nervous state" and unwilling to permit the war to be
mentioned in his presence. George Santayana, however, visiting his
distant cousin on August 5, before Mrs Wharton had arrived, wrote

to his sister, "Howard and his household are as usual. He is less overcome by the war—of which he of course 'disapproves' sadly—than I had expected: in fact everyone everywhere seems to take all this prodigious outbreak very seriously and calmly, with a reasonable sense of how human and how inevitable unreason is." He would remain in Oxford, he wrote, and added philosophical reflections which he would have been unwise to expose outside a private letter leaving England:

My sympathies are naturally with France and England, and with the blameless unfortunate Belgians; yet I feel no anger against the Germans. They are carrying out a brave and heroic determination to be the masters of Europe and to rule by force of arms, industry and character. It is not very different from the principle that has animated strong aggressive nations in all ages: only it is more deliberate and conscious—a little rude and conceited as well. Perhaps the sense of power and of "duty" has turned their heads a little, and they may be rushing to their destruction —or rather to their discomfiture, because no great nationality can be destroyed until it dissolves inwardly. It is hard to say whether what is guiding them is infatuation or consciousness of their destiny. If they win, with all Europe against them, it will be because they deserved to win, being morally the stronger.

Despite Santayana, few Americans in England had that long view, and some, unlike the squire of Qu'Acre, were becoming involved. Even the dead were being put to use, as Bret Harte's "Reveille," written for the Civil War, was still found fresh enough to be reprinted in massive quantities as a broadside to aid British recruiting. "Hark! I hear the tramp of thousands," it began; and it concluded with "the great heart of the nation, throbbing," answering with religious awe, "Lord, we come!" Bret Harte was at last respectable.*

From Rye, James penned impassioned letters in support of the English cause, and took what comfort he could in the company of Peggy and Alex James, with whom he would walk across meadows

---

* Later, Harte's "What the Bullet Sang" (familiar from the *Oxford Book of English Verse*) would perhaps suggest such battlefield verse as Siegfried Sassoon's "The Kiss" and Wilfred Owen's "Arms and the Boy," which, like the Civil War poem, would make much of the quasi-erotic desire of the weapon for the body of the adolescent target.

soon to be within faint hearing of German big guns. It was "inconceivable," he wrote to novelist Rhoda Broughton on August 10, "that just across the Channel, blue as *paint* today, the fields of France and Belgium, are being, or about to be, given up to unthinkable massacre and misery." To Jocelyn Persse the next day he congratulated himself that he had caught Alex "by the coat-tail" just as he was shipping over to Germany on August 1. Now he was trying to arrange passage for both young people "on some safe and convenient basis" in the other direction. "But oh! the appalling blackness of it all, and the horror of having lived to see it!"

Among the American expatriates fleeing what he called "the crumbling of worlds" was a little old man, frail, bearded, with heavy eyebrows, James's friend over two generations, the historian of medieval culture, Henry Adams. The author of *Mont St. Michel and Chartres* had reached England on August 26, where Bernard (*Bernhard* was no longer a popular spelling) Berenson, who had preceded him from France, told him, "I trust that you are satisfied at last that all your pessimistic hopes have been fulfilled." Adams found a country refuge at Stepleton, near Blandford in Dorsetshire, the home of the daughter of his closest friend, Mrs Cameron, where James came to visit him. They talked late into the night, James attempting to induce the ailing old Boston patriarch to share his indignation. Wanton German destruction of some of the glories of Western civilization had only reinforced Adams's cynicism, and James urged in vain, especially when he spoke of England's sacred mission to repel the new barbarians. Like Santayana, Adams had a longer view.

At Lamb House "that gorgeous tawny September," Edmund Gosse wrote vividly of his host's state of mind. James could hear the distant thunder of German artillery across the water,

while the advance of the enemy through those beautiful lands which he knew and loved so well filled him with anguish. He used to sally forth and stand on the bastions of his little town, gazing over the dim marsh that became sand-dunes, and then sea, and then a mirage of the white cliffs of French Flanders that were actually visible when the atmosphere grew transparent. The anguish of his execration became almost the howl of some animal, of a lion of the forest with the arrow in his flank, when the Germans wrecked Rheims Cathedral. He gazed and gazed over the sea southeast and fancied that he saw the flicker of the flames. He ate and drank, he talked and walked and thought, he slept and waked and lived and breathed only the War. His friends grew anxious, the tension was beyond what his natural powers, transfigured as they were, could be expected to endure, and he was persuaded to come back to Chelsea. . . .

Among those in the stream of supplicants to the American Embassy was Amy Lowell. While she sought first-class passage home, many of the others, having fled the Continent with most of their possessions left behind, needed money as well as any kind of passage. "Finally," Miss Lowell wrote Harriet Monroe, "some public spirited American gentleman started a Committee, with offices at the Hotel Savoy, to help stranded Americans. . . . The Committee cashes cheques, gets steamship bookings, suggests hotels and lodgings, provides clothes, meets trains. I cannot write the half it does, but it makes one exceedingly proud. I do not believe that there is an American in London who has not helped the Committee with time and money, or been helped by it." The American gentleman was Herbert Hoover, who organized the effort with five or six business and banking colleagues, their own funds, and the assistance of the American Society in London. With cursing men and weeping women besieging the embassy and the consul general's office, in various stages of need, and more Americans being disgorged by each boat train which arrived in London, every volunteer was useful.

Since she had time on her hands while waiting for her own passage, and publishers were interested in little else but war-related writing, Miss Lowell joined the American Citizens' Relief Committee and cabled to Boston for ten thousand dollars to be put at its disposal. And at Victoria Station, wearing a large placard on her ample bosom announcing "American Citizens Apply Here," she offered assistance to bewildered new arrivals seeking a way out of the war. "Amy was extremely sensitive about her abnormal size," Richard Aldington wrote, "and it must have been agony to display herself in this way. But she had pluck, and went through with it to the end." She even wrote a war poem, "The Allies," on August 14, worked on organizing her *Imagiste* anthology, and on August 27 traveled to rural Chesham, where the D. H. Lawrences lived (warily, for Frieda was a von Richtofen), to confirm the inclusion of seven of his poems.

She dated a "Letter from London," intended for the October *Little Review,* August 28, describing how her London world had changed in less than a month, and appealing for American sympathy. "Neutral we must be," she wrote. But "England is still the mother-country of most Americans. . . . And we love her."

By early September she was at sea. On September 22 her second volume of poetry, *Sword Blades and Poppy Seed,* appeared on schedule in America. The title itself seemed a miracle of foreshadowing, although it had nothing to do with the outbreak of war in the poppy fields of Flanders, and it became a tremendous popular and critical success. And whether her Anglo-American poetic circle were *Imagistes* or only *Amygistes,* her association with Pound and his band had sharpened her technique, encouraged her to use English settings, strengthened her literary connections, and made her a leading figure in American poetry. "Of the poets who to-day are doing the interesting and original work," the publisher's blurb for her *Sword Blades and Poppy Seed* announced, "there is no more striking and unique figure than Amy Lowell." If it referred to her person, Macmillan's claim was accurate; however, it went on, "the foremost member of the 'Imagists'—a group of poets that includes William Butler Yeats, Ezra Pound, Ford Madox Hueffer—she has won wide recognition for her writing in new and free forms of poetical expression."

Pound was outraged. Not only was Yeats unreasonably dragged in, but Pound's own "school" had been mocked. He accused her publishers of "arrant charlatanism" and threatened to sue Miss Lowell for libel. Quickly she disavowed the blurb, but admonished him, "You have only to thank yourself for including me in this group, and it is not agreeable to feel that you only wished the inclusion as long as I could be kept obscure and insignificant." Pound knew he was defeated. A libel action would only give her more publicity, and while she could afford the litigation, he was strapped. Her rise would also weaken Pound further as literary impresario at the very time his own writing was going badly, giving impetus to new grievances, real and imagined, which would further sour his own writing. The "Advertising Manager for a movement," would be T. S. Eliot's description of her "sometimes misguided activity."

By mid-September Eliot had finally given in to Aiken's urging and—like Robert Frost before him—had wandered into Kensington to look for Ezra Pound's address. Aiken had not taken kindly to Pound, but he had tried his other connections without success, baffled not only by the failure of "Prufrock" to interest anyone, but that Eliot himself was "heartlessly indifferent to its fate." Still, Eliot turned up one day at Pound's flat at Holland Place Chambers, a tall, primly dressed, unassuming man of twenty-six, his hair carefully parted in the middle and slicked down. And he came without his poems, perhaps concerned whether Pound could be entrusted with them. Dorothy Pound served tea, the three talked amiably, and on September 22 Ezra Pound wrote to Harriet Monroe that an American by the name of Eliot had called and seemed to have "some sense."

"Send me your poems," Pound had said on ushering Eliot out of the little triangular sitting room. Only then did Eliot agree to relinquish "Prufrock," mailing it to Pound with "Portrait of a Lady." Pound was elated by what he read, Eliot recalling a note from Kensington crowing. "This is as good as anything I've seen. Come around and have a talk about them." They talked, and Eliot then took back his typescripts to make a few small changes for the press, with the understanding that his new friend would arrange for publication. Nothing could be more certain, Pound thought as he announced his new "find" to Harriet Monroe on September 30:

I was jolly well right about Eliot. He has sent in the best poem I have yet had or seen from an American. PRAY GOD IT BE NOT A SINGLE AND UNIQUE SUCCESS. He has taken it back to get it ready for the press and you shall have it in a few days.

He is the only American I know of who has made what I can call adequate preparation for writing. He has actually trained himself *and* modernized himself *on his own*. The rest of the *promising young* have done one or the other but never both (most of the swine have done neither). It is such a comfort to meet a man and not have to tell him to wash his face, wipe his feet, and remember the date (1914) on the calendar.

A few days later Pound again had the two poems, and decided to offer one to Chicago and the other to New York. To Miss Monroe he characterized "Prufrock" as "the most interesting contribution I've had from an American," and postscripted his desire that she would "get it *in* soon." (He sensed that he would have to struggle to get the poem in at all, and did indeed have to press her for months.) To H. L. Mencken on October 3 he forwarded "Portrait of a Lady," and recalling his losing battle with *Smart Set* over Frost, he added, after praising Eliot's intelligence, "I think him worth watching—mind 'not primitive.' "

While war raged across the Channel, Pound was fighting his never-ending battle against the philistines on a variety of fronts, Eliot representing only one major skirmish. In the December *Poetry* would appear his review of Frost's *North of Boston,* which he praised as having succeeded in turning natural American speech into "a contribution to American literature." From Fenollosa's notebooks of Chinese songs and lyrics Pound was adapting a book of eloquently spare poetry to be published by Elkin Mathews as *Cathay.* And he was working with Lewis on a second number of *Blast,* since none of his energies had been redirected by war. As Lewis put it, in talking about how Pound subjected Eliot's writing to a "stiffening," there was nothing Pound did "that did not have a bearing upon the business of writing. . . . He breathed Letters, ate Letters, dreamt Letters." Seeing troops marching off for shipment to France was "a fine sight," but he was uninvolved and even quoted approvingly Yeats's friend Charles Ricketts, who had said, "What depresses me most is the horrible fact that they can't *all* of them be beaten." Jacob Epstein was similarly unmoved by the war. In August he had confided to art patron John Quinn in New York, "My business as I see it is to get on with my work. . . . Everybody here is war-mad. But my life has always been war, and it is more difficult for me here to stick to the job, than go out and fight or at least get blind, patriotically drunk."

By the end of August, Belgium was nearly completely swallowed up, and as an example to towns which did not surrender supinely, the Germans burned medieval Louvain, with its magnificent and irreplaceable library. The French had already suffered hundreds of thousands of casualties, and the British tens of thousands. A million

German soldiers had poured into France, threatening Paris itself until the week-long Battle of the Marne ended on September 12. The Germans would pull back to the Aisne to begin what would be years of wholesale bloodletting in which a few trenches would be exchanged. In Paris, six hundred taxicabs had been commandeered to race troops to the Marne, but London had only become more clogged by traffic and more used to the sight of soldiers and the still-empty threat of Zeppelin raids.

For writers and artists there was a new propaganda office in London which provided a market for their products, but most Americans had not been drawn in. Back in Paris, at her home in the Rue de Varenne, Edith Wharton would write, in November, "*My* sense is completely of living again in the year 1000, with the last trump imminent," and Henry James, returned from Rye, echoed the sentiment. But few Americans took the beginning of the war as emotionally as James. Others did not see it as their war, and for some it was only an outrageous inconvenience.

John Sargent, painting in the Austrian Tyrol, continued undisturbed. He was an American, and an artist. Before long he received word that a friend, an English major, was being held as a prisoner of war, and he intervened—as someone the Kaiser had honored—to procure the major's parole. Then he heard that his niece's husband had been killed in battle. The war was reaching him. He applied in mid-November to the American Embassy in Vienna for an emergency passport and returned to London via Switzerland, working on his Boston Library murals seemingly undisturbed by what he had seen in beleaguered France en route to Le Havre. In London he and James called on an elegant lady whose portrait he had once painted, and although she and her husband were reputed to have pacifist leanings, James launched into an anti-German diatribe which the lady fielded with tact. When the two friends left, a distinct coolness was obvious between them, James impatient with Sargent's lack of enthusiasm, Sargent angry at James's refusal to remain an American neutral.

Ezra Pound, more interested in waging his own campaigns, was busy trying to make a place for T. S. Eliot in the London artistic milieu, still little changed by war, and though at first diffident, Eliot made the most of his new connections and Pound's compulsion to remake writers into his image of what they should be. "He would cajole, and almost coerce, other men into writing well," Eliot thought on looking back, "so that he often presents the appearance of a man trying to convey to a very deaf person the fact that the house is on fire." A master of creative introductions, Pound arranged for Eliot to meet the people who might be useful to him, and Eliot, who was handsome, sophisticated, and gracious, and spoke the native language more elegantly than most Englishmen, was the ideal person for whom to exercise one's patronage. Thus Pound risked nothing in arranging to have Eliot visit Arnold Dolmetsch, whose children danced for him while the American sat rapt; and Wyndham Lewis remembered his first meeting with Eliot, in Pound's flat, as a confrontation with Prufrock himself,

but a Prufrock to whom the mermaids would decidedly have sung, one would have said, at the tops of their voices—a Prufrock who had no need to "wear the bottom of his trousers rolled" just yet; a Prufrock who would "dare" all right "to eat a peach"—provided he were quite sure that he possessed the correct European table-technique for that ticklish operation. For this was a very attractive young Prufrock indeed, with an alert and dancing eye. . . .

The interest I took in any of Ezra's friends was very small, and I did not know what to say to an American. To a *real* American, not an acclimatized Buffalo Bill like Pound. Also I entertained a most healthy suspicion of all Pound's enthusiasms—was I not one of them myself?— and it did not greatly flatter me. So upon encountering another I experienced a certain surly embarrassment. And when later Pound showed me a quantity of poems in typescript by this fellow-countryman of his, most of which he said were bad, but some of which, he assured me, were good, I gazed at them with an unaffected absence of interest. *Prufrock* was among them I remember. This considerably tickled the very conventional malice of Ezra, and caused him to cough about the room in an ecstasy of quietist satisfaction, with a sinological noiselessness of inarticulate mirth, as if chasing a phantom guffaw. . . .

Although Pound indulged the petty malice of Lewis, whose support he needed at the time, he was staunch in pressing Eliot's cause, refusing Harriet Monroe's suggestion that he ask Eliot to "write down to any audience whatsoever," and adding that he was now convinced that his instincts had been sound when he threatened to resign from *Poetry* the year before. Her objection had been that the ending of "Prufrock" was weak, and to John Gould Fletcher she wrote that the poem was faulted by an excess of social polish, and by the atmosphere of Henry James. Pound insisted that it would be false art to make "a portrait of failure" conclude "on a note of triumph." It would take nearly a year to win his point and get the poem about the diffident, absurdly overcivilized Prufrock, who did not have the will "to force the moment to its crisis," published. Yet Miss Monroe had identified the tradition in which Eliot was working, without even knowing that the other Eliot poem which Pound had received, and had sent to her New York rival, the *Smart Set,* had been the Jamesian-titled "Portrait of a Lady."*

Less a public admirer of Henry James than Pound, who would claim to have read, in 1917 alone, all of James's published works, Eliot appears nevertheless to have been suffused with the Master's prose. His poem of the early years in England, "Burbank with a Baedeker: Bleistein with a Cigar," even uses as epigraph (without attribution) lines about Venice from *The Aspern Papers,* and "Prufrock" itself echoed James in its verbal mannerisms. There was the 1909 story, "Crapy Cornelia," in which a middle-aged man muses of the "charm of procrastination," watches himself, and wonders, "Shall I now or shan't I? Will I now or won't I?" and after a long interior monologue confesses his understanding to Cornelia in Prufrockian terms, "You needn't deny it. That's my taste. I'm old." And there was *The Ambassadors,* not only filled with decorous understatements, but with the line "Prufrock" appears to echo, from Mme de Vionnet's parting with Lambert Strether, ". . . we might, you and I, have been friends." At one time Eliot even thought of titling the second section of *The Waste Land* "In the Cage," after James's telegraph girl who can only live vicariously through the messages which cross her counter, like Eliot's Tiresias, borrowed from myth, who

---

* Mencken turned it down, but Pound then offered it to Alfred Kreymborg, who published it in his magazine *Others* in September 1915. Pound also arranged for "The Preludes" and "Rhapsody on a Windy Night," also, like "Prufrock," products of 1910–11, to be published in the second *Blast* in 1915, and for three new poems, written in England, to appear in *Poetry* in October 1915.

knows all but can prevent nothing. Even as late as the rose garden of "Burnt Norton," says an Eliot critic, "it is a quintessentially Jamesian experience which lies at the heart of his work. The tragedy is that of one who can perceive but cannot act, who can understand and remember but cannot communicate." The consolation, as in *The Waste Land,* would lie in memory and in the artistic synthesis of memory and experience—the "fragments I have shored against my ruins."

Eliot would never meet James—Pound did not have that kind of access to the Master—but Eliot already had the vision of personal isolation that is the expatriate's gift and curse, and which James had captured in prose. A Bostonian by heredity, although born in a South-dominated—but French-accented—St Louis and then trans-planted again to New England, he had long known expatriatedom in his own country. "Some day," he would write to Herbert Read in 1928, "I want to write an essay about the point of view of an Ameri-can who wasn't an American, because he was born in the South and went to school in New England as a small boy with a nigger drawl, but who wasn't a southerner in the South because his people were northerners in a border state and looked down on all southerners and Virginians, and who therefore felt himself to be more a French-man than an American and more an Englishman than a Frenchman and yet felt that the U.S.A. up to a hundred years ago was a family extension. It is almost too difficult even for H.[enry] J.[ames] who for that matter wasn't an American at all, in that sense." Later Eliot told Stephen Spender that "James wasn't an American" because, al-though he had an acute sense of the America of his own time, he had "no American Sense of the Past." The real America, Eliot sug-gested sadly, "came to an end when Andrew Jackson was elected president." What Eliot had escaped when he crossed the Atlantic—so he thought later—had been only a vulgarization of the American tradition he preferred to venerate.

In October, while Eliot took the train to Oxford, Pound was al-ready beginning arrangements for the curiously titled *Catholic An-thology*—a reference to the variety of poetry it included, from Irish to *Imagiste.* The principal reason for its existing at all, Pound would later remark, was "to get 16 pages of Eliot printed." In at least one

way Eliot was unprepared for his new academic habitation. Donald
Hall, arriving in England for postgraduate study in 1961, and visiting his famous fellow alumnus in London, was about to take his
leave when he noticed that Eliot appeared to be searching for the
right remark with which to send him off. "Let me see," said Eliot,
beginning a slow, meandering reminiscence, "forty years ago I went
from Harvard to Oxford. What advice can I give you?" He paused,
Hall remembered, "while I waited with greed for the words which
I would repeat for the rest of my life, the advice from elder to
younger, setting me on the road to emulation." Eliot relished a long
pause, then asked, "Have you any long underwear?"

At Oxford, which war was emptying of healthy Englishmen, Eliot
would manage a foreshortened intellectual life, and while the autumn weather was fine, he would go in for rowing, leaving Pound to
press his literary causes. With the regular eights suspended, Eliot
had more opportunity, and future Yale philosopher Brand Blanshard
remembered "a humble race of fours in which his boat won by a tremendous margin; the memory is well burnt in because I was in the
boat that was so soundly trounced."

One class in which he sat was J. A. Stewart's, on Plotinus, the
original membership of which was six, but enlistments and boredom
with Stewart's stuffy manner quickly cut the enrollment to two, Eliot
and future Classics don and civil servant Eric Dodds. Inevitably they
came to know each other better, and one day Eliot "confessed shyly
that he had written some poems himself. I told him that a little
group of us—the Coterie—were accustomed to meet of an evening
for the purpose of reading our poems to each other and having them
torn to pieces critically. Would he care to read us something of his?
He agreed, and a few days later 'The Love Song of J. Alfred Prufrock,' an unpublished work by T. S. Eliot, was read by its author
for the first time to an English audience. We did not tear it to
pieces. We were startled and, yet, a little puzzled, but less puzzled
than excited." An audience was already in preparation for a sympathetic understanding of Eliot's kind of poetry.

The war was reaching England in other ways than casualty lists,
travel restrictions and the emptying of the universities. There were

rumors of Russian troops landing by the thousands in England en route to reinforce the front in Flanders, and in Scotland German agents were reported erroneously to have blown up bridges across the Tweed and the Tyne. To the west, where the Frosts had vacated Little Iddens to move in with the Abercrombies, Mrs Badney, who lived across from the Gallows, knocked at their door one night with the misinformation that the Germans had landed in Portsmouth, and, Frost recalled, "Ledbury was up-side down." But Frost had at last achieved one of his ambitions in settling in England. At the rambling old Gallows he was living under a thatched roof, and even wrote a poem about marital discord which he set realistically in the cottage with its "wind-torn thatch." There, too, he wrote one of his most memorable poems, "The Road Not Taken," which at readings in later years he would introduce as "more about Edward Thomas than about me."

Through the autumn the Frosts lived casually with the Abercrombies. As long as the weather was good they would cook and eat outdoors, where Catherine Abercrombie "sometimes . . . would have an iron pot over a fire with a duck and green peas stewing in it." "Lascelles, John Drinkwater, and Wilfrid Gibson would sit around and read their latest poems to each other," she later wrote, "as I lay on a stoop of hay and listened and watched the stars wander through the elms. . . ." The life appealed less to the Frosts than they would admit. Elinor "kept her precious coffee pot going all day on the stove," American-style, and was always nervously refilling her cup. The Frost children had no playmates (the Abercrombie boys were only three and four) because they could not get along with the local children, and would not return to school with them. Lesley and Carol talked incessantly of their homesickness and their eagerness to return to America, a feeling which Elinor shared but kept to herself. And Robert had a row with Lord Beauchamp's gamekeeper, who not only protected game from poachers but patrolled the preserve, shotgun in hand, to prevent children from picking berries and mushrooms. Feeling an outsider among the already "arrived" writers, Frost quietly resented, too, the close camaraderie of the Georgian poets who clustered about Abercrombie. Gibson, a daily caller, was the worst offender, and his teasing, meant in good fun, was becoming unbearable for Frost. Was Frost's difficulty in finding an audience at home, Gibson once asked, due to the high level of illiteracy in the United States? The atmosphere, although remote from the war, was ridden with other kinds of tensions, relieved for Frost only during the two visits Edward Thomas made before he enlisted, when they warmly renewed their intimacy of the summer months, and confided to each other problems about their professional and marital lives for which each needed a sounding board.

Professionally, Frost's position improved even as he remained reclusive in Gloucestershire, for Mrs Nutt in London had responded to Henry Holt's interest in publishing *North of Boston* in New York by insisting that he could not have the new book without also taking at least a small printing of *A Boy's Will*. "We consider," she lectured Holt, "that under present political circumstances American publishers ought to show some willingness to help English publishers who have had sufficient daring and intelligence to recognize the talent of one of their countrymen. . . ." Holt succumbed.

To keep in touch with the outside world, including Mrs Nutt, Frost made several trips to London. He could not wind up his affairs at a distance, and realized, as he put it bluntly to Sidney Cox, that the war had ended his "little literary game" in England. If he remained another year, while his family grew unhappier, he would be spending money for nothing. "I shall just have to try to get home and live to write another day. I have two fervent hopes. One is that the Germans may not sow the Western Ocean with mines before I cross with the family and the other is that I may find something to do . . . when I get across."

In London there were uniformed men everywhere, even in the Poetry Bookshop, where Frost talked with a very young officer who identified himself as an aspiring poet—Robert Graves. Perhaps in order not to seem unpatriotic, Frost said he was debating with himself whether he should join the army. Actually, he was in London to inquire about passage and—despite Mrs Nutt's injunctions—to try to sell poems to magazines, as the move back across the Atlantic would take much of his remaining money, and he needed funds to live on when he returned. To Harold Monro he sold four new poems for *Poetry and Drama*—"The Sound of Trees" (which referred to

Abercrombie's elms, the "Seven Sisters"), "Putting in the Seed," "The Smile," and "The Cow in Apple Time." England had been good for his writing and he had a stock of new verse to take home.

He evaded Ezra Pound. To Mosher he insisted nonetheless, "Pound is the most generous of mortals," but to Sidney Cox he explained that he was unwilling to be added permanently to Pound's "party of American literary refugees in London. . . . Another such review as the one in *Poetry* and I shan't be admitted at Ellis Island." England had done all it could for Frost, and he had concluded that he could do little for England by remaining. His duty was to further his own work. He explained his feelings in several farewell notes. To Frank Flint, from whom he had been estranged over the *Imagisme* row, he wrote that he understood the long silence but at the least had to "say goodbye to the man who opened England to me." To Harold Monro he wrote that he did not want too much fuss made about his departure or he would feel "as if I were never coming back. I shall be back as soon as I have earned a little more living. England has become half my native land—England the victorious. Good friends I have had here and hope to keep."

Delays in departure were inevitable under wartime conditions, but the Frosts, with fifteen-year-old Mervyn Thomas, sailed from Liverpool on the night of February 13, 1915, on the *St Paul,* as part of a convoy which included the huge *Lusitania.* British destroyers combed the waters with searchlights, looking for mines and submarines until they were well out to sea. Frost was returning to America without a home or a job awaiting him, and he worried besides that he would be considered a coward for leaving England in wartime, and disloyal to America for having published his first books across the Atlantic. Going home could be a mixed blessing for a London Yankee.

The Pin Wheel

It is splendid of you . . . to make this sacrifice for us. You give us the most intimate thing you possess.

—Edmund Gosse to Henry James in 1915

A STRANGER to fame when he sailed in 1912, Robert Frost was as well known as any poet in America when he returned early in 1915. The next year, when *Mountain Interval,* his third book of poems— many of them written in England—appeared, the unknown farmer of 1912 was elected to the National Institute of Arts and Letters. His book would not be offered to Mrs Nutt, who had continued to withhold royalties, for Henry Holt's lawyer had been put to work to rescue Frost's future books from "the fool's contract" he had signed in London. Soon the question would be moot, for the Nutt firm would go into postwar bankruptcy. The fool's contract in any case had established Frost as a poet. His writing income would be vastly supplemented by the public lectures and readings in which he established a persona as Yankee poet sometimes at odds with the private man. And he soon bought another farm in New Hampshire.

From England and later from France, Edward Thomas enclosed in his letters to Frost poems written, while in uniform, as "Edward Eastaway." Having learned from Pound the value of influence, Frost placed several in Harriet Monroe's *Poetry.* Early in 1917, when Thomas's still-pseudonymous work was about to appear in book form, and Frost was arranging for an American edition, Thomas went off to the front with Frost's *Mountain Interval* in his pocket. At Vimy Ridge he was killed. "First soldier, and then poet, and then both," Frost wrote in "To E.T.," bereaved as if of a brother. Only in death would Thomas achieve poetic recognition in his own name.

It was ten years after the war before Frost could face England and its old associations, and he and John Haines "once again . . . climbed May Hill and gazed round that astounding ring of country from Brecon Beacons to Shropshire. . . ." But, Haines recalled, "the wraith of that dead friend was ever before us, 'and the tender grace of a day that is dead' could never come back to us."

"It is perhaps idle to ask," Stephen Spender has written, "whether if Frost had remained in England and if Thomas had not been killed, English poetry might have had a different development. For Frost did bring to England that which the Georgians needed: great critical awareness of the relations between the experience that went into the poem and the technique—the realization through form of things intensely observed." In 1942, in the midst of a second world war, Frost would caution his daughter Lesley, "You mustn't be too hard on the British in their day of adversity. . . . It ill becomes a Frost not to sympathise with a nation that has done so much for our family. Possibly you calculate it has not been all good—good only for me and not for the rest of the family. I have no answer for that. Anyway I am on their side."

He found it difficult to understand Pound, who in his disillusionment had gradually moved to the other side. Still, Frost told Lesley, who was to give a talk on new developments in poetry, "Ezra Pound was the Prime Mover . . . and must always have the credit for what's in it. He was just branching off from the regular poets when we arrived in England."

One branching-off that did Pound little good was his collaboration with Wyndham Lewis on the second and final number of *Blast,* for which, early in 1915, he was prying material from T. S. Eliot. Fortunately for Eliot, the first material he had submitted, which might have been appropriate for *Blast* but which would have aborted his career at the outset, was not used. "Eliot has sent me Bullshit and the Ballad of Big Louise," Lewis wrote Pound. "They are excellent bits of scholarly ribaldry. I am trying to print them in *Blast* but stick to my naive determination to have no 'words ending in——Uck, ——Unt, and ——Ugger.' " The obscene verses may have been part of the saga about King Bolo which Eliot had begun at Harvard and which Aiken had enjoyed, and which Pound referred to years later as writing "which I am afraid his religion won't now let him print." When the second *Blast* appeared in July 1915 it was with "Preludes" and "Rhapsody on a Windy Night," which became Eliot's first published appearance in England.

Lewis remembered confiding his American origin to Pound at about that time. "Oh if the *deah* British public only knew that *three* Americans were responsible for all this disturbance . . . ," Pound laughed—referring to Eliot as well as Lewis and himself. But *Blast* in 1915 had lost the exuberance, if not the bad taste, of 1914. War had shattered the world which had provoked the artistic rebels, and had even begun taking its toll of the rebels themselves. In the second *Blast,* along with a manifesto on art by the gifted Gaudier-Brzeska, was the announcement of his death in action at Neuville-St Vaast. He was twenty-four.

Soon Lewis, too, was in uniform and off to France. Pound would comment, in April 1915, as Hulme and Brooke and others were counted among the dead, that the war was causing a shortage of good poetry. But the problem for Pound was more than a shortage of poets. The literary alliances and friendships upon which he had built his influence had been weakened not only by war service on the part of his allies but by his own fractiousnesss. The *Imagiste* schism and the unanticipated defection of Frost were only symptomatic of his problems. Despite his new friendship with Eliot, his championing of Joyce, and his continuing relationship with Yeats, he was becoming more isolated, and his own creative work was suffering as well. His feud with Aldington, for example, blocked his access to the *Egoist* until Aldington, too, went off to war. Having provided the weapons to writers he had boomed, he confessed to Harriet Monroe about the schismatics, "I certainly should not complain if they use . . . their editorial jobs etc., to attack me. I have only myself to thank for it." Illustrating the paradox, a poem he wrote for the July 1915 *Blast* began,

I cling to the spar,
Washed with the cold salt ice. . . .

"Cowardly editors," he added, ". . . will have my guts. . . ." But even more bitterly,

Friends fall off at the pinch, the loveliest die.
That is the path of life, this is my forest.

The trouble had begun early, but Pound had refused to take the first symptoms seriously. As early as October 1914, publishers' doors were beginning to close, *Quarterly Review* editor G. W. Prothero writing to him, "I am afraid that I must say frankly that I do not think I can open the columns of the Q.R.—at any rate, at present—to any one associated publicly with such a publication as *Blast*. It stamps a man too disadvantageously." Unlike Eliot, who had the good fortune to send the poems which Pound wanted for the second *Blast* at just the time that Lewis was having qualms about the limits to bad taste, Pound continued to rebel openly. Meanwhile, Eliot's substitute material in *Blast* boosted his stock. Richard Aldington later observed that Pound had begun his career "in a time of peace and prosperity with everything in his favour, and muffed his chances of becoming literary dictator of London—to which he undoubtedly aspired—by his own conceit, folly and bad manners." Eliot, he thought, had started in just the reverse of Pound's situation, arriving in London in the enormous confusion of war, "handicapped in every way. Yet by merit, tact, prudence and pertinacity he succeeded in doing what no other American has ever done—imposing his personality, taste, and even many of his opinions on literary England."

Pound's income from October 1914 to October 1915 was a meager £42 10s. Increasingly, he did not fit in. Eliot did. The Yankee Puritan disappeared almost imperceptibly as he discovered that he was really English in behavior, taste, humor, judgment, and vigilant reserve. With Pound's help, Eliot published in the little magazines and reviews, and Pound later edited *The Waste Land* (1922), the most remarkable poem of the century, into shape, but it was the English Eliot who had begun appearing anonymously in *The Times Literary Supplement*.

Poetry could not support Eliot after his fellowship had ended,

and wartime shipping problems had caused him to give up his attempt to return to the United States to take his doctoral examinations. Schoolmastering had been a stopgap, but his clerkship at
Lloyd's Bank was developing into a responsible position when
America entered the war, and he tried, as an American citizen, to enlist from England. The navy refused him as a seaman in its intelligence branch. Army bureaucracy would delay his attempts to enlist,
or to obtain a commission, until the war was over. It was "a crime
against literature," Pound wrote at the time to John Quinn about
Eliot's wasting "eight hours' vitality per diem in that bank." Yet
Eliot was inching ahead, for his *Prufrock and Other Observations,*
thin in size, had a large vogue in 1917.* For Eliot, Pound would
prove a shrewdly tough creative editor. Unfortunately, while Eliot
had a Pound, his friend Pound needed a Pound, too, and had none.
He had leaped into modernism from the unlikely springboard of
nineties aestheticism and Provençal romance, had codified Imagism
and translated Wyndham Lewis's Vorticist images into verbal equivalents. "It is better to present one Image in a lifetime than to produce
voluminous works," he had declared (in *Poetry*) in 1913, but his
wartime writing sprawled despite his new aesthetic of a complex of
"pattern-units." As Eliot would marvel in reviewing Pound's beginnings of his *Cantos*† in 1918, "In appearance, it is a rag-bag of Mr.
Pound's reading in various languages. . . . And yet the thing has,
after one has read it once or twice, a positive coherence. . . ." But
frustrated with an England he found "mouldy" and "dead as mut-
ton," Pound would soon leave, although not for America. In his
famous phrase in *Hugh Selwyn Mauberley* (1919), the war had been
fought for a "botched civilization."

Feeble and ailing but as mentally alert as ever, Henry Adams,
back from London, had complained about his expatriate friends to
his old confidante, Daisy (Mrs Winthrop) Chanler. "I think the reason why I make a moral problem [of], and cast moral aspersions on
H. James, Mrs. Wharton, and the [other] dwellers abroad," he
wrote, "is a certain jealousy of our loss of talent. We are so impov-

---

* Only in 1920 did Eliot's work appear in book form in the United States as
Poems.
† "Three Cantos," in *Lustra.*

erished that we need every intelligence at home . . . instead of being wasted abroad. . . ." It was October 19, 1915, and by then he had cause for special concern about James.

Henry James had plunged passionately into the war effort in whatever ways he could. He spent hours comforting hospitalized soldiers, especially Frenchmen who were not only in strange surroundings but made lonely by difficulties with language. To some he brought gifts; ambulatory patients might be taken to his flat in Chelsea for a meal or to tea with friends. A typical notebook entry was, "Took three maimed and half-blind convalescent soldiers from St. Bart's [Hospital] to tea [at] 24 Bedford Square. . . ." It was the address of G. W. Prothero, who had shut Pound out of the *Quarterly Review*. James's portly presence could be observed at benefits for Belgian refugees and fund-raising efforts for the American Volunteer Motor Ambulance Corps, for which he became chairman. And for *The Book of the Homeless,* put together by Edith Wharton to raise money for refugees, he contributed an essay on his visits to the bedsides of the wounded, "The Long Wards."

Without funds himself, James could only applaud the gifts of others to the war effort. Sargent, scrupulously neutral, would assist only the Red Cross, and offered to do a portrait for a ten-thousand-pound contribution. It was a steep price, but Sargent had not done a major portrait in years, and Sir Hugh Lane agreed to meet it. "What a luxury," James wrote to Dr White in Philadelphia, "to be able to resolve one's genius into so splendid a donation! It isn't known yet who is to be the paintee, but that's a comparably insignificant detail." The war completely absorbed James; his "creative" writing languished. But Pearsall Smith, who had become a naturalized British subject, teased James that it was not really *his* war, but it was now "my war." From time to time he would telephone James and ask such questions as, "When are you coming into the war? How long are you going to sit with the Romanians on a back seat in the Balkans?" Late in the spring of 1915, James discovered the cost of his American citizenship. When he began planning to return to Lamb House, he learned that he would need permission from the police. The Rye area, so close to the Channel, was a zone forbidden to aliens.

He telephoned Pearsall Smith. "Logan, how—you know what I mean—how do you do it?"

"You go to a solicitor," said Logan. And James did, the same afternoon, finding out from Nelson Ward that he would need to apply to the Home Office and produce four householders to vouch for his character and for his proficiency in speaking and writing English. To prepare his family in America, James wrote to his nephew Harry, "I have spent here all the best years of my life— they practically have been my life. . . ." And he added that after nearly forty years of residence in England, and in his precarious state of health—he was a "cracked vessel" who had to carry nitroglycerine pills for his attacks of angina—he saw no chance of ever returning to the United States "or taking up any relation with it as a country." His oldest literary friend, Edmund Gosse, agreed to be a sponsor. "It is splendid of you," he wrote on June 25, "and beautifully like yourself, to make this sacrifice for us. You give us the most intimate thing you possess."

James responded that his decision had brought him "a deep and abiding peace." (Emotionally, the act had all the characteristics of a religious conversion.) For a second sponsor he went to the top. Through Margot Asquith, the Prime Minister's wife, he had begun to visit the Asquith country home, Walmer Castle, and as he wrote her, to be taken by the hand into "the inner circle of political life." Now he asked the Prime Minister to help him "to testify at this crisis to the force of my attachment and devotion to England, and to the cause for which she is fighting. . . ." He could only do so, he wrote, "by laying at her feet my explicit, my material and spiritual allegiance, and throwing into the scale of her fortune my all but imponderable moral weight." George Prothero and J. B. Pinker became the third and fourth sponsors, and Asquith instructed Home Secretary Sir John Simon to facilitate the process. On the afternoon of July 28, James took the oath of allegiance to George V. He was now able to say, he wrote Gosse, *"Civis Britannicus sum!"* He did not feel different, he added. "The process has only shown me what I virtually *was.* . . ."

He had not expected the negative reaction he received from America. His act had been widely taken as one of disloyalty. Even so, he was beyond caring. Yet his new status did not bring him any closer to Lamb House, for the worsening of his heart condition precluded travel. Instead, he remained in Chelsea, writing, despite illness, a preface to a posthumous edition of Rupert Brooke's *Letters from America.* Of the poems which Brooke had written before dying aboard a hospital ship in the futile Gallipoli campaign, James exclaimed to Edward Marsh, one of Brooke's closest friends, "Splendid Rupert—to be the soldier that could beget them on the Muse! and lucky Muse, not less, who could have an affair with a soldier and yet feel herself not guilty of the least deviation." There would rise about Brooke, James prophesied, "a wondrous romantic, heroic legend." Then he turned to the long abandoned novel fragment, *The Sense of the Past,* adding to it intermittently. Finally, in mid-October, he returned to Rye, with his cook, his maid, and Burgess Noakes, now released from the service on medical grounds. It was not a holiday visit, nor was it a sentimental journey. For several days he went through his papers, burning letters, manuscripts, and photographs, in the process suffering acute cardiac distress. He had to go back to London for medical attention, but the task at Rye was done.

The prospect of his own death was now increasingly real. He returned to Nelson Ward to add a codicil to his will, noting his British naturalization, formally bequeathing his portrait by Sargent to the National Portrait Gallery, and directing that should he die in England—then a certainty—his remains were to be cremated and "my ashes afterward laid near those of my parents, my elder brother and my Sister, in the Cemetery of Cambridge, Massachusetts." Since his sister had died in London in 1892, his ashes would not be the first to return.

During one of his walks with his Chelsea neighbor Pearsall Smith, excursions which became more and more abbreviated, Pearsall Smith asked James if he knew George Santayana. The philosopher had been a friend of William's, said the Master, but not one of his own. Living in Cambridge since the war had begun, Santayana had not been able to concentrate upon his magnum opus, *Realms of Being,* contenting himself with shorter essays and poems. (It would not be until 1940 that he would complete the massive four-volume work.) But since Santayana's visits to London were rare, Pearsall

Smith asked James to lunch with them at St Leonard's Terrace the next day.

James traveled the relatively short distance up Cheyne Walk and the Royal Hospital Road by taxi. With Pearsall Smith were his two sisters, wives of Bernard Berenson and Bertrand Russell, and since all four expatriates were American-born, the talk concerned James's new citizenship. Pearsall Smith expressed his contentment at being domiciled during all his adult life with so admirable a people as the English. "Yes," Santayana agreed, "in my opinion the most superior white race, since the Greeks, which has peopled this planet." But there was one drawback, James countered portentously. English people were tongue-tied. For good talk one had to live in Paris. He elaborated further on the theme, then asked his host to ring for a cab.

On December 2, 1915, James suffered a stroke, and the next day a second stroke. His sister-in-law Alice, cabled for, came from America to find him feeble but apparently recovering. In mid-December he weakened, and his mind began to wander. He began to think that he was back in his beloved Lamb House, and dictated strange, disordered imaginings, dredged from subconscious memory, to Miss Bosanquet. While he lingered, Edward Marsh, who had been Winston Churchill's secretary and was now in the Prime Minister's office, read James's preface to the Rupert Brooke volume. Now, hoping that the gesture would not come too late, Marsh asked Asquith whether the Order of Merit might be available for James. It was an honor in the gift of the sovereign, limited in number and reserved largely for intellectuals who might have spurned a knighthood, and the Prime Minister, realizing James's condition, needed no further prompting. Two days later a message conferring the O.M. was sent from Buckingham Palace to Carlyle Mansions. Lord Bryce, a former ambassador to Washington, brought the insignia of the order to James's bedside. The invalid seemed pleased, but his mind drowsily wandered and he was physically helpless with left-side paralysis. For the most part serene in his mental confusion, he lingered on.

In James's last days, his great friend Elizabeth Robins, despite the threat of German submarines, sailed for America. With her was an article she had written which she hoped to publish in a New York newspaper, stressing passionately that England's cause was that of all liberty-loving neutrals, and claiming that its unpreparedness for war in 1914 was proof enough of England's love of, and desire for, peace. "The outside world," Miss Robins declared, "very imperfectly understands her resources, her strength of resistance, above all, her power of enduring. There is no price her destiny can demand of her which she will not pay for free institutions." We misjudge England's strength of purpose, she explained, because our own standards of behavior are different. "Just as over-statement is the tendency, if not the habit, of most people, so [the tendency] of the English is understatement."

In London, Wilson's confidant, Colonel House, had approved of her message. "Would you godfather it?" she had asked him. He promised to see "that it came under the favourable notice of the editor of the *New York Times.*"

If her message to the American people were printed, she vowed, James would see a copy. Aboard with her was James's nephew, Harry, who had been at the bedside in London. They stood together on deck as the *New Amsterdam* steamed into New York harbor. "We looked out over Staten Island, known to Henry James in his youth, and the first of all my remembered playgrounds. Now, the great ship drew into the slip; the gangway went down and several among the waiting crowd pressed on board. Two or three men appeared and drew my companion aside. He came back to me presently. 'They have sent to tell me, uncle Henry is dead.' "

Late in February he had fallen into a coma. A week later, on the evening of February 28, 1916, his brother William's widow at his side, he had died. Elizabeth Robins's appeal for England would appear as a long letter to the editor in the *New York Times* on March 11.

James's funeral was held in Chelsea Old Church, where obsequies had also been held for Whistler. To evade wartime regulations, Alice James smuggled James's ashes past the customs authorities. Later, when his will was probated, there was some surprise that his English estate, including the Lamb House property, was valued at less than nine thousand pounds. The Master had not made a fortune in his adopted country.

By the time that James had gone through with his grand gesture and become a British subject, his oldest American confrere in England, John Sargent, had finally emerged from his artist's ivory tower. Too many young men, scions of families to whom he had long been close, had fallen. More would die, and each new loss would cut through the blur of the long newspaper casualty lists. Among them would be Edwin Austen Abbey II, the nephew and surrogate son of his onetime Tite Street colleague. Young Abbey, educated at his uncle's expense at the best American schools, would die fighting with the British forces as a volunteer. Another casualty would be John Jay Chapman's son Victor, a member of the Franco-American Aviation Corps, who was shot down near Verdun.

Even Ethel Sands, although a neutral American, would abandon her easel to set up, with Nan Hudson, a small hospital in France to treat the wounded evacuated from the front. With no sense of disorientation she would spend January to October each year of the war dressing the stumps of amputees, returning to The Vale for the autumn months to enjoy what remained of the arty set, her Chelsea neighbor Pearsall Smith keeping her in touch with London gossip by letter in the interim. But another American artist, one who had already taken British citizenship, would never get to the war zone. Squat and lumpy in his uniform, Corporal Epstein, Ethel wrote Nan from London in October 1917, was not very handsome in khaki. He had kept out of uniform until he was drafted, his final three months' exemption to complete work in hand becoming the subject of protests in the press, mostly, Epstein claimed, from "bad painters and bad sculptors." Released on medical grounds after a few months, he continued with his experiments in bringing a sense of the primitive to modern art. He was not even wanted as a "war artist."

A generation older, John Sargent had found Post-Impressionist art "hideous" from its first emergence in England. To see "war artists" go off to propagate more of it in the name of patriotism disturbed him, but all that he felt he could do, as a citizen of a nation which in the first years of the war still had diplomatic relations with Germany, was to return his German honors. He asked the American ambassador to London to arrange matters. Walter Hines Page cabled the secretary of state for instructions, and the scrupulousness of American official neutrality can be measured by Robert Lansing's terse response:

Washington, June 23, 1915

Not matters with which the Department or its officers abroad can have any connection.

Sargent should reimburse Embassy for your telegram and pay this reply, five dollars.

Lansing

A month later, as news broke of James's becoming a British subject, Sargent wrote to him with understanding and sympathy, deploring the reaction in America. Many Americans would be shocked by his "step," James responded. He had waited for his government to show some sign of moderating its blandishments of Germany—"the very smallest would have sufficed me"—but the posture of correct neutrality became "at least to me a thing no longer to be borne." With his month-old cable from Washington in hand, Sargent understood.

One large assignment still awaited completion. Sir Hugh Lane had been on the last voyage of the *Lusitania*. His estate, tangled in litigation, included the still-to-be-painted Sargent portrait. James's "insignificant detail" had become the legacy of the National Library of Ireland, which decided, once America entered the war, that it wanted a Sargent canvas of President Woodrow Wilson. The artist had no desire to set up a studio again in the White House, which held unhappy memories of his painting Theodore Roosevelt. Besides, the severe, humorless Wilson was not his ideal of a subject. Nevertheless, with his valet, Nicola, Sargent returned, and Wilson sat, "reposeful" and generally alone. The horde of onlookers of Teddy Roosevelt's days at least had been a diversion, while Sargent, left to match words with Wilson, fell into silence, as did the President. Yet the sittings continued—even after Wilson went back to his desk, for Nicola would slip into the coat Wilson would leave behind for work on the drapery. "It takes a man a long time to look like his portrait, as Whistler used to say," Sargent wrote guardedly to Mrs Gardner in Boston. But the President, and the picture, bored him. Sargent knew he had been wise to retire from portrait painting years before.

The result was not a success. In Boston he had more satisfaction in seeing the ceiling of his hall in the library unveiled, and in going back to studies for the museum dome.

Although in 1916 Sargent had collaborated with the American artist Abbott Thayer on camouflage proposals they brought to the War Office in London, it was not until 1918, when America was already a combatant, that he accepted Prime Minister Lloyd George's offer of an appointment as a war artist, and went to the front. At a grizzled, nicotine-yellowed sixty-two he had no idea how he would adjust to conditions, or how his talents as portraitist and muralist could be utilized. Painting wars was not his forte. Burly, bearded, and balding, he looked in khaki as if he were on the wrong front or perhaps in the wrong war, but he accompanied a division up to the line, and drew what he saw of the wrecked city of Arras, including the ruined cathedral, then little more than bleached white columns that had once supported the main vault now towering over the rubble. He covered notebook pages with scenes of uniformed men at their tasks, and did watercolor sketches meant as studies for larger works; and his *Gassed* was memorable.

After the war Sargent would be asked to become president of the Royal Academy, an office which would bring with it a baronetcy or a knighthood. He had rejected honors which might have cost him his citizenship before, and he did so again, content to live out his last years as an American.* Commending Sargent's intellectual qualities, civic virtues, and social position when the geographical label was more prophecy than reality, James had once described his friend to Jacques-Émile Blanche as "Dear John, an admirable Bostonian." London now became less his home than ever before, as he spent more time in Boston attempting to complete his beloved murals. It was almost as if he had become an expatriate in America.

Expatriatedom in America became the literal situation of other London Yankees in wartime. Frank Harris, in financial straits after the failure of one publishing venture after another (he even went to jail briefly after a libel suit against his *Modern Society*), and in difficulties over his pro-Germanism, a heritage of his student days magnified by his increasing hostility to anything English, fled to New York. There, mixing brazen self-assurance with pitiful requests to such tolerant friends as Bernard Shaw for help, he survived the war. Shaw charitably produced a preface to Harris's *Oscar Wilde,*

---

* Jacob Epstein, long a British subject but never an Establishment figure, would not receive his knighthood until 1954.

which helped sell the book. After Harris lost his job as advertising manager for the Chesapeake and Ohio Railroad in 1916, he acquired *Pearson's Magazine*. There he rebelled against puritanism (many issues were seized), published his imaginative "Contemporary Portraits," and by begging letters and barely legal schemes managed to keep the magazine going for six stormy years. Then he went to France to live out his remaining years writing his much-suppressed and unreliable multivolume *My Life and Loves*.

Elizabeth and Joseph Pennell did not leave until after the United States had entered the war. As Elizabeth put it, explaining their departure after thirty-three years in London, "Zeppelins had destroyed many things in London, no one could tell how much more they might destroy. Why not save the Whistleriana, our greatest treasure, by presenting instead of bequeathing it to [the Library of Congress in] Washington?"

Pennell was a Philadelphia Quaker who never went to Meeting and considered his obligation fulfilled when he sent his yearly contribution to the Germantown Friends, but in the early, emotional days of the war his Quaker pacifism welled up and he was outspoken enough that long-time cronies began avoiding him. At most he was willing to assist as an artist by drawing English shipyards and factories, a collection for which H. G. Wells wrote a preface; the authorities wanted him also to go to the front. "He had no desire to draw the horrors of war," Elizabeth wrote; "they had nothing to do with art. Again, his nights were sleepless, his days torture. The doctor said, 'Get him away' and advised me to let him go without me. . . . He prepared for America. . . ." But he did first go to France, although it proved too full of memories of the past—of etching with Whistler and sketching with Beardsley. When he finally sailed, to do *Joseph Pennell's Pictures of War Work in America* (1918), it was to stay.

Of Henry James's American friends in England, one of the few who survived him was Howard Sturgis, who had left Qu'Acre to do war work in London. Since he was expert in German he was assigned the reading, censoring, and readdressing of German war prisoner correspondence. It was, Santayana wrote, "a marked sacrifice of his comfort and leisure," but that life had become unbearable as the war dragged on. In London, Sturgis would discover that he was suffering from intestinal cancer, and two operations were only an ugly reprieve. As his cousin put it, "It was not difficult to surrender the world." He died at sixty-four, in 1920.

An epilogue to the epilogue remains. Midwife to modern literature, Eliot's *"il miglior fabbro,"* Ezra Pound had left London in 1920, blaming the mental constriction he felt in England. By 1924 he had settled in Rapallo, where he began dating his letters to American friends according to the calendar of the fascist revolution. Postwar Europe seemed to him a chaos that belied faith in democracy, technology, and conventional morality. His solution to the prevailing disintegration combined anti-Semitism and attacks on interest rates—crotchets of his which even preceded *Blast*—and adulation of Benito Mussolini's orderly society. Pound was allergic, William Carlos Williams, M.D., thought, to the "democratic virus."

Pound's poetry, the continuing *Cantos,* became an amalgam of his memories, his erudition, and his cranky philosophies. Few were willing to listen to him when he made a return voyage to America in 1939, on the eve of another war; many thought it charitable to judge him insane. He returned to Italy.

When war came, Pound fulminated over the Italian radio, which introduced him cautiously by declaring that he would not be asked "to say anything whatsoever that goes against his conscience, or anything incompatible with his duties as a citizen of the U.S.A." At the microphone Pound attacked "international usury" and told Americans that Mussolini and Hitler were "your leaders." Monitoring the enemy radio, American intelligence compiled transcripts of his broadcasts, and when he was picked up after the collapse of Italy, he was placed in a prison camp near Pisa. Later he was flown to Washington to stand trial for treason, a charge put in abeyance when a panel of psychiatrists declared him paranoid and mentally unfit for trial.

While controversy swirled about him, Pound remained at St Elizabeth's Hospital in Washington, where he ignored the psychiatrists and continued to write and to publish, seemingly unchanged. Writers who kept their poetry and their politics in separate compartments urged his release, not only because of his already historic place in twentieth-century literature. Since he was declared incurable, they contended, he could never be tried, and his continued confinement became in effect the life imprisonment of a person who was presumed innocent under the law, and therefore cruel and inhuman punishment. But it was difficult, even for poets, to disentangle the cantankerous man from the major writer.

In 1958 treason charges in Federal District Court were dismissed on psychiatric grounds. At seventy-two, Pound returned to Italy. Behind the battle to free him had been poet Archibald MacLeish, a certified liberal, but MacLeish had strategically enlisted Robert Frost to call upon the attorney general and to prepare a statement which Pound's attorney read in court. He spoke especially for his friends MacLeish, Hemingway, and Eliot, Frost had declared. "None of us can bear the disgrace of our letting Ezra Pound come to his end where he is. It would leave too woeful a story in American literature. He went very wrongheaded in his egotism, but he insists that it was from patriotism—love of America. . . . I hate such nonsense and can only listen to it as an evidence of mental disorder. . . . But I think [the solution] should have to be reached more by magnanimity than by logic and it is chiefly on magnanimity I am counting."

It was ironic that two of the surviving Americans of the London years (one of them now "T. S. Elyfunt" to Pound) should have been behind the efforts to assist another. "You and I," Frost had written to Eliot the year before, "shot off at different tangents from almost the same pin wheel. We had America in common and we had Ezra in common though you had much more of him than I. If I was ever cross with you it was for leaving America behind too far and Ezra not far enough."* In Ezra Pound paths had again crossed. When, in Italy, Pound died at eighty-seven (in 1972), stubbornly cranky to the end, he was almost the last veteran of the "pin wheel" that to Frost had been prewar London.

There was still one survivor. Conrad Aiken, who had fought at great financial risk after 1945 to keep Pound in his poetry anthologies, and who in 1914 had brought Pound and Eliot together, had returned to England after the war to live and write in Henry James's

---

* Eliot had renounced his American citizenship and become a British subject in 1928, the same year that he was baptized into the Anglican Church. The officiating priest, the Reverend W. T. Stead, chaplain of Worcester College, Oxford, was an American whom Eliot had met at Ezra Pound's flat in Kensington years before.

Rye, just down the street from Lamb House, until the beginning of another war in 1939. Rye was the "Saltinge" of his time-dissolving autobiographical novel *Ushant,* in which Pound was "Rabbi Ben Ezra" and Eliot was anagrammatically "the Tsetse." Aiken would die at eighty-four, only nine months after Pound.

Possibly no time and no place had ever experienced such an intense cultural cross-fertilization of expatriates from a single nation as had London—and England—by the Americans between 1894 and 1914. The face of art and literature had been profoundly altered in both countries by the convergence. England had possessed the capacity not only to utilize but to absorb the talent to which it had given hospitality. Some Americans were assimilated almost totally. Yet even in spats and morning coat, Bret Harte wrote uninterruptedly about the California frontier that had nearly disappeared, and Henry James, who had become the quintessential English gentleman, continued to write about the American encounter with the sophisticated Old World. But Harte's tales, while often crafted at his highest level, more and more substituted nostalgia for reality, and James's Americans gradually lost touch with the real America that had emerged while the Master polished his prose style in London. Harold Frederic's novels gained in power with distance from New York, then diminished in impact until he was unable to carry off American settings and themes and had to turn to English ones; and Stephen Crane, as the unfinished *The O'Ruddy* demonstrated, was quickly losing touch with his roots as he worked at putting down new ones as squire of Brede. For painters of portraits and draftsmen of pictures, one attractive subject was often as good as another, and art respected fewer national frontiers; but American artists, with only rare exceptions like Epstein, held fiercely to their birthright and refused titles and honors which would have meant giving it up. While that tenacity resulted in American links which might not otherwise have existed, as with Abbey's and Sargent's beloved mural work in Pennsylvania and Massachusetts, the American work was a falling-off. The artist was always more sure of touch in exploiting the terrain he knew best, and that had become England.

For a Frost, whose stay was less than three years, New England never blurred into England, although the subjects he dealt with were often not limited by place. England was opportunity, not raw material, even when he wrote about English experience. For Ezra Pound, a carefully cultivated self-exile was essential to artistic survival. To T. S. Eliot, it became equally essential although accidental in its origins; for a while, at least, Eliot had intended to return. But whether the transatlantic exodus resulted in the artist returning to his homeland, or only in his art returning, the outcome was the enrichment of both cultures. Some critics thought otherwise. An English novelist of the thirties thought that the trouble with the writers of his generation was that "all these people have been influenced by T. S. Eliot, and Eliot is definitely a bad influence. . . . He is an example of the overeducated American, and Henry James is another. It would have been better for contemporary literature if Eliot had stayed in Louisville, or wherever he came from."

It was an "old notion," James had mused, in writing about Henry Harland, that for a writer to have "a quality of his own," he had to "draw his sap from the soil of his origin." In view of his own practice, the Master felt compelled to modify the principle, noting the forces (in 1898) which were alleviating the handicaps of what he called *dispatriation.* "Who shall say, at the rate things are going, what is to be 'near' home in the future and what is to be far from it? . . . The globe is shrinking, for the imagination, to the size of an orange that can be played with. . . ." Yet the artist wrote or painted differently in exile because his American roots were attenuated, and the results would affect both cultures in proportion to the achievement, for there is no more influential example than success.

Would anything have been different had a Harland not gone to London to found a *Yellow Book,* and had remained in New York to write novels as "Sidney Luska"? Would art have been different had not half a dozen American painters converged upon Tite Street? Would poetry have been different if Ezra Pound had not established his informal literary agency in Kensington and become a cantankerous but effective impresario of letters? One can always say that when ideas find their time they also find their progenitors. There would have been poetry and fiction and painting without the London Yankees. Yet given the conjunctions and the interplay of personalities and loyalties, it is difficult to believe that Anglo-American culture would have been the same.

SOURCES

Basically this checklist of sources excludes standard works and editions except where the indebtedness to such works is sufficiently extensive to warrant separate acknowledgment. It also includes reference to manuscript sources except where the supplier of the documentation has insisted upon privacy. Photographic acknowledgments are listed separately.

PREFACE
The Absentees

Elizabeth O'Connor's table talk with Henry James is from her *I Myself* (New York, 1911). Price Collier's comment about English doors being open to Americans is from his *England and the English* (New York, 1910). Emerson's comment dismissing Americans spoiled by Europe is from his *The Fortune of the Republic: A Lecture* (Boston, 1878). Shaw's contempt of "the vagabond artistic American" is from his letter to Molly Tompkins, July 25, 1935, in *Letters to a Young Actress* (New York, 1960). Henry James's letter to William James, Oct. 29, 1888, about the ambiguity of the American writing in England is from his *Letters*, edited by Percy Lubbock (New York, 1920). Gertrude Atherton's assertion that success in London would force her countrymen to acknowledge her is from *Adventures of a Novelist* (New York, 1932). Santayana's public school epiphany is from his *The Middle Span* (1945), in *Persons and Places* (New York, 1953). Julian Hawthorne is quoted from his memoir *Shapes That Pass* in Maurice Bassan's *Hawthorne's Son* (Columbus, Ohio, 1970). The quotations from Thomas Bailey Aldrich and James ("heart of the world") and Hawthorne ("a cold and shivering thing") to Aldrich are from Mrs Thomas Bailey Aldrich, *Crowding Memories* (Boston, 1920). Howells on the "defection" of literary Americans is from his "American Literature in Exile," *Literature*, Mar. 25, 1899. Pound on suffering exile is from his *Patria Mia*, first serialized in the *New Age*, London, 1911. Santayana's disappointment with French snubbing is conveyed in a letter to William James, Dec. 5, 1905, while his letter to his sister Susana is dated Aug. 13, 1901, both in George Santayana, *Letters* (New York, 1955), edited by Daniel Cory. Frank Harris's intoxication with London is from his *My Life and Loves,* vol. 2 (complete edition, New York, 1963). Richard Aldington's T. S. Eliot parody, *Stepping Heavenward,* was printed privately by Giuseppe Orioli in Florence, 1931. Van Wyck Brooks's experience of London is from his *Scenes and Portraits* (New York, 1954). T. S. Eliot's fascination with Sherlock Holmes's London is quoted by Herbert Howarth in *Notes on Some Figures Behind T. S. Eliot* (Boston, 1964). Ford Madox Ford's observation on the warmth of London for American expatriates is from his *Return to Yesterday* (London, 1932).

CHAPTER I
Tedworth Square

Mark Twain and John Bull (Bloomington, Ind., 1970), by Howard Baetzhold, and *Mark Twain in England* (London, 1978), by Dennis Welland, cover Clemens's relations with his audience and with his publishers. Welland publishes much of the correspondence exchanged between Clemens and Andrew Chatto. For the early months in London after Susy Clemens's death there are affecting passages in Clara Clemens's *My Father, Mark Twain* (New York, 1931). Clemens's explanation of his economies, including retention of his Players Club membership, is from a letter to E. C. Stedman, Oct. 16, 1896, in the Columbia University Libraries. Clemens's lectures, interviews, and after-dinner speeches, often reprinted from newspaper reports and transcripts, appear in the valuable *Mark Twain Speaking* (Iowa City, 1976), edited by Paul Fatout. Clemens's encounter with Hamlin Garland is in *Roadside Meetings.* Extracts from the notebooks are from Albert Bigelow, ed., *Mark Twain's Notebook* (New York, 1935). The correspondence with Howells is from *Mark Twain—Howells Letters,* edited by Henry Nash Smith and William M. Gibson (Cambridge, Mass., 1960). Clemens's relations with Bret Harte are recorded in *Mark Twain and Bret Harte* by Margaret Duckett (Norman, Okla., 1964). Mark Twain's "Of Course I'm Dying Interview" is found in *Mark Twain: Life As I Find It,* edited by Charles Neider (Garden City, N.Y., 1961). Clemens's letters to Henry Rogers are in the Columbia University Libraries. Clemens's visit to Lady Monkswell is described by her in *A Victorian Diarist: Extracts from the Journals of Mary, Lady Monkswell,* edited by E. C. F. Collier (London, 1944–46). Logan Pearsall Smith's comment on the American ideal as a Twain-Harte composite is from an unpublished letter (no date) to Joseph Pennell in the Library of Congress. Clemens's "Mental Telegraphy" was published for the first time in *Shaw Review* 17 (May 1974). His jocular invention of the "Twenty-first Century Publishing Company" is from *Punch,* May 31, 1899.

CHAPTER II
Lancaster Gate

Bret Harte's letters, sanitized mainly by omission of letters which do not show him as a loyal family man, were assembled and edited by Geoffrey Bret Harte (Boston, 1926). No collection has appeared since. Eighty-two of his letters to his authorized biographer, T. E. Pemberton, are in the Beinecke Library, Yale University, and additional letters to Pemberton and his daughter are in the Berg Collection. Yale also has Mark Twain's letters to Harte. Margaret Duckett's *Mark Twain and Bret Harte* (Norman, Okla., 1964) deals essentially with their relations before 1894. George Stewart's *Bret Harte* (New York, 1931) and Richard O'Connor's *Bret Harte* (Boston, 1966) are both biographies which lean largely on published material but are more candid about the relationship with Madame Van de Velde. The story about the Harte-influenced visitor to California is from Gertrude Atherton's *Adventures of a Novelist*, and information about the buttonhole flowers sent to Harte when away from London is from Mrs T. P. O'Connor's *I Myself*. Hamlin Garland's encounter with Harte is told in *Roadside Meetings* (New York, 1930). That Lytton Strachey did not know of, or know, his American neighbors is reported to me by Michael Holroyd, who has consulted his Strachey files. The sale of the Strachey Lancaster Gate home is told by Holroyd in his *Lytton Strachey* (London, 1967). John Morgan Richards's biography of his daughter, *The Life of John Oliver Hobbes* (London, 1911), although highly reticent and replete with bowdlerizations of her letters, remains, with his own memoirs *With John Bull and Jonathan* (London, 1905), written in Pearl Craigie's lifetime, the major printed source of information about her life. The best modern study is the chapter about her in Vineta Colby, *The Singular Anomaly* (New York, 1970), which utilizes some of her letters to friends, family, and publishers in the Berg Collection, and Margaret Maison, *John Oliver Hobbes* (London, 1976). I have supplemented these with additional manuscript letters from the Berg and Columbia collections. Information about the *Craigie v. Craigie* divorce suit is taken from contemporary transcripts of testimony in the London press, in particular *Reynolds's Newspaper* and *The Times* for July 4–7, 1895, and Pearl Craigie's letters to friends. Max Beerbohm's parody of a "John Oliver Hobbes" lecture is in the Berg Collection and was first published in Colby. Information about Mary Leiter Curzon and her relationship with Mrs Craigie is from Nigel Nicolson's *Mary Curzon* (New York, 1977). Information about Mrs Craigie's relationship with Owen Seaman is from John Adlard's *Owen Seaman* (London, 1977). Her relationship with Monsignor Brown is detailed in Maison.

CHAPTER III
Cromwell Road

Henry James's recollection of being wooed by the *Yellow Book* editors is from his preface to *The Lesson of the Master,* New York Edition of the *Works,* vol. 15, reprinted in *The Art of the Novel* (New York, 1934). E. F. Benson's recollection is from *As We Were* (London, 1930). James's price for a story is from Harland's letter to Lane, June 15, 1894, in the Lane Archive, Westfield College, University of London. Much additional background material for this chapter also is indebted to the Lane Archive, and its letters from Henry and Aline Harland to Lane. Evelyn Sharp's memoir, *Unfinished Adventure* (London, 1932), reports much of the doings at Cromwell Road, as does Frederick Rolfe's *Nicholas Crabbe* (New York, 1958). The story of women clinging to James when the lights went out is from Elizabeth Robins, *Theatre and Friendship* (New York, 1923). "George Egerton's" letter to Lane is quoted in Terence de Vere White's *A Leaf from the Yellow Book* (London, 1958). Harland's relations with the Stedmans and biographical data gleaned from their correspondence come from Aline Harland's letters to the Stedmans in the Columbia University Libraries, which continue well after Henry Harland's death. Much general information on the Harlands is found in the only biography, *Henry Harland, His Life and Work* by Karl Beckson (London, 1978), referred to hereafter as Beckson. Many letters quoted here from manuscript appear in extract also in Beckson. James's letter to Gosse on Harland is from *Transatlantic Dialogue: Selected American Correspondence of Edmund Gosse,* edited by P. F. Mattheissen and M. Millgate (Austin, Tex., 1965). J. Lewis May's recollections of the early days of the *Yellow Book* are from his *John Lane and the Nineties* (London, 1936), and additional *Yellow Book* background comes from S. Weintraub, *Aubrey Beardsley: Imp of the Perverse* (University Park, Pa., 1976), and James Nelson, *The View from the Bodley Head* (Cambridge, Mass, 1971). Harland's undated letter to Gosse about the "deplorable" sacking of Beardsley is from *Transatlantic Dialogue.* Douglas Ainslie on Harland and James is from Ainslie's letter to Katherine Mix, Apr. 30, 1946, in the Pattee Library, Pennsylvania State University. Biographical data on Morton Fullerton are from R. W. B. Lewis, *Edith Wharton* (Boston, 1976). Data on minor American *Yellow Book* contributors are from K. L. Mix, *A Study in Yellow* (Lawrence, Kans., 1960). Pearl Craigie's letter to Moore announcing her rejection of an invitation to contribute further to the *Yellow Book* is in Richards, while the *Speaker* notice which frightened her off is "A Yellow Melancholy," April 28, 1894. James's "The Story Teller at Large: Henry Harland" appeared in *Fortnightly Review* 69 (Apr. 1898). Harland's manuscript letters to Olive Custance are in the Berg Collection, New York Public Library, and are extracted in Beckson. Letters of Aline Harland in which she claims to be "Lady

Henry Harland," "Aline, Lady Harland," and widow of "Henry Anthony, Fifth Baron Harland," are in the Pattee Library. The purported American bribe to Oscar Wilde's jailer at Pentonville Prison, signed "The Few Anonymous American Friends," is quoted by William White from the manuscript in the possession of London dealer Frank Hollings in *AN&Q,* Nov. 1963.

CHAPTER IV
Croydon Police Court

Testimony from the trial of Kate Frederic and Athalie Mills, and its revelation of the circumstances preceding Harold Frederic's death, is taken from reports of the proceedings in the *Daily Graphic* (the fullest account), *The Times,* the *Daily Telegraph,* and the *Daily News* (all London), between Oct. 20 and Dec. 15, 1898. The G. B. Burgin comment on Frederic's double life appears in *Some More Memoirs* (London, 1924). Robert Barr's long reminiscence of Frederic is "Harold Frederic, the Author of *The Market-Place,"* *Saturday Evening Post,* Dec. 17, 1898. Frederic's letter to Gelett Burgess, June 16, 1898, is in the Bancroft Library, University of California, Berkeley. Mary Curzon's letter to her mother is from Nigel Nicolson's *Mary Curzon,* and Frank Harris's claim of intervention with Frederic in the Venezuela affair is from his *Life and Loves.* Frederic's letters to Stephen and Cora Crane and to Charles Scribner are in the Columbia University Libraries. Other data about Frederic's relations with the Cranes come from Lillian Gilkes, *Cora Crane* (Bloomington, Ind., 1960), Robert Stallman, *Stephen Crane* (New York, 1968), and the *Letters of Stephen Crane,* edited by Gilkes and Stallman (New York, 1960). The best sources of criticism and analysis of Frederic's novels are Austin Briggs, Jr., *The Novels of Harold Frederic* (Ithaca, N.Y., 1969), and the Spring 1968 issue (No. 2) of *American Literary Realism,* which is largely devoted to Frederic, and *Harold Frederic,* by Thomas F. O'Donnell and Hoyt C. Franchere (New York, 1961), which also includes biographical data. There is no biography yet. The C. Lewis Hind anecdotes are from his *More Authors and I* (London, 1922). Arnold Bennett's letter to George Sturt, Jan. 31, 1897, is from the *Letters of Arnold Bennett,* edited by James Hepburn II (London, 1968). Edmund Wilson includes biographical data, apparently furnished by Austin Briggs, in his essay on Frederic in *The Devils and Canon Barham* (New York, 1973). Frank Harris's tale about going with Frederic to see Lord Salisbury is from *My Life and Loves.* Lillian Gilkes and T. F. O'Donnell provide Hall Caine's letter to Cora Crane on the Kate Lyon fund in the *Frederic Herald* 2 (Jan. 1969). Frank Harris's *Saturday Review* editorial on the Kate Lyon verdict appeared on Nov. 12, 1898. Bret Harte's letter on Christian Science to Mrs A. S. Boyd, July 15, 1895, appeared in the *Letters* of Harte, edited by G. B. Harte. The "effeminate old donkey" attack on Henry James is quoted from Frederic by Thomas Beer in his *Stephen Crane* (New York, 1923). Frederic's letters appear in *The Correspondence of Harold Frederic* (Fort Worth, Tex., 1978), edited by George E. Fortenberry, Stanton Garner, and Robert H. Woodward. His letters to the *Daily Chronicle,* May 10, 1894, to Mrs Atherton, July 10, 1898, and to Frederick Stokes, c. July 1898, although all published earlier, are quoted from this edition.

CHAPTER V

Brede Place

The Stallman *Stephen Crane,* the Stallman-Gilkes *Letters,* and the Gilkes *Cora Crane* have already been cited in the notes to Chapter IV. Crane's letters to his brother William are at Columbia. Mark Barr's story about the Brede ghost and about the incident at Delmonico's is from an unpublished memoir in the Berg Collection. Robert Barr's letter about the deaths of Frederic and Crane, dated June 8, 1900, is quoted in full in Vincent Starrett's *Buried Caesars* (Chicago, 1923). Edith Ritchie Jones's recollections were published in "Stephen Crane at Brede," *Atlantic Monthly* 194 (July 1954). The manuscript of *The Ghost* is in the Berg Collection, and additional data about the play were published by the late curator of the Berg, John D. Gordan, in *"The Ghost* at Brede Place," *Bulletin of the New York Public Library* 56 (Dec. 1952). Crane's letters to Sanford Bennett are quoted by Thomas Beer in his *Stephen Crane* (New York, 1923). His letter to Robert Barr from Key West, May 20, 1898, is quoted in part in *The Correspondence of Harold Frederic.* The history of Brede is told by Sheila Kaye-Smith in *Weald of Kent and Sussex* (London, 1966), and the most recent tale of the occult at Brede comes to me from a near-neighbor, Nigel Nicolson's daughter Juliet. I am also indebted to Nigel Nicolson for a firsthand look at Brede. Data about the composition and completion of *The O'Ruddy* come from J. C. Levenson's introduction to the University of Virginia Press's definitive edition, *Essays in Bibliography, Text and Editing,* edited by Fredson Bowers (1975). Data on *The Third Violet* and *Active Service* come from the same edition, edited by Bowers (1976) and again with an introduction by Levenson. Ford Hueffer's reminiscences of Crane are from *Portraits from Life* (Boston, 1937) and *Return to Yesterday* (London, 1932). Crane's "capture" of a Puerto Rican town is described by Richard Harding Davis in his *A Year from a Correspondent's Notebook* (New York, 1898).

CHAPTER VI
Tite Street

Sources for Sargent's life and work basically are the biographies by Charles Merrill Mount (New York, 1955), still the best book on Sargent, Evan Charteris (New York, 1927), and Richard Ormond (New York, 1970). Some of Sargent's negotiations with sitters, and his prices, can be gleaned from letters in the Butler Library, Columbia University. Max Beerbohm's comment on Sargent's withdrawal as a portraitist is from the *Saturday Review,* June 19, 1909. Pennell's life was written about in his own *Autobiography* (Boston, 1925) and in the two-volume *Life and Letters* by his wife, Elizabeth (Boston, 1929). The Pennell Archive at the Library of Congress contains their correspondence with Whistler, Abbey, and others, including their solicitors and their editors (such as *Daily Chronicle* editor W. J. Fisher and William Heinemann). For sources for Whistler in the period after 1894, see my notes to Chapters 30–37 in *Whistler: A Biography* (New York, 1974). For his relations with Abbey, see E. V. Lucas's two-volume, definitive *Life and Work of E. A. Abbey, R.A.* (London, 1921), which remains the major source of data for Abbey's life and includes much of his correspondence with Henry James. (Curiously, the definitive five-volume life of Henry James by Leon Edel includes only two brief references to Abbey.) Data on Romaine Brooks are meager, especially on her London years, but some can be located in Adelyn D. Breeskin's catalogue for the Brooks exhibition at the National Collection of Fine Arts (NCFA) in Washington (1971) and in Meryle Secrest's biography of her, *Between Me and Life* (Garden City, N.Y., 1974). Many of Romaine Brooks's paintings are also at the NCFA, as is her unpublished memoir. James's letter to Mrs Mahlon Sands on how to sit for Sargent is undated but c. 1894 and published in Leon Edel's edition of James's selected letters (Cambridge, Mass., 1974). James's 1897 comment on Whistler's *Irving* is quoted by Viola Hopkins Winner in *Henry James and the Visual Arts* (Charlottesville, Va., 1970). Data on Ethel Sands are from *Miss Ethel Sands and Her Circle* by Wendy Baron (London, 1977), Michael Holroyd's *Lytton Strachey* (New York, 1968), and the *Memoirs of Ottoline Morrell, 1873–1915,* edited by Robert Gathorne-Hardy (New York, 1964). Jacques-Émile Blanche's descriptions of Sargent's relations with his sitters are from his *Portraits of a Lifetime* (New York, 1938).

CHAPTER VII
Lamb House

Leon Edel's masterly biography of James and his editions of James's plays, short fiction, letters, and *The American Scene* are of course crucial. Other James letters appear in *Transatlantic Dialogue* (letters to Gosse) and in Percy

Lubbock's edition of the *Letters* (New York, 1920). James's "I take up my *own* old pen again" comes from the *Notebooks,* edited by Matthiessen. That Ethel Sands was with H.J. on the first night of *Guy Domville* comes from Enid Bagnold's *Autobiography* (Boston, 1969). H. Montgomery Hyde's *Henry James at Home* added detail about the Lamb House period, including rents, property prices and royalties, and "color" about James's domestic life. His relations with Edith Wharton are largely from R. W. B. Lewis's *Edith Wharton* and Mrs Wharton's own *A Backward Glance* (New York, 1934). Further details about James at Rye come from E. F. Benson's *As We Were* (London, 1930) and *Final Edition* (New York, 1940). Data about Charles Yerkes are from the *Chronicle of the Yerkes Family* (Philadelphia, 1904), while that about Emilie Grigsby is from Edel. James's relations with Pearsall Smith are largely taken from *Recollections of Logan Pearsall Smith,* edited by R. Gathorne-Hardy (London, 1949). His relations with Jonathan Sturgis are from Ford Madox Ford's *Return to Yesterday* and *Portraits from Life,* and from Edel. His relations with Howard Sturgis are from Wharton, Lewis, Santayana, Edel, and A. C. Benson's *Memories and Friends* (London, 1924). His relations with Elizabeth and Joseph Pennell are taken largely from their correspondence in the Library of Congress. James's relations with Henrik Anderson and Hugh Walpole are from Edel, while those with Jocelyn Persse are from letters published by Shane Leslie in *Horizon* (London, June 1943). His relations with Alfred Langdon Coburn are from *Alvin Langdon Coburn* by H. and A. Gernsheim (New York, 1966), and those with Elizabeth Robins are from her *Theatre and Friendship* (New York, 1932) and Edel's description of the contents of her papers.

CHAPTER VIII

Church Walk

Noel Stock's *The Life of Ezra Pound* (New York, 1970) is authoritative for dates and places but often uncritical. Patricia Hutchins provides additional detail through 1912 in *Ezra Pound's Kensington* (Chicago, 1965). Definitive details of Pound's expulsion from Wabash College appear in Ernest L. Boyd's "Ezra Pound at Wabash College," *Journal of Modern Literature* 4 (Sept. 1974). Van Wyck Brooks's recollection of London is from his *Scenes and Portraits.* Pound's recollection of the composition of "The Goodly Fere" appears in several places; I have taken it here from Patricia Hutchins. His comment to Malcolm Cowley appears in *Exile's Return* (New York, 1934). The story of Mathews's acceptance of *Personae* is from Stock, as is Pound's comment on Whitman as his predecessor. Contemporary reviews of Pound's work when not directly from the original sources are from Eric Homburger, *Ezra Pound: The Critical Heritage* (London, 1972). References to Pound's relationship with Ford Hueffer and Violet Hunt are largely from Stock and from Arthur Mizener, *The Saddest Story: A Biography of Ford Madox Ford* (New York, 1971); however, the reference to Pound's reading the *Albade* is from Ford's *Return to Yesterday*. Pound's reference to professional "sinning" in a letter to William Carlos Williams is from his letter of May 21, 1909, in *The Letters of Ezra Pound, 1907–41*, edited by D. D. Paige (New York, 1950). Rupert Brooke's comment about Pound is in a letter to A. F. Scholfield, postmarked Oct. 19, 1909, and is published in his *Letters*, edited by D. D. Paige (London, 1951); and Yeats's comment to Lady Gregory is from his *Letters*, edited by Allan Wade (London, 1954). Ernest Rhys's recollection of Pound's reading is from *Everyman Remembers* (London, 1931). William Carlos Williams's memories of his visit to Pound in London are from his *Autobiography* (New York, 1951). Other details of his relationship with Pound are from the *Selected Letters of William Carlos Williams*, edited by J. C. Thirwall (New York, 1957), and Geoffrey H. Movius, "Caviar and Bread: Ezra Pound and William Carlos Williams, 1902–1914," *Journal of Modern Literature* 5 (Sept. 1976). *Patria Mia*, written in 1911 and published in the *New Age* in 1912, was not published in book form until Ralph Seymour did so in Chicago in 1950. The lines from "Sandalphon" about "causing the works to speak" are erroneously quoted in Stock as "causing the words to speak." Jacob Epstein's autobiography, *Epstein*, 2nd edition (London, 1963), and the study by Richard Buckle, *Jacob, Sculptor* (Cleveland, 1963), are the chief sources for data about him; however, his relations with Pound are noted in Stock, in the *Letters*, in Pound's reviews, and in Timothy Materer, "Ezra Pound and Gaudier-Brzeska: Sophie's Diary," *Journal of Modern Literature* 6 (Apr. 1977), and in Jacob Korg, "Jacob Epstein's Rock Drill and the *Cantos*," *Paideuma* 4 (Fall/Winter 1975). Robert Ross's letters in *Robert Ross: Friend of Friends*, edited by Margery Ross (London, 1952), were also useful. Pound spoke of the "hammering" thesis himself in the interview with Donald Hall published in *Writers at Work* (New York, 1963). John Gould Fletcher tells his own story in *Life Is My Song* (New York, 1937) and John Cournos in *Autobiography* (New York, 1935). Background on Hilda Doolittle is from Stock and from *Hilda Doolittle (H.D.)* by Vincent Quinn (New York, 1967), and on H.D. and Richard Aldington from his *Life for Life's Sake* (New York, 1941) and *A Passionate Prodigality: Letters to Alan Bird from Richard Aldington*, edited by Miriam Benkovitz (New York, 1975). Data on Harold Monro are largely from Joy Grant's *Harold Monro and the Poetry Bookshop* (Berkeley, 1967). The details about Miss Weaver and Miss Marsden and the *Freewoman* are in *Dear Miss Weaver*, by Jane Lidderdale and Mary Nicholson (New York, 1970), and in Stock and Fletcher. Pound's relations with Harriet Monroe are spelled out in *Harriet Monroe and the Poetry Renaissance* by Ellen Williams (Champaign, Ill., 1976) and with Amy Lowell in S. Foster Damon's *Amy Lowell* (Boston, 1935), in Jean

Gould's *Amy: The World of Amy Lowell and the Imagist Movement* (New York, 1975), and in Stock and Fletcher. It is Damon who reports Miss Lowell's interruption of Rupert Brooke's poetry reading. Her correspondence with Fletcher is at Harvard, while Fletcher's papers, quoted from in Edmund S. de Chasca's *John Gould Fletcher and Imagism* (Columbia, Mo., 1978) are at the University of Arkansas. Miss Monroe's first purchase of a Pound book in London is described by her in "Ezra Pound," *Poetry*, May 1925. Pound's relations with Joyce are detailed in Richard Ellmann, *James Joyce* (New York, 1959), and in James Joyce's *Letters* vol. 2, edited by Richard Ellmann (New York, 1966), and with Yeats in Ellmann's *Yeats: The Man and the Masks* (New York, 1948), and in Stock. The note on Pound's affirmative response on his marital prospects is from Stock. Both Stock and Hugh Kenner, *The Pound Era* (Berkeley, 1971), discuss Pound and Dolmetsch. For Wyndham Lewis's early career I have utilized *The Letters of Wyndham Lewis*, edited by W. K. Rose (New York, 1963), and *Mrs. Dukes' Million*, edited with an introduction by Frank Davey (Toronto, 1978), as well as Lewis's own *Blasting and Bombardiering* (New York and London, 1947).

CHAPTER IX

North of London

The basic sources for Frost are the *Selected Letters*, edited by Lawrance Thompson (New York, 1964), and the first volume of Thompson's scrupulously honest (and thus sometimes maligned) biography, *Robert Frost: The Early Years* (New York, 1966–76). Additional letters, compiled, quoted, and extracted by Joan St C. Crane, appear in *Robert Frost: A Descriptive Catalogue of Books and Manuscripts in the Clifton Waller Barrett Library, University of Virginia* (Charlottesville, Va., 1973), from which we learn how the Frost children were tutored and/or schooled in England and how Ralph Hodgson introduced Frost to Edward Thomas (letter to Grace Conkling, June 28, 1921). Data about Frost's introduction to Mrs Nutt and his encounter with poets in Monro's shop are supplemented by the interview-based fragment of biography, Robert S. Newdick's *Season of Frost: An Interrupted Biography of Robert Frost*, edited by William A. Sutton (Albany, N.Y., 1976). The description of Mrs Nutt "as if she had just risen from the sea" is from the interviews published as *Frost/A Time to Talk* by Robert Francis (Amherst, Mass., 1972), while the implication that Frost had also explored the alternative of Heinemann was first suggested by Donald J. Greiner in *Notes and Queries* (Aug. 1968). Additional interview-based material, especially valuable for dating the poems, is found in Elizabeth Shepley Sergeant, *Robert Frost: The Trial by Existence* (New York, 1967). Shepley also reproduces Pound's invitation card to Frost. *The Critical Reception of Robert Frost* by Peter Van Egmond (Boston, 1974) extracts the most vital press reaction to Frost's first books and catalogues all of it, while Edward Connery Lathem's edition of *Interviews with Robert Frost* (New York, 1966) reprints almost every such major interview utilized here, including the *Writers at Work* interview by Donald Hall. These include Frost's various explanations of why he went to England in 1912. Pound's correspondence with *Poetry* about Frost is reproduced in *Harriet Monroe and the Poetry Renaissance*. That Pound's review made Elinor Frost weep is from a Sergeant interview with Frost, and Pound's "summary" of Frost's implicit "pay attention to me" prayer is from Donald Hall's interview. Frost's memory of the jujitsu lesson in the restaurant is also from Hall. That Pound may have borrowed a line from Beddoes is suggested by Anya Taylor in "A Frost Debt to Beddoes," *English Literature Notes* 13 (June 1976). That Elinor was a militant atheist is Frost's confidence to Louis Untermeyer in the *Letters* (Mar. 21, 1920). Frost's complaints of being bullied by Pound, and his free-verse parody of Pound to Frank Flint, are in the *Letters*. Frost's comment to Thompson recognizing his streak of malice is quoted in Thompson. Fletcher's and Cournos's memories are taken from their autobiographies, while Gibson's metrical recollection (corrected typographically) is taken from Thompson. Frost's relations with Edward Thomas are taken from the memoir *Edward Thomas* by Eleanor Farjeon (London, 1958), from *Edward Thomas: A Poet for His Country*, by Jan Marsh (London, 1978), from Thompson and Sergeant, and from the *Letters*, where (Apr. 17, 1915) Frost restates his "You are a poet or you are nothing" principle. Edward Marsh's rejection of Frost as a Georgian poet is from Christopher Hassall's *Edward Marsh* (New York, 1959). John Haines's recollections are from his memoir of Frost in the *Gloucester Journal*, Feb. 2, 1935.

CHAPTER X
Bedford Place to Booking Office

Henry James's reaction to the mutilation of the Sargent portrait is from Edel and Hyde. His meeting Ezra and Dorothy Pound is from Kenner. His problems with Amy Lowell are from Damon, Gould, and Ellen Williams as well as Fletcher and Aldington. James's letter condemning *Pygmalion* (to Hugh Walpole, Apr. 21–23, 1914) is in the Humanities Research Center, University of Texas, and quoted in *Shaw: An Exhibit* by Dan H. Laurence (Austin, Tex., 1977). His query to Pinker about D. H. Lawrence is from Hyde. Background on Conrad Aiken is from Malcolm Cowley's correspondence with S.W., and *Selected Letters of Conrad Aiken*, edited by Joseph Killorin (New Haven, Conn., 1978). Background on T. S. Eliot is from

Killorin, from Lyndall Gordon, *Eliot's Early Years* (London, 1977), and from Herbert Howarth, *Notes on Some Figures Behind T. S. Eliot* (New York, 1964). Aiken's offer of "Prufrock" to Monro is from Aiken, "King Bolo and Others," in March and Tambimuttu, eds., *T. S. Eliot* (London, 1948). Background on *Blast* is from Wyndham Lewis's memoir, *Blasting and Bombardiering* (London, 1937), unreliable as it is about specifics; from W. K. Rose, ed., *Letters of Wyndham Lewis* (New York, 1963); from Stock; and from *Blast* itself. Data on the *Imagiste* dinner—in addition to the unreliable Hueffer/Ford—are from Stock, Damon, the letters of Pound and Lewis, and from Cournos, Fletcher, and Aldington. Aiken's picture of London on the eve of war is from his autobiographical *Ushant,* 2nd edition, with key to character identifications (New York, 1971). Information on Eliot's arrival in London is from a letter to S.W. from Valerie Eliot. Eliot's letter to his brother Henry is from Grover Smith, *T. S. Eliot's Poetry and Plays* (Chicago, 1956), and his comment on Lionel Johnson is from his essay "American Literature and the American Language," in the *Sewanee Review* 74 (Winter 1966). (T. S. Mathews's *Great Tom* and Robert Sencourt's *T. S. Eliot: A Memoir* are unreliable about this period, Sencourt even reconnoitering the wrong flat [Ezra had moved] to check where Eliot had first met Pound.) The late interview with Eliot was one of the *Paris Review* series reprinted in *Writers and Their Work.* Aldington's parody of Pound is from the Appendix to Hugh Witemeyer's *The Poetry of Ezra Pound* (Berkeley, Calif., 1969). Chapman's letter to the *Times* is in *John Jay Chapman and His Letters* (Boston, 1937). The Edith Wharton data are from R. W. B. Lewis, and the James reaction to the war is from Edel and Hyde. The information on wartime use of Bret Harte's "Reveille" is from Stewart's biography of Harte. The suggestion about Harte's influence on Sassoon and Owen is from Paul Fussell's *The Great War and Modern Memory* (London and New York, 1977). Amy Lowell's panicky reactions to the war are from Damon, Gould, and—the quotation in which she reacted to being trapped in the crowds—Robert McAlmon, *Being Geniuses Together* (New York, 1968). Epstein's letter to John Quinn is quoted in Michael Holroyd, *Augustus John* (London, 1975). Henry Adams's confrontation with the war and meeting with James are from Ernest Samuels, *Henry Adams,* vol. 2 (Cambridge, Mass., 1964). Gosse's memory of James in wartime Rye is from Hyde. Amy Lowell's letter to Miss Monroe about her volunteer work with the Hoover Committee is from Ellen Williams, with other data from Damon and Aldington. Eliot on Miss Lowell is from the *Sewanee Review* noted above, and Wyndham Lewis on Eliot in Pound's flat is from his essay in the Tambimuttu *Eliot.* Pound's quoting Charles Ricketts is from Stock. Eliot's recollection of Pound's cajoling powers is from his introduction to Pound's *Literary Essays* (London, 1954). Grover Smith suggests the "Crapy Cornelia" relationship to "Prufrock" although not in the detail given here, and Walton Litz in *"The Waste Land* Fifty Years

After," in *Eliot in His Time* (Princeton, N.J., 1973), is the critic who sug-
gests an Eliot response to *In the Cage* and the Jamesian qualities of *Burnt
Norton*. Eliot's letter to Herbert Read is quoted by Russell Kirk in *Eliot and
His Age* (New York, 1971). Eliot's dismissal of James's Americanism is
from a letter to Stephen Spender quoted in his "Remembering Mr. Eliot,"
Sewanee Review 74 (Winter 1966). Brand Blanshard's reminiscence of Eliot
at Oxford is from "Eliot in Memory," *The Yale Review* (June 1965).
E. R. Dodds's classroom note is from his *Missing Persons* (Oxford, 1977).
Eliot's "Marie Lloyd" (1923) is reprinted in *Selected Prose of T. S. Eliot,*
edited by Frank Kermode (London, 1975). Eliot's notes to *The Waste Land,*
however, some of which must be taken with skepticism, claim that at least one
music-hall song borrowed from in the poem comes from an Australian ditty
he no longer could identify. That Pound arranged for an Eliot visit to the
Dolmetsch family is clear from a thank-you to him from Eliot in the
Beinecke Library, Yale University, and that Eliot discovered his need for long
underwear in England is from Donald Hall, *Remembering Poets* (New York,
1978). The poems Frost wrote at The Gallows are described in Sergeant. The
rumor that the Germans had landed in Portsmouth is recalled by Frost in a
letter to John W. Haines, July 21, 1925. His preparations for returning are
from Thompson.

AFTERMATH
The Pin Wheel

John Haines's memoir was in the *Gloucester Journal,* Feb. 2, 1935, while
Stephen Spender's musing over what might have happened if Frost had remained in England is from *Love-Hate Relations* (New York, 1974). Frost's
letters to Lesley are from *Family Letters of Robert and Elinor Frost,* edited by
Arnold Grade (Albany, N.Y., 1972). Wyndham Lewis's letters to Pound are
from Rose. Pound's correspondence with Harriet Monroe is from Williams.
Pound's "I cling to the spar" lines are from "Et Faim Sallir les Loups des
Boys," in *Blast,* July 1915. Pound's rejection letter from G. W. Prothero is
from Donald Davie, "Ezra Among the Edwardians" in *Paideuma* 5 (Spring
1976). Aldington's comparison of Pound's and Eliot's careers is from *Life
for Life's Sake.* Eliot's report to Wyndham Lewis about being refused by the
navy and attempting to enlist in the army is an unpublished letter (Aug. 5,
1918) at the Olin Library, Cornell University. Henry James's last months are
detailed in Hyde and Edel, with the Pearsall Smith material from Hyde.
Elizabeth Robins's memory of being told of James's death on arrival in New
York is from her *Theatre and Friendship.* The Sargent break with neutrality
is described in Mount, as are the last years. James's prediction of Sargent as a
proper Bostonian is from Blanche, *Portraits of a Lifetime* (New York, 1938).

John Jay Chapman's letter to Mrs Winthrop Chanler (Oct. 19, 1915) is in his *Letters*. The death of his son is reported in the Memoir prefacing *Victor Chapman's Letters from France* (New York, 1917). The death of Edwin Abbey's nephew and namesake is reported in Lucas, vol. 2. Ethel Sands's experiences in France and her comment to Nan Hudson on Epstein are from Wendy Baron's *Miss Ethel Sands and Her Circle*. The last years and death of Howard Sturgis are described by Santayana in "My Host the World" in *Persons and Places*. Joseph Pennell's departure from London is described in his wife's life of J.P. The negotiations surrounding the release of Pound, and letters concerning the affair, are in Frost's *Letters*. Aiken's last years and letters are from Killorin. The suggestion that Eliot and James were bad influences on English writers is quoted by Spender in his *Sewanee Review* memoir of Eliot.

ACKNOWLEDGMENTS

Although many individuals, in the line of duty, were helpful in making *The London Yankees* possible, I would like to single out, for special thanks, Karl Beckson, Malcolm Cowley, Harry P. Clark, Fred D. Crawford, Phyllis Dolich, Ellen S. Dunlap, Leon Edel, Valerie Eliot, T. F. Evans, David Farmer, Ian Fletcher, Lois Garcia, Eileen and Alan Hanley-Browne, Serrell Hillman, Fruma Klass, Philip Klass, Llewellyn Howland III, Dan H. Laurence, Sally Leach, Charles Mann, Katherine L. Mix, William O'Donnell, Shirley Rader, Michael Rhodes, Warren Roberts, Richard Schein, Peter Schneeman, Meryle Secrest, Kay Shirk, Lola Szladits, Rodelle Weintraub, and Philip Young.

Most significant among the many libraries and special collections utilized were Amherst College Library, the Jones Library of the town of Amherst, the Berg Collection of the New York Public Library, the Butler Library of Columbia University, the British Library and its Newspaper Library at Colindale, the Library of Congress Manuscript Division, the Fales Collection of the Bobst Library at New York University, the Houghton Library at Harvard University, the Olin Library of Cornell University, the University of Reading Library, the Lane Archive at Westfield College of the University of London, the Pattee Library at the Pennsylvania State University, the Barrett Collection of American Literature at the University of Virginia Library, and the Beinecke Library at Yale University.

Special acknowledgments for permission to use material in their collections, or to copyright material, as specified, are noted as follows:

Henry W. and Albert A. Berg Collection, The New York Public Library (Astor, Lenox and Tilden Foundations): for background material based upon manuscripts relating to Stephen Crane, Pearl Craigie, Henry Harland, and Bret Harte.

Faber and Faber Ltd. and New Directions Publishing Corporation: extracts from Ezra Pound, *Collected Early Poems*. Copyright © 1976 by the Trustees of the Ezra Pound Literary Property Trust. All rights reserved. Reprinted by permission of New Directions and Faber and Faber Ltd.

Harcourt Brace Jovanovich and Faber and Faber Ltd.: for extracts from T. S. Eliot, "Morning at the Window."

⦚ ACKNOWLEDGMENTS ⦚

Houghton Mifflin Company: for extracts from the poetry of Amy Lowell.

The Estate of Robert Lee Frost and *Robert Frost: The Early Years* by Lawrance Thompson. Copyright © 1966 by The Estate of Robert Frost. Reprinted by permission of Holt, Rinehart and Winston, Publishers: for extracts from the poems of Robert Frost.

For photographs and other illustrative material, acknowledgments appear with the list of illustrations.

INDEX